BONDO HIGHLANDER

BONDO HIGHLANDER

By

VERRIER ELWIN

GYAN

ISBN: 978-81-212-9060-9(HB)

Published, 2018

Published by

Gyan Publishing House
5, Ansari Road
Daryaganj, New Delhi-110002
Phone: 011-47034999, 9811692060
www.gyanbooks.com
E-mail: books@gyanbooks.com

Printed at: G. Print Process, Delhi.

PREFACE

THIS book is the first of a series which will aim at throwing some illumination on the tribal life of Orissa, one of the most interesting ethnographic provinces of India. Difficulty of communications, a climate notorious for malaria and blackwater, the temperament of the tribesmen which is often hostile to strangers and intolerant of authority, has led to a general neglect of the anthropology of the province. Much has been written — and has been reproduced over and over again — about one aspect of the ancient culture of the Konds,[1] their attachment to infanticide and human sacrifice, but this, fundamental as it is for an understanding of Kond psychology, is far from being the whole story of this fascinating tribe. The genius of Dalton played but fitfully over the fringes of Orissa; he has some brilliant pages on the Juangs and Bhuiyas, but his explorations did not take him beyond the States into what is now called Orissa but was then Madras. The Ethnographic Survey had little to say about the inhabitants of Ganjam and Koraput; Thurston, in his *Castes and Tribes of Southern India,* has a few pages on the Gadabas, Konds, Porojas and Saoras (Savaras), but most of his information is based on the reports of other people and, though sound enough, is slight and superficial. Risley has a dozen pages on the Konds, whom he calls Kandhs, a little (mostly lifted from Dalton) on the Juangs and Bhuiyas, and a few pages on the Savaras. Russell and Hiralal have something to say about the Gadabas, chiefly the few and uncharacteristic Gadabas of Bastar, the Konds of Kalahandi and Sambalpur, the Parjas (now called Dhurwas) of Bastar State, and the Savaras. Since then there have been some inferior and inaccurate articles in *Man in India,* some notes in the reports of the *Census of India,* and one or two amateur linguistic studies. More recently, however, Orissa has been visited by Dr E. von Eikstedt, who spent some time among the Konds and Saoras, and by Dr C. von Fürer-Haimendorf whose observations drew attention for the first time to the real ethnographic problems involved.

On the Bondos themselves we have a report by May[2] of the Topographical Survey, written in the patronizing tone characteristic of his time, but interesting because it was done so long ago; some useful notes by Henderson, a member of the Indian Civil Service, reproduced in the

[1] I am adopting the spellings Kond for Kondh, Khond or Kandh; Saora for Sarva, S'Ora or Sawara; Didayi for Dire or Didai.

[2] J. A. May, 'Notes on the Bhondas of Jaypur', *The Indian Antiquary,* Vol. II (1873), pp. 236 ff.

Census Report of 1911;[1] some paragraphs in Thurston[2] mainly based on May and Henderson; and a brief account in Bell's *Koraput District Gazetteer*[3] which appears to be taken from the *Vizagapatam District Gazetteer* by Francis, which was published in 1907. None of these accounts do more than stress the unusual appearance of Bondo women and the remarkable organization of the pit-dormitory. It remained for Dr C. von Fürer-Haimendorf to win the honour of being the discoverer, in an ethnographic sense, of the Bondos.[4] It was a study of his reports on their megalithic culture, religion and matrimonial arrangements that first attracted me to them, and indeed I should not have dared to venture on territory which Fürer-Haimendorf had so clearly staked out as his own, had it not been for the fact that his duties in Hyderabad made it impossible for him to extend his Orissa researches.

The present work is essentially a study of the Bondo character. The problem of the presentation of anthropological material is becoming more and more acute. With modern methods of investigation, the ethnographer can collect sufficient information about almost any tribe to fill a small encyclopedia of a thousand pages. In a few cases this is worth doing, but in the majority it is not. To write, for example, a series of monographs on the Orissa tribes, one after the other, each containing — beside a certain quantity of information about customs and beliefs peculiar to the particular tribe — a vast amount of substantially similar material, would not only be unbearably tedious for the author but would soon render his books unsaleable. The ideal thing would be to have a prolegomenon containing general information about an entire ethnographic province, followed by shorter monographs on individual tribes which would not need to repeat what had already been said. I myself, however, have preferred to plan my series of Orissa monographs somewhat differently. This book on the Bondos will lay its emphasis on character and personality, for in this tribe it is the individual who stands out sharply and his human problems which are of special interest. In my *Economics of the Kuttia Konds,* I am stressing the economic aspect of Kond life — food-gathering activities, the problem (in great detail) of axe-cultivation, the preparation of food,

[1] Quoted by J. C. Molony, *Census of India*, 1911, Vol. XII, Part I, pp. 164-7.

[2] E. Thurston, *Castes and Tribes of Southern India* (Madras, 1909), Vol. VI, pp. 207 ff.

[3] R. C. S. Bell, *Koraput District Gazetteer* (Cuttack, 1945), embodying much information from W. Francis, *Vizagapatam District Gazetteer* (1907) and D. F. Carmichael, *Manual of the Vizagapatam District* (1869).

[4] C. von Fürer-Haimendorf, 'Megalithic Ritual among the Gadabas and Bondos of Orissa', *J.R.A.S.B.*, Vol. IV (1945), pp. 149-78 — henceforth quoted as 'Megalithic Ritual'; 'Avenues to Marriage among the Bondos of Orissa', *Man in India*, Vol. XXIII (1943), pp. 158-72 — henceforth quoted as 'Avenues to Marriage'; 'Religion and Ethics among the Konyak Nagas and other Indian Tribes' in *Essays in Anthropology presented to S. C. Roy* (1942), pp. 158-68 — henceforth quoted as 'Religion and Ethics'. There are also some remarks on the Bondos in *The Reddis of the Bison Hills* (London, 1745), pp. 8, 37, 49, 328, 330-5.

the economics of social and religious obligation, debt, bond-service, and so on. In *The Religion of the Hill Saoras* I am attempting a study of primitive religion in a setting peculiarly favourable, for the Saoras are the most religious tribe I know, and here the problems of tribal belief in a Supreme Being, the character of the demigods and demons, eschatology, magic and sorcery, religious conversion, taboo and ceremonial will receive detailed consideration. In a book planned on the Gadabas, I hope to deal rather with the question of sex and marriage, which will of course involve a more intensive study of childhood than I attempt in the other works. Finally, instead of overloading each of these books with a large quantity of myths and legends, I am publishing the whole of my collection in *Tribal Myths of Orissa,* which will be the fifth volume of my series 'Specimens of the Oral Literature of Middle India'.

This plan has the great advantage of providing some variety; it has the defect that no one book will give an encyclopedic picture. In the present work I have sketched very lightly my account of Bondo axe-cultivation, harvesting and the preparation of food—for I shall be describing in the greatest detail substantially the same practices when I write about the Konds. Any differences, and there are some, will of course be carefully noted. I have recorded over seventy Bondo legends; I give some of them here, but the majority will appear in *Tribal Myths of Orissa.* I have not discussed in detail certain aspects of Bondo religious belief and practice, and I have refrained from drawing parallels, because I go into these matters so fully in my monograph on the Saoras.

This book, therefore, will, I hope, be accepted as a strictly limited study of part of Bondo life, an article from the encyclopedia perhaps, but not the encyclopedia itself. I have tried to discover how the Bondo feels and thinks, how he reacts to the great crises of life, what he himself, as a human being, is really like. And, of course, since no individual can be understood apart from his setting, I have had to give some account of the main cultural features of Bondo life.

The Bondo is a difficult person and his is a hard unyielding country. He has brought to a high degree of efficiency the technique of keeping himself to himself. He even invokes the aid of theology against the outsider. Some villages are supposed to be under the spell of a fury so touchy that it is unsafe for any visitor to sleep within his jurisdiction; even the police are careful to camp outside. At certain seasons, notably during the great summer festival of the Giag-gige, no one may enter any village and the paths are barricaded with armfuls of thorn-bushes. My first expedition, in December 1943, was attended by every possible difficulty. I had no maps, for they had all been confiscated by the military. It was very difficult to get supplies of food which would last a month for a large party. I had to waste days by the roadside, waiting for motor-buses which failed to arrive. After reaching Jeypore, I had to leave with my wife and little son on foot for the forty-mile walk to Govindpalle. After a day's journey we were picked up by a bus, which had an engine that actually worked, and this took us part of the way. More time was then wasted trying to get bullock-carts, as no porters were available. After getting to Kadamguda, the first Bondo village in the plains, no one was willing to escort us into the hills. Once in the hills, no one would sell us anything, porters refused to help us move camp, the entire population crowded round us, smiling amiably and begging for tobacco, watching our every movement (I once looked up in a little lavatory of leaves and branches to find myself surrounded by men and women gazing absorbed), but no one was willing to do anything that looked at all like work. Later, my son, then two years old, developed pneumonia and it took us a long week to get him into hospital.

My next tour, in March 1945, was more successful, though I suffered badly from malaria. By then, we had learnt how to handle the Orissa aboriginal and I had an official status for my inquiries. We now got on very well, almost too well. On the first tour we were treated with distant and aloof respect, on the second with drunken familiarity. And the Bondos, especially when a bit high, are undoubtedly alarming. They have no respect at all for human life and, while it is romantic and interesting to number so many murderers among one's friends, I used to feel sometimes rather apprehensive lest one of them should feel the need of a little further practice. One evening, in fact, when I had gone to see some ceremony in a neighbouring village, a group of drunkards invaded our camp and threatened to kill my wife and son; there was no reason for it, except that they were there. Another time, when a group of Bondos were quarrelling and had begun to flourish their knives, my wife went alone into the midst of them and rebuked them with some well chosen words. They were so astonished that they soon made friends. My assistant Sundarlal has been threatened with death on several occasions and on one occasion at least only his quick wit saved him. His presence at Tulaguram during the Giag-gige Festival was considered by the theologians to be affecting the success of the ritual hunt and, since it was taboo to turn him out of the village, he had to be removed by other means. But he sacrificed a goat to Bursung and an old shirt to the priest and they let him off. When a village goes drunk, as it may do at any moment, it is an unpleasant place to be in. I must confess that even if it is expected to be sober, I generally have a slight feeling of apprehension when approaching a Bondo village for the first time.

It was not until the visits of January and February 1946 that I felt I had really got on terms with the Bondos. By this time I had many personal friends among them; Sundarlal and my other assistants had many more; the first suspicions had largely disappeared — no depredation from tigers had followed my earlier visits, there had been no fresh taxation, no policy of prohibition (of which, for some odd reason, I was darkly suspected) had been introduced, no girls had been carried off to the war; we had begun to fit into the picture. In 1946, too, I had the great advantage of being accompanied by exceptionally friendly and helpful people. In January I took with me Mr H. V. Blackburn and Warrant-Officer H. Milham to see the Sume-Gelirak Festival. Val Blackburn, large in heart as in body, has spent a quarter of a century among the aboriginals of Bastar and Orissa. There has never been a more generous employer of aboriginal labour or a more understanding friend of Muria and Kond, Gond, Baiga and Pardhan. Within a few hours of our arrival at Bodoballe he had organized an archery competition, and had been invited to fire a few rounds from his twelve-bore at a hill across the valley to drive away a dangerous demon. His great success, however, was at Bodapada, where he at once became intimate with the notorious double murderer, Miliya Bodnaik, one of the most charming people in the tribe, though apt, when drunk, to get a little fresh.

Harry Milham had seen the Konds, but this was his first real experience of aboriginal India. It was interesting to see how quickly he became *en rapport* with the people, even though he was unable to converse with them; they felt instinctively that he respected and liked them, for this respect, so woefully absent in the attitude of most of their fellow-countrymen, is the real secret of success with the aboriginals. He wrote an amusing and understanding account of his visit, from which I take the following sentences as indicating the reaction of an aircraftsman, who had no anthropological training and certainly no axe to grind. On the dress of Bondo women, he writes: 'Though they wore little I certainly did not agree with the Indians who said their dress was indecent. My reaction was a comparison of their natural modesty with the deliberate provocation of the modern civilized bathing-dress.' On the attitude of the investigator: 'It was essential that we should become a complete part of the village life, if we were to become sufficiently inconspicuous to allow us to see all their daily life and ceremonial.' On the women again: 'Their shaven heads make them appear ugly at first sight, but one soon realizes that some of them are very beautiful and all have really lovely eyes. I did not see one ugly woman in all my tour. The old women are charming. They enjoy far more equality with men than do any of the other oriental women I have seen. They are always happy and have a wonderful smile.' And the conclusion: 'Dear old Miliya! I was really touched when he came along and said good-bye. Then our special pals gave us a farewell grin and they were off in single file down a narrow path. I watched them go, their chatter and laughter growing fainter till at last the end man disappeared and my adventure with these "rude savages" was ended. Sentimentalist though I may be, I had a lump in my throat when they went and with the last disappearing back I knew

I had left a great deal of genuine humanity behind me, to come back where the Bondo " All for one and one for all " is modified generally to " All for one, and that's me ".'

Later I made a second expedition and this time I had with me Shamrao and Kusum Hivale and their adorable children, Suresh and Ramula, who were not only a solace to me, but a perpetual source of pleasure to the people. On this occasion we divided our time between only three villages — Katamguda, Andrahal and Mundlipada — and we managed to witness a number of interesting events, the worship of Pat Khanda Mahaprabhu, the erection of *gunom* stones, two festivals, two ritual beddings, a girl's kidnapping and the addition of a stone to a *sindibor.*

Shamrao Hivale, whose book *The Pardhans of the Upper Narbada Valley* arrived when we were camping in Mundlipada, made a number of independent investigations, for he spent some time alone at Andrahal and Mundlipada. Whatever else the Bondos may think about me, I am sure they regard me as a person who knows how to pick his friends, and Shamrao soon had a number of devoted admirers who, he claims, did not hesitate to tell him all. I particularly value his support and confirmation of my views on the sexual discretion of the Bondos, their estimate of the moral reactions of the Supreme Being, and my general impression of their character which he did much to correct and enlarge.

On these later expeditions my domestic servants were aboriginals from the Central Provinces. Their general attitude was that 'if these are aboriginals, we're civilized' — which is true of the externals, but not of the mind and heart. A Gond exclaimed, 'May tigers munch their bare bottoms *kirach-kirach!*,' revealing a prudery which my R. A. F. friend certainly did not share. My Pardhan cook described the Bondo women: 'like soldiers they carry all their possessions on their backs', which is really very good; another day he said they were 'like overladen little donkeys'.

Every serious writer sooner or later finds himself up against the problem of how to spell. Sir William Jones has been credited with being the first to propose a satisfactory transcription of oriental words : it was he who discovered that Tabriz was a better spelling than Tubburase. At the beginning of the nineteenth century, Solvyns was spelling Ahir — Auhheer, and sepoy — cipaye, and even today we have not reached uniformity. Here our first difficulty is with the names of places. The Census records do them one way, the Sessions Courts in another, the maps in a third, one's ethnographic colleagues in a fourth, and the Bondos themselves complicate the whole thing by calling the villages by entirely different names — Mundlipada is Bodajangar or Serayen, Dumiripada is Gisane, Bodoballe is Bubu-en, Bodapada is Gundrone, Andrahal is Gurone, Kirsanipoda is Gusube, Gokurupada is Omdile. I have decided, therefore, for the sake of uniformity, to follow the spellings (which are the ultimately official spellings) of the maps of the Topographical Survey, even though these often depart drastically from the local pronunciation. I have allowed myself only one liberty; I call the capital of Bondoland Mundlipada (Fürer-Haimendorf calls it Mudulipada in his articles) instead of Mundlapada, for I have got so used to hearing Bondos call it that, that it has got into my mind and thinking.

For the spelling of other words, we are faced with the problem as to how far a word in roman character is intended to appeal to the ear or to the eye. The roman script does not lend itself to accentuation, to lines above or below the line, to those 'damned dots' which confuse the typesetter and the reader. We print *Eugenia jambolana* without an accent; why should we put one on its Indian equivalent *jamun?*[1] We do not disfigure Russian, Italian or German words, when they visit English literature, with phonetic symbols, why must we so ill-treat Hindi, Oriya or Remo? It is another matter if someone like Emeneau, who is one of the greatest of living philologists, expresses everything he has to say in phonetic script. But once we descend to ordinary roman, we confess that we are not philologists and we should have liberty to put our words into whatever shape pleases the eye. I would like to see the greatest possible simplicity in our printing of Indian, and tribal, words just as we write Delhi, Poona and Bombay without any reference to the real pronunciation of these not unimportant place-names. And particularly in dealing with tribal words, I think that their form should as far as possible indicate their linguistic and cultural affiliations.

For example, Fürer-Haimendorf spells the sacramental food of the Bondos *tsoru,* which gives it a definitely Austro-asiatic flavour. But the word is the usual Sanskrit *caru,* or the still more usual Tamil *soru,* and I prefer to suggest this by making a compromise between origin and pronunciation by writing it *soru.* I would not object to writing *tsindibor,* using the initial *t* to suggest something outlandish in the word, but I think *tsoru* (or *tsua* for the commonplace Oriya word for 'well') goes too far in the way of appeasement of the phoneticians.

Another problem that arises is how far are we to give in to the common dialectical variations on ordinary words of Sanskrit derivation? Koppers spells the word more usually transliterated Bhagavan in its dialectical form Bhagwan. Fürer-Haimendorf gives Mahprohu instead of the normal Mahaprabhu. Now if Bhagwan or Mahprohu were genuine aboriginal words, there would be every reason for printing them as they are pronounced. But since they are simply bad attempts at articulating conventional Sanskrit words, of ancient lineage and nation-wide distribution, the use of dialectical forms tends to obscure their origin, which

[1] In his classical *Religion and Art in Ashanti* (Oxford, 1927), R. S. Rattray says, 'As the interest of this volume is primarily anthropological, I have deliberately avoided the use of diacritical marks on words in the vernacular', (p. 9).

is not desirable. Let us translate this into western terms. Suppose I want for example, to write a monograph on Cockney theology. Gerald Kersh, in his novel *The Nine Lives of Bill Nelson* (1942) transliterates the Apostles Creed as recited by a group of London children:

I bleevn Gotherfather or might be
Maker revven nearth,
Than in Jesus Crisis only sonour Lor
Doo was concede by the Yoly Gose
Bore nother Verge in Mary
Sufferedunder punch us Pilate.....

And the Lord's Prayer:

Ow
Farcher Treven,
Harold be Thy name,
Thy kinkum
Thy wilderdun....
Thine skindum pown glory evnever Rah-men.

Now I claim that to write the august symbols Bhagavan and Mahaprabhu as Bhagwan and Mahprohu, not only obscures their lineage, but makes them as ridiculous as Jesus Crisis or Farcher Treven. What would be thought of a serious theological treatise that continually referred to 'Gawd' or 'the Yoly Gose'? It is true that the Bondos, when indulging themselves in the fervour of religious supplication, pronounce the name of the Supreme Being as something like 'Mahprohu'. But in ordinary talk they frequently say Mahaprabhu or even Mahapurub (the normal Bastar way of pronouncing the word). I have preferred, therefore, to write Mahaprabhu throughout the book, as I have given Bhagavan instead of Bhagwan in my account of the Baigas. I have also written Pat Khanda Mahaprabhu in order to stress the affinities of the title to the chivalrous and ancient tradition of Rajput India: *khanda* is the old word for a sword. Pata Konda, given by Fürer-Haimendorf, represents the Oriya pronunciation, but it is not what the Bondos say. Their pronunciation is often nearer the old Sanskrit—I have noticed the same thing among the Baigas—than modern Oriya. But in any case, I do not think that once we have decided to use the roman script, pronunciation should guide us altogether in the transliteration of words. I would like to see a technique developed by which a word-symbol would tell us more of the word's origin and would look well on the page, than attempt to tell us how to say it. The pronunciation might well be indicated, in phonetic script, in a footnote.

In order to discover the basis of Bondo family life and clan organization, I worked on a double method, one (as it were) vertical, the other horizontal. The Bondos do not normally think in genealogical terms and their memories are bad; it was, in the main, only exceptional men who could remember their family trees for even three generations. I recorded 22 genealogies, all in the hill country, and these give a history of exactly 300 marriages. I print a selection of them in an Appendix. But, in addition to this, in order to check the situation as it is today and to cover a rather wider range of information than that obtainable from genealogies, I drew up a questionnaire which was put to 150 male adults, who lived in every part of the Bondo country, including the plains. The two types of investigation confirmed one another in a remarkable way. Thus, the questionnaire revealed that not a single informant had married his mother's brother's daughter or even a more distant cousin than that: the genealogies confirmed this situation, which is in such striking contrast to that among the Gond tribes immediately to the west. Other questions, such as the numerical distribution of the *kuda* and *bonso* and the extent to which clan exogamy has collapsed in the tribe, received almost identical support from both lines of inquiry.

I have already described how the Baron and Baroness von Fürer-Haimendorf, by their intrepid example and the generosity with which they placed their material at my disposal, first inspired me to visit the Bondo country. My obligations to Mr H. V. Blackburn and Mr Shamrao Hivale and his family have been expressed already.

Dr Rama Choudhri and Mr Asutosh Bhattacharyya both made valuable suggestions regarding the Hindu background of Bondo mythology and religion.

On all my tours I was accompanied by my assistant Sundarlal Narbada Prasad. Sundarlal also spent two months in the Bondo country making friends and watching events from April to June 1944 and again spent a month there in May 1945. Sundarlal's knowledge of the Bondos is profound. He established himself as a *moitur-bhai* (covenanted friend) of the Naiko of Mundlipada, the unofficial Raja of the Bondos, a man who at first opposed our inquiries and caused us a lot of trouble but later became an invaluable ally. He succeeded in persuading the Bondos of Tulaguram to allow him to remain with them throughout the Giag-gige ceremonies in 1944. His work throughout, as interpreter, general manager of the camp and ethnographic assistant, was quite admirable.

Ram Pratap Baghel, another of my assistants, toured the Bondo country with Sundarlal in 1944. Gulabdas was the first of my party to explore this difficult area; he went there originally in 1943 to find out villages most suitable for camp, accompanied me on the 1943-4 expedition, and later visited the country in May 1945. Chain Singh Sonwani also went with me, as did Dinabhandu and Gandorbo, Oriya-speaking assistants.

I received much assistance from the Government of Orissa. In 1944 I was appointed Hon. Anthropologist to Government, and in 1945 official Anthropologist. All officials were helpful, but I must express my special appreciation of the help given me by Mr J. Maher, I.C.S., to the late Mr J. W. Nicholson, C.I.E., I.F.S., Conservator of Forests, who did more than anyone to bring me to Orissa and to aid me after I had arrived; to Mr G. V. Rao, O.B.E., Diwan of the Jeypore Estate; to Mr C. Mitter, I.P., Superintendent of Police at Koraput; to Mr A. S. Bunn, I.C.S., Agent to the Provincial Government at Koraput; and to my old friend Mr F. E. A. Taylor, I.C.S., who was at Merton with me and with whom I foregathered after the lapse of a quarter of a century in the Guest House at Jeypore. Mr Sriramamurthy, Supervisor of Civil Supplies, and Mr M. C. Mahakur, Head Clerk in the Koraput Secretariat, gave me invaluable practical assistance.

Mr J. R. D. Tata and Mr J. P. Patel, who have assisted me in the publication of nearly all my books, extended their interest to this one also, Mr Tata making a generous donation towards the cost of the illustrations. I cannot adequately express my gratitude to these two friends for their support.

I must also express my gratitude to the Warden and Fellows of Merton College for their aid towards the expenses of research.

Patangarh V. E.
10 August 1946

POSTSCRIPT

THIS book was completed in August 1946, but after it had gone to the press, certain queries were raised which demanded confirmation. In December 1947, therefore, I paid a brief visit to the Bondo hills, camping at Bodapada (where I learnt to my grief that my old friend Miliya was dead), Andrahal and Tulaguram. I was accompanied by two members of the Department of Anthropology, Mr A. Bhattacharyya and Mr S. Roy: Mr Roy recorded a number of genealogies and his inquiries on the family and clan situation in the tribe confirmed mine. I also had with me my friend Mr D. V. Sassoon, whose delight in the Bondos and human love for them is evident in the photographs which he has generously allowed me to use.

V. E.

CONTENTS

ILLUSTRATIONS

COLOURED PLATES

FIGURES

CHAPTER ONE

INTRODUCTION

1. The Bondos

The Bondos, known among themselves as Remo ('men'), are a small tribe of the type now often called Austro-asiatic, which—at the time of the 1941 Census—numbered only 2,565 persons. Their country is the wild and mountainous region north-west of the Machkund River, and here they have preserved themselves comparatively unaffected by the march of civilization. Indeed by plainsmen and officials the Bondos are regarded as entirely savage, almost as the classic savage type: the strange dress and appearance of their women, their violent homicidal ways, their unfamiliar tongue—they speak a difficult Austro-asiatic language—the inaccessibility of their abode, separate them from the rest of Orissa.

Earlier writers tended to regard the Bondos as an offshoot of the Gadabas, a neighbouring but much larger tribe of similar racial and cultural affiliations. Thus Henderson describes the Bondos as one of the three tribes into which the Gadabas are divided:

> The Gadabas are clearly divided into three tribes, the Bondo Porja, the Gutob (or Bodo Gadaba), and the Parenga Gadaba. I arrange them in the order of seniority as they appear to me. They cannot be mistaken; the Mongoloid cast of countenance is at times very marked, this being the case, as I have noticed, rather more often among the women than among the men, at least among the younger men.[1]

Thurston, who bases his account of the Bondos on the reports of May and Henderson, classifies them as Porojas, but describes them as 'a section of Gadabas, calling themselves Bonda Gadaba and speaking a dialect of Gadaba',[2] but a little later he says that this connexion is 'stoutly denied' by the Bondos themselves.[3] Ramadas, in a slight article on the Porojas of Orissa, says that although the Bondos are usually counted as

[1] C. A. Henderson, quoted by J. C. Molony, *Census of India, 1911*, Vol. XII, Part I, p. 164.

[2] E. Thurston, *Castes and Tribes of Southern India* (Madras, 1909), Vol. XI, p. 209.

[3] ibid., p. 212.

the fifth class of Poroja, 'their habits and dress show that they are quite distinct. They appear to be more akin to the Marias of Bastar State.'[1] Fürer-Haimendorf points out that the languages of the Bondos and Gadabas, though of the same family, are so different 'that they are not mutually understandable'. Both tribes, however, he adds, 'recognize a fundamental relationship, partake of each other's food, and on rare occasions even intermarry. In spite of many divergences in material possessions, social customs and individual religious beliefs, and a certain difference in appearance accentuated by dress and ornaments, there seems to persist among Gadabas and Bondos a similar cultural atmosphere and we can hardly doubt that they are both representatives of ancient Austro-asiatic culture.'[2]

To the north-east the Bondo country merges into that of the Gadabas and the Bondos of this area are sometimes called Gutob Bondos or San (little) Gadabas. They employ the services of Gadaba Dissari shamans. They use many Gadaba words. They make mats and baskets in Gadaba style. At Andrahal I saw a Bondo whose ancestors had for generations been *mahaprasad* with members of a Gadaba family of Onagelu. He had recently been to that village for a funeral and his friend had given him a Gadaba woman's cloth which he was wearing as a shawl. The first member of the Jigri clan was a Gadaba who was adopted by an old Bondo and his wife.

An interesting Gadaba story from Chikanput claims the Bondos as descendants of the first Gadaba couple.

Padum Gadaba and his wife lived in Anchiput. They had five married sons. When all the boys were married, the old woman conceived again and in due time gave birth to a son. Padum took the placenta and cord to Baolidongar and buried them under a stone. From the placenta and cord a boy and girl were born; for six months they lived there, licking the stone. One day Padum and his wife went by and saw the children playing. They thought, 'These are of our race (*bonso*) for they are born of our own placenta and cord, but since they have been born in the jungle (*ban*), we will call them Bando'. They left the children alone and they grew up in the jungle. The boy caught and tamed wild cows and ploughed his fields.

The Bondos themselves look on all the tribes of the area as one family, members of which still eat together, though for purposes of marriage each tribe has become an endogamous unit. One myth of the origin of mankind describes how the twelve Gadaba brothers were born on the banks of the Godavari River and came thence to the Jeypore Hills. The eldest brother was a Bhoi Gadaba, the next an Asur Gadaba, and the

[1] G. Ramadas, 'Porojas', *Man in India*, Vol. XI (1931), p. 248.
[2] Fürer-Haimendorf, 'Megalithic Ritual', p. 161.

remaining ten — Kond, Bondo, Didayi, Jhoria, Parenga, Konda (Dora), Holar, Pengu, Chileri and Maria. Another story recalls the names of only seven of the twelve brothers.

When the earth was made, the first boy and girl became man and wife and the girl conceived. In those days there was no house nor village, and they wandered from place to place. When the day came for the birth of the child, the two sat beneath a sago palm, and here the girl was delivered of twins. At that moment a deer came by and the husband ran to kill it. The deer led him a very long chase, but he caught and killed it in the end. After he had killed it, he cut up the carcass on the spot and sat down to eat the flesh.

The woman watched the road for him, then after a long while she said to herself, 'He has surely killed the deer and is eating; he will bring nothing for me and I will go hungry'. So thinking she put the children down at the foot of the tree and went to find her husband. When she found him she too sat down to eat the fresh raw meat, and they both forgot about the children.

But under the sago palm the two children were crying for hunger. The palm saw their distress and felt sorry for them. The root of the palm went to the ocean and did it service. The ocean was pleased and said, 'What can I do for you? Tell me your desire.' The root told it about the hungry babies and the ocean poured water into the tree. This water climbed up the stem of the tree and dripped down from above into the mouths of the babies. So drinking, drinking they grew up. They married and from them were born twelve sons and twelve daughters. The twelve sons were the fathers of the twelve tribes — Bondo, Gadaba, Kond, Parenga, Didayi, Jhoria, Pengu — the rest we do not remember.[1] The eldest of them was Nangli Bondo.

The origin and affiliations of the Bondos are obscure. But we may accept the possibility that they are members of a group of very old Austro-asiatic tribes which at some remote date took shelter in the wild Jeypore Hills; whence they came, there is no evidence to say, although most of their affinities are with the north-east, nor can we tell how they fared during the centuries they must have lived in their present home. There are no records, no remains, and even the Bondos' own legends seem to me to be of comparatively recent date. But there is every reason to suppose that the Bondos have changed very little

[1] The word 'Poroja' has often been used to describe the Bondos, Jhorias, Gadabas and other tribes. This practice should be abandoned. Fürer-Haimendorf rightly says that 'the term Poroja, which means literally only "subject" or "ryot" and is commonly applied to at least seven distinct populations, all differing in language and culture, has given rise to so much confusion that it seems advisable to exclude it altogether from ethnological usage'. Henderson made a similar protest many years earlier, pointing out that to use, this word to describe the different tribal peoples was 'to make confusion worse confounded, and scientifically as effective as to make a generic class of rayats, and subdivide them into Kapu rayats, Veliala rayats, Oriya rayats and so on'. — Fürer-Haimendorf, 'Megalithic Ritual', p. 161; Molony, op. cit., p. 165.

during their long history and in them we have a chance of studying a type of character and its material expression that may be millennia old. Fürer-Haimendorf, in fact, suggests that the Bondos belong, 'not only in language but also in culture, to that large group of Austro-asiatic peoples who in Neolithic times developed an advanced and complex culture characterized as it seems by the shouldered-stone cult, rice cultivation on terraced and irrigated fields, the art of weaving, the keeping of cattle for purposes of slaughter and sacrifice, and the erection of megalithic monuments in the shape of menhirs, stone-circles and dolmens. It is the culture which to some extent still survives among such Austro-asiatic peoples as the Gadabas, Saoras, Mundas and Khasis and has close affinities to the Austronesian civilizations of the Malayan Archipelago.'[1]

2. The Bondo Hills

The influence of geophysical factors in the development of the Bondo character must not be ignored, for they are far-reaching and important. The remote and elevated plateau on which these highlanders live has isolated them from the corrupting influences of the plains; its open windswept heights has infected them with its own strength and freedom.

The Bondo Hills, many of them about three thousand feet high, overlook the Malkangiri plain to the west and descend sharply on the south to the Machkund valley which divides Orissa from Madras. The hills lie within the borders of the great Jeypore Zamindari, nearly ten thousand square miles in extent and populated by well over a million people, whose Maharaja has his headquarters at Jeypore. The Zamindari is not a State in its own right — the title of Maharaja is a personal distinction held by the present Zamindar — and most of it was formerly included in the Vizagapatam District of the Madras Presidency. When Orissa was constituted a separate province in 1936, Jeypore became officially the 'British' District of Koraput and was made a Partially Excluded Area under the Government of India Act. In theory the fact that a district was an 'Agency' tract or a Partially Excluded Area meant that arrangements could be made for the protection and development of the aboriginal population. A full account of the District and Zamindari Estate is given in the serviceable *Koraput District Gazetteer,* which may be consulted by the curious.

The location of the Bondo settlements in a 'State', for whatever the legal position the inhabitants of Jeypore have never accepted any other status than that of subjects of an Indian Raja, has had an important effect on the Bondo mind. The people are singularly loyal to their ruler, and

[1] C. von Fürer-Haimendorf, *The Reddis of the Bison Hills* (London, 1945), p. 332.

the fulfilment of their duties to him and his officials is one of the virtues regularly impressed on young people. The cult of a sacred sword at Mundlipada is directly linked with the honour done to similar swords in the royal armoury at Jeypore. The absence of obsequiousness and the sense of being in a historic tradition is one of the most pleasing characteristics of State subjects everywhere in India.

Rainfall is moderate — about 62 inches, most of which falls in July and August — but the district is very unhealthy; the prevalence of malaria, and even of blackwater, probably accounts for the elaborate religious apparatus devised by the Bondos for dealing with the demons and furies of disease. The Bondos do not, however, suffer from the yaws which so affects the Koyas and Marias not far to the west. Wild animals are common throughout the district, but there is little game left in the Bondo Hills, which are largely denuded of forest growth. But tigers and bears appear from time to time and are regarded as evidence that the people have offended the demigods or dead.[1]

The best approach to the Bondo country is, to my mind (and I have tried three different ways), through Govindpalle and Kadamguda. It is possible — this refers to 1946 — to go by car certainly to Govindpalle and, if the road has been repaired, to within a mile of Kadamguda, a large and prosperous plains Bondo village about eight miles from Mattili, the police headquarters of the tract. From Kadamguda the traveller can climb into the hills by easy stages, first to Tulaguram at 1,751 feet, then to Goyiguda at 1,993 or Dumiripada about 1,000 feet higher, and finally to the Mundlipada group of villages at just over 3,000 feet. This is easier than the ascent from Mundaguda, which is long, steep and rough, and is more convenient than the approach from the Dudma Falls which, though it involves less climbing, is very roundabout, requiring a journey on foot of over fifteen miles through the forest to Katamguda, the first Bondo village.

By the Kadamguda route the traveller's first glimpse of Bondos will be in the well-to-do villages, Kadamguda, Pandraguda, Puchaguda, Lamptaput, Semiliguda, Pakkanaguda, strung out in line, less than a quarter of a mile apart, along the foot of the hills. Each of these villages stands in a grove of fine trees and is surrounded by broad acres of cultivated land. The scenery is charming, for above the pleasant wooded landscape in the foreground rise the fine hills beyond.

From Pakkanaguda a path winds up the ghat. The Bondos, like the Konds, have a very fair idea of how to align a path and the ascent is not too steep. Half-way up it is possible to rest on a projecting rock and look down over the Malkangiri plain spread out like a map below.

[1] In 1934, 1935 and 1936 the number of human beings killed in the whole district by tigers was 77, 87 and 94 respectively.

The first Hill Bondo village is Tulaguram in its well-watered valley; from here the path goes more steeply through uplands, heavily cultivated by axe and fire, to the beautiful and distinctive Dumiripada on the slopes of a hill which rises to 3,251 feet. From Dumiripada the traveller may go south-west up and down over low hills to Mundlipada, the Bondo capital, with its group of satellite villages, or east to Andrahal and Katamguda, nestling remote and peaceful in their forgotten valley. South of Mundlipada is the beautiful Pinnajangar with its sacred grove and gentle restful scenery, and to the east is Bandapada on the edge of the plateau looking down towards the Didayi villages in the Machkund valley.

There is little diversity in the scene. Everywhere are far-stretching views, blue hills rising against the horizon, mist-covered valleys at one's feet. There are few trees to shut one in. The hills are very bare, shaved clean by centuries of axe-cultivation. Irrigated rice-fields stretch along the valleys and creep up every possible waterway. The villages appear as patches of vivid dark green jackfruit and mango trees. The country has a character and distinction of its own. There is a sensation of being high up, out of the way, above the world.

Geographically, the Bondo settlements fall into three groups, the Bara-jangar group, the Gadaba group and the Plains group. The Bara-jangar group is the most important. Jangar or Bodajangar is one of the names of Mundlipada, or Serayen, the capital of the Bondo country, which is one of a group of twelve villages, the *bara-jangar,* from which the Bondo country is sometimes called the Bara-jangar-des. It is in Mundlipada that the Bondo race came into being; it is about this village and its groves that the most ancient legends cluster; its Naiko is of great authority and is subsidized and supported in his position by the Maharaja. The Naiko has under his jurisdiction Mundlipada itself, Kirsanipada, Tulaguram, Bandapada, Bandiguda, Basupada, Salanpada, Gokurupada, Pinnajangar, Kichchipoda, Dattipada and the low-country Pandraguda, each with its own Naiko who owes him allegiance and must bring him tribute three times a year.

These twelve villages are said to be the original Bondo settlements; some say that each was founded by one of twelve brothers. Among them there is a certain degree of cultural homogeniety. Their citizens, and only they, attend the worship of Pat Khanda Mahaprabhu; they are the most devoted to the Maharaja. Yet although the oldest of the villages, their comparative proximity to the Mundaguda bazaar and the Mattili police station has caused a certain modernization of ideas, definitely 'in advance', if that is the right word, of the outlook of Andrahal and Dumiripada. The villages outside the Bara-jangar group look on it with some derision, and call the people Didayi Bondos, a title that is indignantly rejected. But Didayi influence is certainly stronger than Gadaba in this part, and the gibe has some point.[1] The Bara-jangar Bondos do not usually make mats or baskets.

The 'Gadaba' group of villages includes Andrahal, Dumiripada, Katamguda, Antamguda, and to some extent Bodoballe and Bodapada. These are the most 'difficult' and the most attractive of the Bondo villages. They have come under Gadaba influence, which has modified their language — their vocabulary differs in many respects from that of the Bara-jangar villages—taught them to make mats and baskets, and given them the name of Gutob Remo, or Gadaba Bondo. This group of Bondos does not acknowledge the authority of the Naiko of Mundlipada; it has no interest in the cult of Pat Khanda Mahaprabhu; and it may even keep its festivals on different dates.

The third group comprises the plains villages to which I have already referred. The Bondos here have been in close contact with large numbers of low-caste Hindus for years. It is only recently, however, that they have been made the target of deliberately destructive propaganda, aimed at eliminating everything that is distinctively 'Bondo' in their lives and reducing them to the drab mediocrity of the Hindu untouchable. This propaganda has had some success. A few Bondo families have allowed their women to grow their hair, to pierce their nose for ornaments, to get themselves tattooed, to abandon their home-weaving industry and wear the mill-cloth of the bazaars, to neglect the rules of exogamy and desert the sacred *sindibor*. In just what way these remarkable results, achieved at such great pains by ardent but unintelligent social workers, are expected to benefit the people, it is hard to say. Drunkenness is even more endemic than in the hills; murders are frequent; and the simple truthfulness characteristic of real hillmen is rapidly disappearing. Such is the inevitable result of 'uplift' divorced from brains.

These three groups tend, partly for geographical reasons, to associate mainly with themselves; no Bondo cares to go outside his own area except to meet a girl. Thus Andrahal people do not usually attend the Mundlipada festivals. But boys visit the dormitories everywhere; even from the plains they climb up the hills and go right over to Katamguda. Intermarriage is common among all the hill people at least; I found men at Andrahal had married girls from Katamguda, Bodapada, Antamguda, Dumiripada and Bodoballe of their own group, from Mundlipada, Bandapada, Kirsanipada, Kichchipoda, and Salanpada of the Bara-jangar group, and from Puchaguda and Padua of the plains group. But only two wives had come from the plains, and there is now a tendency on the part of the hillmen to avoid the lowcountry Bondos because of their breach of ancient taboos and neglect of tribal customs.

[1] The Bara-jangar people say they are Mona Remo or Boda Bondo, 'big' Bondos. Bondo men, but not women, may eat in Didayi houses: Didayis of both sexes accept food from Bondos, and thus admit a slight social inferiority.

3. The Bondo Village

A Bondo village is always charming; it generally stretches along or climbs up a hillside; most houses have a view. The dark evergreen of the jackfruit trees, the glorious colours of the mango, rise above the mouse-grey roofs of the houses and their red walls. There is no order in a Bondo village; the houses climb up and down the hillside in complete confusion; there is no arrangement in regular streets; the build-

Fig. 1. Girls clearing a village street with a rake, on which a child squats to give it weight

ings face any way they please and no site is of greater distinction than another. Sometimes there is a rough grouping according to clans — in Bodapada the Bodnaiks lived in one part and the Kirsanis in another — and related families naturally tend to neighbour one another. A Naiko or some wealthy citizen may build a private stone platform in front of his house. But there is no rule about it; in the main everybody lives alike and together. Bondo democracy expresses itself, rather untidily, in its town-planning.

Even the *sindibor*, the sacred megalithic platform which is the centre of the religious and social life of the community, is built wherever it is convenient, not in any special proximity to the house of the headman or priest. But it is always well placed in a shady level spot. Nearby may be the shrine of Hundi, built with a circular rubble wall.

There is no wall or fence enclosing the village; in spite of many feuds Bondo villages are never fortified. But all round are the little gardens of castor trees, tobacco plants, chillies or brinjals. There are manure-pits everywhere and below the settlement a spring or well. Formerly, the girls' dormitory was made on the outskirts of the place, but now the boys' and girls' houses are in the village, no different from any other building, and it is not easy to find them.

But every Bondo village has its own individuality. Dumiripada is one of the most beautiful and distinctive. One day in December I climbed the hill above it. I crossed a stone wall covered with clumps of exquisite blue flowers and pushed my way through masses of spear grass and over hill-clearings sowed with maize. The view from the top of the hill was magnificent. Below, on one side, were the grey roofs of the village set among jackfruit, plantain and castor trees. Away to the west and north was range upon range of hills leading to distant Tulsidongri in Bastar State. I could see nearer at hand examples of the three methods of Bondo cultivation — first, the ordinary fields on comparatively level ground; then the irrigated rice-terracing down the bed of a stream; finally the axe-cultivation on the steeper hillsides.

Dumiripada, like Tulaguram and Goyiguda, has most of its houses enclosed within high bamboo fences, thus encouraging family exclusiveness and independence. At Andrahal and Katamguda, however, the buildings are open and the communal nature of the village is more apparent. These settlements, like Mundlipada and Bandapada, are more like Juang villages, though they lack the fine central darbar hall and the enclosing fence. Andrahal, most fascinating and charming of all Bondo centres, spreads itself over a great area, reaching from a stream in the valley almost to the top of the hill on which it is built. The houses are arranged in terraces one above the other and there are numerous *sindibor*. The village is so scattered that here many houses are able to maintain their little gardens of tobacco or chillies, enclosed within low bamboo fences, immediately around them. Trees grow everywhere, and there are stacks of firewood — wood is a perennial problem in these sparsely forested hills — bundles of grass for thatching, and great bins built up on piles for the temporary storage of *Eleusine corocana*.

Only a mile away down the valley is Katamguda, in its own very narrow defile. On either side rise steep hills, fully cultivated, and the valley bed is well irrigated for rice. The houses clamber up a hillside and are well sheltered by castor trees and sago palms. The path to the west leads to the main sacrifice ground and the *gunom* menhirs, before it disappears into thick jungle. In the middle of the village is the shrine of Hundi, a rubble wall round a central stone pillar, and a little below it is the shaded *sindibor*, a circle of flat stones flanked by menhirs.

Another charming village is Bodoballe. It stands on the top of a windy hill overlooking a deep valley into which some of its houses have overflowed. The hills around are shaven as closely as the head of a Bondo girl, but the village itself is well shaded with trees. The houses are in even more of a jumble than usual, placed where the level of the ground permits, dodging the rocks that crop out everywhere. There are no streets, no lines or rows, no arrangement in terms of procedure or wealth. One or two houses have their own gardens round them, but most stand in the village surrounded only by high bamboo fences.

Bodoballe is high up on its hill, but Pinnajangar is in a valley surrounded by steeply rising slopes, the mountain, Bali, going to 3,250 feet above it. The valley is prettily wooded, though the hillside, when I was there one March, was black with the fires of axe-cultivation. There is good terracing here, some of it supported by stone walls. Near the village is a fine sacred grove and in the middle of the settlement a stone shrine for Hundi and several *sindibor* well shaded and commanding pleasant views of the valley below. Although there are abundant sago palms, this village has a good reputation for its freedom from serious crime and the people are quiet, friendly and obliging.

Mundlipada, the capital, lies in the most thickly populated part of the Bondo Hills, on one side of a gentle valley. On the opposite hill are Salanpada, Gokurupada and Kirsanipada nestling among their trees. Its houses stretch along a hillside and are more open than usual; there is always plenty of light, you feel, in Mundlipada. Behind the village, down the far slope of the hill, is the fine grove of mango trees and the spring called Kingu Bodak (in Oriya, Kappor Chua). Here the Bondo race came into being. Here the women laughed at Sita and were cursed to go shaven and naked. Higher up the hill is another grove where, in a giant banyan, is preserved the sacred sword of Pat Khanda Mahaprabhu.

How far does the general lay-out of a tribal village express the tribe's character? A Baiga or Kuttia Kond settlement, for example, expresses by its carelessness, by its offhand construction and arrangement, the indifference of the people to a particular site, their love of constant change. The Bison-horn Maria village, on the other hand, where every house, or group of houses, stands in the centre of its own cultivated fields and almost forms a village on its own, signifies the strongly individualistic character of this tribe, its love of material possessions, its dislike of grouping. A Juang village again perfectly reveals the communal nature of the people; the houses are jumbled together within a protecting fence and around a central community hall.

The Bondo village is permanent; some of the settlements must be very old. Here we recognize the Bondo love of staying put, his dislike of moving around, his deep attachment to the village unit and the village soil.

The Bondo village is democratic. You cannot tell by looking at it where the important people are, and who has the money. The only tokens of distinction are the occasional private *sindibor*-platforms in front of individual houses.

But at the same time, the Bondo village is a mess. It is very difficult to get about; there are no proper paths, no real communications; you aim at a friendly gate and end up on a dung-heap. But, though this may give a lot of trouble to the visitor, the Bondos themselves do not seem to mind it.

4. The Bondo House

The Bondo house is a self-contained unit in a strongly communal and democratic setting. The buildings are not scattered about over a wide area, each in its own garden, as by the Murias and many Gonds. On the other hand they are not joined together in long rows, as by the Saoras, or round a rectangle, as among the Konds. The general arrangement, as I have already suggested, is not unlike that of the Juangs of the Juang Pirh of Keonjhar State — the houses being grouped closely together, and all opening on to one another with little regular arrangement into streets — but the Bondo houses are more individualistic, for nearly every house has some sort of fence round it or at least a fence round its front compound. In villages like Tulaguram and Kadamguda this arrangement is specially emphasized. Each family enclosure contains two or more huts — one for the parents, one for a married son, another perhaps for another married son, or a poor relation — a cattle-shed and an open shelter where people sit to work and talk. But at Andrahal and Mundlipada the houses are much more open, and there is often only a small fence that makes a sort of enclosure in front.

The walls are of mud with a number of wooden pillars supporting the roof, which is thatched with grass. The veranda is fenced in with an unplastered bamboo wall. The floor is slightly, but only slightly, raised above the ground. The wooden door is substantial and always provided with a lock — as much to keep out enemies as to protect from thieves.

The fenced-in veranda is used for grinding, husking grain, cleaning rice and millet, making mats, and often as a bedroom. In the first room into which the door opens, the people cook, sit and sleep. Above the hearth are two wooden racks, one above the other, for drying fish, new grain, meat or tobacco. Along the far wall is an earthen platform raised some six inches above the ground, on which stand pots of water, gruel and

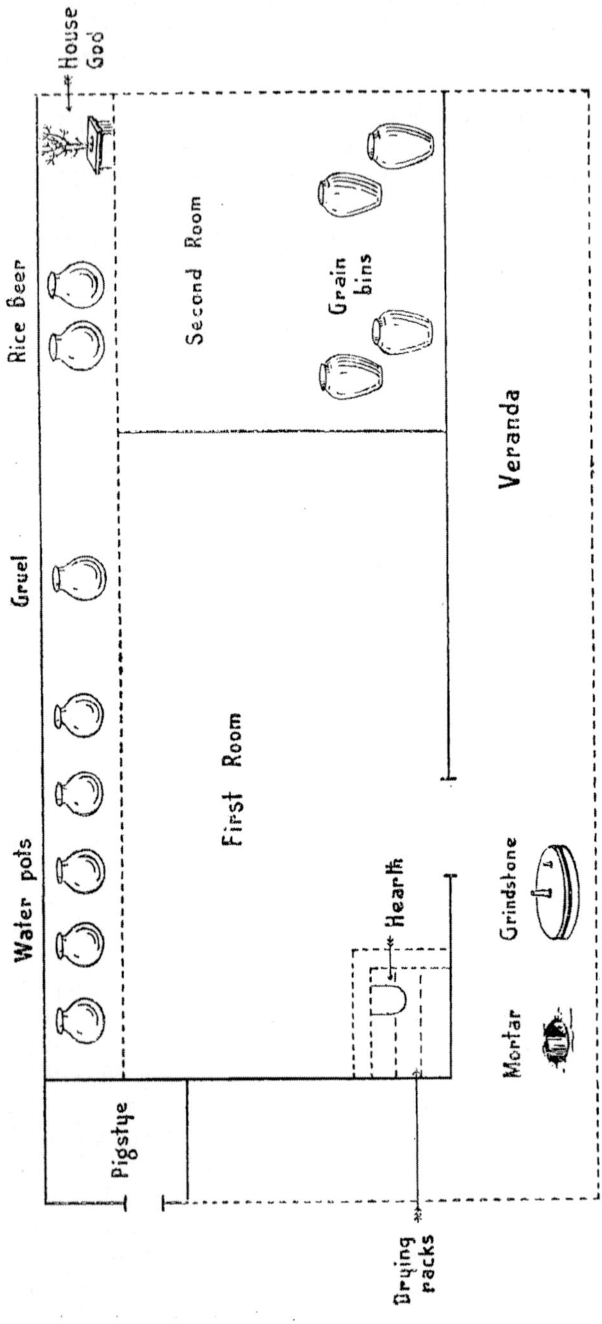

FIG. 2. Plan of a typical Bondo house

rice-beer. In the inner room are grain-bins, and in one corner the traditional branch of *Eugenia jambolana,* with a gourd depending from it to represent a house-god. These rooms are only five feet high, for immediately above is a loft, entered by an aperture in the ceiling of the inner room, where grain and all manner of goods are stored. This ceiling is, of course, flat, and above it is the main slanting roof, which is sometimes double, the lower layer being plastered with mud the better to keep out the rain. Since most Bondos do not observe menstrual taboos, there is no special room for women in their periods and no second door for their use. A pigsty is often built into the veranda, and hens are accommodated with commodious perches. Goats and cattle are given a special shed near by.

Walls are usually built up of mud mixed with straw; sometimes they are of plastered bamboo. In this case the bamboo slats may either be interwoven, as is commonly the case in the Central Provinces, or each piece may be split open with four or five cuts and flattened out. I have noted a similar technique among the Hill Marias of the Abujhmar. Planks of old sago palms are used to fence in open spaces.

When a new house is built, the central pillar is erected first. Mango leaves are tied round it to 'bring the dead and the gods near'. A mat is put over the leaves and this in turn is covered with thorns.

5. Appearance, Dress and Ornament

On the whole, the Bondos are a good-looking people. Boys and young men are often most attractive in appearance. Their fine carriage, magnificent physique, free and open countenance, delightful smile, is captivating. The way they do their hair is specially charming. As they grow older, however, they degenerate a little; the face coarsens, the body is dirtier, the hair is done in a different, and less pleasing, fashion. Like most tribesmen above a certain age, the Bondos let themselves go. In jail, they look terrible.

At first sight a visitor may exclaim that Bondo women are the ugliest he has ever seen. But in a few days, after he has got over the first shock of their rather unconventional appearance, he may revise his opinion. The illusion of ugliness is largely created by the shaven head. But a young girl with something covering her — a fish-basket or a sickle-curved bundle of *kereng* bark — often shows the world a face of character and charm. Little girls, ten or twelve years old, are sometimes very pretty, especially when they decorate their head-bands with sprigs of greenery and white, mauve or scarlet flowers. The chief fault of the older girls (apart, of course, from the lack of hair) is that there is perhaps a little too much of them. Like Baiga girls, they tend more to Audrey than to Tess. They are apt to be plump, rather sleek and smooth, big-lipped, bagpipe-breasted, with ample buttocks, large thighs, thick calves, 'thick as plantain stalks'. Older women are often very charming, with good features and an indefinable attraction that speedily makes one forget the oddity of their appearance.

FIG. 3. Woman's neckband of small brass rings strung on an iron loop

The Bondos themselves give the palm to the girl who gets herself up properly. 'When a woman puts on a lot of clothes like a Dom, we think nothing of her. For us our women are the prettiest. It is when a girl puts on a new bright-coloured cloth and many ornaments that we think her beautiful. Beauty is not in the body, but in its ornaments. For all bodies are at bottom alike, but we can make them different. A girl is beautiful before she marries, but less so after she has had a child.'

This was a Tulaguram judgement. At Mundlipada I was told that 'a girl should have a straight nose, dark eyes, upright ears, chest neither broad nor slender, arms plump and strong, firm belly, navel neither depressed nor protruding, slim waist, large buttocks. Such a girl is beautiful and will be virtuous; she will soon bear children and will be devoted to her home.' On the other hand, an ugly girl 'has a thin pinched face, like a mirror. The tip of her nose turns up, her eyes are too big or too small, she has a fat head, long ears, a thin chest, fat belly, protruding navel stump, coarse waist, scraggy hands and feet. Such a girl is ugly; no matter what she wears she will be unsightly.'

Boys at Andrahal used some rather poetical expressions while attempting to explain the meaning of a love-song. The phrases are probably traditional or at least based on the highly condensed song-technique. They described a girl's body as 'beautiful as a white cloud', her arms and legs 'round and shapely as a bamboo'; her breasts 'sparkling as two fishes'; her shadow 'broad and healthy as a buffalo'. Above all, the beautiful girl is 'useful as the leaf of a giant creeper'—the *Bauhinia vahlii,* from which leaf-cups and plates are made.

An impressive thing about the 'naked' Bondo is the impression of dressiness they give. They do not give one the feeling of almost aggressive nudity — as some Hill Marias or Kuttia Konds do: they seem rather to have too much on. The ornaments of the women cover the breasts and hang down to the navel. The cloth is scanty enough, yet it is remarkable how much it conceals, though a purist might complain that it slips down a little too low over the buttocks. But there is nothing 'indecent' about the Bondo dress, and after a day or two one forgets all about it.

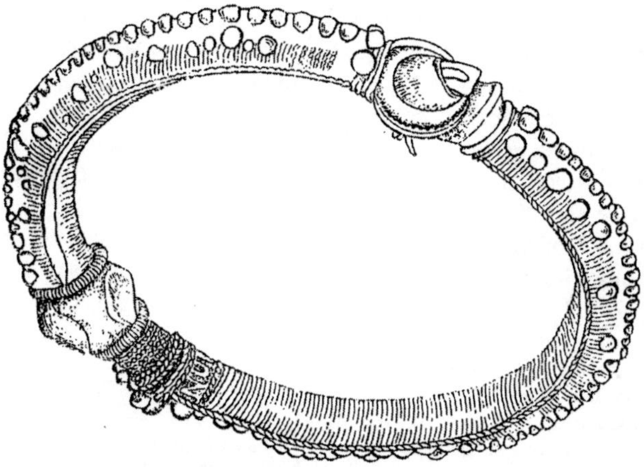

FIG. 4. Woman's brass neckband

It is the women's attire that is remarkable; a very few words will suffice for the men. Men and boys wear the simplest possible loin-cloth, a mere scrap of which is often attached to the waist-cord in front, passed between the legs and hung over the cord at the back. The flap may hang down or be tucked into the cord at one side. Very occasionally, someone back from the Tea Gardens may be seen in a tattered shirt or an old waist-coat, but generally men go as nearly naked as it is possible to be, and are able to display their splendid bodies to the sun and wind.

But no one, not even a little boy, should go entirely naked, and in fact it is unusual to see a child without some kind of rag. Even baby girls must have their minute coloured skirts and these, which are always falling off, sometimes look most diverting. For, so goes the legend,

Long ago two little boys, Bati Mundli and Bati Sisa, were playing together. Their tiny organs were red like raw meat. A kite appeared, swooped down and carried the two organs away with the seed in them. But it dropped them by a stream and mango trees sprang up. The two boys ran crying to their parents and it was decided that henceforward everybody should wear clothes.

There is hardly anything to say about the ornaments of the men. Small rings are inserted in the lobe of the ear and in the upper part of the helix, and from these little brass chains may depend. Bands or rings of aluminium may be worn on one or both arms; I saw one boy wearing an armlet made of a bit of telegraph wire which had been cut in the 1942

Revolution (he paid a Congressman four annas for it) and another boy with an armlet made of the rib of an umbrella. Sometimes you may see a youth with as many as four or five armlets on the right arm. Bondo youths have none of the art of necklace-making which distinguishes the Konds and Murias; round their necks they hang cheap and flimsy strings of tawdry brass. A few rings on the fingers complete the sum total of male ornament, which is in striking contrast to the profusion and variety of the women's decorative scheme.

It has been suggested that the dress and appearance of the Bondo woman is a survival of what was formerly the common practice of all the tribes of this area. C. A. Henderson, who is quoted in the *Madras Census Report* of 1911, has some interesting observations about this and I will quote him in full, in view of our extremely scanty information about the Bondos which is even thirty or forty years old.

> The customs and clothing [of the Bondos] suggest that they are at the stage which the better-known Gadabas passed some time ago. Clothing is to my mind a crucial test. The Bonda Porja taboo, which prevents their women clothing themselves above the waist, is well known. They supply the very patent deficiency by a mass of brass and bead necklaces, and by large heavy circular collars of brass, often of great weight. I sent my specimens to the Museum. These collars are locally made, and are jointed at one side, with a male and female clasp at the other end, which is secured by a bit of string of fibre. The loin-cloth is extremely exiguous, in fact, in fully developed women it does not meet round the hips. It is half suspended from a string, and shifted round the body to meet the exigencies of the moment. They shave their heads from early childhood, and tie round them a fillet of palmyra, or a string with olive shells or little scarlet seeds on it. Compare the familiar Bodo Gadaba (Gutob) found in villages on the main road near Koraput. The women's clothing is distinctly in two parts, a kilt and an upper cloth. A little observation and reflection would, I think, convince anyone that the adoption of the upper cloth is comparatively a recent matter. In the first place the cloths are separate ... in the second place these Gadaba women are not inordinately shy about showing their breasts... On one occasion, riding past, I saw a Gadaba woman coming from a wash. She had only got the kilt on, and the upper part of her body was quite bare...Another point in favour of this belief is that the Parenga women, though they retain their tribal cloth for the kilt, have not adopted, as the Gadabas have done almost universally, a cloth of the same make for their upper garment, but wear an ordinary white cloth on the shoulders. All three, I am convinced, till comparatively recently were unclothed above the waist; and among the remote Bonda Porjas the custom has persisted, backed by a pretty strong taboo...The fillet of the Bondos is common among the Gutob, but the latter have ceased (on my theory) to shave their heads. The Gutob 'bustle' is unknown to the Bondos, why I do not know; neither is it the fashion among the Parengas, because 'God did not give it to us at the beginning of things' or words to that effect.[1]

[1] C. A. Henderson, quoted by J. C. Molony, *Census of India, 1911,* Vol. XII, Part I, p. 164.

The woman's cloth is so important that I devote a separate section to it. Here we may note that the narrow skirt is held in place round the loins by a waistband, to which it is attached in front but not behind, where it slips down low over the buttocks. The girdle is nowadays bought in the bazaar and is sometimes made of little brass or iron bugles strung together. Formerly the women made rough cords of *kereng* fibre, strips of creeper or anything else available. There do not seem to be any special traditions about this girdle or rules for its use. Bondo women do not, even during the menstrual period, wear a pubic cloth between the legs.

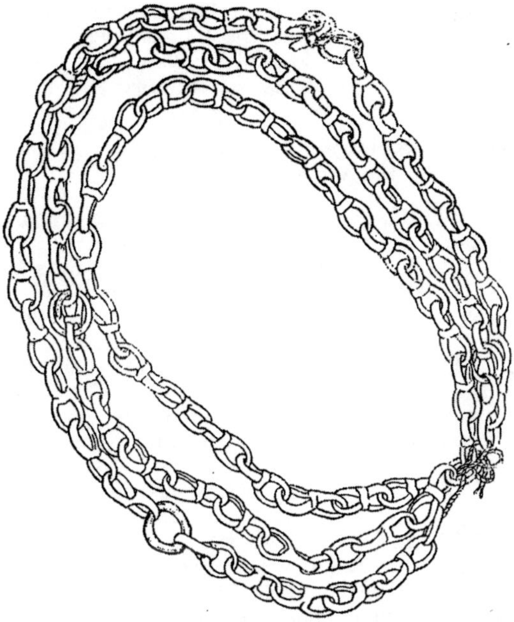

FIG. 5. Brass chain worn round a woman's neck

As I have suggested, the skirt is the least part of a Bondo woman's dress. She covers herself from the head downwards with a variety of ornamental devices. Round her shaven head she wears a number of bands—simple palmyra strips or woven and plaited fillets. Into these bands the younger girls put flowers, older women may stick leaf-pipes. They balance their sickles on their heads, with the blades thrust through the bands, when they go to the fields.

The Bondo woman wears no nose-ornament and does not seem specially concerned about the ears. This is probably connected with the obligation to be 'naked on top'. A few aluminium rings, with chain or pendant, in the helix or a brass button in the lobe is deemed sufficient. On both wrists, however, a woman wears a great many broad brass bangles, separated by bands of old cloth to prevent them from rubbing: I counted twenty-six on the left arm of one young woman and twenty-eight on the other; even then, she said, she had several more in the house. The Bondo tradition is that these bangles have a magical effect on child-bearing and the symbolism of the arm thrust into the bangle is too obvious to need emphasizing.

There were Bondos living in Theranaru and their numbers grew. In those days Bondo women did not wear bangles on their arms and for this reason when the Sisa offered sacrifice the demigods were not pleased and did not let the women conceive. One day Mahaprabhu came to the place and the Bondos complained to him that the demigods were giving them a lot of trouble and stopping children from being born. Mahaprabhu said, 'Call the women here'. They came and he examined them; he saw they had no bangles. 'This is the reason,' he said. 'If you put bangles on their arms you'll soon have plenty of children and good harvests.'

On the other hand, it appears to be taboo for a Bondo woman to wear anklets. The reason is given in the following legend.

There was a Naiko with a little daughter whom he loved very much. The mother was dead, and the sons married, and the girl used to live lonely in the house. There was a Dom in the village; he too had a daughter. This girl made friends with the Naiko's daughter. The Dom girl had anklets on her feet and the Bondo girl was envious of them and wanted to wear them too. A merchant came when only these two girls were in the house. The Naiko's daughter bought some anklets, exchanging them for grain. But directly she put them on she fell ill, for Dagoi was angry. The following day she died. Since then no Bondo woman has worn anklets, for Mahaprabhu told us, 'If your women wear anklets, Dagoi will kill them all'.

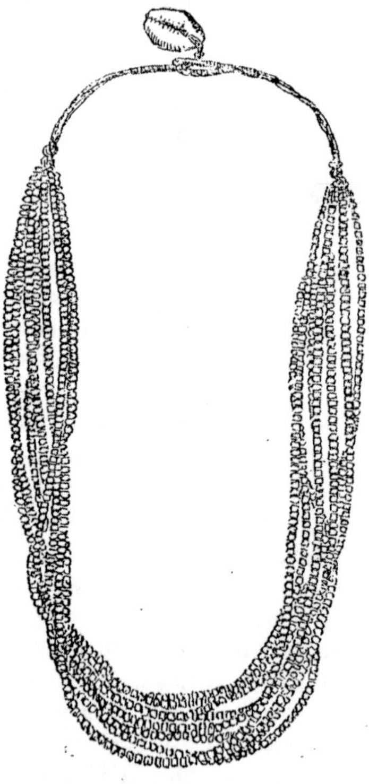

FIG. 6. Bead necklace with cowrie fastener

It is on the ornamentation of her neck and bosom that a Bondo woman lavishes her greatest care and takes her chief pride. She puts on a great mass of brass and beadwork; so heavy that she does not usually carry herself very well, for the weight of the ornaments disturbs the erect posture and flattens the breasts a little. There are heavy brass collars of several different patterns: a woman may wear six of these at once. Brass chains long enough to hang in half a dozen loops, eight-foot strings of coloured beads looped round and round, necklaces with beads arranged in regular patterns Muria-style, strings of shells and beans, cover the entire bosom and hang down to and even below the navel. The prevailing colour of these decorations is green, blue and yellow; red occurs, especially in some villages, but does not predominate. A girl often has a ruling colour so that the visitor can speak of 'the red girl' or 'the blue woman'.

These neck-decorations, which average in price a hundred or more rupees, are the most valuable form of property the Bondos have. When a woman dies, her daughters inherit her ornaments, but if there are no daughters, they are divided — those that came originally from her parents' house return to it, and the other ornaments given by the husband are claimed by him or by his family. It is a tradition that a girl should go fully clad in ornaments to her husband's house. The husband is not expected to give his wife money for beads, though he ought to produce the price of thread to string them on and coloured yarn for her skirt. He may, however, give his wife rings and bangles. It is a common custom to leave a little grain on the threshing-floor at the end of a harvest for the girls of the family. They collect and divide it, make it into flour and sell it to the neighbours. The proceeds are always used for the purchase of ornaments.

The ornaments are obtained from local Ghasia brasssmiths or Kammar blacksmiths — there was a thriving colony of Ghasias at Dumiripada in 1943 making brass ornaments for the Bondos by the *cire-perdue* process — and from the bazaars in the plains. During the war, however, there was a great shortage, and merchants even attempted to buy in the brass rings and collars of the Gadabas and Bondos in order to resell the metal at a high profit in the towns.

A girl may win rings during the games in the dormitory or receive them as presents from her lovers. But there does not seem to be any custom of giving wedding-presents or gifts at any other ceremonial occasion.

Bondo women must keep their heads shaven from babyhood till death. They seem to be curiously indifferent to the disposal of the hair so carefully removed, but this may be due to their comparatively modest dread or sorcery and witchcraft. The general practice is for old women to shave the heads of their juniors; one day in Katamguda I watched an elderly body attend to half the women in the village all through a long morning. Sometimes, however, an old man — a father or a father's brother — may shave the head of a little girl. But men are not supposed to do this (though they sometimes break the rules) once a girl is mature. 'Men are great and women are small,' I was told. 'So how can we shave their heads?' In some villages, a husband is allowed to shave his wife.

Little boys also have their heads shaved, but once a youth becomes of dormitory age he is very careful to have his hair long and dressed

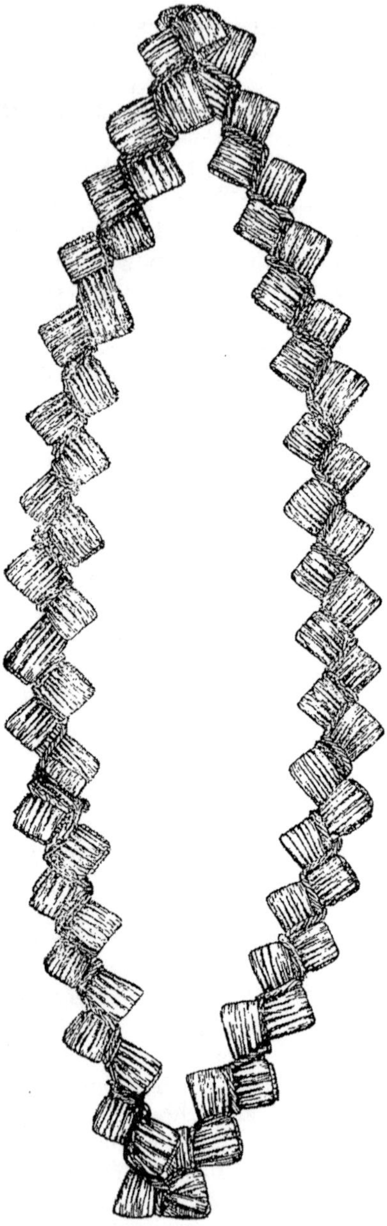

FIG. 7. Head-band, of plaited caryota fibre, worn by boys or girls.

attractively. The traditional method is to wear it long, hanging down to the shoulders round the head, perhaps held in place by one or two decorative bands. It is sometimes tied back into a little knob; I have seen a boy with the tush of a barking-deer attached to his bun as an ornament, and another with the feathers of the scarlet minivet sticking out of it. 'Then a boy looks handsome,' I was told at Andrahal. 'Then, when girls see him they are excited and think of marriage.' This is important in a tribe where a boy is expected to win his bride by his personal attractiveness; until their marriages are arranged all Bondo boys have to be on their toes. At Tulaguram new fashions in hair-dressing were strongly condemned. 'If a boy does not let his hair grow, he'll never get a fresh girl, but only a widow or someone's cast-off wife. If he ties up his hair in a bun or shaves it in front, we say, "He's become an old man" and none of the really good girls will look at him.' For now what they call 'Assam fashion'—they use the word 'fashion'—has begun to spoil the good old tradition and some boys even part their hair in 'Bengali' style or the 'English' or 'bulbul' manner.

But after marriage a boy first ties his locks in a bun at the back of his head and later gets someone to shave the front in conventional style. Men do not usually shave their heads after a death. But if a man has been excommunicated for going to jail, being beaten by a Dom or getting maggots in a wound, his *samdhi* may shave a little of the hair at his temples. The Bondos use a locally-made razor (which is described in a riddle as 'something that eats black grass and sleeps in a hard place') and makes a lather of his own spittle.

The Bondos wear moustaches 'for strength and beauty'; a few men have beards. The moustache gives a man self-confidence and during a quarrel he twirls it at his enemy.

In the hill villages the custom of tattooing has almost disappeared, though I have seen a few old women with the marks in Andrahal and Mundlipada. In the plains villages the Bondos tattoo one another with thorns and a mixture of charcoal and the sap of the *Bassia latifolia*. At Andrahal there was a vague tradition that,

> Formerly the Doms used to tattoo us. But one day Mahaprabhu said, 'Show me your hands'. Those who had tattoo marks on the backs of their hands he caught and dragged away. Since then we have given up the custom.

This suggests that wounds went septic and people died; the practice was found dangerous or troublesome and so abandoned. This seems to me more likely than the tradition that tattooing was given up on account of the 'naked on top' curse. For after all, most tattoo marks are 'below'.

6. External Influence

Not only civilization, but the primitive culture of the surrounding tribal populations has had singularly little influence on the externals of Bondo life. In the hills the Bondos, especially in the Andrahal group of villages, are constantly in touch with the Gadabas, Didayis and Konds. Yet they have shown no inclination to imitate the Gadaba style of architecture (which is an improvement on theirs) or their beautiful and varied dancing or the elaborate feasts in memory of the dead. They have remained equally unaffected by the Konds' interest in wood-carving or their distinctive style of village-planning. Konds are rather feared as sorcerers and the Didayis are hated as rivals; no decent Bondo would model his way of life on them.

The Bondos probably look and behave just as they did hundreds of years ago. But many of them *think* very differently. Their minds indeed are much more conventional than their bodies. The Doms, degraded missionaries of a lofty faith, have imported the Hindu religious ideology and a Hindu eschatology into Bondo culture, which has accepted without always assimilating it. Indeed the steady imperceptible pressure of Dom influence is a far more important agent of culture-change than the puerile reformist evangelism of self-conscious Hindu propagandists in the plains, which I have already described.

In the hills, the Doms are the most important. Then there are the police. Every murder advances the cause of 'civilization' a little further. A party of Hindu and Muslim policemen invade the village, camp there and are entertained free of charge for several days. They point out the evils of Bondo culture; they sneer at the pork, the beef, the palm-wine; they snigger at the dress and ornaments of the women; even the best of them thoroughly despise the 'savages' they have come to interrogate. Sometimes a Sub-inspector expounds his own theological and social theories. In this way the Bondos learn by experience the character of modern civilization, that the primitive should be economically exploited and culturally despised, and he tends to withdraw more and more into the shelter of his own community and throw up barriers against the outside world, even though at the same time he assimilates some of its ideas.

There are two other important instruments of culture-change. The first is Assam. The Tea Gardens attract the aboriginals because there is a way of earning enough money to pay a bride-price, or to escape from embarrassing domestic or economic complications, or to find an arena for adventure. The Bondos like going to the Tea Gardens (they also enjoyed going to Manipur during the war) and they are obviously well treated there. Out of 150 men interrogated, 27 had made the expedition. The effect is largely in externals, shorts and shirts which rapidly wear out, an umbrella which soon breaks and yields up its ribs for the manufacture of armlets, perhaps an old solar topee which will be brought out amid shouts of applause in the middle of a dance. Men returning from Assam, however, both here and among the Saoras, have a bad reputation for being wild and lawless and of caring little for their civic or tribal duties.

Prison life has a curious influence. On most aboriginals its effect is deplorable; it coarsens, hardens and degrades the splendid Maria, it reduces the unhappy Kond to a cowering frightened animal; but it occasionally does a Bondo good. The Bondo returns home and is received — after the appropriate penalties have been remitted — with open arms. His social position is now assured. He has seen the world. He has got about. He has contacted civilization and survived. He has learnt another, perhaps more than one, language and now can hold his own with police and revenue officials. In some cases — I think of Sonia Sisa (comrade and ally of Shamrao Hivale), Miliya Bodnaik (H. V. Blackburn's friend), Muliya Dangra-Manjhi (the intimate of Christoph von Fürer-Haimendorf), all murderers, all damned, all very courteous, charming and interesting friends — the ex-convicts remain simple, unsophisticated, with their tribal loyalties unimpaired. Moreover, they possess the advantage, which to the visitor is of incomparable merit, of talking a non-Austro-asiatic language. They can be understood. As informants their value is discounted by the impact of Hinduism which they have received from their fellow-prisoners. Most Indians grow a little devout in jail, and the Bondo convicts return with an entire new world of demigods and furies, rites and sortilegia with which to confound the old uninstructed Sisa or Dissari.

But whether from jail or Tea Garden, untouchable Dom or pietist reformer, Hinduism is on the march. What has it done ? It has brightened up the Bondo vocabulary; the Sisa can now address the divine Singi-Arke in bilingual terms, the Dissari can confound a fury in almost classic Oriya. The great personages of the *Ramayana* have banished the petty and anonymous tribal heroes from Bondo mythology; the wolf-bellied and Falstaffian Bhima steps from the august pages of the *Mahabharata* into the Bondo sky, whence he rains down seed and fertilizing showers. Hinduism energizes the Bondo festival from a mere orgy of beef and beer into a sacrament of fecundity in which the womb, the soil, and the arrow are alike consecrated by blood and supplication.

On the whole, the impact of Hinduism, by the various means I have described, has been for the good; it has enriched Bondo culture, just as it has changed the stark and rather infantile life of the Marias into the superbly complex and engrossing civilization of the Murias. For it cannot be denied that the Hindus have an incomparable technique; they have no compeers in the world in the art of gesture, in knowing where to put the hands, in the exact use of words, in the skill of genuflexion. In dealing with the gods, you must apply flattery with a trowel, and the modern luxurious display of Bondo ceremonial, so alien to so economical a tribe, is probably due to inspiration from without. The social influence of village Hinduism has been less beneficial.

CHAPTER TWO

THE ORGANIZATION OF SOCIETY

1

BONDO society is divided and controlled by no fewer than three different exogamous affiliations. There is first and foremost the relationship of a man with his own village community. To the Bondo a village is an almost sacred entity; its members are bound to him by special ties; its boundaries are protected by magic rites; at certain seasons no stranger may enter, no householder may leave; to visit an alien village is always risky; only at home is there security and peace. A man's neighbours are his *soru-bhai*, brothers who have eaten the same sacrificial food, a privilege that is rigidly restricted to members of the same village.[1] *Soru* is obviously the Sanskrit *caru,* which is defined as an oblation of rice, barley and pulse boiled with butter and milk and offered in sacrifice to the gods and ancestors. *Soru* is also an ordinary Tamil word for 'food', used mainly of poor people's food, but without any sacramental reference. For the Bondo, *soru* is any kind of dedicated food prepared for festivals; it does not apply to wedding or funerary feasts where many visitors are invited, though on these occasions special *soru* food may be prepared for an inner group.

This sacramental fellowship of the village community is of the utmost moral and religious importance, for since it makes the village an exogamous unit it exercises a profound influence on the men and women who compose it. 'The women of our own village are our mothers and sisters' — and this belief is taken very seriously indeed. Men do not make indecent jokes in the presence of their own women, though they are ready enough to do so elsewhere. There are no flirtations between neighbours and only rarely a breach of the rules that may lead to marriage. For the Bondos consider it really important that marriages should be concluded between people who are attached to different *sindibor,* who are strictly separated from one another during the *angto* days of the great festivals, who partake of a different *soru* food. The institution of

[1] At the festivals of Pat Khanda Mahaprabhu a special *soru* meal is prepared by a member of the Kirsani clan in the name of the god, and the Naikos of all twelve villages composing the Bara-jangar group can share it.

the girls' dormitory, with its open invitation to youths of other villages and the taboo on the local boys, impresses this on every child; marriage with someone in the same village is regarded almost as seriously as the crime of incest. The only official exception to the rule is where families have migrated from one place to another; when they do this it is some time before they are permitted to share the *soru* of their new home and during this interval marriages with their neighbours are not forbidden.

These rules are very strictly observed. Of the 300 marriages recorded in the genealogies not one, and of the 150 discussed in the questionnaire only two, were real breaches of *soru*-exogamy. In some villages like Andrahal and Dumiripada there are a number of immigrant families which have not yet entered the new community and these have intermarried within the village. Both the breaches of the rule recorded in the questionnaire came from the low country, where Bondo social life is rapidly decaying under external influence — and one of these was an elopement and irregular in any case.

A woman enters her husband's *soru*-group and if she is widowed, she can re-marry someone from her original village.

Village exogamy is common throughout Orissa; it is strictly observed by the Juangs; the Konds go so far as to name a betrothed girl by the village to which she will go; and most other tribes observe the rule with more or less fidelity. In this therefore, the Bondos are in line with the general tradition of the area.

2. The *Kuda*

Bondo society is still further subdivided into a number of exogamous patrilineal clans, which — following a common Orissa custom — take their names from those of village functionaries, such as the Bodnaik, Challan, Dangra-Manjhi, Kirsani, Mundli and Sisa. A few of these *kuda*, as they are called, such as the Dora, Jigri and Mandhara, probably represent the inclusion within the tribe of members of other communities.

There are many stories about the origins of the different *kuda* and it will be well to quote these as showing how the Bondos explain their existence to themselves. I myself have no doubt as to their origin; they are a comparatively modern borrowing, dating from the time of the first Dom settlements in Bondo villages. This rather curious division of near-Hindu Orissa society seems to have developed from the need of saving the village headman from too great a pressure of public business. All aboriginals shrink from the performance of civic duties, but someone had to keep order in the village, official visitors had to be entertained, reports had to be taken to the police, taxes had to be collected and paid, the gods had to be appeased. So the portfolios were divided; an assistant headman, the Bodnaik, was appointed; the Challan was put in to help him; the Dangra-Manjhi had to see that the young men did their share; the Kirsani had to carry loads for officers.

The following story, from Gokurupada, is important for the light it throws on Bondo psychology.

On Malyagiri seven brothers and seven sisters were born and came thence into these hills. When they saw the streams and forest they were pleased and built their village here. Then Pat Khanda Mahaprabhu was born at Mundlipada and revealed himself in a dream to the eldest of the brothers. At that very moment in Jeypore the Maharaja had a dream that Mahaprabhu had been born on earth and he sent his men to worship him. But when they arrived we ran away and hid in the jungle, for we were afraid that the work of looking after them would be too heavy for us. But they chased us and brought us back to the village and it was agreed that the business of looking after the village on the one hand and of entertaining officials on the other should be divided. So the eldest brother was named the Mundli and became the Naiko of Mundlipada, the chief of all; after him the Challan was appointed to help him, the Kirsani to carry the officials' baggage, the Dangra-Manjhi to see that the young men (*dangra*) brought wood and water for any visitor. Another brother became Sisa to perform the worship of Pat Khanda Mahaprabhu and yet another, the Pedda Naiko, to help the Naiko. There were no Doms in those days, so a Kantaru (in Oriya, Bariko) was appointed to take reports to the police; when the Doms came we gave this work to them.[1]

Later, as the number of people increased, the descendants of the brother who was made Kirsani went to live in Kirsanipada, the descendants of the Challan separated to Salanpada and the Mundli people remained in their first home, Mundlipada.

A rather similar story accounts for the origin of the Mandhara *kuda*.

The twelve Bondo brothers were in a quandary. Who was to go at Dassera to take the Maharaja's tribute to Jeypore? Each said to the other, 'You go, you go,' but not one of them was willing. They decided at last to go out and find someone else, determined to send him by force if necessary. They took their bows and arrows and went across the hills. When they reached the Machkund River, they saw a Didayi woman; she had just finished bathing her little son; he was standing on the bank and she was naked in the river. When she saw the twelve brothers she was frightened and ducked under the water and was never seen again. The child began to howl and the brothers went to comfort him. They said among themselves. 'This is just what we want. Let us take him home and bring him up to carry the tribute to the Maharaja.' They did so and when he was old enough they got him a Bondo girl for wife. Then

[1] This arrangement still holds. The village headman is called the Naiko but, though in Mundlipada itself this office is always held by a member of the Mundli clan, in other villages the Naiko may belong to any of the *kuda*. The Bodnaik, a corruption of Pedda or 'little' Naiko, and the Challan, assist him. The important duty of Bariko is now always fulfilled by a Dom.

the brothers clubbed together to buy a goat and they collected rice and two rupees in cash and sent the boy with these things to Jeypore. When he returned they called him Mandhara — giver of *mān,* honour — and his descendants have ever since performed this duty for the tribe.

The Dora *kuda* also, as its name implies, originated in the adoption by a Bondo of a strange child from another tribe.

A Dora with his pregnant wife went with a load of bamboo baskets to the Bondo Hills. They sold them and got a lot of grain, as much as they could carry. But on their way home, the woman's pains began and she gave birth to her child by the path. Now the two of them thought, 'How are we to take the child home? A baby in the womb is easier to carry than a baby at the breast. We can't take both grain and child; if we leave the grain somewhere these Bondos will certainly steal it. We will have to leave the child.' They made a bed for the baby under a thick creeper, covering him with leaves, then made their way quickly home.

After they had gone an old Bondo and his wife came along. They saw there was something under the creeper and they searched and found the child. That wife had never borne a child and, when she saw him, she was very happy and cried, 'Now Mahaprabhu has at last given us a son. Let us take him home and when he is big, he will look after the goats and cattle.' They picked up the child and took him to their house.

The Dora and his wife put the grain in their bin and went back quickly to fetch the child. But when they reached the place he had disappeared and, thinking a tiger had taken him, they returned in tears.

The Bondo woman fed the baby with goat's milk and looked after him. When he grew up he went to the dormitory and found a girl. They made him the father of the Dora *kuda.* But now they are true Bondos; we do not let them marry members of the Dora caste.

The first member of the Jigri clan was a Gadaba.

A Gadaba had three sons; two were big and one very small. One day the parents went for wood to the jungle, and the two bigger boys were playing somewhere. The youngest went after his parents, but got lost; an old Bondo couple found and adopted him. He grew up and married a Bondo girl. When his foster-parents died, he took the property. He had many sago palms and used to sell the wine. A man who taps palm trees for profit is known as Jigiriya, so this man became the first of the Jigri *kuda.*

The original idea seems to have been that every Sisa priest should be a member of the Sisa *kuda,* every Naiko headman a Mundli, every watchman a Kirsani or Dangra-Manjhi, and this arrangement still holds in Mundlipada itself. Furthermore Kirsanipada was to have been the home of the Kirsanis, Salanpada that of the Challans, Mundlipada that of the Mundlis. But the exchanges of matrimony and the pressure of economic need were too strong for this tidy plan and by now it has generally broken down. There are today Sisas and Challans in Katamguda, Mundlis and Kirsanis in Tulaguram, Dangra-Manjhis and Sisas and Kirsanis in Andrahal; in fact, members of the different *kuda* are widely distributed throughout the villages.

The fact that the *kuda* and territorial systems were at first more or less coterminous has given the *kuda* rules considerable authority and, as we will see, they are less frequently broken than the others. Whenever a Bondo has to give his name officially, he attaches to it the title of his *kuda;* in some of the great feuds, as at Andrahal, the combatants divided, largely though not exclusively, along *kuda* lines; in some villages members of the different *kuda* live in separate quarters. At festivals and the major sacrifices a representative of each of the *kuda* in a village is chosen to assist the Sisa and sometimes each representative has to make a levy of grain from the members of his own clan. Members of a *kuda* have their memorial menhirs placed together, apart from those of other clans.

The stress laid on the *kuda* organization is not, however, due to its original association with a scheme of territorial exogamy; it is much more likely to be based in the fact that it is not native to the Bondo but has been borrowed from what is regarded as a superior civilization. When a Bondo tells you that his name is Sonia Sisa, he does not mean to remind you that he is a member of an ancient Austro-asiatic tribe; he implies that he is in touch with the modern world. For the Doms, who are to him the real representatives of civilization, have the same system, and so have other communities; the Bondo may despise them socially, but he has no doubt that they are more in touch with modern life.

3. The *Bonso*

The *kuda* is a loan; the system of village exogamy may have arisen by imitation or on psychological grounds — that it is wise to keep the boys and girls of the same place away from each other. But the *bonso* (race) system is to my mind fundamental and old. Bondo society is divided into two great moieties, the Cobra (Ontal) and the Tiger (Killo or Kukusa). There is a vague tradition, particularly in the low country, of other *bonso* groups — the Sun, the Monkey, the Fish, the Bear. But of the 300 marriages examined in the genealogies, only one was with a woman of the Bear *bonso*: all the others were between Ontal and Killo.

The neighbouring tribes have other *bonso* — the Gadabas, for example, have Bear, Fish, Sun and Monkey groups; the Didayis have a Bear and Monkey; the Parengas have a Monkey, Vulture and Sun group, in addition to the Tiger and Cobra. Wherever, therefore, the Bondos talk of other *bonso*, they probably refer to members of these groups who have been taken into the tribe. They themselves are divided between the Tiger and the Cobra. 'As sometimes two chicks are hatched from a single egg,' said a Bondo at Andrahal, 'so are Ontal and Killo born together and live in a single nest.'

Today the Cobra people are far the most numerous. Of 300 men and women examined in the questionnaire, 206 were Ontal, 92 were Killo and 2 were doubtful. A similar proportion was observed in the genealogies.

The *bonso* are, as their names imply, totemistic. Thus members of the Tiger race should never kill a tiger; they say: 'When we are out hunting, we feel very embarrassed if we meet a tiger; we just don't know what to do and our weapons fall of their own accord from our hands. The tiger also feels awkward and goes away.'

But I suspect a certain apprehension on the part of the Bondo that, while he himself may be strictly orthodox, the tiger may not be equally observant of the rules.

Each *bonso* has a myth behind it. The origin of the Tiger people was explained to me at Bodapada.

An old couple had three sons. The youngest boy was a man from the waist down, but his head and shoulders were those of a tiger. The two elder boys married and their wives came to the house, but the tiger-boy used to sit lonely by the hearth. While the other boys were sporting in the dormitory, he sat lonely by the hearth. But he always got his food first.

One day the whole family went to their hill-clearing to thresh millet and only the eldest brother's wife was left in the house. She cooked the gruel and when it was ready the tiger-boy came in and asked for his share first as usual. Now this was one of those girls who are known as food-stealers; she loved to take more than her share and to eat at odd times. So when the tiger-boy asked for his food, she lost her temper and picked up the cooking-pot and broke it over his head, burning him badly. He leapt onto the girl and killed her, then broke his way out of the house through the roof and dragged the corpse to the threshing-floor where the family was at work. He threw the body down there and ran away into the jungle.

Now the old parents were specially fond of this boy, he was so unusual, and they went after him. When they found him he showed them his burns. 'Look what she did,' he said. 'And now I'll never come back, for my brother will certainly kill me. But you go home,' he added. 'I'll be all right here. And if ever you are in any kind of trouble, come and tell me and I will help.' The old people went home and there was a tremendous row, for the other boys were jealous of their parents' affection for the youngest. 'You told him to kill my wife,' shouted the eldest brother; he was beside himself with rage, and in his frenzy he killed both mother and father.

When the tiger-boy heard of this he came to the house. First he killed the goats and cattle, then his two brothers. But there was a girl left and she was pregnant. He thought of killing her too, but when he recollected her condition he had pity on her and took her to the jungle to live with him. The child was born and when he grew up, he became the father of the Tiger people.

Members of the Cobra race declare that they cannot even look at a cobra, still less kill one, 'for it is our brother', though their eyesight is unimpaired when they see other snakes. The origin of the moiety is described in a tale from Bodoballe.

Long ago a man and woman grew old without having a child. But in her full age the woman conceived and in due time gave birth to a cobra-child and a human boy. Of the two the parents loved the cobra-child the more, for he was the elder of the twins and most beautiful, and they were always spoiling him with little chicks and birds' eggs to eat. The human boy grew up and went to the dormitory; he found a girl and they were married, and the new wife came to the house. He had not told her anything about his cobra-brother for fear that it would put her off.

One day, soon after the wedding, the youth went to the forest with his parents, leaving his wife in the house. It was morning and as the girl was cowdunging the floor, the cobra, not realizing she was there, came out of its hiding-place. When it saw her, it tried to escape but she, in fright and not knowing who it was, struck it and in a fit of temper it bit her and she died. Then the cobra said to itself, 'I have killed my sister-in-law. When my brother returns he will kill me.' So thinking, it left the house and made its home in a hole in the ground out in the jungle.

The parents returned and when they saw their daughter-in-law dead and their favourite cobra-son gone, they went weeping through the forest in search of it. When the cobra heard them weeping, it came out of its hole and told them what had happened. They begged it to return with them but it said, 'No, I will not come home, for we two brothers will always be quarrelling and we might well destroy each other. I will live in the jungle and since we will not meet often we will remain friends.'

The two old people went home and said to their human son, 'Son, your brother has gone to live in the jungle. Should you meet him, do not lift up your hand against him; do not strike him or do him any injury or you may die as your wife has died.' Since then the Cobra people have never injured the cobra and the cobra never injures them.

There is a certain resemblance between these two stories. In each there is a non-human son in the family; in each he kills the elder brother's wife; in each the parents have a special love for their strange offspring and, when he goes to the jungle, follow him and try to persuade him to return. Some of these motifs are not unknown to Indian folklore. The similarities in the stories suggest the close interdependence of the moieties; their lack of originality suggests that they may be modern.

4. The Observance of the Clan Rules

Let us turn now to consider the strength of these different affiliations and the control that they exercise on marriage and society. What, in the first place, of the distribution of the moieties and clans ? The following tables, which are based on the questionnaire presented to 150 adult men in all parts of the Bondo country (figures for women are for the first wives of these men), will give some idea of the comparative strength of these divisions.

Table I

DISTRIBUTION OF 150 MEN AND 150 WOMEN ACCORDING TO *bonso*

Bonso		Men	Women	Total
Ontal (Cobra)	..	114	92	206
Killo (Tiger)	..	36	56	92
Doubtful	..	..	2	2

The genealogies also revealed the great numerical superiority of the Ontal clan, for there were 436 Ontal people as against only 163 Killo and 1 doubtful (a woman belonging to a Bear *bonso* who was originally a member of another tribe).

The *kuda*-clans are more equally divided, though the Kirsani and Sisa are the most numerous. Those clans, which, like the Dora and Mandhara, represent the recent adoption of members of some other caste into the tribe, are — as we might expect — but weakly represented.

Table II

DISTRIBUTION OF 150 BONDO MEN AND 150 WOMEN ACCORDING TO *kuda*

Kuda		Men	Women	Total
Bodnaik	..	12	21	33
Challan	..	21	10	31
Dangra-Manjhi	..	3	4	7
Dora	..	2	2	4
Jigri	..	4	2	6
Kirsani	..	45	51	96
Mandhara	..	4	2	6
Mundli	..	14	29	43
Sisa		46	28	74

Is there any relationship between the *bonso* and *kuda*? Is there any kind of pattern whereby some of the *kuda* are attached to the Ontal and others attached to the Killo *bonso* ? Would every Sisa, shall we say, be an Ontal and every Kirsani a Killo ? The following Table shows that this is not so. I take these figures from the questionnaire and they are fully confirmed by the genealogies. The Mandhara *kuda*, however, which here appears to be exclusively Killo, is shown by the genealogies to be distributed between the two *bonso*.

Table III

RELATIONSHIP OF *bonso* AND *kuda* IN 300 CASES, MEN AND WOMEN

Kuda		Ontal *bonso*	Killo *bonso*	Others
Bodnaik	..	21	11	..
Challan	..	24	3	..
Dangra-Manjhi	..	5	2	..
Dora	..	1	3	..
Jigri	..	5	1	..
Kirsani	..	83	10	2
Mandhara	..	..	7	..
Mundli	..	32	11	..
Sisa	..	28	44	..

These figures are based on the questionnaire, which gives us an up-to-date picture of the situation. Let us now turn to the genealogies to see how the different groups have intermarried during the past two or three generations. There has evidently been a considerable breakdown in the system of Bondo exogamy, as Table IV will show.

It will be seen that the *kuda* rules are fairly well observed; breaches occur chiefly among the very numerous Kirsanis and the powerful Sisa and Mundli clans. But the *bonso* rules are largely ignored.

The reason for this is no doubt partly the freedom of youths to choose their partners at will in the dormitories and partly the unequal strength of the different divisions. There are not enough Killo women to go round, and many Ontal men therefore had to marry within their own *bonso*. On the other hand, the comparatively small number of Killo men had plenty of Ontal girls to choose from and only broke the rules in half-a-dozen cases.

Table IV

SOCIAL AFFILIATIONS IN 300 BONDO MARRIAGES

Number of marriages between men and women of	
their own *bonso* and their own *kuda*	25
their own *bonso* and a different *kuda*[1]	123
a different *bonso* and a different *kuda*	128
a different *bonso* and their own *kuda*	24
Number of cases in which	
Ontal men married Ontal girls	142
Killo men married Killo girls	6
Ontal men married Killo girls	76
Killo men married Ontal girls	75
Ontal men married others	1
Number of cases in which	
Bodnaik men married Bodnaik girls	1
Dangra-Manjhi men married Dangra-Manjhi girls	1
Kirsani men married Kirsani girls	20
Mundli men married Mundli girls	12
Sisa men married Sisa girls	14

5. A Dual Organization

The existence of dual organization in India has long been a puzzle to anthropologists. In a recent article,[2] Koppers has attempted to demonstrate, in opposition to Ghurye,[3] that an ethnological dual organization cannot be found in peninsular India, most of the supposed moieties being unestablished by modern research or found on examination to be endogamous rather than exogamous. But Ghurye's contention that in former times there was in southern India a wide prevalence of dual organization with matrilineal descent, based as it is on a careful study of kinship terminology, cannot be lightly dismissed. And I suggest that it is possible that he gains some support from the division of Bondo society into the Ontal and Killo moieties, if this can be established as a genuine dual segmentation. But before this can be accepted as a fact, certain points of evidence and inference must be discussed.

[1] The questionnaire revealed a less drastic indifference to the rules, though the general picture is the same. Thus, while the genealogies show that *bonso* exogamy broke down in 47 per cent of cases, the questionnaire gives a figure of only 37·3 per cent: in nearly two-thirds of the marriages the rules were kept. The proportion in the case of marriages between members of the same *kuda* was almost the same; the genealogies give 16·3 per cent and the questionnaire gives 14 per cent.

[2] W. Koppers 'India and Dual Organization', *Acta Tropica*, Sep. Vol. I, Nr. 1/2 (1944), pp. 72ff.

[3] G. S. Ghurye, 'Dual Organization in India', *J.A.I.*, Vol. LIII (1923), pp. 79ff.

In the first place, is Bondo society really bisected into two divisions? Koppers defines 'the fundamental characteristic of an ethnological dual classification system' to be 'the division of the tribe into two exogamous moieties'. Is this condition fulfilled here? As we have seen, in all but one or two doubtful cases, the Bondos are divided into Ontal and Killo; out of 300 men and women whose affiliations were revealed in the questionnaire, 206 were Ontal, 92 were Killo and there were only 2 others. But do these 'others' represent once flourishing *bonso* which have now died out? The neighbours of the Bondos, as we have seen, also have *bonso* divisions, but these are invariably multiple rather than dual. The Gadabas have some half dozen *bonso,* including the Bear, Fish, Sun and Monkey; the Parengas have several similar groups, so do the Didayis. But none of these groups have died out in the other tribes, and it is surely more reasonable to suppose that when we find in Bondo society a rare example of a *bonso* other than Ontal and Killo it represents the entry of a neighbour into the tribe. This is what the Bondos themselves affirm. Of the 300 marriages observed in genealogies, in only one of them was an alien *bonso* — the Bhalu or Bear — involved. I have also recorded one member of a Hanu or Monkey *bonso* and one of a Suraj or Sun *bonso*: these were stated to be Gadabas who had been assimilated by marriage into the tribe. On the borders of the Bondo country and in the plains a few other examples may possibly be found, but I think that it can be affirmed with some confidence that for all practical purposes the Bondo tribe is divided into two great, though numerically asymmetrical, moieties.

But, further, are these moieties really exogamous ? There are here two problems to be considered. In the first place, as we have seen, Bondo society is divided by three different systems of exogamy, each independent of the others. The rule against marrying within the *soru*-fellowship of the village community is the one most strictly observed; the division into nine *kuda* clans is less carefully obeyed, but still seems to exert considerable influence; *bonso*-exogamy, however, has largely broken down. Can it then be claimed that the *bonso* system is of sufficient importance to rank as a real dual organization ? I think it can, for I suggest that this system is the oldest of the tribe's exogamous regulations and in former times chiefly controlled them.

Territorial exogamy, so common among the Orissa tribes, may owe much of its rigorism among the Bondos to the influence of neighbouring peoples; the partaking of the *soru*-food — which is the essential factor in the system — is a classical Hindu custom, and may have come in with the growth of Hindu influence in recent years.

Kuda-exogamy too appears to be of modern origin. It is an obvious borrowing from the near-Hindu castes which have settled in the vicinity; the Doms and Panos also divide themselves into Bodnaiks, Challans, Dangra-Manjhis, and so on. Since the division is, according to the legends which account for it, related to the demands made on the people by the administration, it is hardly likely to have arisen before those demands began to make themselves felt, in comparatively recent times. The fact that certain villages are now associated with *kuda* names, such as Mundlipada and Kirsanipada, and that there is a tradition that all the Mundlis should live in the first and all the Kirsanis in the second, does not argue against this, for the real Bondo name for Mundlipada is Bodajangar or Serayen and that for Kirsanipada is Gusube.

The evidence is scanty enough; it is hardly more than a hint; but coupled with the fact that only the *bonso* have genuine Remo names — Ontal and Killo or Kukusa — I think it is sufficient to suggest that the original organization of Bondo society was along *bonso* lines and that the other systems came in afterwards.

But, it will be said, the *bonso* today hardly serve their exogamic purpose. I agree; there is a serious breakdown. But perhaps that is just what one would expect if it is true that the *bonso* division is very old and half-forgotten before the more clamant demands of its modern competitors. Moreover there are groups of Bondos, arrogant and restless, who break every rule, and the figures in our tables are to some extent inflated by the antinomian traditions of certain families. Thus, in the family of Muliya Dangra-Manjhi, the murderer, of 24 marriages recorded, 19 broke the *bonso* rules. In Mogla Kirsani's genealogy not a single Killo occurs; every marriage is between Ontal. On the other hand, out of 36 marriages associated with the gentle law-abiding Raja of the Bondos, Lachhim Mundli (Genealogy I), 24 observed the *bonso* regulations, while in the family of Lachhim Kirsani of Bodapada, out of 12 marriages all but 2 observed them.

The terminology of kinship, says Ghurye, often 'preserves types of social organization in fossilized forms'[1] and some Bondo usages, though partly explicable on other grounds, certainly suggest an original dual organization; at the least, they are not inconsistent with it. Although the mother and her sisters or father and his brothers are not grouped together, entirely different terms being used, a dual organization is suggested by the community of words for the children of the father's brother and the children of the mother's sister, which are *māng* and *ming* in each case.[2] This is what we would expect if, for example, there were two Killo sisters who must originally always have married Ontal husbands, with the result that their children and those of their Ontal husband's brothers must all have been Ontal. So also the mother's brother's son is *marenger*, her elder daughter is *ming*, his younger daughter is *kui*. The father's sister's son is also *marenger*, her elder daughter is *ming* and

[1] Ghurye, op. cit., p. 79.
[2] For a list of relevant terms, see Appendix I

her younger daughter is *kui* — for where there are only two divisions to a tribe, the mother's brother's children and the father's sister's children must belong to the same group.

Equally suggestive are other terms. The father's brother and the mother's sister's husband are known by the same words — the elder being *busān,* the younger *kakka.* Similarly the mother's sister and father's brother's wife are each called *busān boi* (elder) and *umbuk boi* (younger).

Again the father's sister is *wāng* and the mother's brother's wife is also *wāng;* the mother's brother and the father's sister's husband are both known as *māmung.* This might be the result of the cross-cousin marriage, but in that case we would expect the father-in-law also to be *māmung,* whereas he is actually *unkui* (it is significant that *māmung,* alone among Bondo relationship terms, is of Oriya derivation). Moreover, as Rivers says, this feature of relationship 'may follow directly from the dual organization and be independent of the cross-cousin marriage. Where there are only two social divisions, the husband of the father's sister must be a man having the status of the mother's brother, and the wife of the mother's brother a woman having the status of the father's sister.'[1]

And further, there is no cross-cousin marriage among the Bondos. This is no argument against the existence of dual organization. Rivers himself, who was partly responsible for connecting the two systems, later decided that there was no necessary relation between them,[2] for — as Westermarck says — 'it is difficult to understand why dual organization should have led to the marriage of first cousins to the exclusion of marriages between other members of the two exogamous moieties.'[3] Not a single cross-cousin marriage could be traced in the genealogies recorded and not one of the 150 men examined by questionnaire admitted to a marriage with even a second cousin. The reason is, of course, that marriages among the Bondos are arranged by children instead of parents, and it is the eager impulse of the youthful heart rather than the Table of Affinity that regulates the matrimonial affiliations of the tribe.

The division of a dual organization is frequently asymmetrical. Ehrenfels says that 'such reciprocal groups usually look upon each other in a mixture of aggressive pride and dependent comradeship at the same time, thus producing a marked sense of rivalry. The stressed reciprocity of all these groupings seems to have root in the idea of magic fertility, since

[1] W. H. R. Rivers, *The History of Melanesian Society* (Cambridge, 1914), Vol. II, p. 24.

[2] See Rivers, 'The Marriage of Cousins in India', *J.R.A.S.*, 1907, pp. 623ff. and op. cit., Vol. II, p. 122.

[3] E. Westermarck, *The History of Human Marriage* (London, 1925), Vol. II, p. 79.

warfare between the two marriage-classes plays a similar role as human sacrifice or head-hunting in lunar-mythological fertility-rites... One of the two parties in a genuine dual system is often found to be either more skilled, powerful, numerous or superior.' There is also, he adds, a marked association with totemism.[1] Some of these features are absent from the Bondo system. There is no apparent rivalry between Ontal and Killo. But hostility between dual groups is by no means universal. There is no evidence of it between the two moieties of the dual organization in America.[2] But the Bondo arrangement conforms to the classic pattern in that the Ontal are overwhelmingly superior in numbers and both moieties are closely associated with totemism.

On the whole, therefore, although the social picture is not quite in the sharpest focus, I believe that we have in the Cobra and Tiger bisection of Bondo society a relic of a genuine dual organization with patrilineal descent.

6. The *Moitur* Friend

Throughout Orissa, as elsewhere in Hindu and tribal India, there is the custom of making ceremonial friendships. These have often been described and there is no need here to do more than to emphasize their existence also among the Bondos. As we might expect in Orissa, the *mahaprasad* engagement is the most popular and important. *Prasad* is anything given by a god or an offering of food presented to him and afterwards distributed to the worshippers. *Mahaprasad* is specially applied to the *prasad* of Jagannath, to whom the great Puri temple is dedicated, and technically the two contracting parties to a friendship should partake together of some of this sacred food brought to them by returning pilgrims. But even in Orissa the use of the words has been enlarged, and it is now applied to any pair of life-long friends who have entered on their friendship by a solemn covenant.

In general this relationship is taken very seriously. The missionary Gordon says that 'after an acquaintance with the people (of Bilaspur) of fourteen years, he could recall only one instance in which such a friendship was broken. Like David and Jonathan, the parties stand by each other, they are bound together for better or worse.'[3] The friends must not speak of each other by name; they must support each other under all circumstances; it was 'hinted' to Gordon that there was a

[1] O. R. von Ehrenfels, 'The Dual System and Mother-right in India', *Anthropos*, Tome XXXV/XXXVI (1940-1), pp. 655f.

[2] Rivers, *Social Organization* (London, 1932), p. 29.

[3] E. M. Gordon, 'Notes concerning the People of Mungeli Tahsil, Bilaspore District', *J.A.S.B.*, Vol. I (N.S., 1905), p. 188.

community of possessions which extended even to a community of wives. Since the *mahaprasad* of Jagannath is distributed to all, without distinction of race or caste, the *mahaprasad* friendships are often made between persons of different communities: Captain Brooke, an administrator of the Sambalpur District in the 'seventies, did not consider this was altogether a good thing. Too often — I have noticed it myself — the friendship is formed with a predominantly utilitarian motive. 'On taking charge of the district,' says Captain Brooke, 'the recurrence of the word *mahaprasad* in official documents struck me. I was warned that one person could not be trusted in relation to someone else, because he was his *mahaprasad*. Unfortunately no individual is restricted in the number of his *mahaprasads*; men of wealth or influence have many and, as might be expected, native Government officials, from their position, are eagerly desired. Rumour also says that the tie is bought and sold. Instances are known of the connexion being established on the eve of a trial, to secure the neutralization of hostile evidence. The indigenous native officials seem peculiarly imbued with a lust for this sacred friendship and it may be questioned if among them there is a single individual whose *mahaprasads* are not in a measure proportionate to his position and standing in the Government service.'[1]

I doubt if this rather unsympathetic account would correctly describe the Bondo's attitude to the *moitur* or *mahaprasad* friend. For him it is a very genuine alliance of affection and mutual support, even though he may occasionally contract such a friendship with an official or outsider for business purposes. But normally these friendships are only rarely made; they mean too much; they are apt to be expensive. Two *moitur* friends cannot marry their children to one another; a *moitur* has to make ceremonial gifts at a marriage in his friend's family — he may sometimes have to go so far as to produce a buffalo — and he has obligations at his friend's death. Throughout life also he must remain the firm ally and supporter of his friend, an important point in a tribe of so many vendettas, and at all times when *moitur*-brothers meet, they exchange token presents and ceremonial gifts of liquor and food. The *moitur*-brotherhood does not, however, supersede the *soru*-brotherhood; *moitur*-friends of different villages cannot share the same sacramental food.

The ceremony of covenant is similar to that conducted elsewhere. The neighbours are called in, and a Sisa or Dissari cowdungs a little patch of ground, laying upon it a leaf-plate with mango leaves and flowers. The two friends sit on a mat before this altar, and each is attended by a witness. The Sisa asks, 'Do you truly wish to be *mahaprasad*?'

[1] W. S. Brooke, 'Note on the Custom of Mahaprasad in the Sambalpur District, Central Provinces', *The Indian Antiquary*, Vol. VII (1878), pp. 114f. At this date Sambalpur had not been transferred to Orissa. In tribal society there is a general tradition that a man should not have more than one *mahaprasad*.

and when they reply that they do, he makes them stand up and addresses Mahaprabhu in a brief prayer.

O Mahaprabhu, O Pat Khanda Mahaprabhu, these two have somehow or other come together in a surprising friendship. Let this friendship never be broken. Let their affection for one another be equal. Let there be no deceit between them. If this friendship should ever break, then let my own eyes be broken.

Each friend then puts a pice into the leaf-plate before him and they sit down together again. The Dissari throws a cloth over them and passes some water in his cupped hands round their heads. He marks their foreheads with rice, splits the mango leaves and folds them into two little bundles, tying one round the wrist of each. He puts flowers and the pice already offered at their feet. Then the two friends rise and each puts a flower behind the other's ear. They salute all present. They exchange small gifts and give each other cups of liquor. Before drinking they let a few drops fall to the ground in honour of the *sairem* and the gods.

Boys and girls also form flower-friendships, which are taken less seriously and result in less serious consequences. These are normally a simple expression of mutual affection and regard.

CHAPTER THREE

A SELF-SUFFICIENT ECONOMY

1. The Life of Highlanders

Bondo life is a life of highlanders, free, simple, arduous, on the whole happy, controlled by the routine of the seasons and the cycle of festal and ceremonial events. Economic activities, religious duties, social obligations combine in a coherent and not undignified way of life which in many ways is well suited to people living at this particular stage of development, in such isolated hills, with just so much available in the way of material resource.

Although the Bondos have no commercial sense (they have no idea of how to make money and sometimes appear remarkably indifferent to it) they are adept at providing for their own wants and are an unusually self-sufficient community. They make most of their own cloth, even though they now buy a little coloured cotton to improve the pattern. They have to get a few pots and cooking-vessels and brass and bead ornaments from outside. But they themselves make many ornaments of bark or fibre; they do not use shoes, lanterns, or any form of transport; their rain-coats and umbrellas are of bark or leaves; gourds often usurp the place of pots and vessels; they prepare most of their own liquor or obtain it from the palms that grow prolifically on their hills; they get their knives and other implements of iron from local blacksmiths almost as primitive as themselves; they grow their own tobacco and smoke it in the simplest of pipes fashioned from rolled-up leaves.

For food the Bondos depend mainly on agriculture. The physical character of their surroundings has forced them out of the food-gathering stage by providing extensive open country available for cultivation, but not offering sufficient opportunities for the gathering of roots and fruit or the hunting of game. The Bondos now rarely hunt except at festival time, and there are few streams large enough for fish. Mango, tamarind and jackfruit trees are common in the neighbourhood of most villages and their fruit is eagerly collected; such other fruit trees as are to be found in the scanty forest provide fruit during the hot weather. Roots and tubers are a useful addition to the diet, but they are not — as among the Konds — its main feature. Wild vegetables, bamboo-shoots, and mushrooms are collected and eaten. The Bondos do not seem to be specially fond of honey. 'If we find some, we take it and eat it if we're hungry.' I could not discover any charms to ward off bees. The Bondos are fond of red ants and even more fond of the date-palm grub; you may see a boy home from the jungle with a grub dangling at his waistband: he goes to the fire and roasts and eats it as a tit-bit between meals. I once saw a boy roast a fat dung-beetle and suck the rich hot juice. Silkworms are regarded as good for any swelling of the stomach. Rats are fattened in cages or hunted and killed at festivals.

The Bondos keep cattle, goats, pigs, and poultry; they do not milk the cows or goats, but they eat beef and almost every animal or bird is dedicated to some ceremonial purpose, a fact that makes it difficult for the traveller to buy local supplies. The Bondos eat carrion with avidity, with the curious result that it is rare to see a vulture or kite above their villages, and hens with large and flourishing broods wander at large, free of danger from the sky.

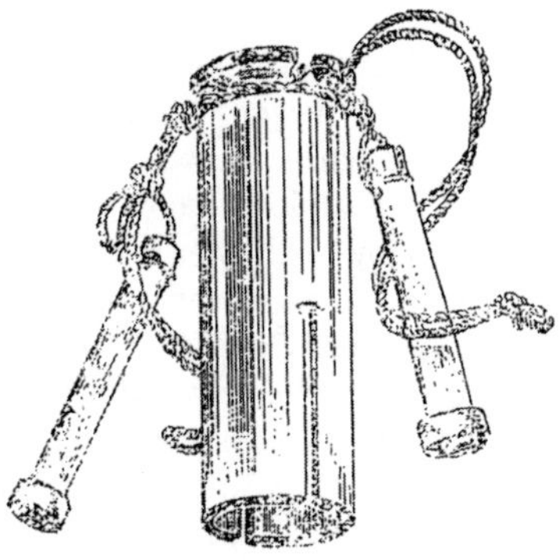

FIG. 8. Bondo cow-bell

The routine of Bondo life is controlled by the seasons, and varies according to the work that must be done or the holidays that must be enjoyed. All the year round, the women get up very early, 'after the cock has crowed a second time', and the men too rise only a little later 'while it is still dark but light is on the way'. A woman gets up, wipes her eyes with a dash of water, lights the fire and begins husking and cleaning grain. She sets a pot of gruel to simmer on the fire, and cleans and puts the house in order. If there is ploughing to be done, the men take the cattle out immediately, but otherwise leave them tied up till nearly midday; if there is no ploughing the first male duty of the day is to go out to the sago palms for the morning drink. Ploughmen, however, usually postpone their drink till the morning's work is over. When there is something to be done in the irrigated fields, the women follow the men there, taking the children with them, and carrying food for the morning meal. When they feel ready for it, the labourers collect in a corner of the field and take it from leaf-cups. The Bondos are rather individualistic about food, and when they eat at home, the meal is often divided into a number of cups which each member takes when he feels like it and sits alone, often outside, drinking out of the cup which he holds in the left hand while he eats a little chutney or vegetable with the right. Two girls, close friends, may sit together feeding each other out of a single cup.

In the Andrahal area men make mats and baskets, preparing the bamboo slats with a small knife on a sort of tripod, and making the complicated twilled pattern expertly. A man anxious to finish his work on a mat in time for the bazaar may be up before sunrise while it is still cold and damp. But when the drinking parties start for the palms, few remain behind. There is no rule about the early morning wash; the morning drink is much more important. Actually both men and women wash and clean their teeth (with twigs) at any convenient time during the morning. In the hot weather they bathe almost every day, and it is common to see mothers bathing their babies, making a couch for them between their legs and pouring water on their wriggling bodies from a gourd.

If the people have been working in the irrigated fields, they often get home about midday and may then have something more to eat. After this they may go out to the more distant hill-clearings. When there is no work in the fields, they go direct to the clearings, but in that case they do not start so early, for they expect to stay longer. During the afternoons Bondo villages are often practically deserted, except for a few old women sitting at their looms. The people begin to trickle back, each with a load of wood or leaves, in the late afternoon. Men go at once for their evening drink of palm-wine, women grind, husk grain, fetch water, and cook. At about eight o'clock the family has its evening meal, but again in a very individualistic manner, and then the boys and girls retire to their separate dormitories and the elders sleep.

FIG. 9. Bondo pestle

Work is shared by men and women, but the women labour more, and for longer hours, in addition to work in field or clearing, they have to fetch water and cook and care for the children, and whenever they are free they must be at the loom. Certain activities are taboo to men. They are not usually supposed to extract fibre from the *kereng* bark, but this rule is not always observed, for I have seen men doing it. But I do not think they ever weave. They must not husk or grind, and they should not ordinarily cowdung the floor of a house. They should not bring wood from the forest in the Hindu month of Jeth, just before the rains. They should not cut the hair of adult women. Women, on the other hand, are not allowed to plough, though they are permitted to take their part in almost every other agricultural process. They must not climb trees or onto the roof of a house, or place a carrying-pole over their shoulders. A woman must not offer *gige* (sacrifice), though she may attempt to divine, but not treat, a disease. Women may not make mats, nor carry out a corpse nor hunt. They may not cut the taller trees in the clearings. They may dance, but they may not beat drums or use any musical instrument other than the jew's harp. If they do any of these things, I was told, 'it is *bissas* (sin or pollution) and we will lose by it'.

Such is the daily routine; the sequence of events throughout the year can most conveniently be indicated by a calendar, though it must, of course, be remembered that such a calendar is only approximate: its events are not engagements in a programme which is adhered to punctually. The weather, the state of the crops, the dreams and inspirations of a shaman, may seriously disturb the routine. But, on the whole, things occur in this order and at about this time of the year.

2. The Bondo Calendar

January

Reaping and threshing of the rice harvest. Threshing *Eleusine corocana* and the smaller millets. At the end of the month or the beginning of February, at the full moon of Pus, is the Sume-Gelirak Festival, during which occurs the Merer-Susum, the First Fruits Feast of the new beans. After this, grass may be cut and *kereng* branches brought from the forest.

February

Seed-beds are prepared in the irrigated fields and rice is sown in them. Ploughing begins. Spinning and weaving fills every spare minute of a woman's time. Weddings and the final bringing of brides to their husbands' houses. Ceremonial beddings. *Gunom* ceremonies. New clearings are cut.

March

Heavy work in the fields. Ploughing. Transplanting of rice-seedlings. Spinning and weaving. Weddings. *Gunom* ceremonies. New houses are built.

April

Work in open and irrigated fields completed. The great festival of the Giag-gige begins at the full moon of Chait and lasts over a fortnight. Ceremonial hunts. Dancing. The First Fruits of the new mangoes. After the Giag-gige (and in some places even before it) forest-clearings are fired and it is permissible to sow *Eleusine corocana* and *Panicum miliare* and other small millets, and to thatch the roofs of houses. Weaving continues.

MAY

Work in hill-clearings continues; unburnt wood is collected and burnt; millets are sown. Weaving. Bamboo and grass is brought in. Houses are carefully thatched against the rain. Firewood is collected.

JUNE

The rains begin. Ploughing of level fields and sowing of dry rice and the millets in them, and in the clearings. Preparations for the rains.

JULY

Weeding begins and occupies a great deal of the women's time throughout the rains. Gersum-gige, the feast of the new mango kernels, gourds and roselle, after which bread and gruel can be made with kernel-flour. From the end of Sawan (July-August), spinning and weaving is taboo till the following January. Sprouting shrubs are removed from the hill-clearings. Gadar-gige is celebrated to protect the cattle from disease.

AUGUST AND SEPTEMBER

Boys begin their visits to the girls' dormitories in other villages and continue to do so till the end of the year. Love-affairs, betrothals and kidnappings. Weeding in fields and clearings; the task of guarding the crops imposes a heavy burden on all. First Fruits Feast of the maize crop. Women collect bamboo shoots. *Guizotia abyssinica* is sown.

OCTOBER

The larger and more advanced millets are reaped, and roasted, husked and eaten at a ceremonial feast. Tribute is sent to the Maharaja of Jeypore at the Dassera Festival, which is also observed after a fashion in the Bara-jangar villages.

NOVEMBER

Crops are guarded day and night and the villages are almost deserted Gewursung Festival, corresponding to the Hindu Diwali, now or in October. Brides are sometimes brought now to their husbands' homes.

DECEMBER

Reaping of rice, millets, and crops in the hill-clearings.

3. CULTIVATION

The nature of the Bondo uplands makes three kinds of cultivation possible — the raising of rice on irrigated and terraced fields, the growing of dry crops on fairly level ploughed fields of the ordinary type, and axe-cultivation on the steep slopes of the hills.

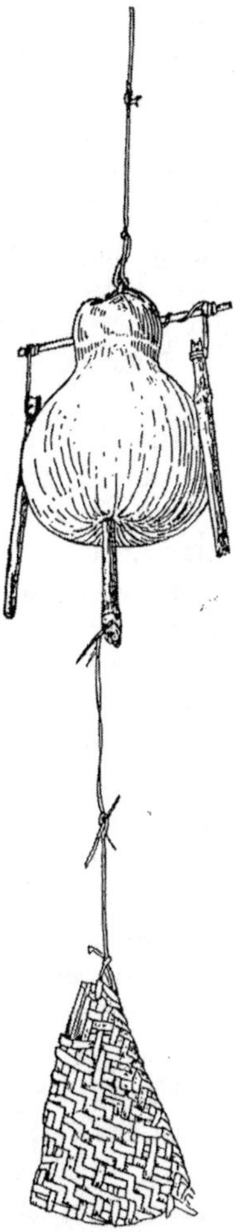

Fig. 10.
Scarecrow

Tribal opinion, but not the Zamindari Estate, recognizes private ownership of the hill-clearings. The population has now increased to such an extent, and the entire countryside has been so burnt over, that it is no longer possible for the Bondos to practice 'shifting' cultivation in the usual sense.[1] Each household 'owns' a number of sites on the hillsides, which are not necessarily within their own village boundary, and uses these in rotation. All chance of any substantial regrowth has long since disappeared, and the most that can now be expected is a fairly heavy growth of shrubs and grasses to provide the manure when burnt. The clearings are thus almost like fields; the result is that there is no annual gathering, as among other tribes, to settle where the forest shall be cut, and no wandering at will over the hills; a clearing has become a personal possession which must be preserved and can be inherited. The Bondos sell their clearings to one another and mortgage them, of course without legal sanction: indeed any kind of axe-cultivation is officially forbidden throughout the Jeypore Estate. A poor man may 'hire' a clearing for a few years; he pays no rent, but makes presents of meat and liquor at the beginning and end of his tenure; the owner is allowed to help himself to cucumbers and gourds. A hard-working family can keep three clearings, each representing a different year of development, going at once.

As I hope to deal with the problem and technique of axe-cultivation in great detail in my monograph on the Kuttia Konds, I will here only lightly sketch the Bondos' method of raising their crops.

[1] In 1872, H. G. Turner, Special Assistant Agent, spoke very strongly of the effects of *podu* cultivation. But R.C.S. Bell writes: 'The administrative experience of three-quarters of a century shows that Mr Turner exaggerated the rapidity with which forest destruction is affecting the climate and appearance of the Koraput country. Though *podu* cultivation is by no means extinct, the 3,000-foot plateau is still well watered and summer crops of rice are grown in nearly every village... Early reports show that when Koraput was chosen in 1870 as headquarters the country round it was completely bare of tree growth as it is now. It seems likely that the transition from evergreen jungle to the bare hill slopes that are now to be seen was spread over centuries rather than decades.'—*Koraput District Gazetteer,* p. 105.

The official moment for the commencement of axe-cultivation is at the end of the Sume-Gelirak Festival, when the village priest ceremonially initiates the task of cutting the clearings. Nowadays this is not very heavy work, for there are few big trees, and the main business, which is done by both men and women, is to clear the grass and cut shrubs and saplings. Mango, jackfruit, tamarind and sago palms are spared, but everything else is cut. In March or April, men fire the now dry grass and branches. They do not rake the ashes over the ground, nor do they — so far as I know — bring branches from neighbouring woods to increase the quantity of ash. The Bondos, like the Konds, prefer to cut and fire bamboos, for they believe the wood yields the best manure and the roots prevent erosion.

During the Giag-gige ceremonies in April, there is a little rite for the collection and re-burning of half-consumed stumps of trees and branches. Men and women then go to their own clearings and work at them until they feel that the area is reasonably burnt over. During the time of waiting for the rains, men erect small field-huts, sometimes high in a tree, though they seem to be taking less trouble over these nowadays, perhaps because the menace of wild animals is now so small.

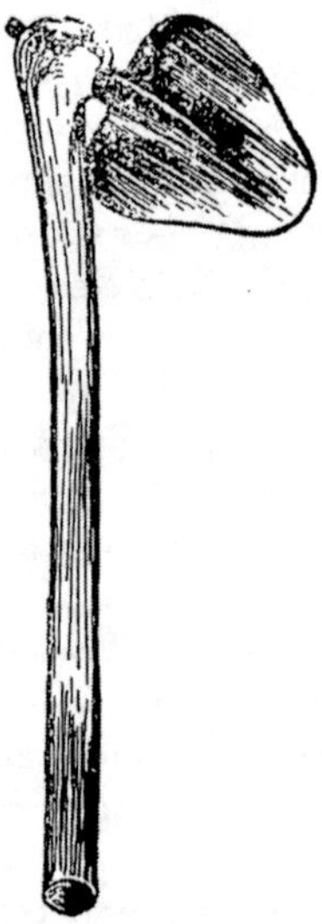

Fig. 11. Bondo hoe of older type

After the breaking of the rains, the Bondos sow the first seeds. They often first offer fish and rice in the clearings to promote the fecundity of the seed, which itself has been consecrated at more than one ceremonial. They broadcast several different kinds of millet, including *Eleusine corocana, Panicum miliare* and *Panicum italicum,* with *Sorghum vulgare* and *Penisetum typhoideum,* all mixed together, from a basket slung over the left arm and scattered with a flick of the right wrist. After this sowing, men and women rake up the earth with hoes, of which the Bondos use two varieties, both shouldered, but one is attached to the shaft by a tang and the other by a handle-hole.

After the broadcasting of the small seeds, the Bondos proceed to plant pulses of various kinds including *Cajanus indicus* and *Dolichos biflorus,* cucumbers, gourds and castor trees, dibbling holes in the ground with a stick and treading down the earth afterwards. They do not usually sow beans in the clearings, and we do not find, therefore, the 'ghost-forests' of dead trees which, left standing to support the bean-vines, are so conspicuous a feature of the landscape in the Juang and Bhuiya Pirhs of Keonjhar and Bonai.

This is the custom during the first year's life of a clearing; in the second year, only small millets are sown, and in third and subsequent years the clearings are permitted to produce more or less what they like; they are cleared and fired, but sown, if at all, very casually.

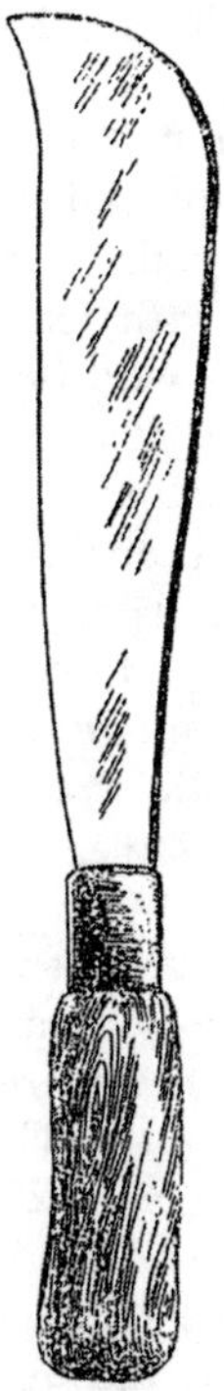

FIG. 12. Hatchet to cut grass and shrubs

From the beginning of September, when the first small millets ripen, the Bondos reap a small quantity every day, just enough for the day's food, threshing it with their feet on the veranda, husking, cleaning, cooking and eating it immediately. Thenceforward the main crops slowly mature, and the business of reaping begins.

Below the hill-clearings, and often in the neighbourhood of a village, are fairly level fields, and the Bondos plough these in the ordinary way — there is nothing characteristic about the Bondo plough, which is an obvious importation from the plains — and raise crops of dry rice and *Eleusine corocana* upon them. They also sow the black oilseed *Guizotia abyssinica*, but they grow no wheat.

There are finally the irrigated fields and terraces. The Bondos are less adept at terracing than the Saoras, but they carefully utilize the streams and the beds of their numerous valleys for wet rice-cultivation, building up every yard of space available into fields that lead from one to another with drops of two to six feet. There is some good terracing at Andrahal; the walls are roughly riveted with stone and stand six to eight feet high, but they lack the finish of Saora work. The irrigation arrangements are carefully made; canals are taken across and round the fields, and the water is often carried over the drop by a gutter of hollowed bamboo or caryota wood.

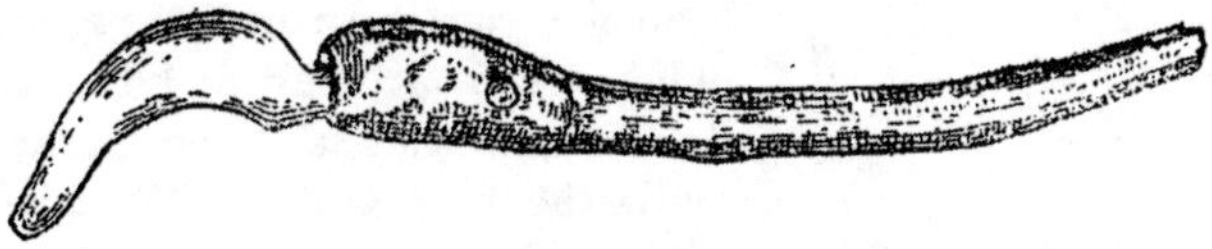

FIG. 13. Another type of hatchet

The Bondos flood a field to a depth of a few inches and plough it twice; then they flood it again with as much as two feet of water and drive heavy wooden harrows over it to ensure a perfectly level surface. They use a wooden leveller worked by hand to remove any inequalities of surface round the edges of the field. They devote special care to the preparation of seed-beds which they plough and level several times.

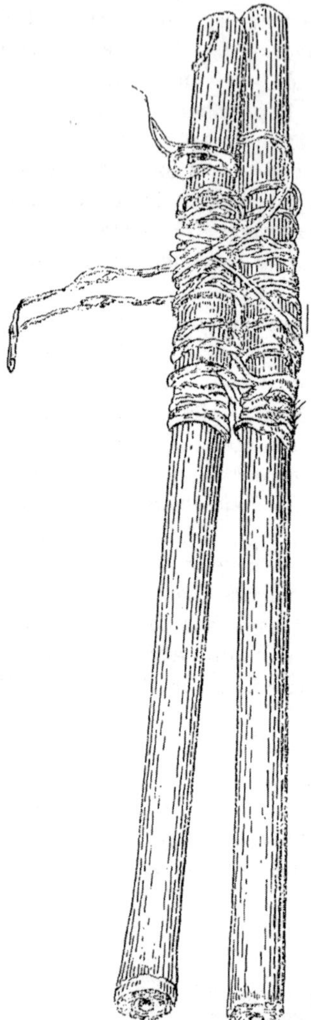

FIG. 14. Instrument for castrating bulls

They prepare the seed by first cleaning and then damping it with water in a pot for a week. Then they tip it out into a basket, and cover it with leaves, from time to time sprinkling it with warm water. After three days, they let out the water from the seed-bed and sow the rice by throwing it forward (not with a sweep of the hand) into the damp soil. They do not make any attempt to cover the seed with earth, but they guard very carefully against birds. A little water is gradually let into the beds as the seedlings come up.

When the seedlings are sufficiently mature, women pull them up and carry them in bundles to the main fields, from which the water has been drained. They stand in long rows, each with her sickle thrust through her headband, singing melodiously as they plant out the seedlings. Water is again let into the fields to a depth of two or three inches and is then adjusted from time to time so that the heads of growing stalks are just above the surface. They let out the water for weeding, and then allow it to fill up again.

For reaping, it is customary for a married girl to return to her parent's house; when she goes back to her husband she takes with her a large basket heaped with the new grain. The chief peculiarity of Bondo harvesting is that, in common with the Konds, they do not usually cut the stalks low down, but cut or break off the ears at the top.[1] This means that there is always a famine of straw in Bondo villages.

[1] The plains Bondos, however, generally reap in the conventional manner.

The Bondos take most of their crops in bundles direct to the threshing-floors, but they store the unthreshed *Eleusine corocana* on raised platforms fenced in with grass walls, for this crop has to be gathered, though not necessarily threshed, before the Sume-Gelirak Festival can begin.

The threshing-floor is guarded by various taboos. The men working there must not do any other work; they must cook on the spot and no cooked food may be brought from the house. They must not eat meat, though fish is allowed, and they may only drink palm-wine, but not beer or spirits. They may talk among themselves but not to others. During the threshing period they must observe sexual abstinence. The actual work of threshing and winnowing is performed in the way common throughout tribal Orissa. *Eleusine corocana* is beaten with long poles; other crops are threshed by the feet and by small droves of cattle, muzzled with rope or small bamboo cages, which are tied together but not attached to a central pole. The Bondos winnow by shaking the grain down from a fan held above the head and also by fanning piles of grain on the ground. If when fanning a man hits the grain with the fan, the others exclaim, '*Poloi*', which means 'Come back, don't go away!', for there is a belief that grain hit by a fan will go away to one's parents' house. The winnowers smooth the heap with the offending fan turned upside-down and must abuse the careless worker. If there is insufficient wind for the winnowing the Sisa offers a fowl to Ispur, a Sky God, on the floor itself. Sometimes a forked branch of bombax is erected and the winnower stands upon it.

FIG. 15. Symbols of a plough and sickle made on a heap of grain at the ceremony described here

When the grain is ready, it is heaped up in a long mound which may be as much as ten feet long, four broad and two feet high. The labourers make criss-cross patterns along and over the mound with ash, and rough symbols of the sun and moon, a plough and a yoke. They put a winnowing fan face down at either end of the mound and make a kind of altar of agricultural implements — a billhook, a knife, an axe, a rope to tie the cattle, a cow-bell, a broom.[1] Ash of burnt straw is used everywhere to keep away hostile ghosts.

[1] Similar practices are common throughout India. Some sort of covering must be placed on a heap of winnowed grain. In Hindi this is called the *chhattur* from the word meaning an umbrella. In Benares this is a mere cake of cowdung; elsewhere it is a shoot of grass, a dry stick of *arhar* pulse, or a leaf of the *Asclepias gigantea*. A spear may be struck in the ground beside the heap. Cf. H. M. Elliot, *Memoirs of the Races of the North Western Provinces of India* (London, 1869), pp. 235, 239.

I was present at a ceremony in Kadamguda on 18 December 1943, where the Naiko (who acted as his own priest) prepared his rice crop for removal to the bins. He built an altar in the way I have described, and placed before it some smouldering sticks of ebony wood. Beside them he put ten leaves of the same tree, each with a little cooked rice and some bits of roasted crab. Then, in front of the winnowing-fan at the north end of the grain-mound, he made a pattern on the ground with coal-dust and red earth. On this he offered an egg and some more rice and crab in the name of Bursung and the dead. He repeated these offerings at the south end of the mound and in front of the altar of implements. An assistant took an egg and crab-meat to the border of the field, threw down these offerings there and broke the egg, which had not smashed, with his axe. Finally the Naiko offered crab-meat and another egg at the western side and scattered parched rice, freshly made in his own house, over the entire mound. He sacrificed a fowl and walked round shaking the blood over the grain. He broke an egg and scattered both white and yoke. Three times he picked up a handful of grain, blew on it and threw it back. This was the end of the ceremony; the rice was now ready to be taken to the bins. The Naiko first removed a winnowing-fan full of grain with his own hands and then his relatives and servants began shovelling it into baskets. On the first basket the Naiko placed a leaf-cup with an egg in it and some crab-meat.[1]

Fig. 16. Ganangpa charm to protect a garden

[1] I witnessed an almost identical ceremony, four years later, in the same village, but on this occasion the winnowed grain was intended for seed and so parched rice was used for crab-meat. A symbol of the moon was made with ash on the mound of grain, for 'the moon is a woman, and she will look after the seed as gently as a woman'.

I was told that if it is not possible to remove all the grain which has been threshed and winnowed that very day, the householder should burn some chaff and, holding his breath, sprinkle the ash over the grain. This prevents it from escaping. The idea that grain, and especially rice, is always trying to get away, occurs in the legend, quoted later in this book, about rice having wings.

The Bondos cultivate their small gardens, digging up the soil with hoes and carefully manuring it from the dung pits that are maintained throughout the year. In the gardens they grow maize, a little tobacco (they are not very ardent smokers), beans, chillies and gourds. A garden may be protected by a sort of supernatural scarecrow called Ganangpa. A branch is tied to a mango tree to guard the fruit; a grass doll with an egg and a bit of *Semecarpus anacardium* is hung from a pole among the tobacco plants; then if a thief comes he will get sores or bad eyes.

4. Hunting and Fishing

Seventy years ago, the Bondo Hills were rich in game. May, writing in 1872, reports that,

> Game is plentiful, as must be the case in a country so thinly populated. The bison, sambhar, pig, axis or spotted deer, the ravine deer, bears and occasionally the wild buffalo, and tigers, roam at large and fearless of man, with whom they are so little acquainted. Peafowl and other wild fowl are abundant. The otter also is to be found, but only on the banks of the larger streams.[1]

But today, though the Bondo never stirs out of his village without his bow and arrows (which are also intended to protect him against human foes), there is little left for him to shoot. The forest has gone and past generations have stripped the countryside even of its sparrows. Mr H. V. Blackburn, whose opinion may be accepted as authoritative, says that Bondo youths are the quickest and sharpest of any aboriginals he has seen; their eyesight is wonderful, and they are after the smallest target in a flash. In a shooting competition at Bodoballe, 75 per cent of the contestants hit a cigarette packet with their arrows at a distance of 30 feet; at a greater distance their aim was not so good: at 50 feet only one scraped it.

[1] May, op. cit., p. 238.

Bird-lime, made of the milky sap of the jackfruit, is used for catching little birds; many kinds of traps are prepared and ensnare birds, hares and rats. Hunting proper is almost confined to the great ritual expeditions of the Giag-gige, which I describe fully in a later chapter.[1]

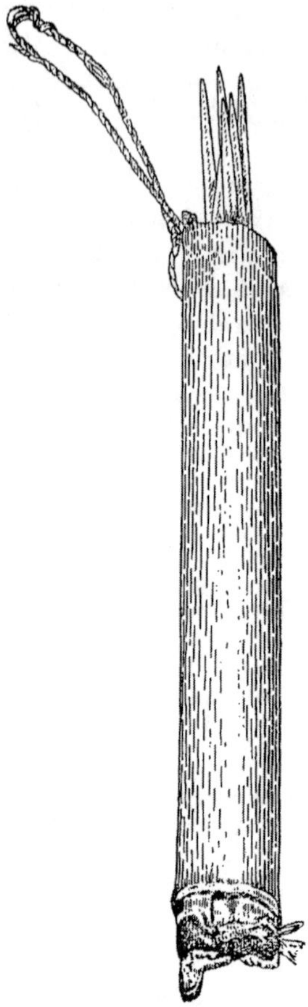

FIG. 17. Bamboo container for bird-lime

Fishing is restricted by geographical conditions. There is a broad stream down the Tulaguram valley and a little tumbling rivulet at the foot of the Andrahal hill and yet another running out from sacred Kingu Bodak. But the high Bondo plateau is not a good place for fish; more commonly found are the crabs hiding in the rocks of stream and rivulet. These play an important part in Bondo ritual and diet. They are not only eaten eagerly whenever found, but they are offered in the name of the dead at the first reaping of the new rice, on the threshing-floor before the winnowed grain is taken to the house, should the *Eleusine corocana* crop be diseased, and when the sap of a sago palm begins to fail. Crabs and fish are offered to the dead inside a house on most festal occasions.

There is a ceremonial drive for fish during the Giag-gige Festival, and throughout the year women go fishing from time to time. Before they start, it is their custom to spit on a little ash and throw it away or to make a ring of date-palm leaves, put it on the path, place a few thorns inside it and step over it as they go and return. When they catch their first fish, they spit on it and throw it back into the water.

The Bondos use traps and a net. They are all of the common pattern. A *tundor* is a bamboo trap set in a flowing stream. The *gira* is a basket which women use to sweep a pool, chasing the fish into it or catching

[1] In Andrahal I found a curious belief that if a man has a father or elder brother living, he must not eat the liver of any creature taken in the chase — 'for it is as if he is eating his own father's or brother's liver' — but should give it to them to eat for him.

them by a concerted drive across. They also dam up a stream and bale out the water, leaving the fish helpless in the mud. Men use a large net

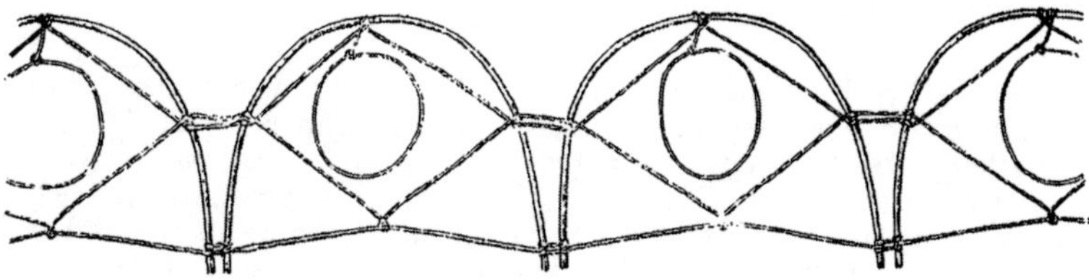

FIG. 18. Snare for catching birds and rabbits

attached to a bamboo frame, which they lower by a cord into the water and then pull up. They sometimes poison the water with bits of the broken bark of the mango and *Eugenia jambolana*; this is said 'to make the fish drunk' and they are then easily caught.

5. Wine, Beer and Spirits

'Wine is sweet in the mouth and tender on the stomach; spirits burn the liver and drive men to blows; beer fills the belly and makes one lazy.' In this way the Bondos distinguish the three kinds of alcoholic refreshment available to them. They might have gone further and pointed out that beer is the drink for weddings, funerals and festivals; spirits must be bought from the bazaar or secretly distilled; but palm-wine is always ready at one's door, the generous and abundant gift of mother earth.[1]

The Bondos have several legends to account for the existence of the delicious tree, *Caryota urens,* whose plentiful sap is perhaps the chief solace of their lives. The following story comes from Mundlipada.

Originally the sago palm was very small and had long roots. When Mahaprabhu wandered in the jungle he used to dig up the roots and eat them. One day, as he was digging, one of the roots broke and some juice came out; Mahaprabhu tasted it and liked the sweet flavour. After that he used to camp by the trees and dig up the roots and drink their juice.

Sita grew impatient and went to find her husband. When Mahaprabhu saw her coming he was afraid and ran away. When Sita saw the palms she guessed that it was because of them that her husband did not come to her. She was angry with them and kicked the roots right away into the sea. She tugged at a tree with both hands and it stretched out and went up into the air, very tall.

[1] Throughout the book when I use the word 'wine' I mean the fermented sap of the *Caryota urens,* by 'beer' I mean either *li* or *pendam* made of rice or millet, and by 'spirits' I refer to the liquor distilled from the corollae of *Bassia latifolia.*

When Mahaprabhu saw what she was doing, he ran back and caught hold of his wife. Sita cursed the tree: 'From today your juice will come from your top, not from your bottom.'

Another story comes from Dumiripada.

The seven brothers were out hunting. They grew weary and sat down to rest beneath a sago palm. Presently a little sap dripped down onto one of them. He had his pipe in his hand and he unrolled the leaf and caught a little of the sap. He tasted it and found it sweet and refreshing. He climbed up and cut the tree a little and more sap came out and there was enough for them all. But they found it troublesome to stand beneath the tree and try to catch the sap in leaves, and soon they learnt how to tie a pot up in the branches and collect it that way.[1]

At Andrahal the Bondos suggested that the roots of the palm go right down through the earth to the ocean that lies below. The water flows up and is matured into sap as it rises through the stem. 'The sago palm',

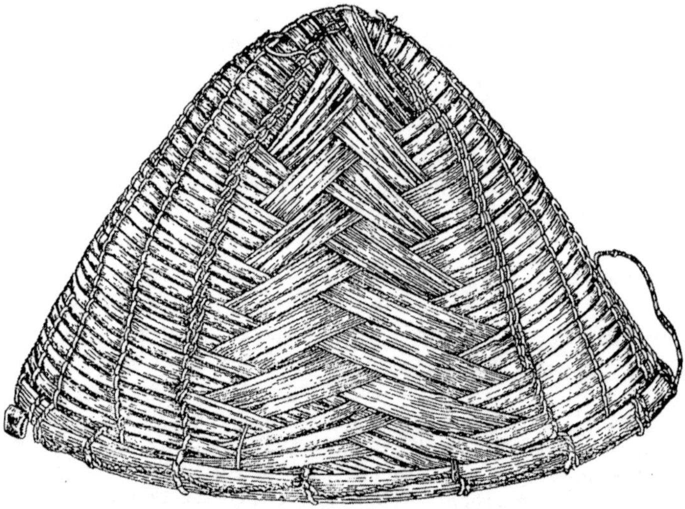

FIG. 19. Basket used for catching fish in a pool.

they said, not without reason, at Bodoballe, 'is our mother and it is on her milk that we feed and live.' Miliya Bodnaik confessed that when he was in jail he longed for his drink of wine every morning and evening throughout his sentence; it was the only thing he really missed. Sonia

[1] For an account of similar stories and traditions in Bastar, see my article, 'The Sago Palm in Bastar State', *J.R.A.S. Bom.*, Vol. XVIII (1942), pp. 69-78, and *The Muria and their Ghotul*, pp. 53ff.

Sisa told me that it was this that dominated his dreams. A Bondo at Mundlipada described his idea of a perfect day to Shamrao Hivale: it was 'to go to the palm trees in the morning and sit there for an hour chatting and drinking; to come back and slumber on the *sindibor*; after a good meat meal, to take one's wife apart and lie with her; then at sunset return for the evening drink of wine'.

Every palm in the Bondo country belongs to someone; it is a most valuable form of private property, though I doubt if the Courts would recognize a right of possession, and many quarrels and not a few murders derive from uncertainty of ownership or thefts of the juice.[1] At one time a tree could be bought for one or two rupees, but the price in 1945 was at the least five rupees; the palm under which Muliya committed his ferocious murder[2] cost him ten rupees. The trees are inherited along with other family possessions; if a father has two trees and two sons, each gets one; if he has three trees, each takes one and they divide the produce of the third.

When a new tree is to be planted, a Bondo brings a seedling from the forest, it is considered very lucky if his wife is suckling a child at the time. He makes a hole in the ground, offers a fowl to Bursung and drops some of the blood into it, then plants the tree; after this it is expected to grow rapidly. When the tree is ready for tapping, a ceremony called the Saphung Sunungbok-gige is performed. The owner goes to the tree in the morning and offers rice and a fresh egg in the name of Bursung at the foot; in the evening, he offers another egg for Singraj, a water-spirit. Then he cuts the first spathe and lets the sap fall to the ground throughout the night. Next morning, another man — not the owner — sacrifices a fowl and sprinkles the blood round the tree. He climbs up and fixes a small gourd to the spadix with a thread and descends. Presently, as the gourd fills, the weight of the sap breaks the thread and projects the gourd to the ground where it is smashed to pieces. The owner of the tree offers another egg and now he himself climbs the tree and ties an earthen pot in place among the branches. Later, when they judge the pot to be full, the owner and a few friends assemble at the foot of the tree. They sacrifice another fowl, bring down the pot, warm it on a fire near by, offer a few drops to the dead, and drink.

If the sap does not flow freely, another fowl may be offered to Kittung

[1] Donkar Sisa of Semiliguda had a palm at Tulaguram which he leased out, first to Soma Mundli of that village and then to one Lachmi Bodnaik, but failed to tell Soma about the new arrangement. Lachmi went for the juice, but Soma objected and Lachmi, anxious to avoid trouble, left the tree alone. Soon afterwards, however, the flow of juice ceased and Soma decided that the outwardly complaisant Lachmi must have secretly performed magic or given some medicine to the tree. He went to kill him, but Lachmi shot him first. This was at Tulaguram on 9 November 1945. Lachmi got five years.

[2] See pp. 237-9.

or Ispur, a Sky God. If this has no effect, crabs and fish are sacrificed to the dead, with the following charm:

> *Hānum*! From the horn of the palm let the pot overflow and fall to the ground! Let the water of the ocean come! Let the spring water come! Let the pot overflow! I offer crabs: I sprinkle (water); I offer fish.

The trees are climbed either by a very long bamboo pole, which is slung from a hook attached to a branch high up the trunk, and is hidden in a neighbouring thicket when not in use, or by a bamboo ladder consisting of a pole tied tightly against the trunk with strong bands of fibre. Great bundles of thorns are often attached to the trunk to deter thieves.

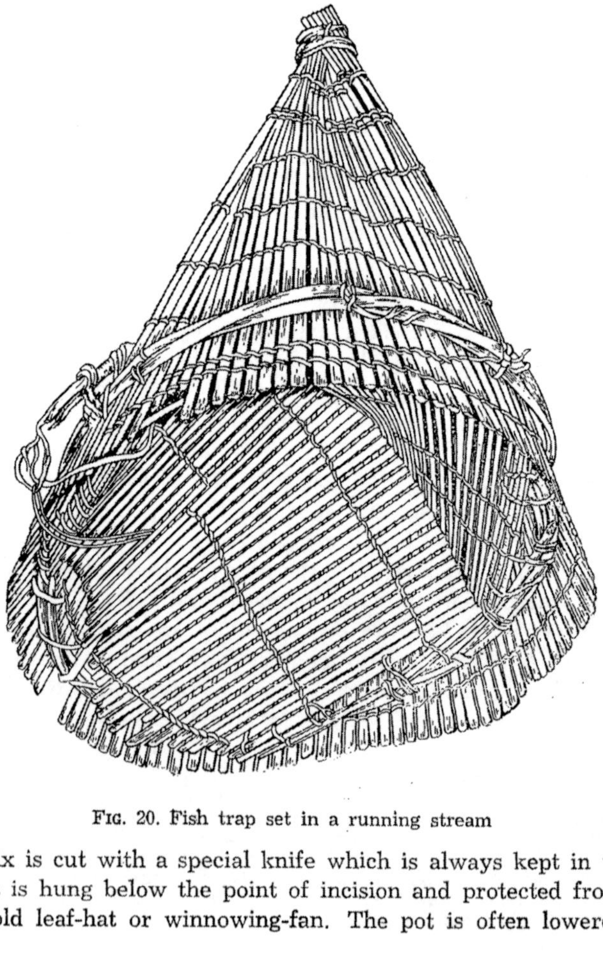

FIG. 20. Fish trap set in a running stream

The spadix is cut with a special knife which is always kept in the tree and a pot is hung below the point of incision and protected from birds with an old leaf-hat or winnowing-fan. The pot is often lowered by a cord to someone below and when it has been emptied is drawn up again and returned to its place. Before cutting a new spadix, it is an advantage to jump up and down on it daily for a week or two in order to loosen it thoroughly.

The wine is usually taken hot. 'If we warm it,' I was told, 'we can drink more and it has the effect of food; the belly feels satisfied, hands and feet are strengthened, and we can get drunk more quickly.' Above all, there is no hangover. 'If we take it cold,' on the other hand, 'we feel sick and lazy and have a headache the next day.' Friends sit round a pot helping themselves with gourd ladles, somewhat on the Saora pattern but smaller and less elaborately made: these ladles must be held by the handle, not by the bowl, or one may get a headache.

Shamrao Hivale recorded two songs sung to wives by Bondos as they return from drinking below a tree.

I go to the palm tree to drink wine. Make it hot and then it will warm me.
Walk straight and not reeling to and fro, however much wine you may have drunk.
I have been wandering about, I have climbed the tree and now I am tired.
Give me my food, for the day is passing and I must work.
I must tether the cows and buffaloes,
I must shut the pigs in their stye and drive the fowls into the house.

Another song stresses the physical effects of the drink.

Give me rice, give me gruel, for I must eat.
The wine has set my calves trembling, my thighs trembling,
My very loins are trembling.
To me it is already night, for I feel tired and sleepy.
Let me eat and sleep; give me my food quickly.
Sweep the floor and spread the mat and we will sleep together.

When an old tree ceases to give sap, the owner makes an incision in the trunk and removes some of the pith. He wraps it in leaves and places it amidst the hot embers of a glowing fire. When it is cooked he examines it carefully to see whether it is fit to be made into sago flour. If it is, he cuts down the tree, divides it into blocks, splits these into sections; then his wife removes and shreds the pith, beats it with a mallet, husks it in a mortar until it is reduced to a fine flour, then mixes it with flour of *Eleusine corocana* to make bread or gruel.

Like other tribesmen the Bondos use the wood of the palm to build cattle-sheds, to fence in a veranda and sometimes for rough doors. The fibre is made into a fine cord and used in making headbands and combs.

Rice-beer

The Bondos make two kinds of rice-beer, *li* (the Mundari *ili*), 'the best drink of all, very delicious and intoxicating', and *pendam*, which corresponds more or less to the Bastar *lānda*.

Before making *li* it is necessary to abstain for twenty-four hours from sexual intercourse. The best *li* is made with old mountain rice which has been roasted three months previously and put aside to mature in a special jar. On the day the brew is to be started, the housewife gets up very early in the morning and goes alone, and while it is still dark, for the 'medicines' to mix into the compound—bark of *Bassia latifolia, Terminalia tomentosa* and *Diospyros melanoxylon,* and roots of *Phoenix sylvestris* and *Baliospermum axillare.* She brings them home and cuts them into small pieces. She fills a pot with water, and puts into it the materials of the 'medicine'; into another pot which has at the bottom a hole closed with a bamboo sieve, she puts the rice which has been carefully washed. She places the first pot on the hearth and the second above it and lets it steam after carefully closing its mouth with leaves. Presently she makes a little hole in the leaf cover and sniffs at it; if it smells sour she knows it is ready. She removes the cover, stirs the rice with a wooden spoon, tips it into a basket and puts it by the hearth. Then she boils the medicine for a long time until it thickens, when she takes it out and smears it all over the inside of yet another pot. Into this she drops a few bits of root tied up in leaves, pours in the steamed rice and puts the pot in a dark cool corner of the house.

Six days later the woman removes the rice and husks it until it is of the consistency of flour. This she puts into a fresh pot, filling it up with water, and lets it stand for three or four days. At the end of this time, she examines the brew and if she finds worms in it 'as long as half your finger', it is pronounced ready.

Any of the smaller millets, or *Eleusine corocana,* can be used instead of rice and sometimes a mixture may give very satisfactory results.

Pendam differs from *li* in being somewhat simpler to make and in requiring an artificial fermenting agent instead of the various roots and bark employed in *li.*

The woman boils the rice or millet in the husk and dries it in the sun. Then she husks it and puts it in a pot of water to boil. In another pot she puts some water with leaves of *Momordica charantia* and boils them until there is a thick sticky mixture which she smears over the inside of another pot, into which she puts the boiled rice. She grinds up five or six balls of the artificial ferment (*osad* in Oriya, *surong* in Remo), mixes it in with the rice and pours water over it. She ties up the mouth with leaves and puts it aside to stand in a cool place. After a week she tastes it, and if it is a little bitter she knows it is ready. She strains it through a bamboo strainer and when she has warmed it, it is fit for drinking.

This is rather different from the Maria beer, in the making of which no artificial ferment is used, but I gather the result is very much the same, and I myself have noticed little difference in between taste and potency of Bondo *pendam* and Maria *landa*. Both are an enormous improvement on *mahua* spirit.

Ardent Spirits

The Bondos trace the discovery of ardent spirits (distilled from the corollae of the *Bassia latifolia* tree) to Mahaprabhu himself.

When Mahaprabhu sowed the seeds from which sprang every kind of tree and shrub, he forgot to plant the *bosisum* (*Bassia latifolia*). After a long time he discovered the seeds tied up in a leaf-bundle in the roof of his house, and he took them to the forest and planted them. In due time the trees grew and bore flowers and fruit. One day when Mahaprabhu was examining his forest, he noticed how many and how beautiful were the flowers of this tree and he picked a few and ate them. Soon he felt drowsy and lay down under the tree and went to sleep. Presently he got up and said to himself, 'How nice and peaceful one feels after eating this. If I give it to men they too will feel happy and restful.' So he called the peacock and jungle fowl and maina and told them to scatter the seeds all over the world. 'Eat as much of this as you can,' he said, 'and then let the seeds fall in your droppings everywhere.' The birds ate and began to dance, and as they danced they ate more and more until their bellies were full. The peacock and jungle fowl let their droppings fall in the forest near by, but the maina flew all over the world dropping the seed.

Then Mahaprabhu called Soma Bodnaik and told him, 'This is the *bosisum*. Eat the flowers and fruit and feed your children on it. You will get drunk on the juice. It is the tree of plenty and delight.'

The Bondos distil their own spirit — under the present laws, illegally — at home or in one or other of the numerous secret streams and gullies that thread amidst their hills. For the Bondos are as adept at this as at brewing rice-beer or tapping the sago palm, and even the bravest excise officials shrink from interfering.

The *bosisum* flowers in March or April and the Bondos often burn the grass under and round the trees in order to facilitate the task of collecting the fallen blossoms. The trees are most plentiful below the hills, in the villages of the open country; the hill people have only a few trees, but often bring their supply from below.

When they have gathered enough, they soak the flowers in water for three or four days and then boil them in an earthen pot, over the mouth of which another pot is placed upside down so that it rests mouth to mouth, the join being carefully tied round with a bit of cloth and plastered with mud to make it airtight. From a small hole in the side of the upper pot, a bamboo tube leads down to another vessel which is also carefully closed except for a small opening to admit the pipe. As the mixture boils, water is poured over the vessel to keep it cool, and the steam passes down the pipe and condenses there as spirit. Sometimes this home distillery is set up in the bed of a mountain stream, partly for security against excise officials and partly because of the water-cooling apparatus that is thus automatically provided.[1]

I have written at some length about this because of the great importance that alcohol has in the formation of the Bondo character. The women drink, but not to excess; the men drink more heavily, consistently and enthusiastically than any tribe I have yet visited. A boy begins to taste the sweet flavour of palm-wine while he is still at his mother's breast; as he grows up it is a proud moment when at last he is allowed to accompany his elders to the family palm, a prouder still when he is first sent up the tall tapering trunk to bring down the pot of sap. Throughout the turbulent exciting days of youth, alcohol assists him in the long labour of the plough, in the dramatic quest for love, through the tedious business of the marriage ceremonial. As he grows older, it is his support through the routine of religious ritual; it anesthetizes him against the sorrow of a funeral, the distractions of a family feud, the worries of an official visit. In age it tranquilizes his memories, supports his failing limbs and fortifies him against the approach of the Constables of Death.

6. Cloth and Its Taboos

The turbulent and often lazy life of Bondo men is in sharp contrast to the pacific industrious existence of the women. From my camp at Katamguda in 1943 I remember watching the varied activities of the sexes. On one side the women were busy all day long preparing their yarn from bark fibre, weaving, stitching leaves into cups and platters, fetching water, making brooms. On the other side, a little way off, were the men; some of them lay asleep, others smoked and gossiped, only two were working at their mats. At Dumiripada, while the men reclined comfortably on the *sindibor,* the women hurried to and fro on their many chores. In the most strenuous hours of a woman's day, in the early morning, the men everywhere are enjoying themselves beneath their palms. Where a man fills in his spare time with drinking, a woman occupies every minute at her spindle or the loom.

[1] The Bondos, like other tribes, use the *Bassia latifolia* for several other purposes. If the flowers are dried in the sun they will keep for weeks, but it is possible to increase their keeping properties greatly by frying them until they are sticky and then making them into balls. These are used for food and often prove an invaluable stand-by in time of want. The seed is used for making oil.

There are three kinds of Bondo home-spun and home-woven cloth. The most striking is the coloured strip which serves as a woman's skirt. A plain white sling a foot wide and about four feet long is made for the special purpose of carrying babies. And there is a man's loin-cloth, generally plain white with a red line border, about three-and-a-half feet long and nine or ten inches broad.

The woman's skirt is something more than just a bit of cloth. It is the badge of the tribe, established in the mythology, enforced under penalty of stringent sanctions; to weave it is the supreme occupation — after child-bearing — of the Bondo woman; all her art goes into this one form of self-expression. There may not be very much of it; a grown woman's cloth is not more than three feet long by ten inches broad, but she makes a great fuss of what she has. She is proud of the varieties of stripe and colour, and when a new skirt is ready it is eagerly examined and discussed; everyone tries it on, little girls measure it round their waists, older ones hold it against their bodies as if they were trying on a frock, some look envious, others openly admire.

The earliest account of this cloth was by May, of the Trigonometrical Survey, and I will reproduce his description here since, despite its rather patronizing tone, it shows what the Bondos looked like over seventy years ago.

> The women are extremely ugly, both in feature and form, which is rendered more repugnant by their short hair, and the scantiness of their attire, which consists of just a piece of cloth either made of the *kerong* bark and manufactured by themselves, or purchased from the weavers of the country, about a foot square, and only sufficient to cover a part of one hip; it is attached to their waists by a string on which it runs, and can be shifted round to any side. A most ludicrous sight has often been presented to me by a stampede among a number of these women, when I have happened to enter a village unexpectedly where they had been collected in the centre space, usual in their villages, intent upon their occupations. On my approach, each one and all hurried to their respective dwellings, and, as they ran in all directions, endeavoured to shift this rag round to the part most likely to be exposed to me. They are necessarily very shy, and are seldom to be met with out of the village, except at midday when engaged in assisting the men in the preparation of ground for cultivation, and when there is the least possible chance of meeting with strangers; but among themselves they do not seem to be at all particular.[1]

May goes on to describe the legend of the origin of the cloth, and concludes:

> My informant gave me to understand that one of the Government

[1] May, op. cit., p. 231.

agents in these parts some years ago insisted on a young woman being properly clothed, the result was that she survived the change only three days. This story, which is declared to be strictly true, has unfortunately had the ill effect of confirming these people in their superstition.

Today the cloth seems to be a little longer than it was in May's time, but we have no means of knowing whether there has been any variation in its general pattern. Nowadays it is woven in vertical stripes and considerable variety is achieved by changing the colours and the distance between them. When May wrote, such colour as there was must have been obtained by the use of vegetable dyes prepared at home; these are still used — especially indigo and the bark of *Morinda citrifolia* — but most of the colour now comes from bright cotton yarn in the warp, red, yellow, brown, black and blue, which is brought from the bazaar or purchased from itinerant Dom merchants. In colour and fastening, this cloth resembles that worn by Konyak Naga women, but the Konyak cloth is not made of bark-yarn, is thinner and its stripes are horizontal and not vertical as among the Bondos. The Konyak loom also is different; it lacks the Bondo breast-beam, being attached to the weaver by a band round the waist.[1]

There is an absolute taboo on a Bondo woman wearing any other kind of cloth round her waist, and those who — under the influence of a so-called reform in the plains villages — have broken it are regarded as untouchables and classed with the Doms. The origin of the prohibition is given in a number of slightly differing stories, which may be divided into three main cycles. In the first, the shaven heads and half-clad bodies are the result of a curse, the penalty for laughing at a bathing goddess; in the second, the scrap of cloth is regarded not as a punishment but as an advance on complete nudity; in the third, a woman, who has removed her clothes to husk grain on a warm day, jumps below the earth to avoid being seen in the nude by her brother; he catches her by the hair, and it comes away in his hand, and the woman is left hairless and with only a tiny rag she was holding to wipe off her sweat. There seems to be no way of reconciling these stories with one another, or of deciding which is the earlier; although curse stories are known in connexion with cloth I think these motifs in their particular form are not found elsewhere. Each cycle includes some tales in which the protagonists are unnamed, but in others the chief characters are Rama, Sita and Lakshman, who are imagined as being in exile in the forests of the Bondo hills.

[1] There are other, at least superficial, similarities between Bondo and Konyak culture. Both have the dormitory; the Konyaks have stone seats for their high priests, and large platforms where the men sit. Temperamentally, the two are not dissimilar. But the differences far outweigh any resemblances.

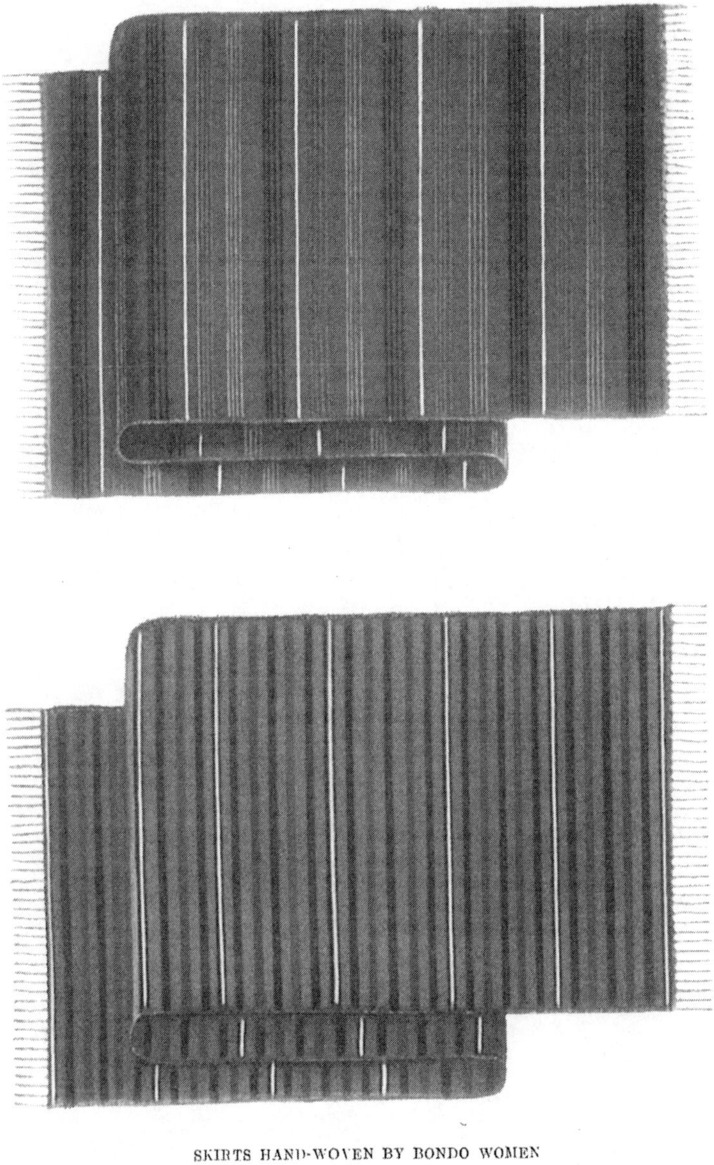

SKIRTS HAND-WOVEN BY BONDO WOMEN

As an example of the anonymous stories of the first, the 'Curse' cycle, I give the following from Dumiripada:

A woman of Mundlipada, the wife of the eldest of the first twelve brothers, went to fetch water at the Kingu Bodak grove. The goddess of the spring was bathing and her thin cloth clung to her body; the woman saw the breasts and laughed. When the goddess asked why, she replied, 'Because your cloth looks thin as a spider's web.'[1] The goddess said, 'This is not a spider's web, but it is silk shining like the sun, and because you have mocked at the sun, go live naked in the jungle!' As the goddess said this, the woman's hair shrivelled on her head and the cloth from her body. She hid in a hole beneath a rock.

Now the twelve brothers had gone out to hunt; when they returned each went to his wife, but the eldest brother could not find his. After a long search he found her in the cave and she told him what had happened. The brothers went to Mahaprabhu and the eldest wept before him. When the wife of Mahaprabhu saw his tears, she measured a bit of her own bark-cloth against her arm and tore it off. She gave it to the eldest brother and said, 'Your wife and all your women must wear this for ever; otherwise your race will be destroyed'. Since then the descendants of the eldest brother have been called Nangli Bondos, the chief of all the Porojas.

The next version, from Mundlipada, is modernized and the characters have been renamed.

In the days when Rama, Sita and Lakshman were living, Rama used to go secretly to the village and listen to what the people were saying. There was a poor potter; one day his wife was late preparing food, and her husband fell into a passion and abused her. But presently she said to him, 'Very well, come and lick my privates'. The potter replied, 'That isn't my work; it is Rama who does that sort of thing'. Rama went home and told Lakshman, 'Take Sita away, for if even a potter can talk like this about me, I am not a fit person to have a wife'. But Lakshman said, 'How can I take her ? She has a child in her belly.' Rama said, 'If you won't take her, I'll take her myself'. Then Lakshman prepared to take Sita back to her mother's house. On the way they reached the Kingu Bodak grove and rested there. Lakshman prepared their food and Sita went to bathe. Her cloth clung to her body and her breasts and swollen belly could be seen. Some women came from Mundlipada for water, and when they saw Sita they thought she was bathing naked and they clapped their hands and laughed, for they were excited at seeing the wife of such a great Raja bathing naked like themselves. When Lakshman heard them he became furious and cursed them: '*Mund-landi, phen-bandi*; be

[1] There was an odd commentary on this one day when I was camping with the Hivales at Andrahal. Kusum Hivale showed some Bondo women one of her silk saris, thinking they would be interested. Instead they ran in all directions screaming, 'Spider's web! Spider's web!' and would not return till the sari was put away.

shaven above and naked below!' At once the hair was burnt from their heads and the cloth from their waists. They hid weeping among the stones round the spring. But Sita was sorry when she saw what had happened and called them to her. She tore off the coloured border of her sari and gave it to them. 'Wear just this much,' she said. 'Weave it with your own hands. If you wear more than this, if you buy from the bazaar, your race will be destroyed.'[1]

In the second cycle of tales there is no offence and no curse; the Bondo skirt is a gift of Mahaprabhu's mercy. It is at least an advance on complete nakedness.

One day Mahaprabhu went to a village to beg for fire. A Bondo woman was sitting naked; they were all naked in those days. She was preparing *honda* (in Remo, *eyosam*, a delicacy something like *halwa*, but not so sweet). When she saw Mahaprabhu she hid her privates with one hand and gave him fire with the other. When Mahaprabhu's wife saw this, she tore off a bit of her own cloth and gave it to her. Mahaprabhu laughed and said, 'She is not a *honda* woman; she is a *bonda* (naked) woman'. Since then we have been called Bonda (naked).

The use of the Oriya *honda* for the Remo *eyosam* dates this little tale; it may even be a Dom invention calculated to amuse some constable on tour.

[1] Both in the original *Ramayana* and in later Hindu tradition, Lakshman is described as never looking into the face of Sita but as casting his eyes to the ground in her presence. On one occasion only Sita accused her brother-in-law of desiring her. When the demon Maricha, about to be slain by Rama, cried to Lakshman for help in Rama's voice, Sita begged him to go to the rescue, but he, understanding the deception, refused to go. Then Sita abused Lakshman, saying that he did not want to save his brother as he himself was in love with her. (See *Srimad-Valmiki-Ramayana*, ed. Krishnacharya, Bombay, 1911, Vol. III, pp. 248f). But this accusation was never taken seriously.

My friend Mr. Saurindranath Roy, of the National Record Office, however, has drawn my attention to a remarkable passage in the Khotanese version of the Rama legend which was discovered by H. W. Bailey among the Pelliot collections of Central Asian Texts in the Bibliothèque Nationale and edited and published by him in *The Bulletin of the School of Oriental and African Studies*, Vol. X, Parts 2 and 3. In this version Sita appears not as the ideal Hindu wife, but as a mistress held in common by the two brothers Rrisma (Lakshman) and Rama. 'When they saw the woman lovely to behold, their minds were greatly distracted. They remained bound by love. She did not go but stayed there. They asked for the woman, they led her far away. She dwelt in a most excellent garden. Together with her they did the common deed, act of a lay person, improper, contemptible.'

To the aboriginals of Middle India, Lakshman is the classic type of the husband's younger brother who, in most communities, is licensed to enjoy an intrigue with the elder's wife; there is an excellent example of this in a story given by Shamrao Hivale, *The Pardhans of the Upper Narbada Valley* (Bombay, 1946), pp. 99-102. Here, as in the Khotanese story, Sita is regarded as accepting the relationship, but Rama does not appear as *mari complaisant*. In Bondo society, however, Lakshman and Sita would be in a forbidden relationship to one another; hence Lakshman's anger at the women's jests which, in a Gond setting, would merely have amused him.

The third cycle of legends turns on a motif common in Indian folklore, but given a new setting by the Bondos. This is the motif of a sudden and drastic descent below the earth, leaving the hair sticking up above ground. This is, in Ho, Santal, Manjhi, Birhor and Uraon stories, an attempt to account for the origin of sabai grass and is usually associated with the murder of a sister by her brothers.[1] In Bondo tradition also, the motif is connected with the relations, not of murder but of propriety, between a brother and sister. The Bondos repeat the tale with different characters and to explain various things. One day it is Pat Khanda Mahaprabhu and his sister, and is intended to show why Pat Khanda lives as a sword and his sister as a rock; another time it is Bhima and his sister, and the story explains the existence of a small crater with two exits on the Cherubiding Hill.[2] The Gadabas are always telling stories about their Bondo neighbours, and I give the following from the Gadaba village of Onagelu, not far from Andrahal.

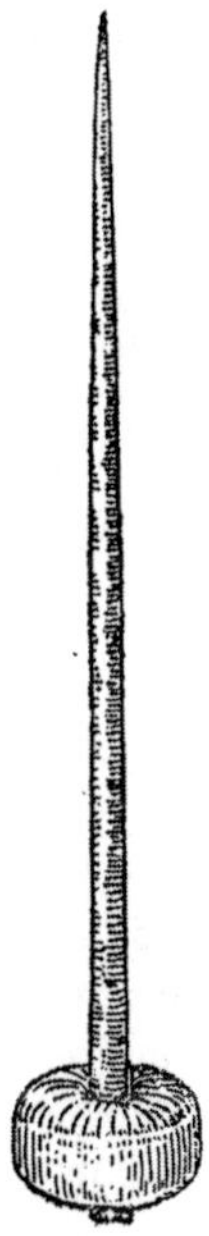

FIG. 21. Wooden spindle for preparing bark yarn

Long ago the sister of Lakshman Mahaprabhu was sitting naked in front of her house, busy husking rice. She had thrown off her skirt and only had a scrap of cloth to wipe the sweat from her body as she worked. Presently Lakshman Mahaprabhu came along the path, carrying two mountains over his shoulders. From afar he saw his sister working naked, so he put down his load and shot a pellet at her as a warning of his approach.

But she took no notice, so he fired an arrow. It stuck in the ground before her, but she still took no notice. At last Lakshman sent his dog and then she realized that her brother was near at hand. She could not reach her skirt in time, so she jumped into the mortar holding her scrap of cloth in her hand. She went down under the earth until she came up again at Kingu Bodak. As she went the earth sounded *dal-dal*.

When Lakshman Mahaprabhu saw what had happened, he went in search of his sister. At Kangu Bodak he found her still below the ground and only her hair sticking out above it. He took hold of it to pull her out and it came away in his hands. He threw it away and it turned into thatching-grass.

[1] See C. H. Bompas, *Folklore of the Santal Parganas* (London, 1909), pp. 106 and 466; S. C. Roy, *The Birhors* (Ranchi, 1925), p. 427; *North Indian Notes and Queries,* Vol. III, p. 65; A. Grignard, *Hahn's Oraon Folk-lore* (Patna, 1931), p. 77; W. G. Archer, 'Sabai Cultivation in the Rajmahal Hills', *Man in India,* Vol. XXVI, pp. 12ff; Verrier Elwin, *Folk-Tales of Mahakoshal* (Bombay, 1944), pp. 367ff.

[2] May, op. cit., p. 236. Bhima and his sister usually laboured in a state of nudity, and Bhima 'to prevent unseemly encounters' had a string of bells round his waist to warn her. One day she accidentally appeared before him naked and they fled precipitately in opposite directions. 'The two outlets to the little basin are the respective paths taken by this highly modest couple.'

Then his sister appeared with no hair on her head and dressed in nothing but the little scrap of cloth. She stood behind her brother and he said, 'Because your head is shaven and you are wearing that tiny skirt, your children will be called Bondo'.

In a Bondo version of the story, recorded at Goyiguda, the characters are not named, and the brother pulls off the hair as his sister jumps into a pit, not a mortar. When she reappears, Dharmo (the Sun) curses her to live always like this. The brother does not recognize her in her new garb and the two became man and wife.

The taboo on wearing anything more than the narrow strip of cloth enjoined in the legends is not absolute, though it is forbidden to make any variation on the skirt. There are times when something more is allowed, even required. A woman may use a cloth-sling to carry a baby on back or hip. In pregnancy when her condition becomes embarrassingly obvious, she may wear a sort of bib (generally of Dom manufacture) hanging down over her belly. When it is very cold, early in the morning or at night, she may wear a Dom shawl. In the plains women wear similar shawls when officials visit a village or a 'reformer' is directing his voyeurist eyes upon them. Everywhere, when women go to visit a burning-ground to examine the bones of a cremated corpse, they are expected to put on a roll of cloth like a bandolier. A similar roll may be worn at wedding dances, and it is usually customary for women to put on shawls at a dance.

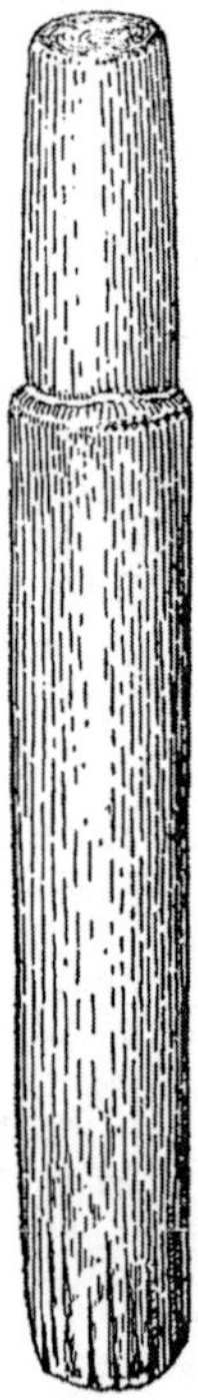

FIG. 22. Wooden mallet used for beating bark-fibre

Bondo cloth is woven of yarn spun from the fibre derived from the stem of the deciduous shrub called *kereng* (*Calotropis gigantea,* R. Br.). It is taboo to cut the shrub or bring the branches to a village at any time except between the Sume-Gelirak and Giag Festivals, that is, between January and May; it is equally taboo to weave with new thread except between these two limits, though old thread may apparently be used at any time. On the Friday after the Sume-Gelirak Festival, women (in Mundlipada I was told that men could go also, though in other villages this was denied) go to the forest and cut the *kereng* branches. They bring them home, split them down the middle with a sharp knife and bury them in mud or leave them in a pond for about a week. They bring the soaked and softened branches back to the house and spread them to dry on the roof. After a few days a woman takes a bundle of the now dry sticks and sits down to shred them. She does this with a sharp-edged bit of bamboo or a piece of *kereng* itself. After breaking up the fibres she separates them delicately with her fingers, and then rolls them into a large ball which she beats against a stone with a heavy wooden mallet. When she judges that the ball has received sufficient punishment, she undoes it and coils the fibre inside a basket, joining the strips together as she does so. She moistens the fibre with a little water, then takes a spindle — a very simple implement consisting of a length of bamboo thrust through a small flat circular stone which helps it to revolve and begins to spin it into yarn. She revolves the spindle by rubbing it against her thigh, generally allowing it to spin on the ground or against a basket. When the spindle is full, the woman winds the yarn onto a double-forked stick. Later she unwinds the yarn across her knees, minutely inspecting it as she does, and finally winds it in double thread into a ball. If the yarn is to be coloured, she prepares a dye from the bark of *Morinda citrifolia*, boiling it to a pulp and soaking the yarn in it.

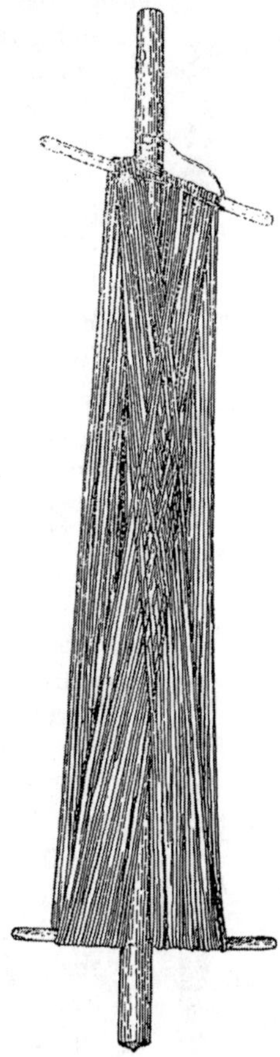

FIG. 23.
Yarn wound on a stick

The loom itself is set up out of doors; it may be in the garden, or behind the house against a wall, or in a front courtyard. As most of the weaving is done during the cold weather, and the Bondo weather can be very cold, the looms are generally in the sun; if the heat becomes troublesome, the weaver erects a screen of mats and baskets to give her shade. If she has to leave her work for a time, she covers the half-finished cloth with a basket or a leaf hat.

The Bondo loom is what is called a tension loom. Its size is adapted to the modest scraps of cloth which are to be made on it. Four stakes of *Grewia tiliaefolia* wood, each some 30 inches long, are driven into the ground, often being knocked firmly in with a pestle. The exact size of the loom, that is the distance between the stakes, varies with the size and style of the cloth to be made, but it is generally in the neighbourhood of 21 inches broad and from 24 inches to 28 inches long. Facing the weaver a breast-beam 30 inches to 36 inches long is tied to the front stakes about a foot above ground, and another horizontal beam of the same length, and at the same height, is tied to the back stakes. This is the frame of the loom. The rest of the apparatus consists of two bamboo bars which are fixed between the front and back stakes at either side and hammered down to force them apart to the desired distance; two forked bamboo twigs to support the heddle rod; a polished bamboo sword; a shed stick; and a horned bobbin. The bobbin is a bamboo stick about two feet long with forked ends; there are several of them each wound round with different coloured threads.[1]

The weaver begins her work by passing a double thread of fibre yarn in fairly tight loops over the two beams to make the warp. She attaches every alternate double thread to the heddle rod (which is supported across the loom on two bamboo sticks), lacing them to it by a single thread. Then she passes each double thread alternately over and under a shed stick, runs it over the warp beam, then back underneath and round and over the breast beam. When she has prepared sufficient warp, the weaver beats down the bamboo bars which thrust apart to the fullest extent possible the front and back stakes, thus tightening the warp to the required tension. She raises the heddle rod as far as it will go and supports it on either side on forked bamboo twigs. She is now ready to begin her work.

FIG. 24. Bobbin

During this process of preparation the woman usually squats well back on her heels, but now she gets close to the breast-beam and sits upright with her legs outstretched under the loom. Occasionally she brings a leg back and tucks the foot under her buttocks, but the normal attitude—as for spinning—is to sit with the legs extended straight in front.

The weaver begins a new cloth by inserting a bamboo slip between the odd and even threads, beating it up against the breast-beam; she inserts a second slip between the opposite threads and beats this up also. Then taking the bobbin in the right hand she passes it through the shed. The shed itself is formed by the sword which she turns on edge near the breast-beam, thus separating the odd and even threads, and making just sufficient room for the shuttle to pass through. Since the bobbin has no point, but rather a projecting horn at either end, this is a clumsy business. Then the weaver raises

[1] The Bondo bobbin is the simplest of the three types described by Ling Roth, the filament being wound round it more or less lengthwise, parallel to its axis. It resembles the Ainu pattern, though the Bondo loom is more elaborate in having breast and warp beams.—H. Ling Roth, *Studies in Primitive Looms* (Halifax, 1918), p. 4.

the pick with the sword if she is using fibre yarn (as for a man's cloth) or with her fingers if she has coloured bazaar thread. She brings the shed stick which hitherto has lain well back, up to the heddle rod, thus changing the position of the threads. She turns the sword on edge again, returns the bobbin and beats up the pick once more. Then she pushes the shed-stick back and the tension reasserts itself, and the warp is again in its first position. This is indeed the secret of the tension loom; there is only one heddle rod and the operative rod is a shed stick which lies behind the heddle and passes below the free threads and above those attached to the heddle. This stick produces a counter-shed and when the heddle is raised by shifting its position, even though this may be only a fraction of an inch, the relative position of the two sets of thread is changed.

When the weaver is using different coloured threads, whenever the colour is to be changed, she breaks the thread and uses another bobbin with a different coloured thread, tying the new thread to the old. When a red border is to be put on a man's cloth, the weaver first threads the red yarn through the warp from both sides. The two ends hang down on either side and every time a pick is shot the red thread is wound over the end, and thus forms a border running along the side of the cloth.

When the weaver judges that she has made enough she measures with her hand the unwoven warp between the two ends of cloth (for, of course, by now the finished cloth has worked back underneath the loom).[1] She generally leaves two hands-breadth. She brings the two rods very close together in the middle of this space and runs a sharp knife between them; the threads are cut and the cloth can be removed from the loom. The woman carefully ties the ends together, knocks up the bars between the stakes and carefully gathers all her impedimenta and takes it indoors.

It takes two or three days fairly consistent work to weave one of the coloured skirts, for the thread has constantly to be broken to make the changing pattern, and the shot is beaten up with the fingers instead of with the sword, a very slow and tedious process. But a piece of plain

[1] There is a useful note on bark cloth in R. H. Lowie, *An Introduction to Cultural Anthropology* (London, 1934), pp. 120-2. The technique of beating bast, the inner bark of trees, into cloth is found in Africa, Central and South America, Indonesia and Oceania. This is not, of course, woven but beaten out into sheets. The work is confined to men in Uganda, to women in Polynesia. The Matchi and Chisak sub-divisions of the Garo tribe make a sort of bark blanket. Bark cloth is still used by the Veddas and Nicobarese. In Orissa, the Alekh sect of Hindu ascetics use it. There are many references in the ancient literature. Men were instructed to cut the branches, women to peel the bark and prepare the yarn, scenting it with coconut and turmeric and the juice of a fragrant mountain vine. See P. Mitra, *Man in India*, Vol. XI, p. 231; J. K. Gan, *Man in India*, Vol. XIII, p. 47, quoting Ankermann, 'Kulturkreise und Kulturschichten in Africa', *Zeitschrift für Ethnologie*, Berlin, Vol. XXXVI, p. 62; H. Ling Roth, op. cit., O. Jones, *The Grammar of Ornament* (London, 1910), p. 14.

white cloth can easily be finished in a day. At Katamguda I timed two women on 7 March 1945. They were working side by side, and each wove from 11 o'clock in the morning till just after 6·0 in the evening, with hardly a break. They finished together. One of the women, a young girl, produced a cloth 42 inches by 10 inches; the other, an older and more expert weaver, finished in the same period a cloth 52 inches by 11 inches.

CHAPTER FOUR

THE QUEST FOR LOVE

THE Bondos, who are such he-men in other ways, are a little timid when they approach the act of sex. I would not call them particularly moral, but they are quite exceptionally discreet. Sexual experience is difficult, dangerous and expensive; while the Gond or Baiga often thinks of copulation as little more than a pleasant experience, the Bondo regards it as a very serious matter. There are several reasons for this. The Bondo youth is bound by the strictest of taboos from having anything to do with the girls of his own village; when he meets the girls of other villages, he does so — as we shall see — in public and under conditions of the strictest conventionality. This places an effective brake on those casual every-day affairs which are the normal recreation of village boys in other parts of India. Then again sexual intercourse is a risky matter; it involves the introduction of the most precious of life's possessions into an unknown and alien world. This is something fundamental in the psychology of the tribe; the Bondo cannot bear going abroad. That is his real torment in jail; that is why he is so unwilling to carry your baggage to another village — I once saw a group of women weeping in utter despair because a member of the household was carrying some of my things to a village only four miles away. Like other tribesmen, the Bondo has the strange and sinister legend of the Vagina Dentata, which is of course closely connected with the fear of castration. According to one legend, the penis originally had a tongue which was ultimately stolen by a snake; in another it was of enormous length and a woman chopped off all but a hands-breadth; in a third, a girl mutilated many youths with her fierce dentated vagina until at last a young hero, who had the wit to sheath his own organ in a condom of iron, broke off the teeth and turned them into crabs. These are not just dirty stories calculated to raise a hiccoughing chuckle on the *sindibor*; they are the attempt of Bondo fiction to suggest the risk of sex.

But the most potent influence against promiscuity is that the girls will not have it. It is generally admitted in other tribal societies — and I believe it is largely true — that it is the girls who lead men on. But this is not true of the Bondo girls. To them sexual intercourse in the pre-marital period implies a serious intention; it is almost equivalent to a betrothal. The Saora youth drives an arrow between the breasts carved in wood on the pillar of the house where his beloved lives; after that she is his. But if the Bondo youth translates this symbolism into actuality, he is caught; he is hers.

All this is characteristic of the eastern group of tribes, who are remarkable for their sexual reticence. The Saoras have the same outlook, so do the Juangs, Gadabas and Marias (who are in many ways distinct from their Gond cousins). But the Gond group, whether from some racial defect or because of the culture-contacts to which they have been exposed, have a very different tradition. The Gonds, Pardhans, Konds and other allied tribes regard the expression of sexual passion, however delightful it may be, as a comparatively trivial affair, to be indulged as a passing whim, unimportant (provided certain conventions are observed) in its effects.

It is against this background that the Bondo dormitory must be considered. The dormitory is, I believe, a symptom of a certain stage of cultural development rather than indicative of any particular racial affiliation. Indeed it would be difficult to develop any racial theory about an institution which flourishes alike in Indonesia, the Philippines, Assam, Africa and South America.

But the dormitory assumes very different forms in these varying cultures. In one it is a guard house; in another a training school for warriors; in a third a place for temporary sexual association.[1] Generally it is the boys' house which is important, the girls' house being definitely subsidiary. But among the Bondos it is the girls' house — the *selani dingo*[2] — which matters; the boys' house, the *ingersin,* is simply a base-camp for adventure, from which they go out in search of love and happiness; the centre of the male life of the village is the stone platform, the *sindibor.*

For the Bondo dormitory is nothing more than a sort of matrimonial agency. There are no signs that it was ever a central institution, inspired with magic power, where tribal affairs were conducted. It is not a village guest house; it does not exist to promote the arts of recreation; its organization is sketchy. There are no official leaders of boys or girls, and the members are not given dormitory titles. They do, of course, work for the public good; boys assist at marriages, funerals and the ritual hunts, while the girls prepare leaf-cups and platters, or cook and prepare rice-beer. During the Sume-Gelirak Festival, two of the boy members have ritual duties throughout the long-drawn ceremonial. Boys

[1] For a full account of the dormitory in different countries see *The Muria and their Ghotul,* pp. 269ff.

[2] *Dingo* is the name for the pit of former days. Now that this has disappeared, the house is often called by the Oriya *dangri-basa.* Both houses in fact are often called *basa,* which simply means 'sleeping-place'.

go to fetch a bride and girls escort her to her new home. Boys and girls together attend at the consummation of a marriage. In fact, as Fürer-Haimendorf has said, 'The dormitory system of the Bondos is not only of the highest value for the regulation of family and social life, but acts also as a stimulant to economic activities'.

But these activities are only incidental to its main purpose. I have already pointed out that the peculiar psychological attitude of the Bondos towards sex is an important factor in dormitory life; to this we must

FIG. 25. Carving on the door of a house at Kadamguda

add the equally unusual belief of Bondo parents that their children are most likely to be happy in marriage if they choose their own partners. A Bondo boy has an unprecedentedly wide field from which to select his future wife. He must not have anything to do with a girl in his own village, and he should normally avoid a girl of his own *bonso* or *kuda*, but he is not tied down — as are most of his neighbours — by obligations to a cousin or other relative or by his elders' tiresome desire that he should marry money or improve the family status by marrying well. The Bondo boy is free. But this freedom presented the tribe with a serious problem: how were the boys to meet girls? The answer is given in a most significant statement which I recorded at Andrahal.

Since they could not marry in their own villages, how were the boys to get wives ? It is no good marrying unless a girl and a boy like one another; otherwise they will be unfaithful and tigers will destroy us. So we made a separate place for the girls to which boys could come and dance and play, sleep and get to know them.

The classical Bondo dormitory was a place of ordeal; it was a practical expression of the Test-theme motif of the folk-tale. It was a pit, roofed over and entered by a small aperture, where the girls spent their evenings and entertained boy visitors from other villages. It corresponded to the Under World where so many legendary heroes have had to go to win a bride. Here the Bondo hero was tested, and the heroine was proved; if they passed the test, a life-long relationship was established.

I have been unable to see any specimens of the older pit-dormitories, for they no longer exist. But I was shown where they had been, and was given various accounts of what they were like. At Dumiripada I was told,

We used to dig a large pit at Dassera time and roof it over with bamboo, matting and palm-leaves. We covered this with earth, smoothed it down and cowdunged it. There was a small hole to serve as door with a bamboo shutter and a ladder to climb up and down. Before it was used the Sisa had to sacrifice a hen and a pig inside the pit and sprinkle the blood round it and over the roof.

The foundation of the dormitory is attributed to Mahaprabhu, and its general religious associations are emphasized in the following account from Andrahal.

It was Mahaprabhu himself who made the first pit. Before houses were built he lived in such a place. One day when the boys were hunting, they saw the pit and thought, 'If we make such a pit we will not feel cold' and they made one to use in the winter months. But when they first dug the pit, great rocks came out. Then Bursung gave the Sisa a dream saying, 'Sacrifice in my name and the pit will be ready'. After that we never made a pit without giving an egg to Bursung and a fowl to Hundi. When a new pit was made the girls had a feast and the Sisa (but not the boys of the village) shared it. An old woman used to go with the girls and stay with them until they wanted to sleep. Then she would climb out, close the door with a big stone and go to her house. In the early morning she would return, remove the stone and let the girls out.

This pit-dormitory came to an end, not as the result of any 'reform' but for an entirely practical cause. It was found to be too risky to keep the girls on the outskirts of a village near the forest which in the old days was infested with wild animals. There are many different tales of the tragedy that led to the change of custom. One describes how a boy visitor went out to relieve himself and a tiger killed him. Another says that it was as the girls were entering the pit that a tiger attacked them and carried one of them away. A tale from Salanpada is probably exaggerated.

At Salanpada when the girls were sleeping, the old woman who looked after them went home and forgot to shut the door. A tiger came and crouched by the opening. A girl went out to piss, she saw the tiger and, thinking it was a dog, tried to drive it away. But the tiger sprang on her and both fell into the pit. The tiger killed most of the girls, but two or four escaped by pretending to be dead. In the morning, when the old woman came she saw the tiger and ran for help. The villagers came with their bows and arrows and killed it; when they opened the roof, they found only three girls alive.

In Pinnajangar I was told that the tiger was inspired by the *sairem,* the ever-watchful dead, who were outraged because a married woman slept one night in the dormitory.

FIG. 26. Carving on the door of a house at Kadamguda

But whatever the exact details of the incident, I think it probable that some tragedy occurred, though it is just possible that Dom influence had something to do with the change of custom. At Gokurupada I was told that Doms had declared that Government officials would shoot any boys and girls found sleeping in the pit. Such childish scares often have a far-reaching effect.

At all events the picturesque custom was abandoned, and today the girls live in any house available to them; sometimes it is built specially, sometimes it is borrowed from someone who does not need it. The boys make a camp on someone's veranda or borrow a house; they rarely erect a building of their own. Since the change from pit to house, the time when dormitory life flourished has also changed; the girls used to sleep in the pit from October onwards for about six months — for it was obviously a barracks for the open season. Nowadays dormitory life begins in August and continues to January or February. Otherwise there does not seem to have been any very great change in custom.

May gave an account of the dormitory as he saw it seventy years ago. Some of his facts seem to be dubious, but he rightly stresses the serious matrimonial purpose of the institution.

> Marriages are consummated in a very curious manner. A number of youths, candidates for matrimony, start off to a village where they hope to find a corresponding number of young women, and make known their wishes to the elders, who receive them with all due ceremony. The juice of the sago palm in a fermented state is of course in great requisition, as nothing can be done without the exhilarating effects of this their favourite beverage. They then proceed to excavate an underground chamber (if one is not already prepared), having an aperture at the top admitting of the entrance of one at a time; into this the young gentlemen, with a corresponding number of young girls, are introduced, when they grope about and make their selection, after which they ascend out of it, each holding the young lady of his choice by the forefinger of one of her hands. Bracelets are now put on her arms by the elders (this has the same signification as the wedding-ring among European nations), and two of the young men stand as sponsors for each bridegroom.[1]

This description does not agree with the tradition or practice of the modern Bondo. The boys' visits are much more casual and the elders do not play the part attributed to them. In fact, the most important thing about the Bondo betrothal is that it should be an affair of young people.

Today what happens is this. Every evening excited, happy boys gather in their little dormitories and decide where they will seek adventure. Each village has a group of dormitories which it visits regularly, but one boy may have met at a marriage or bazaar a girl of whom he wants to see a little more, another may wish to put his fortune to the test by pressing bangles on a long-admired acquaintance. The choice is unrestricted, and sometimes the boys go very far afield; they may climb up the great hill, all the way from Kadamguda to Andrahal, or from Puchaguda to Dumiripada. The girls have palm-wine and little tit-bits of food, some roasted rats perhaps or parched gram, ready for their visitors and it must be an exciting, and sometimes anxious, time as they wait to see who is coming. If parties from two or more villages arrive on the same evening, it does not matter; they are all entertained.

1 May, op. cit., p. 237. There is a better and more credible account in Bell, op. cit., p. 76.

The visitors in their turn bring gifts of rings, beads and mats; many Bondo boys have bunches of little rings always hanging at their girdles.

An evening's programme may include a dance — though the Bondos do not seem to be very fond of this; they prefer to sit indoors round a cheerful fire. There they sing, often antiphonally, tell stories, listen to an expert playing the fiddle or jew's harp, and indulge in a good deal of horseplay. Bondo boys are very rough and the girls, provided that certain conventions are observed, do not seem to mind being knocked about. I remember an evening at Bodapada, when I sat, on the end of a plough, for some hours (it was from midnight to about three in the morning, and I — unlike the Bondo — am no night-blooming flower) in extreme discomfort, my eyes pouring with tears from the pungent wood-smoke that filled the house, watching the scene and comparing it with the spacious and dignified life of the Muria *ghotul*. The room was crammed to capacity with boys and girls; it was impossible to move about; anything less likely to lead to the tender transports of private affection could hardly be imagined. The boys spat in the faces of the girls, smeared their faces and breasts with ashes from the fire, slapped them, thumped them with the clenched fist; they sang, told dirty yarns, roared with laughter; they were all very hearty. Here, it seemed to me, was a very practical reason for the comparative lack of what we call sex in the Bondo dormitory; there was no room. But it was great fun — if you like your pleasures tough.

The singing was good; above the smoke and flying ashes and breast-grabbing arose the haunting melodies of Bondo music; this is most beautiful: it has a dying fall, and at its best can compare with any tribal music. The recording of the songs, which was done for me by Shamrao Hivale, was enormously difficult. It was almost impossible to obtain a definitive text. The boys would sing something and every time the words were checked, they would alter them. In the end, we had to fall back upon a paraphrase. The boys told us what they were singing about, and though this does not represent an exact translation of a song, it is a translation of their interpretation of one and thus illuminates the sort of thing they say. Here is one such paraphrase.

The boys sing first.

O parrot, come away from this pit to our country and its warmth.
In our country we have stripped the forest of trees and grass, and now we have nothing to do but sit and sing.
It was there that light was first made by the chick hatched in the warmth of a man's belly;
It cried *kuku-kuku* sitting on his arm and the day was born.
We ourselves were strangers when we first went there.

But cross our boundary and you too will belong to us.
Give rice and salt, give tobacco to the elders, and you will belong to our country.
Come sit with us and drink our wine, enjoy our food, our curry rich in juice.
Then we will lie together and be happy.
I will keep you happy always, in showers of rain, in dry weather and in the cold.

The parrot (which represents the girls) replies:

Certainly I will come to your country and give you happiness.
I will cross the Tulsi, Akulo and Thakur mountains for you.
I will come to the land that is called Samay, Arang and Kindago,
And there I will give you your first-born son.

Another song follows the same technique of using a large number of proper names which presumably have romantic associations to the hearers.

O girl, let us live in sport and laughter, for you are my starling.
O girl, we will live to see many buffaloes killed,
We will see many a forest grow again, my starling.
O girl, you will go to catch crabs and fish while I lie on the *sindibor* at ease, for you are my starling.
O girl, let us lie together on the great rocks Tumlaida, Tirada and Usume, for you are my starling.
Let us go to the meeting-place of the Sunadak and Bunadak and drink it's water from a single cup, for you are my starling.
Let us go to Budingber, Pesangber, Pasangre, Talang and Marangre, where the rocks make music as of drums.
Let us offer leaves on the *runnukbor-sanaibor,* for you are my starling.
Let us walk together on the paths Gugusing and Ogiksing, for you are my starling.
O girl of Andra, Sisa and Sampe, you are my starling.

And another song, much simpler, runs thus:

O goddess help, do help us.
From our own village we go to an alien dancing-ground.
The girl has gone to the stream; call her and persuade her.
Put flowers on her head and we will dance with her.
When our work here is finished
We will go elsewhere, to another village.

It is said that boys must be able to sing the songs of the villages they visit; they must learn words and tune. If they sing new songs, or if they cannot respond to the singing of their hosts, it is regarded as a breach of etiquette, as something not done, a failure in good manners.

There is obviously some pretty sentiment in these exchanges, for it must be remembered that though there is not here an exact translation of the songs, there is an exact translation of the Bondos' interpretation of them. This is how the Bondo youth thinks about his girl. Sometimes he goes further.

> Come, let me give you some rice-beer and tobacco
> And we will pass our time alone in the forest.
> Holding your shoulders, twisting your breasts,
> I will have you on my knees.
> I will have you in the forest where I can embrace you shamelessly.

But apparently this is just their fun; the song is greeted with screams of ribald laughter, but few actually adventure on the shameless embraces in the forest.

The chief sexual recreation of the Bondo dormitory is what the boys call 'breast-play'. There are parallels here to the *metza* of the Zulus, where boys and girls are permitted to work themselves into a state of extreme, but unconsummated, sexual excitement. The Bondo boy not only grabs the breasts of every girl he can get at; he also fondles the breasts of his beloved, and this is generally all she will allow him. This is indeed all that is required in view of the fundamental purpose of the dormitory; a certain gentleness, a tender pressure instead of a vulgar tug indicates one's intentions, the delicacy of one's touch makes all the difference between matrimony and a bit of fun.

There is a legend about this which is worth recording. It comes from Andrahal.

Once the breasts of women were each a cubit long. There was a young girl who had two boys in love with her. They were for ever visiting her in the dormitory and there they fondled her breasts all night as they sang and played. Even when they were eating a boy would hold a breast in one hand and eat with the other.

The girl enjoyed this attention at first, but after a time she wearied and longed to die. One night in despair she took a knife and cut off her breasts and died.

From the blood that flowed from her breasts there sprang up an orange tree. Since then women have had smaller breasts, beautiful and round like oranges.

But, as I will show presently, the Bondo youth has to stop there. In all this area the taboo on the female breast is comparatively weak.[1] It is said that a Saora woman has no objection to being touched on the breast, but greatly resents a hand placed on her shoulder. I was told the same story in Bastar. There was a violent quarrel in Andrahal, when a Bondo youth from Dumiripada touched a married girl on the shoulder.

All this, however, is only preliminary or adjuvant to the real purpose of the boys' visits, which is to find the right girls as wives. If a boy finds an unbetrothed girl whom he likes and who seems to respond to him, he persuades his friends to go to the same dormitory again and again. Then, as I was told at Andrahal,

> The boy says to himself, 'Does this girl like me or not?' He lights a leaf in the fire and burns her as she sits by him. If she is unwilling she abuses him and goes to the other side of the fire. But if she likes him she says nothing, but quietly herself lights a leaf and burns him. He must not make a sound. Sometimes they burn each other with bits of bamboo. Then the boy makes another test. He takes a bangle or ring and offers it to her, catching her by the hand. If she accepts it, they are betrothed. The boy goes home and tells his father. He says, 'Do what you will my son, if you are happy'.

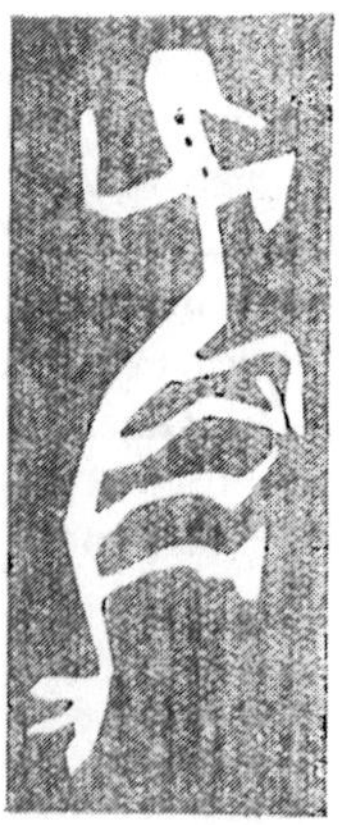

FIG. 27. Carving on the door of a house at Goyiguda

A common formula used by girls when a boy offers her a bangle is: 'Are you a boy who uses fresh leaf-cups or used ones?' In other words, 'Do you enjoy your food in your own house or are you a servant somewhere else?' Sometimes she says, 'Do you eat from a leaf-cup or a brass dish?', that is, 'Are you rich or poor?'

If a girl refuses a bangle and the boys consider that this is simply due to shyness and that she is really worthy of their friend, they force it on her. I have seen this done; there is a tremendous struggle and the boys are very rough indeed. The bangle has no legal force but it is a big step forward in the direction of marriage.

Girls continue to attend the dormitory after they are betrothed, during the long ritual of the *sebung* marriage-ceremony and even after they are married if their husbands are immature. Boys too continue to visit the dormitories after they have been accepted by a girl and sometimes,

[1] But when the Bodapada boys saw photographs of Saora and Maria women with breasts exposed, they uttered cries of excitement and grabbed at the pictures, making as if to squeeze the nipples with their fingers. Yet similar photographs of Bondo girls left them unmoved.

as we shall see, they change their minds and break off their engagements. Girls too sometimes have their minds changed for them. Young married men may visit the dormitories and if one of them wants to take a second wife, he may behave exactly as if he was a young unmarried boy.

When Lachhim Kirsani of Gokurupada, for example, wanted a second wife, he accommodated himself with his cousin at Bodoballe and went every evening to the girl's dormitory. There he found a girl he liked and offered her a ring. She accepted it and eloped with him. Her brother followed her and took her home saying, 'We are ready to give her to you, but let the due rites be performed'. So Lachhim went for her with baskets of meat and rice and they sent her back with equivalent gifts.

It is clear, therefore, that the real aim of the Bondo dormitory is marriage and this fact governs all the relationships between the girls and their boy visitors. The Bondo *selani dingo* is, in fact, the very opposite of the Muria *ghotul*. The relationships of boys and girls in the *ghotul* should never lead to marriage; those in the *selani dingo* should never lead to anything else. The Murias allow parents absolute authority, the Bondos allow children absolute freedom, in the choice of partners. The Murias forbid intimacy between betrothed couples; the Bondos allow it only to the betrothed. Pre-marital pregnancies are a serious problem to the Murias; I was unable to obtain the record of a single such pregnancy among the Bondos. Though they showed no hesitation in discussing matters of sex, even matters rather discreditable to themselves, not one of the 150 men examined admitted to having himself been embarrassed or of having known of any girl suffering from this particular scandal. I checked this — for I was surprised at it — by private inquiries from the Doms who never lose an opportunity of discrediting the Bondos, but they confirmed my information. It would be hard to imagine a greater difference between the two types of dormitory.

For the truth is, as I have already suggested, that the Bondos indulge but rarely in pre-marital intercourse.[1] This is the kind of problem, of course, about which 'impressions' and the vague reports of officials and casual visitors may lead to the worst kind of misrepresentation and I will, therefore, document the point with extracts from life-histories of a number of informants when (it must be remembered) they were talking off their guard and had no motive to conceal or distort events that had happened long ago. Indeed men who were ready to boast of recent

[1] This discovery was so unexpected that I asked Shamrao Hivale to make special independent inquiries on the point during his month's visit to the Bondo country. He was on confidential terms with a number of Bondo youths and his information entirely confirms mine.

erotic triumphs admitted themselves dismal failures when confronted with the stubborn virginity of the dormitory girls. At the beginning of the chapter I have hinted at this; I will now go into the subject, with examples, rather more deeply.

All my informants admitted visiting the girls' dormitories regularly when they were young and having a great deal of fun there. But it was strictly circumscribed fun. The girls put a definite limit to the liberties allowed, and the boys — who were often smaller and younger — were frankly in awe of them. Kissing is apparently unknown to the Bondos, the chief form of sexual expression being — as we have seen — the fondling of the breasts. This is allowed. But beyond that it is dangerous to go. The girls are armed — both arms are covered with heavy brass bangles, a blow from which can break open a boy's head. And, as several Bondos have told me, the practical difficulties are enormous. There is no room inside the dormitory, and if a boy takes a girl out the others follow him to see what he is up to.

But not only are the girls obstinately chaste until they are certain that an admirer intends the serious business of matrimony, the boys too are not always very assiduous in pressing their attentions to their right true end. This may be due to the sense of risk in sex; it may be that boys do not want to commit themselves too far; there is also a slight but definite homosexual strain among them. This, while not surprising in view of the quite extraordinary beauty of many Bondo boys, is most unusual in tribal India. I doubt if the usual physical manifestation of this tendency can be found among the Bondos. But they certainly form passionate and romantic friendships and express them with embraces which are less discreet than those they bestow upon their girls; it is common to see boys lying in each other's arms.[1]

Let us now consider some actual examples of dormitory experience. Soma Kirsani of Basupada described how he used to visit all the dormitories in the neighbourhood of his village 'for fun', but he added, 'I never lay with any of the girls'. One evening at Bandapada, however, he got very drunk and forcibly embraced a girl; she hit him so hard with her bangle-fortified arm that the scar has remained to this day. 'I had to let her go and after that I never went to that dormitory again. I used to go instead to Gokurupada. After I had got to know the girls there, my mind set itself on one of them, whom I liked very much. I put a bangle on her arm and as she liked me too she let me do it.

[1] Laubscher notes the homosexual element in the Tembu stick-fight which is not unlike the Castigation of the Sume-Gelirak. 'I have frequently observed in the stick-fights among young men that they rush at each other and rub their bodies together, chest to chest, and then jump apart and rain blows upon each other.'— B. J. F. Laubscher, *Sex, Custom and Pathology* (London, 1937), p. 282. Bondo youths do exactly the same.

Once she was sure of me she let me have her. I took her out of the house while the others were playing. She slipped out first and I followed. We had to go a long way, for when anyone leaves the dormitory the other boys follow to see what he is doing. In the dormitory, the girls used to sleep on one side, the boys on the other. I lay at the end of the boys' row, nearest to the girls, and when everyone was asleep I used to go to my girl. It was very difficult for we were all crammed together, but my girl was clever and shifted away a little from the others. Afterwards I married her.'

Lachhim Kirsani of Dattipada was also very careful in his dealings with girls. 'Already, when I was a boy, the dormitory was no longer underground. I used to visit the girls' houses at Mundlipada, Basupada, Dumiripada and Bandapada. In those days we were really frightened of girls but they did not mind so long as we only caught hold of their breasts and fondled them. I only once had a girl all that time. It was at Bandapada. For a whole month I tried for her. At last, one night, when all the boys and girls were drunk and were staggering round the room pretending to dance, I took her outside. At other times I used to go as far as Pinnajangar and Kichchipoda, where I played breast-games and beat the girls. This made me very happy. In the end I put bangles on a girl at Pinnajangar, but I never had her till we were married.'

Every account emphasizes the fact that Bondo girls are not 'easy', either for matrimony or for love-making. Soma Kirsani of Kirsanipada described how 'when I was a boy the dormitory was underground. I went to all the neighbouring villages to play with the girls. I tried to put bangles on girls at Mundlipada and Basupada, but they wouldn't let me. I never lay with a girl in the pit. When I found the girls were so obstinate I got disgusted and gave up visiting the dormitories altogether. But one day when some Dumiripada girls came to dance at our place, three of my friends captured one of them and I forced some rice into her mouth and she agreed to live with me as my wife.'

Budha Sisa of Katamguda told me that he never once lay with a girl, though he visited every dormitory in the hills in the days when they were underground. 'I never lay with a girl, though I always played with their breasts. For we believed that a girl would only give herself after a boy had put bangles on her. We didn't dare take a girl by force, for fear that she would break our heads open with her heavy bangles.'

It was always the same story. Each informant remembered one triumph of his young days, vividly remembered because it was so unusual and exciting. Sonia Bodnaik of Bodapada said one day, 'I used to play with the girls' breasts, but I only once had intercourse. And even then, it wasn't very good, for she was drunk; it was on the way home from the bazaar and I had her among bushes near the path.' Hadi

Kirsani of Bandapada used to make a circuit of four or five dormitories, but only once at the time of the orgiastic Sume-Gelirak Festival, after making her thoroughly drunk, did he seduce a girl.

But it is not only a boy's fear of physical assault from the strapping wenches who are often older and larger than himself, that makes a boy hesitate; he is also influenced by the general tradition that sexual intercourse is a very significant thing, a prelude to marriage or at least the token of a betrothal. Muria hypocrisy exclaims only at impregnation; Bondo realism recognizes the importance even of copulation. Certainly in many cases an act of intercourse has led a Bondo youth into the trap of marriage.

Soma Mundli of Bodapada seems to have been a rather unsuccessful little boy. 'I tried to have a couple of girls at Katamguda, but all they did was to tick me off and I felt rotten. At Kuriguda there was a girl ready for me, but I didn't like her; her hands and feet were thin as a string and her belly was big as a fish-basket. Boys younger than me got girls, but I didn't and when I saw them at it my mind felt as if it was being fried on a hot fire. For two months I went to the Semiliguda dormitory and, after I had poured honey and ghee over her for weeks, a girl who was much older than me began to respond. I couldn't get anyone else, so I slept with her. She gave me liquor and some plantains; I gave her a ring. After we had been together she agreed to come to my house. We fixed it that I should wait for her by the spring the following Monday, and that's what happened. She came with her water-pot as if she was going to draw water, and when she saw me she threw it away and we went off together.'

Budha Challan of Kadamguda, down in the plains, had a similar experience. 'When I first met the girl I married, she was very frightened of me. She used to go shifting round and round the fire out of my way. But one day I met her at the Mundaguda bazaar and she asked me for a present. I bought her parched rice for half an anna and one plantain. That seemed to please her and next time I went to her dormitory she gave me some liquor to drink. The following evening I gave her four rings — it was rather a lot but I thought I'd better. And in fact that made her ready. She went outside to piss and I followed and had her on the veranda. But the other boys and girls caught us, right in the act, and there was a lot of ragging and laughter. I said to the girl, "Now we've been shamed before the world; we'll have to go away together". She agreed. I said, "Tomorrow at sunset go to the spring and wait there for me". She did and we went off together.'

After Sonia Bodnaik of Bodapada had seduced his girl on the way home from the bazaar, she took it for granted that she was to marry him. But a youth from Kirsanipada kidnapped her and took her to his house. But Sonia always felt that the girl really belonged to him and she reciprocated his affection. 'She didn't like the Kirsanipada fellow; he was weak and didn't do the work with enough vigour. At last she came to my house in a great temper and that night I had her three times. In the morning she drank water from the pots in my house and said, "I won't go away; I'm going to stay with you".' A big result for a drunken correspondence on the Mundaguda hill.

In the not uncommon struggle and rivalry between different groups of young men for a popular girl, it seems to be the boy who succeeds in actually seducing her who wins her permanently. Budha Sisa of Kadamguda finally won his wife at a wedding dance in Bodapada. 'There was a girl there whom I liked enormously. Directly I saw her I gave her some tobacco. During the dance she in turn gave me a little of her own tobacco, and she laughed at me and pulled a ring off my finger. I whispered, "Bring me something to drink; if you do I'll stay here all night". So when it got dark she brought me some liquor and we drank together and she lay with me. But that very night, later on, a party of dirty fellows from Dattipada captured her and carried her off. She escaped from them and hid in the jungle. In the morning she made her way to Tulaguram and met me as I was going down the hill to my home. I said, "Come back with me". She did and I made her my wife. I gave her father two cows and two-and-a-half rupees.'

Another youth from the same village, Sonia Kirsani, won his wife in a similar fashion. 'For three months I regularly visited the dormitory at Semiliguda, climbing up that great hill every evening. When we played there, one of the girls always used to push and hit me, and I began to think after a time that she must mean something by it. So one night I dropped a ring, as if by accident, and she picked it up and put it on. I bought her some parched rice and gave her liquor. Then I made her very drunk and took her to our forest-clearing. We hid there together for two days and after that I married her.'

In these cases the act of intercourse takes the place of the regular engagement. In other cases a girl who has hitherto proved adamant allows her lover to possess her once he has offered and she has accepted the formal betrothal bangle in the face of the whole company.

When a youth has succeeded in persuading a girl to accept his bangle, he may wait until his family can perform the long and complicated ritual of the regular marriage or he may, if he is impetuous, or poor, or if there is danger of his intended being carried off by someone else, take her forcibly to his house and marry her there at once by the simplest of rites. The bangle transaction has the effect of a betrothal and seems to give a boy some rights over the girl — for example, as we have seen, he may now enjoy some freedom of intercourse with her, but it is not finally binding and if such a betrothal is broken no compensation has to be paid.

In practice, where so many youths are competing nightly for so many girls, it is not surprising that both boys and girls should change their minds and that jealousies and disputes should arise between different groups. Lachmi Kirsani of Gokurupada, for example, first put bangles on a girl in the Bandapada dormitory. 'But after a time I met a girl in the Salanpada dormitory whom I liked better. So I gave her a bangle and she let me lie with her. But in the end I went to visit the Kichchipoda dormitory and there was the best girl of all, and it was she whom I ultimately married.'

The fact that a girl is already betrothed by this method, therefore, does not prevent another group of boys from kidnapping her and marrying her to one of their friends. This often happens and serious quarrels sometimes result. Sonia Kirsani, to whom I have already referred, used to go not only to Semiliguda but also to the Andrahal dormitory, for his first love was there. One evening he gave her palm-wine and persuaded her to accept his bangles, whereupon he took a party of friends to bring her to his house. But when he got to Andrahal, which after all was a very long way off, he found that a party from Bandapada had forestalled him and that his girl was gone. Another girl met them and said, 'Brothers, what are you looking for so anxiously?' They told her what had happened, and carried her off instead for another of the group.

Soma Jiggri of Katamguda used to visit the Rasavada dormitory. There he managed to win a girl who was very fond of him and was anxious to go to his house. But while he was making up his mind to carry her off, a party from Chindiguda took her away. After a time, Soma met her in the Mundaguda bazaar. She told him that she was not officially married yet and that she wanted to come to him. They went off together and she hid for a week in a friend's house, after which they celebrated a simple but binding marriage.

A young man of about twenty, Sukra Kirsani of Semiliguda, landed himself in jail as a result of one of these disputes. He had put bangles on a Rasavada girl and was actually on his way to her parents to pay the bride-price of two cows and two-and-a-half rupees, when he heard that a rival, Ghasi Sisa of Kuriguda, had taken her to his house and had made her eat rice — an act which is as binding as a formal marriage. Sukra returned home without saying anything, but he was very angry. Some days later a party of dancers came from Kuriguda to Semiliguda to dance and Ghasi was among them. They all got a little drunk and then Sukra started a quarrel, asking why the other had stolen his girl, on whom he had put bangles. Ghasi is said to have replied, 'Because I was strong enough. If you don't like it, come and pull out my pubic hairs.' This was unforgiveable; Sukra went to his house, got an axe and wounded Ghasi so severely that he had to spend a month in hospital. What happened to the girl I did not discover.

These stories are obviously very different to those recorded in *The Muria and their Ghotul.* In the pacific and ordered life of the Murias, controlled by parental authority, such incidents simply do not occur. I doubt if they occur even in societies — such as the Didayi, Jhoria and Kond — where there is a somewhat similar tradition of youths visiting the girls' house to win their wives. But among the Konds, for example, such visits are quiet and tame affairs compared to the turbulent invasions of parties of Bondo youths.

The Bondo dormitory, alike in its restraints and its excesses, is a mirror of the Bondo character. It is an essential part of Bondo life for, as Fürer-Haimendorf says, 'The friendships made in the *selani dingo* are the only conceivable avenue to marriage and any breakdown of the dormitory system would be tantamount to a revolution of social life; indeed it is probable that in the place of mutual attraction, family interests and considerations of wealth would become the decisive factors in the conclusion of marriage'.[1]

A NOTE ON BONDO DANCING

The Bondos, like the Saoras and Konds, attribute to the dance a vaguely religious purpose.

Soma Bodnaik and his two wives lived on Samudra Hill. They were the first and after them the rest of mankind was born, and Mahaprabhu to make them happy taught them how to dance. Soma danced with his two wives, and called the other men and women to join them. One day Mahaprabhu said, 'When you sacrifice or hold festival, on such days dance through the night till dawn, so that the old men and women and the demigods will be pleased'. They did so and the demigods were pleased. But when the people scattered into many different villages, they stopped dancing and the demigods were angry and troubled them. The Naikos assembled and went to the sky to ask Mahaprabhu to help them. 'We are having a lot of trouble; what are we to do?' Mahaprabhu said, 'It's because you've stopped dancing. Go and do as you did before, and all will be well.' The Naikos returned to their homes and set the people dancing again, and after that there were good crops and many children were born.

But the demigods must be easily pleased, for Bondo dancing is wretched stuff. There is little rhythm, no variety, no dignity. The Bondos evidently are not very good at recreation; for there are few games, and no organized games, no toys or masks, no attempt at drama, and the dancing, as I say, is deplorable. There are three possible reasons

[1] op. cit., p. 172.

for this. The first is that the Bondos, like the Hill Marias, dance only on ceremonial occasions — at weddings, festivals, funerals — and they are generally a little drunk at such times, and often pre-occupied with the thought of quarrels. Secondly, although dancing is one of the pastimes of the dormitory, it does not seem to be a very popular one. The climate is against it — for the dormitory period is in the rains and early cold weather — and the boys and girls prefer to take their fun indoors. But dancing is not an easy art and without constant, daily practice, the dancers do not become proficient. It is only by such continual effort that the Murias and Gadabas have developed the intricate and beautiful dances which help to make their dormitory life so well worth living. Thirdly, the rule forbidding boys and girls of the same village to dance together is hardly calculated to encourage the art; since boy visitors come only during part of the year, girls must in any case be often left without opportunity. In form and atmosphere, Bondo resembles Saora dancing — a general drunken muddle and a lot of noise. It is a perfect expression of the orgy. But whereas the Saora dance is a procession, this is a round, probably because the Saoras dance down the narrow village streets and the Bondos in the open space before the *sindibor*.

The general pattern of a Bondo dance is simple. A group of unmarried girls stand in the centre huddled together and singing simple ditties with endless refrains — *Lele lolo lele lolo* or *Rasurilo basurilo*. Round them moves an unbroken circle of boys (who must be in a marriageable relationship) and outside this circle stampedes a procession of drummers, dancers and old women. The girls are motionless, still at the centre of the cyclone; the inner circle of boys moves with some restraint — they go sometimes in file, more often in an expanding and contracting circle which rotates slowly about the girls; they face inwards and move in either direction. But the great procession which thunders round the circumference of the dance circle has little order about it. Within the main movement each individual dances as he will, whirling and stamping, prancing and hopping, now bending low, now leaping in the air. Drummers go for a time in pairs, facing each other so that one has to retreat before his fellow's approach; then they swing round and form into lines and columns.

In villages where Dom influence is strong, a dance may develop into a kind of 'Demsa', the low-country dance, not unlike the Muria Hulki, where a long line of women, each holding her neighbour's shoulder, or clasping her round the waist, weave patterns within and through a circle of men and drummers.

At weddings girls do a dance of their own, waving branches of the red cedar and the shrub *Colebrookia oppositifolia*, and dressed in bandoliers of rolled cloth over their shoulders.

The drummers either process with the dancers or sit to one side on the *sindibor*; one man has the large *kinding* drum — he holds it and another beats it with sticks; a third taps the parchment moon of a gong;

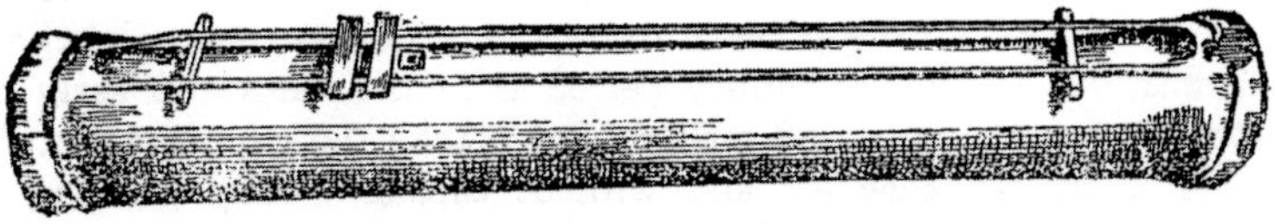

FIG. 28. Bamboo ideochord

a fourth bangs the little *tamuk* kettle-drum.[1] Others blow buffalo horns and flutes or whistle shrilly through their fingers. A faint accompaniment of song, almost drowned in the general confusion, continues throughout the dance.

There is no special dress, but everyone gets himself up as well as he can. The women put on all their ornaments and fill their headbands with flowers; the boys tie bells to their ankles, fix plumes of feathers round their heads, and wear turbans with long streamers hanging down behind. Every boy or man must have something in his hand, and sometimes he will have both hands full with his bow and arrows, an axe, a chopper, a threshing-hook, a heavy stick and a long murderous knife. As the dancers gyrate they flourish their knives and wave their sticks in a ferocious manner; every now and then a watchful wife or mother darts into the crowd and relieves a dancer of his weapon. At a dance of little boys in Bodapada, they were all disarmed by their parents who were obviously on edge and nervous for fear of trouble.

For all round the dance stand anxious women, the home guard, watching for the first sign of trouble. It is charming to see a young wife hover about her husband, tying up his bells if they come off, straightening his head-dress, consoling him if he is in a temper, refreshing him with beer or water. A Bondo dance is the most sexually decorous dance I have witnessed anywhere; indeed husbands have little opportunity to misbehave under the watchful eyes of wives, and the unmarried have to act with great discretion. During the great festivals, I believe, there is a general relaxation of this standard, and of course dormitory boys do sometimes succeed in seducing a girl during a dance. But in the main, the Bondo dance is curiously sexless.

[1] Bondo musical instruments are of the conventional type. They have a split-string ideochord of bamboo, played with a small stick in one hand and plucked with the other. The *kinding* is a double-membraned drum of the *dhol* type; one face is of goatskin, called *jangjang* and beaten with the hand, the other face, of cowhide, is *dungdung* and beaten with a stick. The *tamuk*, the ordinary *timki* kettle-drum, is made of earthenware covered with cowhide. There are two stringed monochords: the *tolia* is a guitar and played by plucking; the *kusang* is played with a small bow. Flutes are of the ordinary pattern with five or six stops. Girls use small bamboo jew's harps, which they play with great skill, giving a low sweet note.

CHAPTER FIVE

THE ESTABLISHMENT OF LOVE

1

THE Bondo attitude to marriage is, so far as I know, unique among the tribes of Middle India. These sensitive and emotional people have decided that the essential thing in any permanent marital relationship is less the alliance of families through the economic exchanges of the cross-cousin marriage or any other exploitation of the Table of Affinity than the union of hearts in the bonds of mutual attraction and desire. Bondos marry, not because they are related to each other, but because they love each other. This is a fact of enormous importance for the understanding of their complex psychology; it is the foundation of their comparatively lofty moral standard; it explains more than one of their religious rites; it has its indirect influence on the nature of their crimes.

The marriage ceremony is equally adapted to the needs of so affectionate and romantic a tribe. The great majority of youths win their wives by a dramatic performance known as the *gubai-godo-rungone,* a version of the widely-distributed 'marriage by capture'. The *gubai* procedure imports into the legal and ordered atmosphere of modern times the authentic thrill of 'cave-man' antiquity. It is a surrogate for kidnapping and rape — under conditions of the strictest conventionality. The young hero who has passed the tests of fire and torture in the 'Under World' of the pit-dormitory (or its modern substitute) is not denied the excitement of carrying away his bride and winning her like the prince of any folk-tale.

Domestic life is guarded and fenced about by religious ceremonial which aims at binding and rebinding the partners in their adventure of fertility and love. These sanctions are reinforced by the opinion of society, which makes it rather expensive to change one's mind, and dreads the possible supernatural disasters that follow adultery or divorce.

We must now turn to a detailed inspection of every aspect of Bondo matrimony, to its ritual gateway and the home that lies beyond.

2. The *Sebung* Wedding

A regular marriage (*sebung*) between a boy and girl of well-to-do families, where everything is regular and socially approved, where the choice has been made by the children in the dormitory with the subsequent consent of the parents, is an elaborate affair and the entire ceremonial may last for several months. It is so expensive that only 5 of the 150 marriages investigated were of this type. There is a complicated series of ritual visits, the payment of a token fee which precedes the handing-over of the full bride-price, the exchange of ceremonial gifts, the sacrifice of a buffalo, the escorting of the bride to the bridegroom's house, and the formal bedding of the happy pair. It is not quite clear at what point the couple are actually supposed to be man and wife, for in spite of all the ceremonial there is no real ceremony; I think that probably the marriage is not really clinched until husband and wife are forced to sleep together, although compensation has to be paid if the girl elopes with someone else at any time after the payment of the token fee.

The Bride's Visits. After the preliminary discussions have been completed — the dormitory wooing done, the bangles forced onto the girl's wrist, the parents consulted and their consent obtained — a small party goes to fetch the bride for a visit to her future husband's house. When they arrive, there is the usual show of resistance: the girl hides, the parents raise difficulties. But the visitors must not be daunted, and while some of them invade the kitchen to get something to eat, others search for the girl until they find her. They take her, with a girl chaperone of the same age, back to their village, but on her first two visits she must not eat or sleep in the house of her betrothed. She gets her food from friends and sleeps with the other girls in the dormitory. Then for four successive days she has to perform certain domestic tasks, possibly the relic of a former ordeal when a wife was tested before acceptance. On the first day she husks grain, on the second catches fish, on the third fetches wood, and on the fourth gathers bundles of leaves. Finally the boy's father gives her a present of rice and sends her home under escort of the boy himself and one of his dormitory friends. It is not unusual for boys to make the best of this journey. 'Whenever I went to fetch my wife or take her home,' said Soma Kirsani of Basupada, for example, 'I used to enjoy her on the way.'

The position is now reversed and the boy is the visitor. He does not at first go to the house, but when his future father-in-law hears that he has arrived he sends for him and gives him a feast, making him sit in the middle of the company and giving him palm-wine to drink. He is indeed treated with the greatest respect and honour, as sons-in-law are treated all over India. His hands are washed by one of the girl's brothers, to whom he gives a ring in return.

Next morning the father calls the boy, and his friend, and pulls his leg a little. 'Well,' he says, 'now you can go home. You have got a wife. But what about your friend? What has he got? Nothing but some wasted time, a handful of rice and a little liquor.' The friend is supposed to answer, 'As you sent a girl with your daughter, so I have come with our son-in-law. Even tigers have their companions; how should a human being be without one?' The boys have something to eat and return home.

After a fortnight these visits are repeated and precisely the same programme is fulfilled — an example of something we will notice more than once in this book: the Bondo's love of repetition.

The Sāgur Tanka. The next incident in the proceedings is when the boy's father goes to meet the girl's father, his *samdhi,* (they use this almost universal word), with a gourd of palm-wine. He says 'Your son-in-law has eaten in your house, but my daughter-in-law has not eaten in mine. But now after a week I will give you the *sāgur tanka* and then the girl must eat in my house.' He returns home and the family spends a busy and not unpleasant week preparing rice-beer. When it is ready a party of ten to fifteen men go dancing, drumming and singing with the beer to the girl's house. The boy's father makes a formal presentation and adds one rupee as a token payment of the bride-price.

The presentation of this rupee marks an important step forward towards the conclusion of the marriage. Before it is paid the bride may not eat in her betrothed's house, for once she has done that, once she has taken rice, she is virtually married and then, if there is any change, compensation will have to be paid. But now after the two visits and the many discussions, it is presumed that she knows her mind and she is permitted to eat but not yet to sleep there.

The Bridegroom's Visit. The bride has been tested twice and has survived the ordeal. Now it is the groom's turn. He goes with the usual companion to his father-in-law's house, and is allowed to eat there, though he must sleep in the boys' dormitory. He has to work in the fields to prove his skill with hoe or plough; then he must fetch wood and leaves. After three days of this the girl's father kills a bullock and gives a feast. Then the boy returns home, taking his bride and her chaperone with him, and carrying presents of beef for his parents. This time the girl stays for three days, sleeping in the girl's dormitory but eating in the house.

All this has been going on during the hot weather, and we may suppose that it is now June, the busiest time of the year, with the rains approaching. Yet another party goes to the bride's house with gifts of meat and beer and one of them says, 'Now the days of heavy work have come. What is the point of our daughter-in-law remaining in your house ? Let her come now and work for her husband.' They take the girl, with more gifts of meat, rice and liquor, and this time she spends a whole month in her future home, working and eating in the house but sleeping in the dormitory. There is a convention that she has not yet had sexual connexion with her betrothed.

The nails are being slowly driven home. One party has presented a rupee; the other has contributed a month's free labour; both have offered and accepted costly presents. These things must not be wasted.

The rains pass and the cold weather comes, and now the youth begins to build a hut for himself where he and his wife can live a comparatively independent life. He sends messages calling the girl to join him, but the parents reply, 'We will not send her now. But in Phagun, when the leaves wither and the water dries and the dust flies through the air, at that time we will send our girl.'

The House-warming. When at last the time comes, not so much for the marriage — for that to all intents and purposes is accomplished — as for setting up house together, the first business is to get a buffalo. Everything is now done — according to an invariable Bondo habit — by the days of the week. On a Monday in Phagun, the boy's father buys a suitable animal. He ties it up near the *sindibor* and boys and girls come from neighbouring villages and dance round it, and drink all night. This goes on throughout the week, while the elders are occupied in brewing beer and husking rice for the feast at the house-warming. On the Sunday, the parents go down to the Mundaguda bazaar to buy extra food-stuffs and presents. On the Monday, the mother's relatives and the father's *moitur* friends pay ceremonial visits. Each group, if they can afford it, should bring a buffalo and gifts of rice and beer.

On this day the groom's buffalo is decorated with garlands and the Doms cover it with a new haldi-coloured cloth and feed it with rice and beer. There is a great dance lasting all night.

The next day, the Tuesday, the people feed the three buffaloes with rice and beer again, and the people of the groom's own house go with his buffalo to visit their relatives. A Dom has the privilege of dragging the animal round and he may eat its leavings. Everywhere the buffalo and its escort are received with food and liquor. The other buffaloes are also taken round amid the usual medley of drunken brawls, the revival of ancient grudges, sentimental exchanges between old friends, anxious mothers, giggling girls, excited boys.

The songs sung at this time cannot be said to reach a very high level of poetry. One of them goes something like this:

We have sold our field and our garden;
We are ready for the marriage.
If you are willing, put on your bangles.
If you are unwilling, do not put on your bangles.
You have come but for a day,
How can I wear your bangles ?
Come another day
And then I will wear your bangles.

The groom's buffalo is now brought to the front of the house and killed. As it dies there is a wild struggle to cut off bits of the tail and scraps of flesh from the mouth. The boy's father stands by with a long bamboo stick shouting, 'Be careful, let's have no quarrels', and others sing,

O mother, maternal uncle has come,
Paternal grandfather has come.
O starling,
You are beautiful as a starling.

Now begins an orgy of meat-eating and drinking. The buffalo presented by the maternal relatives is sent as a gift to the bride's father. In turn he sends yet another buffalo as a gift and also returns the buffalo he has just received. Both buffaloes are killed, and the maternal relatives get half the flesh of their own buffalo.

On the Wednesday morning the buffalo contributed by the *moitur*-friends is killed and they too get half the flesh. Both relatives and friends must cook and eat separately. Shares of meat are given to the dancers and the rest is divided among the *soru*-neighbours and near relatives.

Nothing happens on the Thursday and Friday, but on the Saturday the bride makes a somewhat belated appearance on the scene. It is noticeable that all the fun and feasting has lacked her presence and that of her relatives. But now the groom, and his father, and a large party of men and women burdened with gifts of meat, rice and liquor, go to fetch the girl. She hides, naturally, but is careful to be found and her father hands her over ceremonially to the groom's father, saying,

Now we are giving you your flower. Today your expectations are fulfilled. Why should I deny your hopes any longer ? All these days I have been guarding your flower, fearful lest some thief should come and pluck it. Now the flower is in your hands. Care for it well. But whatever happens after this is no fault of mine.

Then they escort the girl to her new home with drums and singing and the girl's mother sends presents of food to be shared by the people. When the bride reaches the house she at once goes to fetch water in a new pot, and cooks a feast for the girls of the dormitory whose hospitality she has so often enjoyed. There is the usual dancing and drinking to a late hour and the bride slips away quietly to the dormitory. She is presently taken to her husband and the two are shut up together; I will describe this incident in a separate section immediately.

The marriage is now complete, but one important duty remains. The bride-price, of which only a token payment has so far been made, has still to be paid. After about a week, therefore, the boy's father goes with whatever has been agreed — cattle, beer, grain and cash — and with the special compliment of several baskets of cooked rice and meat. The girl's father accepts the price and the gifts, and, emptying the baskets of meat and rice, refills them with new grain from his own store.

The above account of a full-dress marriage, which comes from Mundlipada, reveals a complex and expensive programme of events which continue for an almost incredibly long time. Sometimes the business is despatched somewhat more expeditiously, yet all Bondo ceremonies tend to be long-drawn out; the Giag-gige lasts a fortnight, so does the Sume-Gelirak, and funerary ceremonial may go on for ten days after every death. The Bondos, in truth, jump at any excuse for taking a day off.

But there may be a deeper reason for the lengthy correspondence of marriage ceremonial. The Bondos allow their children to marry for love, because they apparently believe that love is the surest foundation of a happy and permanent marriage. But they know too that love, especially young love, is a fickle and uncertain thing. At the same time they have a rather exaggerated horror of domestic change and are keenly alive to the supernatural dangers of adultery. These dangers are minimized by a long period of testing; if a boy and a girl can survive the visits, the tests, the eating and drinking, the endless discussions, the publicity, they are likely to survive also the tensions of married life.

3. Other Marriage Procedures

Only 5 of the 150 marriages investigated were of this elaborate character, though other procedures also subject the betrothed couple to various ordeals in order to test their mutual affection. There is a simplified version of the *sebung* marriage, in which the main features — the parents' consent, the payment of a bride-price — are the same, but the programme is shorter and less expensive. This is the *damung-jang,* as it is called in Remo, the Oriya term being the *dālabhāt,* the pulse-rice marriage, to indicate its economical character. No buffaloes are killed; the number of visits is reduced to a minimum; the gifts of meat and rice are limited to a single exchange. 30 of my 150 informants, or 20 per cent, were married in this way. A slightly more expensive version of the *damung-jang* is known as *tessagur*; this involves certain additional exchanges of liquor, but is otherwise the same.

When a group of youths carry off a girl already betrothed to someone else, or if a girl breaks her engagement and elopes with a new lover, the resulting alliance is known as *udala-rungone* or *urosagga,* the *udaliya* or irregular marriage of other communities. A technically 'adulterous' marriage, where a woman leaves her husband and goes to live with another man, sometimes forcing herself into his house, is called *uda-oini* or *dāk-iro,* corresponding more or less to what is known elsewhere as *paisa-mundi.* Widow-remarriage is approved, and indeed generally required: it is often celebrated with the husband's elder (not younger) brother and is called *guisung-gui.* The ceremony in these cases is simple and resembles that of the *gubai-godo-rungone* which I will now describe.

The dramatic, exciting, turbulent marriage by capture, the *gubai-godo-rungone,* as I have already suggested, may be regarded as the typical Bondo method of uniting a man and woman. It expresses the Bondo's love of taking things into his own hands. Its clinching ceremony is the feeding of the bride with rice cooked in the bridegroom's house. Social and economic adjustments are made later. This type of marriage covers those occasions where boys raid a dormitory, force bangles on any pretty girl they see, even if she is not betrothed and carry her off, as well as those where, as often happens, after a boy has 'proposed' to a girl and she has accepted him, it appears that the parents are likely to make difficulties, or if there is not sufficient money for the *sebung* ceremonial, or even if the couple are in a hurry and want to get together as soon as possible, the boy enlists the help of half a dozen friends and kidnaps the girl in a bazaar, in the fields, after a dance or from the dormitory. In as many as 105 instances out of 150, this was done.

When this happens the girl, of course, is expected to make a great deal of fuss; she weeps and screams, but somehow she usually fails to make a very effective resistance and is taken direct to the would-be husband's house. Here she is offered a meal of rice. She may refuse it, especially if she is in love with someone else, but since she is generally prepared for what is going to happen, she takes the food and this is regarded as equivalent to a betrothal, almost equivalent to the marriage itself. The girl stays in the village till the next morning, but not apparently with her lover, and she is then permitted to go home.

Next day the boy's mother and one or two women go with palm-wine to see the girl. If the parents are not hostile to the proposed match they receive the visitors honourably and at once begin to discuss the bride-price.

Plate I Group of boys at Bodapada D. V. Sassoon

D. V. Sassoon

Plate II

Plate III Boys peeping through the wall of the visitors' hut *D. V. Sassoon*

D. V. Sassoon

Plate IV Lachhim Kirsani of Bodapada

A few days later a party of men take to the girl's parents whatever price has been agreed — this must always include one rupee, the *sãgur tanka* — and say, 'We have brought the bride-price. Both boy and girl desire this match. According to the custom of the days of old we have brought the price.' There is a long discussion; the parties bargain as if they were purchasing a cow; the elders are called; but in the end the amount is accepted and the date fixed when the girl is to go to her new home.

When the day comes, the boy's parents call women and girls and two boys to their house and after giving them food and liquor send them to fetch the girl. I was present at Andrahal on 12 February 1946 when my friend Sonia's representatives went to Dumiripada to fetch a wife for his younger brother. The father, Gulong, sat down before offerings of palm-wine and beer and recited over them the following incantation:

Giving honour to the Maharaja we live in his kingdom. Giving honour to their *samdhi* these people have given us a girl. When we bring this girl, let us live and eat for twelve years and thirteen ages. In the *samdhi's* house the flower has blossomed; we are going to bring that flower. If the *samdhi* gives it willingly we will return wearing it in our hair. At such a time as this, our *samdhi* is great and we are small. O Mahaprabhu, witness of good and evil, men great and small are sitting before you. Today the *samdhi* is great and we are small. One day perhaps we shall become great and then the *samdhi* will be small.

When he had said this, Gulong touched the threshold with cups of wine and beer; he drank a little himself and the messengers departed.

When the party arrives, it is customary for the girl's parents to greet them and ask why they have come. They reply, 'For our daughter-in-law'. They sit down and drink together while the mother bustles about preparing gifts of food to send with her daughter. Presently the father takes the bride by the hand and makes her stand before the visitors and says, 'Look, according to your desire we are giving you this girl. From today we have no more responsibility. If she does no work, she will be yours. If she becomes a food-stealer, she will be yours. If she goes squint-eyed, she will be yours. Whatever she may turn out to be, she will be yours. *Nena mund denga, pena gondi denga*; her head is ours but her body is yours.' The visitors reply, 'However she may turn out, she will be ours; no blame will attach to you'. Then, taking the girl with them, they escort her with drumming and singing to her husband's house.

4. Consummation

February seems to be a favourite month for bringing a bride for the last time to her husband's house, not now for a visit but for an occupation. Under the full moon of the nights of Magh, processions wind to and fro all over the Bondo hills, their sweet plaintive songs echoing each other. I remember one night at Andrahal how down the hill above the village came a long line of women, bringing a bride to her new home in the moonlight, singing in the beautiful Bondo fashion. They made the girl sit in the street before the house, while her husband sat by the door watching her. This girl was in a sort of spiritual quarantine, and it was necessary to disinfect her before she could be allowed indoors. For on the very night that the boys had originally kidnapped her, a leopard had carried off a dog from the village, and the Dissari suspected that it was her fault; she must be possessed by a Rau.[1] Accordingly, there was a little ceremony. The Dissari made husband and wife sit together, he put a rice-mark on their foreheads, sacrificed a black chick in the usual way and said,

O Mahaprabhu, after this let no Rau remain here to trouble us. May these two eat and live happily. Let them soon have children and be happy. Let this girl be like the washed rice and a blooming flower. O Mahaprabhu, let the Rau leave her.

Then her parents-in-law formally greeted the girl and took her into their home. 'This is your house now,' they said. 'Today we put it into your hands. Work well and live happily here. Look after us old people.' They made her cook some rice and bamboo-shoots in a new pot, and the family and some of the *soru*-neighbours shared the food, which is regarded as very lucky. While they were eating, the bride slipped away to the dormitory.

On a similar occasion at Dumiripada, I recorded another 'lecture' given by the parents when they took the girl into the house.

O girl, somehow or other we have brought you here and married you to this boy. He is our son; you are our daughter-in-law. Reverence the old men and women and all who visit us. Give them food and water. This is your hearth, your broom, your pot, your pestle, your grindstone; the whole house is yours.

Now the elders have done their part and youth takes charge. The marriage must be consummated with due publicity. One group of boys goes hunting for the bride, another for the groom. They catch them and bring them struggling in a desperate but vain resistance to any available hut, which has of course been discreetly vacated for the purpose. At Mundlipada, the boys told me, the custom was to tie the couple together, the girl with her arms round her husband, but leaving his

[1] A Rau is a vaguely-imagined demon of hill or forest.

hands free. They lay them down on a mat and pour several pots of cold water over them saying,

From today you two are husband and wife. Live happily together. May you have great strength. Go to it hard and have children, many and soon. You must have a child within a year. Grow fat and strong, both of you, for you will need all your strength for the copulation you must do.

Then shouting with laughter and excitement the boys bang the door and run away, leaving the unfortunate couple to undo themselves and get warm as best they can. This is the last of the marriage ordeals and it is a very real one. Soma Kirsani of Basupada recalled how the boys tied him tightly to his wife, poured two pots of very cold water over them, fastened the door securely on the outside and ran away. It took him a long time to free himself and he was then 'so cold he could do nothing'. He and his wife went to sleep separately in their respective dormitories and the 'wedding night' was postponed. And when Lachhim Kirsani of Gokurupada, who had had intercourse with his wife ever since he had put bangles on her, was officially 'bedded', the boys threw him on the ground, tied his wife on top of him and said, 'You don't know how to do it; your wife will have to teach you'. Then they turned the couple over so that the boy was uppermost and pushed his legs up and down saying, 'Go to it with vigour and there will soon be children'. They doused them as usual and ran away.

I have watched this scene on various occasions, but always in Andrahal, where the procedure is a little different. One night — it was 13 February 1946 — the girl was taken first into a small hut; then her husband struggling violently was carried in by an excited crowd and pushed through the door. The boys snapped the bride's waist-band and pulled off her cloth, slapping and thumping her naked body till she was crying loudly. Then they also stripped the boy and pushed him on top of his wife and ran out, banging the door behind them. Another evening, I watched a long and desperate struggle to get the husband out of the boys' dormitory where he had taken refuge. It was a real fight, for the boy spat and bit and kicked, threw bits of burning wood at his tormentors, pulled their hair and contested every inch of the way. He had to be carried up the hill to his house. Here the girl had hidden herself in the loft among the grain-bins and it was impossible to get her down without spilling the grain; every time they approached she knocked some of it onto the floor — it was an effective check. So at last the boys had to shut the door and go away. Even that was difficult, for the husband pushed a blazing stick through a hole in the door to prevent it being latched.

This custom is widely distributed among the Orissa tribes and in Bastar. The Juang ordeal is even more severe than the Bondo. The Marias and

Murias, however, are content to shut the bridal pair up together and do not torment them.[1] However, they steal a fowl from the groom's house as a reward — a thing the Bondos do not seem to have thought of.

5. Guppasing

A great deal of trouble has been taken to ensure that husband and wife should get on well together. But domestic harmony is not everything and a further effort must be made to free the house and family from any supernatural dangers that may attach to the new bride or to the very occurrence of so important an incident as a marriage. For this purpose sacrifice must be offered to Guppasing.

Guppasing appears to be a house-god, for various kinds of offerings are made to him when a building is erected. When a new house is being built, 'when it begins to look something like a house', no one should cook within its walls until Guppasing has been propitiated. After a child-birth, when the house has been to some extent defiled, the father offers — on the day the umbilical stump sloughs off — a pig or fowl to Guppasing above the pit where the mother has been bathing. After this she can enter the house and cook — a thing that was taboo before.

In connexion with marriage, offerings to Guppasing seem to have a two-fold purpose. One is to purify the place of danger; the other to admit the bride into her husband's *bonso* and *kuda* and the fellowship of her new *soru*-neighbours.

At Andrahal I was told how necessary it was to take these precautions. There may have been some broken taboo, some neglect of the gods. 'For many years,' said my informant, 'such a girl has been living with her parents and has been sleeping in the dormitory. Who knows what she has been up to there ? Any sins of that period must be put far away. Now she has come in her husband's house; she will be working near the house-god, she will be touching the seed-grain. It is essential that no harm should come of it. So we sacrifice to Guppasing to put far away any defilement that may be clinging to her.' This sacrifice is not offered by the Sisa or Dissari, but by any male member of the household; the food that is subsequently prepared is regarded as something very special, and only husband, wife and celebrant may eat it.

On 18 February 1946 I was present at a Guppasing rite at Mundlipada. Mangla Mundli brought his wife home on the 13th; he was bedded on the 14th and on the 18th he had the ceremony, performed by his own father. The wife was made to sit on the threshold and the husband near by.

[1] Cf. my 'Notes on the Juang', *Man in India*, Vol. XXVIII (1948), pp. 102ff, and *The Muria and their Ghotul*, pp. 129ff.

The celebrant sat before her, holding branches of three different shrubs with which he sprinkled her with water. He put little piles of rice on the heads of both wife and husband, and made a fowl eat of them. Then he took the wife into the house, made her sit by the hearth and repeated the process. Finally he killed the fowl, and the girl cooked it, and the three of them ate it.

The following charm was recited during the ceremony;

> *Hānum* ! O Guppasing Arlangsing, defilement has gone, sacrifice is done.
> Let the harvest be abundant; let children be abundant.[1]

But there is another, perhaps more significant, purpose of the Guppasing rite. The food cooked after the sacrifice is regarded as a very special kind of *soru*-food and once the new wife has partaken of it, she becomes a member of the *soru*-fellowship of the village. She also now changes her *bonso* and *kuda*, automatically taking those of her husband. Sometimes, I was told, when the stress was on this aspect of the rite, the sacrifice was performed in the place where the newly-married couple had been made to sleep together on their wedding-night, and the celebrant exclaims, 'On behalf of the *soru*-brothers, I sacrifice to Guppasing'.

6. Motherhood

The Bondo is born, as he lives, hard. The mother continues with her ordinary work almost to the very moment of delivery and resumes much of it immediately afterwards. She has very few privileges or duties during the months of pregnancy. She should not go out of a house during an eclipse and she is supposed to observe some simple rules of diet; she should avoid mangoes, the jackfruit, which might make the child dribble later on, the brinjal, which will give it itch, a spotted fowl, which will infect it with its spots, and any kind of carrion. The father is not permitted to eat the head or feet of anything sacrificed or killed in the ceremonial hunt.

The process of childbirth is taken equally simply and is unencumbered by the usual apparatus of magic tricks and charms to get the

[1] *Hānum*, an ejaculation used at the beginning of many Bondo charms, is probably one of those sounds in which what Otto calls 'the numinous feeling' is articulated. So is the holy syllable *Om* which, like *Hānum*, has no sort of conceptual connotation, but is 'really a sort of growl or groan, sounding up from within as the quasi-reflex expression of profound emotion in circumstances of a numinous-magical nature, and serving to relieve consciousness of a felt burden, almost physical in its constraining force.' R. Otto, *The Idea of the Holy* (London, 1926), pp. 194 ff. Hivale describes how, similarly, the Gond or Pardhan magician exclaims '*Occha*' or '*Ojhha*' as he falls into trance.— Hivale, op. cit., p. 66.

child out of the womb. When the pains begin, the other women — who must be exclusively Bondo — take the mother into a corner of the ordinary living-room of the house. Sometimes they tie a rope to the roof for her to cling to. They make her sit on her knees. Two women hold her and persuade her to cough violently. After presentation, some older woman — again it must be a Bondo woman — makes a ligature round the cord and cuts it, with an arrow if it is a girl, with a sickle if it is a boy. The women make a small pit inside the house for any blood, but bury the placenta and cord, wrapped in a large leaf, in a pit (which must be more than an arm's length deep) under the eaves behind the house. They bathe mother and child with warm water, rub the child with oil and warm it before the fire.

A face-presentation is regarded as particularly fortunate. 'It is good for the child to come bowing down to the Earth and touching her feet. For then the Earth is pleased and always gives the child plenty to eat.'

The mother should not touch the cooking-pots until the child's umbilical stump falls off. This is the signal for the little rite known as Dibok-gige. The purpose of this seems to be to bring the mother's family into somewhat closer touch with the father than hitherto, for up till now the mother's father may not eat in his daughter's house. There is also some idea of interesting the *sairem* in the child's health and prosperity.

A week after the falling of the stump, the child's father goes to his father-in-law and says, 'Now a child is born in my house. Give us a feast.' The father-in-law produces a cock if the child is a boy, a hen if it is a girl, and the younger man returns home. When he reaches the house, the mother brings out the child and sits with it on the threshold. The father waves the fowl round them and says, 'This fowl has been sent by my parents-in-law. Let their grandchild grow fat. Let it not cry too much. Let it live happily. Let it grow old as its grandfather. Let it be fat and strong as he is.' He then kills the fowl in front of the house and they cook and eat it. The taboo on the father-in-law is now lifted and after a few days they invite him to drink rice-beer and enjoy the usual repast of crabs or fish.

A few other details about babies may be noted here. Twins are called *baton*. Two boys are said to have been *moitur*-friends in a former birth and so fond of each other that they arranged to be reborn in the same womb. Both children are given the same name, based as usual on the day of the week when they were born. Two girls are also supposed to have been special friends in a former birth. A boy and a girl are said to have been an exceptionally affectionate brother and sister who never quarrelled. But twins seem to be rare, and I was unable to hear of actual instances. One informant indeed exclaimed indignantly, 'Is a woman a bitch or a she-goat that she should litter two or three children at a time ?'

When a child's first teeth drop out, the mother throws them on the roof saying, 'May he soon get new ones'. Sometimes, however, the father takes them to a cross-roads near the village and buries them in a little hole.

When a very small child dies or is stillborn, the women themselves sometimes bury it near the hearth inside the house, and the father offers a fowl in the name of the *sairem.* But it is said that if the child is buried directly under the hearth, even this simple offering is unnecessary. Somewhat older babies are taken to the usual burning-ground and cremated within little hearths of stone.

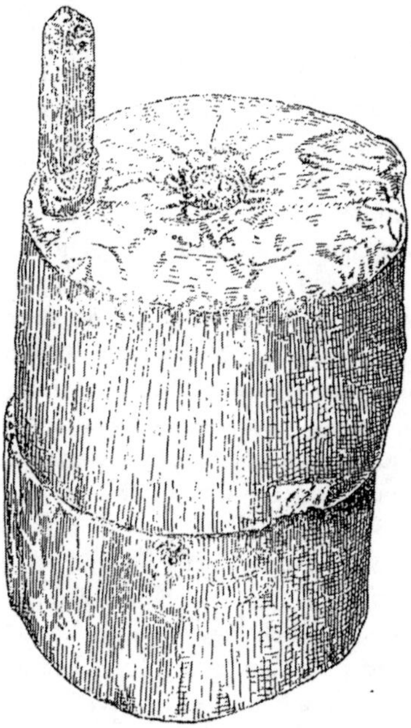

FIG. 29. Grindstone

In some villages there is a rule that after a child is born, no seed may be taken out of the building until it is named.

The Bondos are excellent parents. They adore their children and are wise enough to give them a great deal of freedom. Fathers are almost as good with the babies as the mothers. As the children grow they make little toys for them — animals out of jackfruit with sticks for legs, little propellers with leaves, model axes and ploughs; they teach them the simple games of poverty — mud-pies, rice-husking with dust, houses, hide-and-seek. Mothers pet and spoil their children, delight in making them look nice and fuss round them to protect them from harm. During a dance mothers hover anxiously around, to adjust a fallen plume or check a quarrel. At the Castigation ceremony of the Sume-Gelirak (see pp. 177-8) mothers wait with pots of oil, and when their offspring seem to have had enough, catch hold of them, drag them from the fray and anoint their scars. Should there be any young boys in a party of porters shifting camp, the mothers come with cups of gruel and follow the party, watching it out of sight, sometimes with tears.

But the best gift of Bondo parents to their children is the gift of freedom. I have noticed in consequence a very friendly pleasant relationship between fathers and sons.

7. Name-giving

An important moment in the development of a Bondo couple towards complete domesticity is the giving of a name to their first child. This is done sometimes on the very day of birth, sometimes after five days, sometimes when the umbilical stump falls off. The date depends on economic rather than ceremonial considerations: whether or no rice is ready for a feast, if there is a supply of beer or wine at hand, whether a fowl or pig can be obtained. The actual business of naming is done by a maternal relative; the mother's brother or sister and her brother's son or daughter usually take part. After the usual sacrifice of a fowl, one of them puts an uncooked leg of the dead bird in the child's hand and names a number of dead ancestors — few beyond the grandparents are remembered — slowly one by one. Should the child clench its hand round the drumstick it is a sign that the person named has been reborn and his name is given. But if the child gives no sign — and it is obvious that this is what usually happens, if indeed the rite is often performed nowadays at all — it is given a name based on the day of the week on which it was born.

For here again we see the Bondo's extraordinary attachment to the days of the week. The week-days revolve round the Sabbath bazaar at Mundaguda like a magic circle, blessing each new-born baby with the most conventional of names. The result is that it would be hard to find anywhere a smaller variety; some of the older men have strange Bondo names, but the younger men and women show a distressing monotony. In a recent murder case, where two Bondos were charged with murdering two other Bondos, the names of the murderers — Sankar Kirsani and Soma Kirsani — were identical with the names of the victims, who were also named Sankar Kirsani and Soma Kirsani. The consternation of the unfortunate Sessions Judge, who had to write a more or less intelligible judgement, may be imagined.

The names based on days of the week are these:

Sunday	Adi, Hadi, Odwari
Monday	Soma, Somra, Somri
Tuesday	Mangla, Mogla, Mangli
Wednesday	Budha, Budhai
Thursday	Lachhim, Lachhma, Guru, Guruwari
Friday	Sukhra, Sukhri
Saturday	Sania, Sona, Sonia, Soni

D. V. Sassoon

Plate VI Sonia Sisa of Andrahal

D. V. Sassoon

Plate VII Two young boys

Plate VIII Bondo boys

Plate IX Budha Sisa of Andrahal

Plate X Sonia Kirsani of Kichchipoda

Plate XI Sonia Sisa of Andrahal, shortly after he had completed a sentence for homicide

The recurrence of names among the 150 men interrogated by questionnaire was as follows:

Sunday	15	Thursday	23
Monday	25	Friday	18
Tuesday	15	Saturday	18
Wednesday	15		

The days of the week,[1] therefore, comprising only eight different words, accounted for 86 per cent of the names. Among the others there were five men called Muliya, four Ghasis and only twelve others. From other sources, however, I collected the following list of names; many of them are nicknames; some show modern Oriya influence; some occur only in the early stages of the genealogies.

Apla
Bhuta (ghost)
Bira (strong)
Boli
Bondkalang
Bursakiye
Butki (small)
Dalmaru (cutter of branches)
Dambu (Dom)
Datu
Dengarupa (tall and handsome)
Dondri (plump as a fish trap)
Dongu
Donker
Dungap
Gaigussong (she wanders like a bitch)
Garboisan
Ghasia
Godra
Gopa (cow herd)
Gulong (peon)
Gussung
Jagbandhu (friend of the world)
Jhali
Kaila
Kaliya (black)
Khandaru
Killub
Killupsup
Kimpa
Kindri
Kinker
Komolsan (seated on a lotus, Brahma)
Kujai
Kukra (cock)
Kurri
Lepa
Losam
Mila
Milaboi
Miliya (maker of bangles, Ghasia)
Nari
Ontaru
Pandu (light-coloured)
Podu
Sannyasi
Salai
Sankar (the Hindu deity)
Sobha (handsome)
Tiglai (a joker)
Tio
Tamio (an only child)
Ujje
Urkuri (mad)

Bhuta is a derogatory name, meaning ghost or evil spirit, given in true Hindu fashion to discourage demons from attacking the child. Ghasia and Miliya, the title of a caste which for some reason is regarded with particular detestation by Hindus and aboriginals alike, and Dambu or Domu, are also intended to give the denizens of the other world an

[1] A reference to Eric Linklater's *Poet's Pub*, though frivolous, is almost inevitable. Sir Colin Keith had seven sons; the first was born on a Sunday, the second on a Monday and so on till the sixth arrived on a Friday. 'When Lady Keith became pregnant for the seventh time, Sir Colin's excitement grew with every month. "He'll be born on a Saturday", he said, "and that will make a good deed for every day in the week. I've worked harder than God, for He rested on the seventh. If the boy's dropped on a Saturday I'll call him Saturday. By God I will!"' And so he was, and so his father did, and Saturday Keith became the hero of a first-rate novel.

impression that the baby is utterly worthless and thus not worth molestation. Sannyasi may have been given because a Hindu ascetic visited the village on the child's birthday. Tamio is a name given to an only child, long after its birth, whose mother is called 'plantain-sterile', *kadali-bãnjh,* an Oriya word suggesting that she is like a plantain-stalk which bears one bunch of fruit and then decays. Gaigussong, as a girl's name, hardly requires comment.

When a child's name has been finally determined, the mother's brother or sister (whichever is there) puts some chicken curry and cooked rice in a leaf-cup, and taking this in the left hand and a stick in the right, goes behind the house. He strikes the wall with the stick and calls loudly to the parents who are sitting inside, 'What is the baby's name ?' They answer and when he has heard the name he sits down outside and eats the food which he has so prudently brought with him.

8. The Dagoi-gige

Before proceeding to a discussion of those fascinating tensions and attractions, repulsions and anxieties that make up the normal pabulum of domestic existence, it will be well to clear out of the way a number of religious proceedings which are intended to safeguard the married pair from supernatural dangers. There are, alas, no such ceremonies to protect husband and wife from the wayward impulses of their own hearts; no religion has yet devised a sacrament to nullify the pangs of jealousy; the marriage-bed can be guarded against demons but not against frigidity; there are prayers to improve the rainfall and to effect the conversion of the Jews, but none to increase mutual passion or the conversion of a nagging wife.

But since the Bondos think that the supernatural protection of a married couple is important, it is our business to think so too, and we must consider with due sympathy their arrangements for fertilizing themselves, their cattle and their crops. The modern Western world has lost a good deal in being no longer able to dismiss devils to their proper place; it was such an easy way of curing our inferiority complex before the stupendous unknown. The Bondos have not yet attained the frustration and boredom of unbelief; they are still at the exciting and heroic stage of being able to see devils everywhere and know just how to deal with them.

To check the activities of a troublesome demon called Dagoi, every married Bondo may perform three times in his life a sacrificial feast known as the Dagoi-gige, once for himself with a bullock, once for his wife with a cow, and finally for both with an egg-laying hen. The occasion for the feast is the realization that all is not going well with one's economic-domestic life: the wife is barren, so are the cows, the crops are failing, the goats are dying and the hens devour their brood; there is sickness in the family which the Dissari is at a loss to diagnose: it does not seem to be due to a restless *sairem* or a breach of tribal taboo. On such occasions the Dissari generally points to the sinister and mysterious Dagoi.

No one knows very much about Dagoi, except that he is a deity connected with the house — 'Dagoi lives in the home' — and has the special property of making things barren: women under his influence do not bear children and fields do not yield their crops. I do not know whether, if at any time the Bondos should come to recognize the advantage of limiting the population, their attitude to this contraceptive deity might change.

Once the three celebrations in his honour have been performed, Dagoi never interferes again; there cannot be a fourth celebration of the Dagoi-gige. The only exception to this is where a man has a number of wives; every polygamist, whether in Hollywood or Mundlipada, has a lot of troublesome expense. A cow may be given for each successive or contemporaneous wife. Thus Lachhim Kirsani of Dattipada had to give a cow for his elder wife because she had a pain in the chest, another cow for his younger wife because her child had rickets, and a bullock for himself.

Dagoi in fact often emphasizes his displeasure by activating the streptococcal infections, but, properly appeased, he proves himself a valuable chemotherapeutic agent. For example, Hadi Kirsani of Bandapada had a suppurating wound on his foot, his wife an obstinate pain, probably of chancroid origin, in her chest. Soma Kirsani of Katamguda had a great sore on his thigh — the Dissari treated it with his own prescriptions and sacrificed a pig to Hundi, but it was no use. He grew steadily worse for two years, until in despair the medicineman advised the celebration of the Dagoi-gige. Within a fortnight the enemy was routed and Soma was a new man. Soma Mundli of Bodapada had bad crops and a wound in his arm for two years; things only improved after a Dagoi-gige. Gudra Bodnaik of Dumiripada suffered from 'weak legs' and his wife with a wound in the breast; they sacrificed to Dagoi and recovered. Two years later, however, their son fell ill, so they made a supplementary offering of a fowl. Arung Mandra of Dattipada lost his cattle, the crops failed, he developed a septic foot and his wife suffered from chronic indigestion. The Dagoi-gige set everything to rights.

It is not ordinary sickness that calls for the Dagoi-gige; there must be a general dislocation of domestic affairs. It will be noted that in most of the above examples the patients were suffering from some form of disablement that would prevent them working in the fields or caring properly for the cattle, thus indirectly causing a loss of fertility.

Sometimes the occasion for the sacrifice falls early in life; sometimes husband and wife grow old before it becomes necessary; a few dodge it to the end, partly to avoid the expense and partly because the even course of their lives has not demanded it. But in any case it is definitely a joint performance of husband and wife, an enterprise through which they face together their common troubles and overcome them. As such it has its place in supporting the stability of Bondo marital life.

On 20 March 1945 and the following days at Mundlipada I witnessed two celebrations of the Dagoi-gige; the first was in the house of Mangla Mundli and was performed for his wife Pandri; the second was celebrated by the Naiko himself. On these occasions a householder has a good deal of expense. In addition to the usual supply of wine and beer, he must provide a bull and a crowing cock if it is for himself, a cow and an egg-laying hen if it is for his wife. In a fertility rite the offerings must be appropriate.

In the early morning of 20 March, then, a Pujari — as they called him — belonging to the same *kuda* as Mangla, and a *soru*-brother of the same village — came with his similarly qualified assistant Sonia Mundli. He brought an arrow with a ring strung on it, a chisel, an adze and some rice in a leaf-bundle. The two men made a sort of camp on the veranda of Mangla's house, and Sonia prepared a hearth and lit a fire. Mangla's brother's daughter brought water in a new pot and Sonia put it on the fire and began to cook the sacramental rice. The Pujari pottered about a little, had a drink and then led the way to a field behind the house where some of the villagers and visitors who had already assembled were inspecting the cow (for the ceremony was for Pandri) which was to be killed. A young man — there is no rule about such a man's position or relationship with the householder — he may be anyone expert in the task — took his axe and struck the cow a sharp blow with the blunt edge on the back of the neck, killing it instantly. In order to sell the skin at a fair price, great care is taken not to break or tear it, and it is possible that what I suspect was once a very wide-spread custom of hacking a sacrificial animal to pieces has disappeared for a purely economic reason. After this someone killed a fowl. The Pujari sprinkled a little of the cow's blood on his bundle of rice. He cut off the cow's right ear.

Then he returned to the house and made Mangla and Pandri sit on a ploughshare under the eaves in front. Before them he placed a bundle containing every kind of seed used in their fields. He threw over them a little of the blood-stained rice and then, placing his chisel successively on head, both arms, knees and feet, tapped it with his adze 'to drive away all disease, danger or mistake'. The effectiveness of this rite obviously depends on the use of the iron implements, iron being a well-known demon-scarer.

The Pujari returned to the field and waited till the others had skinned the carcass and had begun to cut it up, whereupon he removed a number of strips of flesh from the ribs and hung them at either end of two bits of bamboo which he slung over his shoulder like a carrying-pole.

He returned to the house and repeated the rite of the iron tools; this time he supplemented it by hanging the meat-sticks over the couple's shoulders. After this he put a little rice from his bundle into leaf-cups and offered them to the four quarters of the earth, the threshold, the field, the domestic implements in the house and the cattle-shed. When he had finished he packed everything up and put it in a basket.

Meanwhile out in the field there was a scene of great activity. Girls were fetching water, men were standing over a long pit which they had filled with burning logs and were placing pots of rice and meat upon it. Others were measuring rice, already cooked, on great mats. The Pujari helped himself liberally to meat and rice and returned to the house. He handed tooth-twigs to Mangla and his wife and they cleaned their teeth. Again he made them sit down, hung the meat-sticks over their shoulders, knocked them all over with the iron tools, offered rice as before, gave them water to wash their hands and then gave them some of the *soru*-rice that had been cooking all the while on the veranda and had some himself. He also gave them generous helpings of the meat and rice which he had brought from the field.

When the meal was over the Pujari went through the entire routine again and once more collected his impedimenta in his basket. Presently Mangla's brother's daughter came and tied on her back a cloth filled with cooked rice — her perquisite — and bundled together everything that had been used during the ceremony, the pot used for the *soru*-rice, the ploughshare, the arrow, iron tools and strips of meat. She hoisted the bundle onto her head and went away quickly looking round.[1]

All this, of course, took time. Between every incident there was discussion, some quarrelling and much drinking of wine and beer and it was not until about 3 o'clock in the afternoon that the Pujari was ready for the concluding rite. Now he took a bit of the cow's liver and some rice out of the village along a path towards the east. The guests followed him, most of them wearing leaf-cups like caps upside down on their heads. A couple of youths staggered along under great loads of meat. The Pujari and his assistant sat down apart from the others and offered

[1] Loud cries of protest greeted my attempt to photograph this part of the ceremony, though no one objected to my camera at other times. I did, however, take a photograph, but when the spool was developed, although the rest was in good order, nothing whatever registered on the negative exposed to this *angto* object!

rice and liver to the four quarters, then broke off bits of the liver and ate them. The others made a fire and roasted the meat they had brought, eating it on the spot. They had already taken a large meal of meat and rice in the village, but this was a sort of picnic to round off the ceremony. Mangla provided more wine and beer to wash it down.

This was the end of the day's ceremonial, but the feasting and drinking — and quarrelling — went on late into the night. There was no dancing or singing. Mangla took the cow's stomach, which had not been cut open, with great care to the house and placed it out of harm's way on the roof.

Early next morning, Mangla and Pandri sat down together with the cow's stomach and the bundle of seed, which I have already mentioned, before them. Mangla offered rice exclaiming, 'Let the crops be good; let us soon have children; let us eat and live happily together; let there be no kind of trouble in the home'. He slit open the stomach, spread the dung on the ground and they both searched in it for undigested grain. This time they were fortunate enough to find the seeds of *Panicum miliare, Eleusine coracana* and *Solanum esculentum.* Mangla's crop of these things, it was believed, would be particularly successful during the coming year.

The seeds were carefully separated and placed in a leaf-cup; afterwards they were mixed with the seed to be sown later. Mangla offered rice to the Departed and the Pujari ended the proceedings with a rather beautiful benediction:

> May you have many children. May your harvest be good. May your cattle live long. May your fowls prosper. May Thakurani Bokarani bless you. As the flowers blossom, as the washed rice shines white, so may this sacrifice achieve its end. May the beanstalk never break. May the golden cock ever crow in your house.

There is one disadvantage about the Dagoi-gige; it cannot be repeated more than three times, unless, of course, there is a plurality of wives. But an ordinary couple, who have averted the dangers that beset them three times, can rely on this rite no longer. This happened to Somra Challan of Katamguda. He had for some time been in difficulties. His first wife had borne him three sons and a daughter, but they had all died within a few years and soon afterwards she followed them. Six weeks after her death Somra went to the trouble and expense of marrying again, but it was not till three years later that the new wife produced a daughter. She was not pregnant again for two years and grew more and more sickly. Somra was fond of her: he had exhausted his quota of Dagoi rites, and did not know what to do next. In his anxiety he sent for a special Dissari. The expert declared, 'Your fate is bad;

Gurang is out to trouble you. That is why your first wife and children died. This woman too will go mad and die if you are not careful. There is only one way to improve your fate and that is by the path-marriage.'

Somra Challan agreed. The Dissari initiated the proceedings by making husband and wife sit together in their house while he tied a string round them. They then promised in his presence that if their child was born safely and survived they would celebrate the path-marriage. The Dissari sacrificed four fowls to Gurang and he and the neighbours ate them, but Somra and his wife were not permitted to share the feast, for from that day till the child was born neither of them might touch meat or fish.

At last, at the end of 1944, a male child was born. On the eighth day, the umbilical stump dropped off, and Somra called the Dissari to conduct the Dibok-gige. He himself made a small pit, the mother washed her hands and feet above it, and the Dissari sacrificed a she-goat, a pig and three fowls (for Somra was sparing no expense to 'improve his fate'), letting some of the blood fall into the pit. The stump was thrown in and covered with earth. On this day, but on this day only, Somra and his wife were allowed to break the taboo on meat and they shared the feast, which was a good one, with their neighbours.

Mother and child continued well, so on Sunday, 4 February 1945, the Dissari came to fulfil the promises of the path-marriage. For this a lot of paraphernalia had to be prepared. There was a sheep, five fowls, a large gourd, a cucumber, three bamboo fans for Gurang, Jamjamra and Lullibhut, a basket, a fishing-rod, and a fish-trap. The Dissari led the worshippers along the path to the south-west of Katamguda, through charming wooded scenery, till he came to a point where it forked and ran up a little over an incline. Here he halted and constructed his temporary temple. He erected a booth, with four pillars about three feet high covered with a little roof, and placed by each pillar a stylized 'royal umbrella'—forked twigs tied round with thread. Inside the booth he put two pots. In one was rice, water and ground turmeric; in the other unhusked rice, water and turmeric roots; the mouths of the pots were closed with leaves. An assistant erected a swing near the

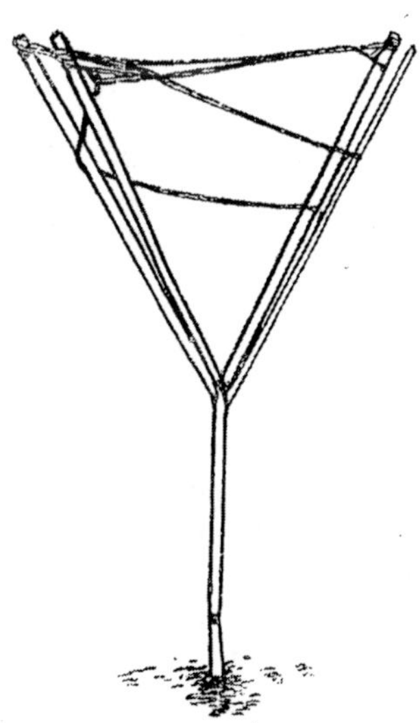

FIG. 30.
Ceremonial 'umbrella'

booth; the seat was woven with thorns, sharp and upright. On the other side of the booth he put a young bombax tree decorated with a bit of bazaar cloth in honour of Jamjamra. Somra Challan and his wife, fasting, sexually abstinent and dressed in their oldest clothes, stood by nervously expectant.

Suddenly the god fell upon the Dissari and he leapt onto the swing, apparently indifferent to the thorns, and rocketed to and fro. Wearying of this, he got down and made Somra sit on the ground, his wife in his lap, the child in hers. He waved rice round them, then took Somra

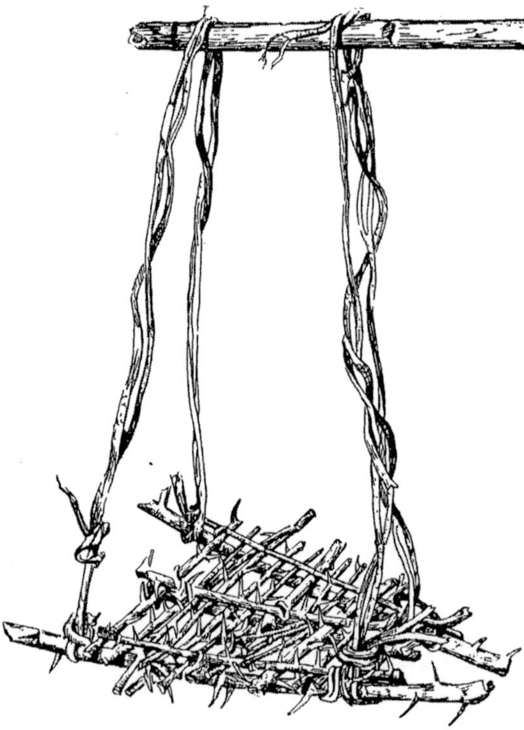

FIG. 31. Magician's swing, its seat made of thorny branches

into the booth and made him squat on the pot of rice with his wife on top of him; the child was given to a kindly neighbour and rewarded her as babies will. The Dissari then took upon himself to climb into the goodwife's lap, as she sat on her husband and he on the pot of rice, and supporting himself by the roof of the booth executed a remarkable lap-dance. When he had finished he made the long-suffering couple

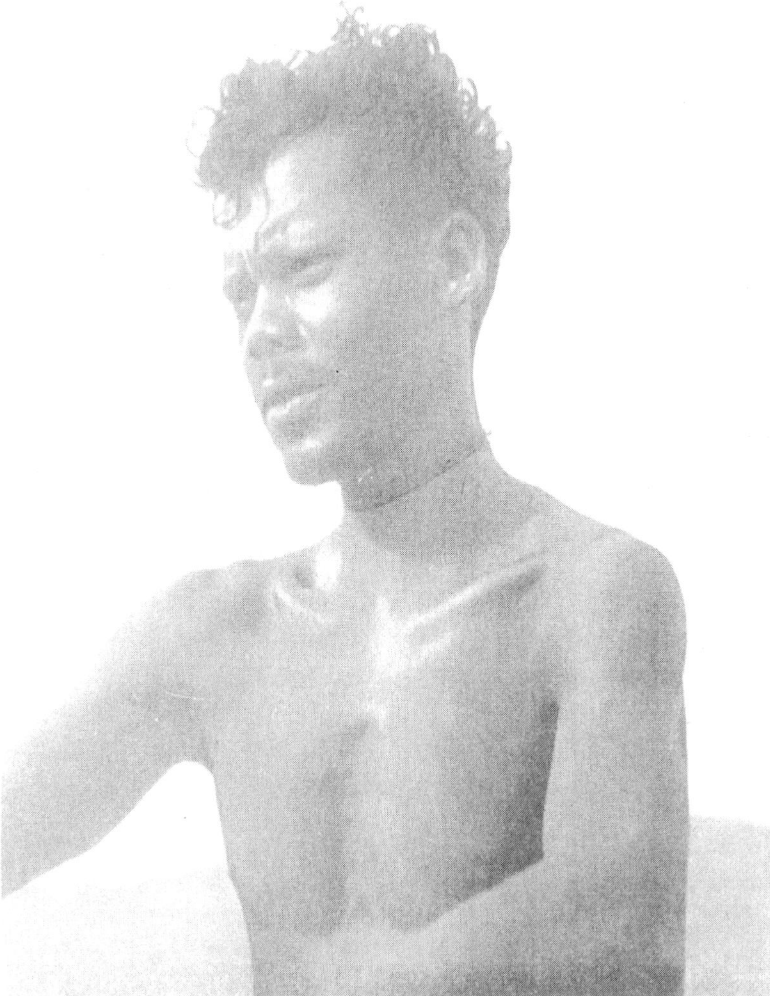

Plate XIII Muliya Dangra-Manjhi of Mundlipada

Plate XIV *D. V. Sassoon*

Mogra Kirsani on his release from imprisonment for homicide

Plate XV

The Naiko of Mundlipada,
chieftain of the Barajangar villages

The Naiko cuts a friend's hair

Plate XVIII Sonwari of Andrahal carrying the upper portion of a wooden grindstone

Plate XX Old woman of Katamguda

sit on the spiked seat of the swing and threw a lot of water over them from the consecrated pots within the booth and shouted, 'Now the path-marriage is done!'

Somra and his wife went down to a trickle of a stream near by and took an exiguous bath; they threw away their old clothes and put on new ones; the wife's fresh bark-cloth, bright with red and yellow stripes, was much admired.

The Dissari now got down to the real business of the day—the food. He sacrificed two fowls and a sheep to Jamjamra, a white hen to Singi-Arke and a black hen to prevent any witch from obstructing the proceedings. Gurang, however, who had been originally detected as the author of all the trouble, for some reason only got one white hen.

Finally the Dissari made a little cart and two mud buffaloes and a mud man and woman to drive them. He put flowers, a model fishing-rod and fish-basket in the cart and tied the bullocks to it, setting the man and woman up as drivers. Then he shooed them away saying, 'Go, let us have no more trouble'. After that everybody relaxed and, when the sheep and fowls were cooked, enjoyed an excellent meal. The Dissari got two helpings and the new pots and cloth from the bombax tree as his perquisites.

This kind of ceremony is of great importance in promoting the harmony and stability of married life. Husband and wife face tragedy together and together they strive to overcome it. Each celebration, like the jubilee celebrations of other cultures, reminds them of the first days of marriage and revives the old happiness. I do not know of any case of separation of a couple which has passed through a series of Dagoi sacrifices. The marriage ceremony itself is casual, noisy and drunken; bride and bridegroom do not appear together till they are bedded. The later ceremonies unite man and wife with far more publicity; it is as though they were joined and rejoined in mutual love, the duties of fertility, and the war against the furies.

9. The Psychology of Domestic Life

We have seen the young Bondo and his girl setting their feet firmly on the path of a legal, lifelong and romantic association for comradeship, child-bearing and mutual aid in economic activity. They are inspired, not by the dictation of parents or the tyranny of family obligations, but by love; they are supported not only by the opinion of society which admires fidelity and abhors its opposite, but by every kind of supernatural sanction. Are they happy? Does the glow continue? What are their real feelings and reactions, tested in the day after day struggle with poverty, anxiety and disease?

The Bondo marriage system is the exact opposite of that of the Murias of Bastar State.[1] The Muria boys and girls enjoy almost unrestricted freedom of intercourse during the pre-marital period; they are allowed to fall in love and they are generally forbidden to marry their lovers. In the great majority of cases their marriages are arranged by the parents with prescribed relatives. Bondo boys and girls appear to be remarkably abstinent during the pre-betrothal, if not the pre-marital, period,[2] but they marry for love and they commonly ignore the claims of family or society to dictate their future lives. Which type of marriage is the more successful ?

It is hard to say. This is not a thing that can be weighed in the balances of a laboratory; even a large number of reports can only give an approximate picture. If I may venture on an impression, I would say that Muria life, both before and after marriage, strikes me as the happier. Murder of the domestic partner is practically unknown in either tribe; suicide for domestic reasons occurs in both and the incidence is not dissimilar. But it seems to me that violent quarrels between husband and wife are more common among the Bondos and the separation rate is higher. We need not be surprised at this in view of the fact that Bondo marriage is based on mutual desire. Love means tension and a love-marriage must be often balanced precariously on a razor-edge of attraction and repulsion. Bondo marriage soars to the heights and sometimes crashes to disaster; Muria marriage walks across the plains.

Yet even so Bondo marriages are fairly stable. The separation rate is only five per cent, which is higher than the Muria or Juang, but far lower than the Gond, Baiga and Pardhan populations of the Central Provinces. Polygamy is over seven per cent, which is rather high. I have only heard of one wife-murder and that was twenty years ago. I could find no one who remembered a wife murdering her husband.

Bondo domestic life is affected by two very unusual factors — the first is the fact that the wife is often older than the husband, the second is the liberty allowed to the husband to intrigue, not as usual with the elder brother's, but with the younger brother's, wife.

The reasons for these strange arrangements are not easy to discover. 'In every village,' says Fürer-Haimendorf, 'you can see fully grown girls with husbands hardly more than eleven or twelve years old and the Bondos are emphatic that the girls themselves have chosen these

[1] For a detailed study see my *The Muria and their Ghotul* (Bombay, 1947), pp. 614ff.

[2] Naturally there are exceptions, and I have recorded some of them in this book. But it cannot be denied that there is a world of difference in the sexual outlook of a Bondo youth who enjoys perhaps half a dozen surreptitious acts of intercourse during the betrothal period, and the Muria who indulges himself nightly with complete social acquiescence.

partners. I was assured again and again that such uneven matches were of the girls' own making and older women have told me that they like marrying small boys: "for then we have young husbands to work for us when we are old". This is probably only half the truth and a stronger motive may be the girls' desire to prolong the happy days in the dormitory. For young wives of immature boys continue to sleep in the *selani dingo,* and there they no doubt find compensation for the lack of marital bliss.'[1]

But this cannot be a very strong reason, for as Fürer-Haimendorf himself says, 'not all young men are eager to intrigue with other men's wives', and the bliss to be found in the Bondo dormitories can in no way compare with that offered, for example, by the Muria *ghotul.* The boys who visit the *selani dingo* are generally in search of wives and they find it difficult enough to establish relations with the unmarried girls, still less with girls whose affiliations might lead to every kind of complication. It is not uncommon for a party of youths to kidnap a betrothed girl from the dormitory; I have never heard of them molesting a married girl.

It is possible that Bondo women are under-sexed. The dormitory girls certainly repel advances; the lack of murders and suicides for sexual motives suggests that the general libido of the tribe is weak; girls do not seem to desire to begin their sex-life and to face the burden of child-bearing too early. Marriage with an immature husband is the simplest of all contraceptives, and the counter-attraction to domestic happiness is not so much the pleasant life of the dormitory (in which after all male company is only available for half the year) as the carefree liberty of life in one's own home.

The custom is fairly common. Out of 150 cases examined by questionnaire there were

Boys marrying younger girls	..	36
Boys marrying girls of about the same age	..	15
Boys marrying older girls	..	99

Bondo women give a number of reasons for this. At Pinnajangar I was told that a girl preferred a young husband 'for he will work better, feed his wife better and do what she tells him'. At Andrahal the women said that a girl considers an older boy 'as an old man: he does his hair differently; how can we love him?' At Mundlipada, they said that girls were afraid of intercourse with big boys; they could rely on younger boys to introduce their attentions gradually, 'not more than one node

1 Fürer-Haimendorf, 'Avenues to Marriage', p. 172. That this is not a result of a disordered sex-ratio of the present day is indicated both by inquiries and genealogies; the Bondos say that, as far back as their traditions go, wives have usually been older than their husbands.

of the bamboo at a time'. There seems to be a real dread of the act of defloration; the Bondos are among the few tribesmen that recognize the existence of the hymen; 'if a girl cries out with pain, she will be ashamed'; it is better therefore to begin with the timid and gentle penetrations of little boys.

A ribald tale, which is known to more than one tribe in Middle India,[1] supports the girls' opinion.

There was a Bondo father and son, and the son's mother. The boy was married to a pretty girl, but she had not yet come to live in the house. One day the father said, 'It is very troublesome for your mother to bring the gruel every day to the hillside. We had better bring your wife to help her; I will go and fetch her.' The boy agreed. The father went to his *samdhi's* house and asked for his daughter-in-law. They gave him food and wine and father and girl started home. On the way they passed a Hindu shrine to Mahadeo. The father said to his daughter-in-law, 'Ask for some gift here; ask that you will have many children'. The girl said, 'Yes'. Then he said, 'I'll go and collect dry wood. You go and bathe, then stand before the shrine and ask what you will.' But the father went into the shrine and shut the door. The girl bathed and returned to the shrine and cried, 'Give me many children'. From inside the old man answered in a deep voice, 'You have your father-in-law with you. Lie with him and you'll have all the children you want.' Presently the girl went to get some water to drink, and the father slipped out; he picked up a few pieces of wood and joined her. 'What did the god say?' he asked. She told him. They went on their way and after a time they came to a field of wild hemp; the stalks tinkled in the wind. The old man took her there and as he worked there was the sound of the tinkling hemp. That night when the son went to his wife she said, 'You are a good lover, but there is not the sweet sound of tinkling hemp as when your father did it'. Since then boys have worn bells to delight their girls. But now women only marry younger boys, because one of them was once deceived by an old man.

The effect of this disparity in age is not necessarily bad, though it is interesting. 'What of the relative ages of husband and wife?' asks Stekel. 'There should not be more than five years' difference either way. A man of twenty-eight married to a girl of twenty-four or twenty-five may be considered a good match in years; many of the happiest marriages are between an older woman and a husband a few years younger.'[2]

But although the disparity in age may not make for married unhappiness, it has other results. In the first place, it promotes polygamy, for a man finds his wife growing old while he himself is young—it must

[1] I give a somewhat similar tale in *The Muria and their Ghotul*, p. 417f.

[2] W. Stekel, 'The Dangers of Married Life', in A. Forbath, *Love, Marriage, Jealousy* (London, 1938), p. 233.

not be forgotten that aboriginal women age very soon — and he still desires youthful companionship. It is natural then for him to take a younger wife.

Then the fact that so many of the wives are older than their husbands has the obvious result that it is more common for wives to be jealous of their husbands than for husbands to be jealous of their wives.

Yet another result, arising, I think, directly from this, is the lifting of the taboo on the younger brother's wife. This is a thing almost unheard of in other communities, which allow a man the greatest freedom with his elder brother's wife but ban him by stringent sanctions from the younger brother's establishment. But among the Bondos an elder brother's wife would probably be too elderly to be attractive, whereas the younger brother's wife, though possibly older than her own husband, would be more of an age with the elder brother and so more available for an affair. I do not know that such affairs occur often, but they occur sometimes, and thus they are important. Serious quarrels sometimes arise as a result and I will give one or two examples of the way they go.

One day Budha Sisa returned to his house at Kadamguda with his younger brother's wife who had come over from Pandraguda on a visit. When she saw the girl his wife immediately suspected that he had seduced her on the way. Budha took every possible oath that he was innocent, but his wife refused to believe him and when he asked for dinner she smashed the cooking-pot in which it had been prepared. 'Then I beat her so hard,' recalled Budha with relish, 'that she fainted. But when I threw water over her she was all right. Since then we've only had the ordinary little tiffs that everybody has.'

Dukku Sisa was another man who had trouble with his wife for a similar reason. His home was in Puchaguda at the foot of the hills and his younger brother lived at Dumiripada two thousand feet above. One morning in May 1945 Dukku went to his clearing on the hillside near the path from Dumiripada to collect the unburnt wood for further burning. That very day his younger brother had a violent quarrel with his wife and she left the house, and was hastening down to Puchaguda to tell the other family all about it. On the way she met Dukku and they retired together into the woods. There was 'nothing wrong' in this, as Dukku was careful to point out, but unfortunately someone saw them. In the evening Dukku and the girl went home together. Dukku's wife said nothing at the time, but after the girl had left the house next day she said to her husband, 'You two have been up to something. Why didn't you have me last night? Why were you so exhausted?'

At the quarrel which followed my assistant Sundarlal was present and was able to make notes of the main exchanges. Dukku denied that he had had anything to do with the girl. 'I simply met her on the way and she was crying, so I brought her to see you. It was for you I did it.'

This the woman would not believe, so Dukku had to swear on his own son, and beat the earth with his hand. 'If I did anything,' he cried, thumping the ground with vigour, 'may my own son turn into earth.' That did convince the suspicious wife, and she said nothing more about the matter till the afternoon when she went into the village and there met the person who had seen Dukku and the girl going off into the woods together. She came home furious. 'You took an oath and beat the earth with your hand; you lied to me.' Dukku responded by asking for his dinner. His wife picked up the cooking-pot full of food and threw it at him; it smashed and the dinner was ruined. 'You swore to me and yet you did lie with your brother's wife. Now our child will die. What's the use of my going on living here ? Go and bring that other woman and have her for a wife.' Dukku, deciding that his best course was stout denial, protested. 'I never did anything of the kind. Who saw me ?'

'The one who saw you told me about it. What's the matter with my organ ? Is hers so much better ? Is mine so worn out that you must climb onto every woman you see ?'

In all aboriginal disputes two things are essential. There must be someone who actually saw and is prepared to testify to an incident; without an eye-witness nothing can be established. But at the same time it is a point of honour never to give away the name of your informant. The eye-witness is necessary, yet can never be produced. This inconsistency is a valuable factor in making for the stability of tribal marriage. Dukku and his wife were thus playing the game according to the rules.

But Dukku was losing his temper; after all he had just lost his dinner. I'll copulate with your mother,' he declared. 'You're only fit to be the wife of a dog. Why are you accusing me like this for no reason whatsoever ? Who saw me ? Mention a single name. I'll break your bones, eater of my excreta.'[1] And so saying he began to beat his wife. She

[1] Bondo bad language is very bad indeed. The most popular expressions refer to intercourse with forbidden relatives or to the eating of dirt. Thus, a man threatens to copulate with his opponent's mother or sister or he calls him the result of a dog's copulation. He may say, 'Eater of my excreta', 'eater of the smegma off my penis', 'eater of your own wife's vagina'. The most insulting taunt is 'eater of my wife's excreta'. References to the pubic hairs are common, though they do not seem to be quite so explosive in their effect as in Bastar. The Bondos also use such Oriya expressions, probably picked up in jail, as 'brother-in-law', 'copulator with your own sister', 'dog', 'bitch' and so on. It is remarkable that they do not abuse women with expressions reflecting on their virtue; they do not seem to say 'noseless', 'wanton', 'whore'. They have no homosexual abuses and they do not use the word 'bastard'. In the Rasavada murder of 1945, Guru Dora shouted '*Dur-dur-dur*' at his enemy, calling him as if he was a dog. It cost him his life.

screamed, 'What are you beating me for? Why lay your hands on an old woman like me? Go and bring that fresh young bitch.'

But Dukku went on, as all aboriginal disputants go on and on, with the one strong point in his defence. 'When I went to that girl, who saw me? Bring out your proofs or I . ıll break the vulva of your mother.'

The wife too relied chiefly on repetition. 'You went to another woman and yet you swore by your own child and now my child will die. Go and bring that bitch to the house, and if she won't come, at least go and lick up her excreta.' She began to weep then and Dukku more angry than ever picked up a bit of wood and beat her again. Now she cried, 'Yes, it's true I didn't see you; no one saw you; I won't say anything more about it'. Dukku stopped beating her, and she put the child whom she had been holding in her arms, on the ground. The boy began to scream, but she refused to pick him up and console him by putting him to the breast. The noise exasperated Dukku more than ever. 'Get out of my house,' he shouted in fury. 'Get out, you seducer of a dog, you breaker of pots. Get out and I'll get a new wife tomorrow. I'm not going to keep you any longer.' 'Certainly,' screamed the wife. 'I won't prevent you. I'll clear out this very moment.'

For three hours the quarrel lasted, well into the night. Then, exhausted, the two sat down together and had some sort of meal. The woman put the baby to her breast and soon afterwards, says Sundarlal, they were laughing and discussing their everyday affairs with the utmost good humour and at last went to bed together.

The Bondos do not, of course, confine their occasional romantic impulses to their younger brother's wives, though it is always nice to be able to intrigue with a clear conscience. Ghasi Mundli of Mundlipada once annoyed his wife to distraction by having an affair with a young girl at Bandapada. 'I had gone', he told me, 'to the Mundaguda bazaar and I met this girl there. I gave her a plantain and some parched rice and when it was time to go she walked along with me. On the way I took her aside into the jungle. Unfortunately I didn't get home till rather late; it was already dark. My wife said, "Why are you so late today?" I said that I had been busy drinking palm-wine at Salanpada. But it so happened that some of our Mundlipada people had seen me giving parched rice to the girl and they got talking and of course in time the story came round to my wife. She didn't hesitate; she went for me at once. "What a liar you are! You said you were drinking but actually you were eating—eating that girl's excreta. Why not bring her here and marry her? May you die soon! May the gods and the *sairem* devour you." I got very angry at that and beat her till she fell down. She hit her head against a stone and fainted. I tried to rouse her by throwing water over her. Then I put some gruel in her mouth and she recovered. Since then we have had no big quarrel, but of course plenty of little ones.'

Sonia Bodnaik had a serious quarrel with his wife for a less serious reason. 'One day the girls of Kirsanipada came to dance. I had a lot of fun with one of them and caught hold of her breasts. But by bad luck my wife saw me. When I got home that night she was very angry and abused me with filthy language. I wasn't drunk, so I gave her a good beating. She went off sulking and for a whole week wouldn't talk or sleep with me. I found it very difficult to bring her round.'

These are the serious distractions of domestic life. Yet they do not seem to be common. A man may remember one such quarrel in a long lifetime of companionship. The Bondos are not a promiscuous people, and infidelity to the marriage tie is dangerous supernaturally and socially disapproved. The Bondos are not particularly jealous, for there is so little occasion for jealousy. Even where there is, the emotion does not seem to go very deep, and — despite the Bondos' notorious indifference to the value of human life — does not seem to excite those dark and passionate outbursts which in the Bison-horn Marias result in the murder of many erring wives.

Among aboriginals jealousy of the future, the desire to prevent one's widow from marrying again, is rare. I recorded one such case, the only one — so far as I remember — in my experience, at Mundlipada. Budha Mundli was stabbed in the stomach by his treacherous friend Hadi Mundli. His wife made him lie down on the veranda and tried to revive him with a little gruel — the universal remedy in all emergencies. As she sat by him Budha, knowing that he was going to die, began to weep a little. He had two small sons and two daughters and there was no one but his wife to bring them up. The wife said, 'Don't weep because that sinner has robbed you of your life'. Budha replied, 'What of my four children? You will go to another man when I am dead and who will care for them?' The wife said, 'I will never leave your children for a man'. Budha did not trust her and made her take an oath. She pulled a thread out of her cloth and, holding it in her hands, declared, 'If ever I leave my children for a man, may my life break as I now break this thread'. She broke it and laid her hand on the ground saying, 'Mother Earth is witness; may she devour me if I am unfaithful!' She touched her eyes and said, 'May my eyes burst if I look at another man'. She made the children sit by their dying father and placed her hand on the head of each in turn saying, 'May these too die if I am unfaithful to you.'[1] When this was done she persuaded Budha to take a little more

[1] It is said that if a man of the same village marries a widow, the dead man's ghost troubles the new husband, saying, 'And where am I to live?', and often makes him ill.

Plate XXI Girl at Katamguda fetches water in gourds

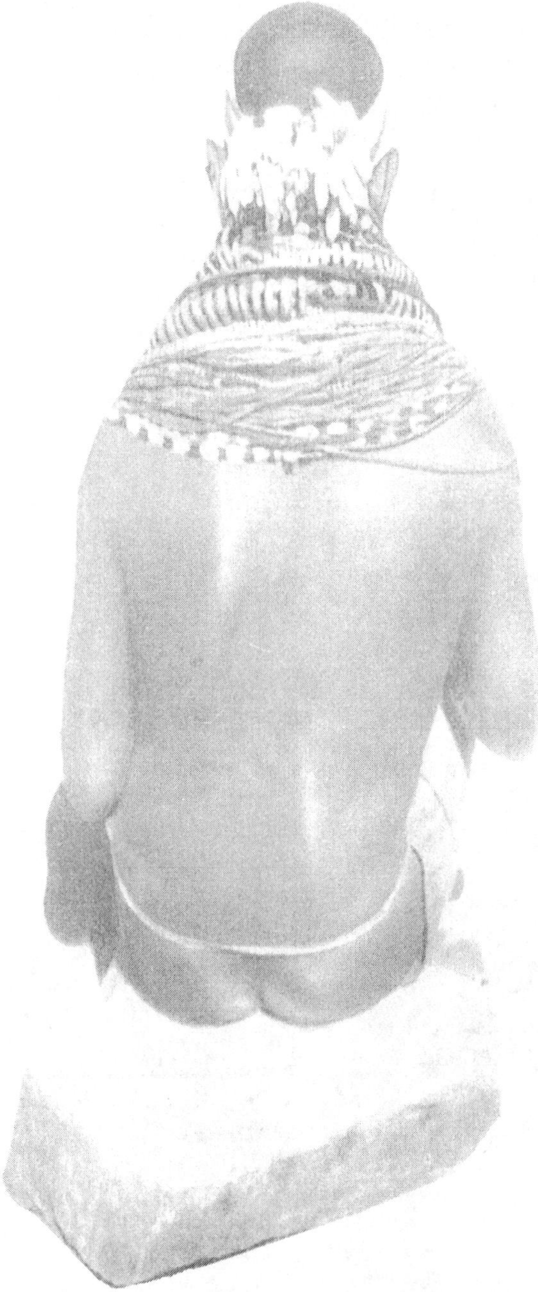

Plate XXV (*Above*) Mr H. V. Blackburn, Mr H. Milham and friends at Bodapada. (*Below*) Mr D. V. Sassoon at Andrahal

Sundarlal talking with boys at the Mundlipada *sindibor*

Plate XXVI

Shamrao, Kusum and Suresh Hivale with Bondos at Mundlipada

Plate XXVII Two girls, Guruwari and Adiwari, share a leaf-cup of gruel at Mundlipada

Plate XXVIII Kindring and Sukri, young Bondo girls, prepare brooms at Andrahal

gruel, and next morning the neighbours put him on a rough stretcher and started off to the Mattili hospital. But half way there the unfortunate man died. When the woman knew he was dead she told the people of her oath, which she has faithfully observed.

In this pathetic incident the element of jealousy is not obtruded but it cannot be ignored. Budha's children would probably have fared better had his widow remarried; what the dying man could not tolerate was the thought of his wife and children and property passing into the control of another. The jealousy here probably had a basis of possessiveness rather than of sex.

Quarrels and disputes about food, unpunctuality, relatives-in-law, slackness in work are much more common among the Bondos; many of them are, I think, the natural result of the nervous tension of the love-marriage. A few examples may be given. Not infrequently a wife breaks out in protest against her husband's drinking excesses — for Bondo women drink very much less than Bondo men. At Basupada, for instance, Soma Kirsani's wife abused him and smashed the cooking-pots because he was always drunk and did no proper work. He broke her head open with a stick, but he was a better man afterwards. Lachhim Kirsani of Gokurupada was very poor and had the distressing habit of cadging for drinks anywhere he could. One evening he came home drunk on rice-beer and asked his wife for something to eat. She abused him and his elder brother came in and supported her. '*Thu-thu*, sister-betrayer, you spend your whole life like a dog. You can't get food for yourself and you don't get any for your wife. Brother-in-law to a dog, there'll never be food in your house. So you'd better eat my dirt, for that's all you'll get tonight.' Lachhim was naturally annoyed and hit his brother in the face. They struggled and Lachhim cut open the older man's head and would probably have killed him had not his wife flung her arms round him and dragged him away. As it was, he got six months in jail. It is noteworthy that here it was the elder brother supporting the younger brother's wife, and there may have been additional motives, which did not come to light, for Lachhim's assault.

A rather similar dispute led to the only wife-murder that has been recorded. It was twenty years ago, at Katamguda. Godra Kirsani was a habitual drunkard and did no work. One day, his wife who was much younger than he, wearied beyond endurance by the poverty and misery of the home, abused him. He lost his temper and beat the girl with a heavy stick. She was pregnant and one of the blows fell across her belly and killed her.

10. Menstruation

In most tribal societies the fact that woman is a menstruating being is of great psychological importance. The dangers associated with the catamenial blood render its subject at once fascinating and repulsive. One reason why the pregnant woman is so attractive to her husband is that she is temporarily free of this disturbing influence. The monthly holiday that the menstrual period imposes on a married couple is of incalculable value; it increases the woman's desire through abstinence and it gives the man a much-needed respite from his wife's importunate sexual demands.

But the Orissa tribes—such as the Saora, Gadaba and Bondo—are astonishingly careless about a taboo that is so rigidly enforced elsewhere. While the Gond group of tribes—including the Konds—regards a menstruating woman as one of the gravest magical dangers that can menace a household, some even making a separate door for her to use or segregating her in a wretched little hut outside the village or in a small kennel on the back veranda, the Bondos (except, of course, for special groups which have come under alien influence) appear to be indifferent alike to the aesthetic and the magical disadvantages of this condition.

The Gadaba woman wraps an old bit of cloth round, but not between, her thighs. The Saora woman puts a dirty skirt underneath a clean one. The Bondo woman does not even do that. She has no idea at all of a pubic cloth. She lets the blood trickle down her leg and wipes it away with a soft leaf from time to time. She is allowed to cook; she can go to the *sindibor* or approach a shrine; her husband may hunt or, if he is a Sisa, perform his ordinary ceremonial duties. Some Bondos say that they do not have intercourse during the period, but others admit that they are free to do so if they want to. At the end of the period, there is no ceremonial bath and the skirt is not washed.

In Mundlipada, however, I was told that a little ceremony was performed at the menarche, but this seems rather for the celebration of a girl's maturity than to avert any possible danger from her condition. 'When a woman is in her period,' I was told, 'it means that Mahaprabhu is visiting her. The first time is a *biru* (sacrifice).' One of the male members of the household, usually the father, makes the girl sit down before a hen which has never laid an egg, and a bundle containing seven different kinds of wood. He kills the hen, sprinkles the girl and the wood with the blood, waves the bundle round the girl and then takes it out of the village and throws it away. The offering of the sterile hen suggests that the rite is intended to prevent a premature pregnancy.

According to Bondo legend, menstruation is the result of the bite of a rat.

In the old days woman's organ was very small; men had to do it on the belly. There was a Raja who had a pet rat. One day when the Raja was away at Nandpur, the rat went between the Rani's legs and nibbled away till there was a hole and blood flowing from it. Since then blood has flowed every month.

Another story attributes the menses to an act of incest. A brother raped his young sister on a hillside and, breaking the hymen, made her blood flow copiously. She died, but it was the beginning of the monthly embarrassment for all other women.[1]

This attitude to menstruation is, I believe, the original Bondo attitude. In places where Dom influence is strong, or where the Bondos think they may be laughed at, customs and ideas are changing, or at least there is a pretence of change. I have no doubt that in a few years the cooking and water taboos at least will be adopted. But at present, the absence of strain and anxiety in connexion with the menses is something which probably promotes domestic happiness.

11. Polygamy

The Bondos find it as difficult to make a success of polygamous relations as anyone else. Polygamy is comparatively common — seven per cent of the men investigated by questionnaire had embarked on this difficult enterprise and had succeeded in keeping two wives at once for a time at least. I think that one reason for this rather high incidence of the practice is the custom of youths marrying girls older than themselves. The wife grows old too soon and the husband, still often only a boy, finds himself wanting a sexual and social companion nearer his own age. Very occasionally the elder wife suggests the 'employment' of a partner in order to save spending money on a servant and to give her some relief from work, but most plural marriages are attended by a depressing history of petty quarrels. I will give a few examples to illustrate how the institution works.

Lachhim Kirsani of Gokurupada married a girl much older than himself. When she grew elderly and lost her beauty 'his whole mind was not on her'. 'So I determined,' he told me, 'to get another wife. When she heard about it my first made a great row. When I brought the new girl into the house, my first hit her over the head with her arm which was heavy with bangles and went to live on the veranda. It was only when my second went out that my first would come in. When the old

[1] Yet another Bondo story is given in *Myths of Middle India*, p. 274, where there is also a full discussion of menstruation legends in other parts of India.

wife cooked the food, the new wife didn't get enough to eat; she was always fighting with the poor girl. "*Thu-thu*, you bitch," she used to say. "I suppose you've come here because you want to eat my dirt. Couldn't you get any other husband? I suppose no one but my poor half-starved goat would look at you. Has he got two organs that he can please us both?" She used to go for me also. "I know; you're tired of me; I'm just an old woman; so you've brought this wanton. You want to burn down my home." At night when I lay down with my second, the first would put herself on the other side and turn me over so that I had to sleep facing her. After a bit I got rather tired of this and I told her to clear out. "If you come back again," I said, "I swear that your father and brother will die." So she went home and her brother and father came and killed one of my pigs and took it away. She married a man at Bodoballe, so now we are all happy.'

I believe that it is a recognized convention that when the new wife arrives in a house, the old one should crack her over the head with bangles, and thus work off some of her rage in this preliminary gesture. It is not only when a woman leaves her husband that her relatives may come and kill a pig; it is said that if two co-wives are always quarelling, the father of the aggrieved girl may come and kill a goat or pig and feast upon it. The fear of this expense is supposed to put some check on these quarrels. For Bondo society, which is intensely interested in personal happiness, does not altogether approve of these entanglements, and it tries to make them difficult. 'To have two wives is just like prostitution,' said a young Bondo back from Manipur.

Sukro Mandro of Dattipada also had an elderly wife. 'When she was young, I was a baby; when I was mature she was elderly and bearing children. She did not satisfy me.[1] There was no pleasure in it. So I got a second wife. The two women were not unhappy together, but the new girl was a food-thief and a wanton, and after a time I turned her out. To get rid of her I had to let her father take one of my goats and give him a rupee.'

When Miliya Bodnaik of Bodapada came back from jail, he found his wife had aged with poverty and loneliness during his absence. 'She was much older than me; after all that time in jail I wanted someone younger. So I said to her, "I'll get another woman; don't mind her; she will just be a servant and will do the work while you take your ease". But she said, "All those years you were in jail, I lived alone waiting for you and never went to any other man. And now that you return you find me old". I felt ashamed, but all the same I got a second wife to help in the work.'

[1] 'She could not satisfy my *buffu*'. *Buffu* is the expressive Bondo word for libido in the widest sense.

Sonia Kirsani of Basupada took his younger brother's widow as a second wife. The first wife was elderly and had two sons. When the younger brother died, the neighbours said to Sonia, 'Here is a nice girl; don't let her go to some stranger's house. Why not keep her yourself?' Sonia had actually often enjoyed himself with the girl and was very fond of her, so he followed this congenial advice. The older woman, however, was very annoyed. 'I used to like the new girl,' said Sonia, 'and I took her about with me everywhere. But my first was jealous and refused to give me anything to eat. Sometimes she used to sulk for days at a time, she wouldn't cook or do any work, but just sat about. Then she began breaking water-pots and smashing gourds. That was too much and I turned her out. Her brother and father came and killed my fattest pig.'

The excuse that an extra hand is needed for the housework or the fields is often made. Lachhim Sisa of Mundlipada assured me that in his case the excuse was the true reason. 'I took a second wife simply because there was so much work to be done. I was afraid that if we employed an ordinary farm-hand he would take an advance of money and then go off to Assam. But I thought that if I took a wife, then even if she ran away I would be able to recover my expenses.' But the two wives did not get on well together, perhaps because — in spite of Lachhim's motives being so entirely economic — he found it necessary to sleep every night with his new farm-hand.

But the wife of Soma Sisa in the same village actually begged her husband to get a second wife. 'She said to me, "How can I manage the field-work with all these children to look after? Get another woman to help me. You can do whatever you like with her. I won't mind." So I got a new girl and now I do all the outside work with her. We go together to the forest and work together in the fields. I like her best, for she is young and has never had a child. When I go to bed, I don't lie down with either of them; I go off by myself and then later on I go sometimes to one and sometimes to the other, occasionally to both. And when I go with the younger girl to the jungle in the day-time I always take the opportunity of lying with her there.'

These instances suggest that the pattern of Bondo polygamy is not substantially different from that of other primitive communities. Sometimes the motive is economic: to promote a man's importance and to increase the number of labourers in his fields. Often disparity of age prompts him to take a younger wife. The childlessness of the first wife, so common as a cause of plural marriage elsewhere, is not mentioned in the above examples, but has doubtless also played its part.

Bondo polygamy is marred by jealousy and sulks. It is not regarded enthusiastically by Bondo society. It generally concludes with the departure of one or other of the wives.

12. Suicide

It was not possible to obtain statistics of Bondo suicides and case-records were not available. I had to depend therefore on personal inquiry; this was not easy, for the people naturally were unwilling to reveal any details which might, they feared, lead to a re-opening of tiresome investigations by the police.

In any case, suicide is rare among the Bondos and its light incidence in a tribe where the homicide rate is so high gives some confirmation to Laubscher's theory that 'suicide has some basis of a racial constitutional nature, and that races who are prone to the externalization of aggressive propensities in an impulsive manner, have a low rate of suicide'.[1] The psychological basis for this is that there is among such races less introjection of sadism.

I was only able to obtain some account of five suicides. But these, such as they are, are instructive. Each of them was the result of domestic unhappiness, for the Bondo believes with Dr Johnson that 'to be happy at home is the end of all ambition' and to fail in that is to fail in everything. Four out of the five suicides were women, not perhaps surprising when we remember Havelock Ellis' dictum: 'There can be no doubt that the sexual emotions of women have a profound influence in determining suicide.'[2]

My first example is the remarkable case of the woman who hanged herself because her husband thought she was too fat. One day in Cheliguda eight or nine years ago, Hadi Challan came home from the sago palm where he had been drinking with his friends and looked at his twenty-five year old wife, who had never borne him a child and was getting fatter and fatter every day. He felt he could bear it no longer and began a long tirade of abuse. 'Here you are, with no children, and you're as fat as a sow. How long am I to put up with such a gross creature in my house? How long am I to go on stuffing you with food? I'll get another wife and you can get out' and so on and on until the final, unforgiveable thing: 'If you don't get out of this house, you'll have to eat your brother's flesh.' No Bondo can tolerate this insult, and

[1] B.J.F. Laubscher, *Sex, Custom and Psychopathology* (London, 1937), p. 308.

[2] Havelock Ellis, *The Sexual Impulse in Women*, p. 1. The police later gave me details of two other Bondo suicides; one was a man, Pandra Dora, who hanged himself to escape the torment of acute pain in the eyes; the other was a woman of about 25 years, Moti Dora, of Pangam who hanged herself on 5 February 1941 because, as the official report says, 'she remained unmatured'.

that night when Hadi was asleep the woman hanged herself above him from the roof.

The same kind of insult led to the death of Hadi Kirsani's wife at Gokurupada a year or two later. This wife was about twenty-eight years old and the mother of three sons. She was not fat, but Hadi thought, rightly or wrongly, that she was lazy. One day the whole family came in late and weary after a long day's sowing in the forest clearing. Tempers were strained and Hadi abused the mother of his children. 'You never work properly,' he shouted. 'You spend all day just sitting on your arse. If you're not careful I'll kick you up the - - -.' He seems to have gone on for a long time, as aboriginals in a temper will, and then he too said the unforgiveable thing. 'If you don't go away, you'll have to eat the flesh of your own sons. I'm going to get another wife.'

The woman went weeping to the little hut in their field and brought a long creeper from the neighbouring forest. She tied it to a beam of the hut and hanged herself. Hadi followed her and cut her down, but he was too late; his attempts to revive her were of no avail. The police were summoned as usual in such cases, and Hadi told me how the Sub-Inspector threatened to arrest him on a charge of murder. But he sold his two bullocks and gave the policeman twenty-five rupees and so got the case registered as one of suicide.

In two cases suicide followed a quarrel with a daughter-in-law. Dengarupa, Kirsani's mother, a woman of about forty-five years, was always at loggerheads with his wife. After a time Dengarupa wearied of the constant friction in the house and gave his mother a good beating and told her to get out. The old woman was given no food for two days, but she refused to go; at last, when the others were asleep, she hanged herself in the house. When Dengarupa and his wife awoke they saw her body hanging above them.

Kurri Mundli of Mundlipada, a man of fifty-five or more, hanged himself after similar disagreements with a young woman. Kurri suffered from a peculiarity unusual among the flesh-loving aboriginals — he could not bear the taste of fish or meat. His wife used to adjust the cuisine accordingly, but she died, and Kurri was left to the care of the wife of his only son who lived with him. This girl seems to have conceived the notion that if she could make her father-in-law, who was probably a very tiresome old man, thoroughly uncomfortable, he would go somewhere else and they would have the house to themselves. So she started putting little bits of meat or fish, the claws of crabs, scraps of skin and gravy, into his gruel, thus making it intolerable. The poor old man would taste it and, finding it uneatable, put it in a corner of the inner room. For nearly three weeks, I was told, the pile of wasted food accummulated. Kurri got hungrier and hungrier and more and more annoyed, until at last he could stand it no longer and hanged himself above the heap of food which he could not bear to eat.

My last case was a recent one and I was able to get fuller details. It is the pathetic story of a girl who could not make up her mind, and whose vacillation created such entanglements that she hanged herself, on 6 May 1944, at Dumiripada, her birth-place and her parents' home.

Her name was Budhai and a year previously she had been married to a handsome young fellow called Sobha Sisa who hailed from Antamguda, a small village about two miles distant across the hills, whence the unmarried boys paid frequent visits to the Dumiripada dormitory. After the usual delays, Sobha took his wife to his house, and all went well until the day before the Giag Festival was due to begin; then they quarrelled. Sobha beat the girl and she ran away, not to her home, but to Mundlipada. She arrived tired and hungry — for it is a long way — only to find that the Giag ceremonies had already begun and she could not be admitted inside the village. The Mundlipada people asked her if she was ready to marry one of their boys and she said she was. 'Then come back when the festival is over,' they said. 'But go away now; if you do, you can marry anyone you like when we have finished.' Budhai then went wearily along for another three miles to Bandiguda, where the Giag had not yet started and stayed there in her mother's brother's house.

When the Giag Festival at Mundlipada came to an end, one Soma Dangra-Manjhi collected a party of youths and they went over to Bandiguda to kidnap the girl. After an exciting struggle in the dormitory, they brought Budhai back to Mundlipada, apparently very much against her will, for she refused Soma's bangles and declared that she would not touch his rice. When she reached the village she said, 'Yes, it is true that I was ready to marry anybody, but now I don't want to'. But Soma forced her to stay in his house, gave her plenty to drink and finally persuaded her to eat some rice in the company of a group of elders. Once Budhai had eaten the rice, she became, of course, for all practical purposes Soma's wife. But in less than a week she slipped out of the house and went back to Sobha at Antamguda.

When Soma discovered this he was very angry. 'Look,' he said. 'I have spent five rupees on this worthless girl and all that's happened is that she's gone back to her first husband.' He called the other youths. 'Come, let's get a pig from Antamguda and have that much consolation.' This is the usual custom when a girl leaves her husband, though the position here was somewhat complicated by the number of husbands there were. Soma and eight or ten youths went off to Antamguda. They had their bows and arrows and they shot the first pig they saw and carried it off. They met with no opposition; the Giag Festival

Plate XXIX

Plate XXX

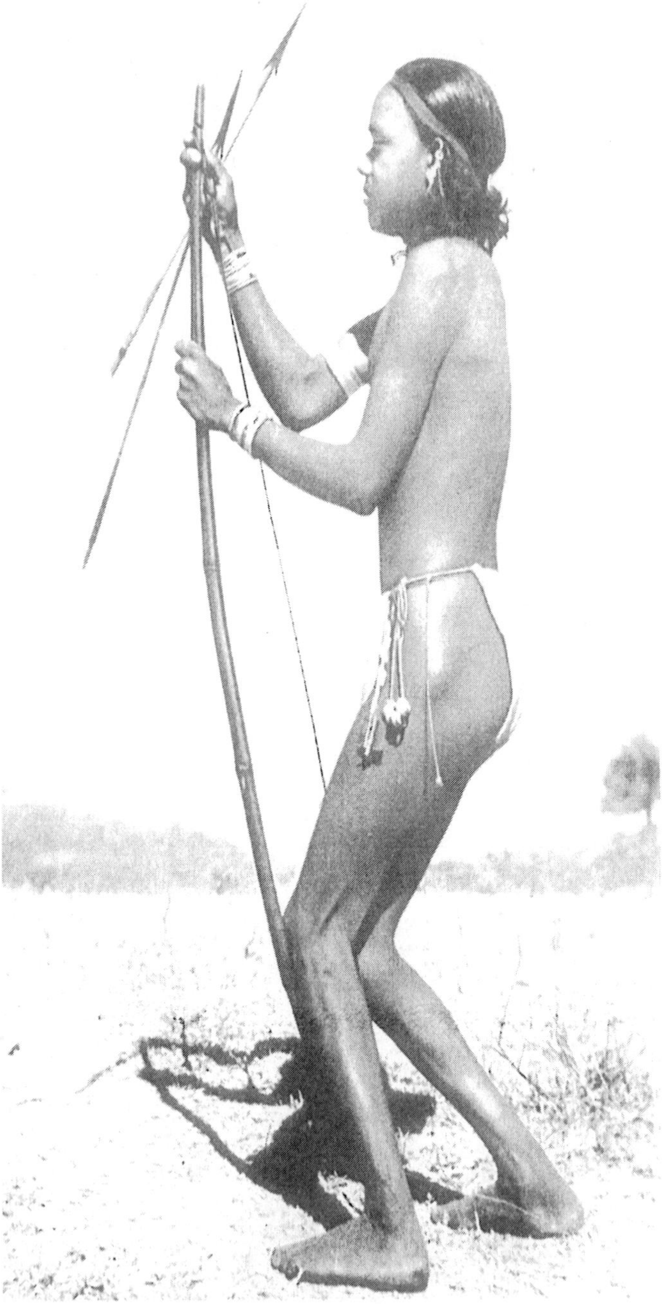

Plate XXXI

Plate XXXII Corner of Bodoballe village

D. V. Sassoon

Plate XXXIII Winnowing at Kadamguda

D. V. Sassoon

Plate XXXIV Ceremony on threshing-floor at Kadamguda described on pp. 49ff.

D. V. Sassoon

Plate XXXV Woman at Andrahal threshing millet with her feet

Scenery at Mundlipada

Plate XXXVI

was still in progress in this village and the men were out hunting; only the women were at home. But Soma and his party broke an important taboo (that no outsider should enter a village during the festival, still less remove anything from it) and this caused general apprehension as well as particular annoyance to the owner of the dead pig.

And not only to him. He went at once to Sobha and said, 'Due to your wife's silly behaviour, I've lost my pig. I don't care what happens to your wife, but I must have compensation for my pig or there'll be trouble.' Sobha was annoyed at this and naturally worked his temper off on poor Budhai who was so remarkably incapable of making up her mind. 'When you've gone and married another man, what do you want to come back and worry me for?' he shouted at her. 'I'm not going to pay for any pig.' Budhai's parents would have to pay, he decided, and off he went to Dumiripada, which he ought not to have done—for not only should no one go in but no one should go out of a village during the Giag Festival—but Sobha and indeed all of them were past caring about *angto* rules at that moment. Sobha went to Budhai's parents and rudely demanded the price of the pig. They refused to give it and there was a noisy and excited quarrel, in which half the village joined.

Sobha came back from Dumiripada in a passion and dragged Budhai out of his house and beat her. She escaped from him and ran away to Dumiripada. The Sisa was in despair. All day people were going out of the village and carrying its prosperity away with them; there would certainly be a wretched crop that year. Budhai went to her brother's house. But she found no sanctuary there. Her brother and his wife abused her and called her own mother in to help. The mother said, 'We've spent a lot of money on you already. Isn't one marriage enough for you? Why do you want to change from man to man and cost us a lot more? Anyway don't come here: we don't want you. Why don't you go back to your new husband?'

Budhai went out feeling that there was no happiness for her anywhere. In the afternoon she told her family that she was going back to Antamguda. But on the way, as she passed the burning-ground, she went off the path and hanged herself above the ashes of the dead in whose chill company she was now to wander.

13. The Unsuccessful Marriage

The number of unsuccessful marriages among the Bondos is appreciably higher than that of other Indian tribes at a similar stage of cultural development. For the Bondos, the separation-rate is 6 per cent; for the Juangs only 2 per cent; for the Murias 2·4 per cent.

The reasons for the breakdown of marriage partnerships are much the same as those discoverable elsewhere. In one case the husband was impotent;[1] in another the wife, according to the Dissari, was the real cause of the family's poverty and the death of her three sons. A common cause is the disparity of age between the partners. Mangla Mundli of Bandapada, for example, said, 'My wife was much older than me and used to go to other men, for how could a young boy satisfy her? One day I caught her at it, but I was not big enough to beat her. She even used to give away my food and liquor to other men.' Panda Dora of the same village said, 'I was too young for my wife, so she ran away. She did her best to force me to it, but I couldn't and at last I fell really ill with the effort. So she left me and married a man in Dattipada. I took a couple of cows from him as compensation.' But in the case of Soma Kirsani of Kurriguda the husband was the elder. 'I was much older than my wife and she did not care for me and ran away. She was always falling in love with young men; one day I caught her and gave her a good beating, so she ran away and married one of her youthful lovers.'

Many excursions in polygamy end in the departure of one of the wives; indeed, in tribal society polygamy is often a confession of matrimonial failure. For example, Lachhim Challan of Kadamguda, who had four wives, turned one of them out because she would not bring wood and water properly, and another because, he said, she was so exacting in her demands upon him that he could never get sufficient sleep. Sonia Sisa of Andrahal had two wives, but the younger used to quarrel with her colleague and sulk with him. Presently she refused to serve him with food when he came in from the sago palm and then stopped cooking altogether and denied him intercourse. Sonia sent her back to her parents with a bullock and a brass dish.

There does not seem to be any formal ceremony of 'divorce'; separation is effected when a woman definitely leaves her husband's house, if he forcibly turns her out, or if she attaches herself to another man. The Bondos have a custom, which I have not observed outside Orissa — though it is common within the province — of penalizing a man who turns his wife out of his house. Such a wife returns to her old home and her father or brother goes to the husband and asks what has happened. 'What was the matter with her? Did she refuse to work? Was there something wrong with her hands and feet?' The husband makes

[1] Impotence seems to be rare among the Bondos; at least I heard little of it. I was told of a youth at Mundlipada who was cured of it by eating the penis of a bear cooked in milk with a long straight root — obvious symbols of erection and semen. It is said that if a man dies while in this condition, his ghost is very restless; if it can meet a pregnant woman it makes its way into her womb and kills the foetus. The symbolism is again clear; impotence, unable to create life, is ever dissatisfied and, jealous of the life it has been unable to make, destroys it.

his complaint and the others tell him to produce his witnesses. 'If she was as bad as that,' they tell him, not believing a word of it, 'you ought to have killed her.' They generally attempt to persuade the man to have the woman back, but if he has made up his mind he says, 'Talk as much as you like; I'm not going to have her'. He gives them a rupee and sends them away.

But now they have a right to shoot a pig. It may be any pig they see. If it is the husband's pig, it does not matter; but if it belongs to someone else there is a loud quarrel and the husband has to pay compensation to the owner. After this, the woman is free. When she remarries, her former husband does not get any part of the bride-price, 'because it was his fault; he himself turned her out'. The price is paid to the parents instead. But if a woman elopes of her own free will, the husband can claim heavy compensation from his supplanter. When a widow remarries, the bride-price is paid to the deceased husband's elder brother; a son cannot claim it.

Disputes about the economic consequences of marital separation are often complicated and sometimes end in tragedy. A disaster of this kind occurred in Mundlipada in 1941. A girl called Sunki was married to one Lachhmi Mundli and he paid a bride-price of two cows and a rupee for her. In 1940 Lachhmi was drowned and the widow was married by an elder brother, Budha Mundli. But after a time Sunki got tired of Budha and went back to her father's house. The question of compensation was raised by Budha's elder brother, Hadi Mundli. He insisted that, since Sunki had now left the family circle, the original bride-price paid by Lachhmi should be returned. But the other party argued that this would not be fair, for the girl had not eloped with some other man, but had simply gone back to her own father. If she married yet again, the matter could be reconsidered. This seems fair enough, but Hadi would not have it; there was a row, a scuffle and in a burst of rage Hadi ended the discussion by killing one of Sunki's cousins.

CHAPTER SIX

MAN AND THE IMMORTALS

1. The Character of Bondo Religion

Bondo religion today presents a pattern familiar to all students of the tribal faiths of peninsular India, a symbiosis of very old indigenous beliefs and practices with the traditions of modern sub-Puranic village Hinduism. A Supreme Being, with a Sanskrit name, equated with the Sun, of limited power and somewhat ambiguous character, has below him (but not subject to his control) a number of departmental and local demigods presiding over stream and forest, village and home. The unseen world is still further populated by demons or furies and the uneasy ghosts of the recently dead, who make their presence known by ruining the crops, sending wild animals to harry the cattle, and affecting the living with disease. The Bondos deal with these tiresome intruders on their otherwise happy and fairly prosperous existence through shamans who detect the cause of any trouble and priests who conduct the prescribed ritual. The demigods are located in stones and trees; a few shrines, usually of stone, are made; but the most important megalithic monument, sacred to Mother Earth, is the *sindibor,* the stone platform where much important civic and religious business is concluded. Feasts and holidays, often with the serious purpose of improving the fertility of the crops, diversify the somewhat monotonous routine of the agricultural year: their most obvious features are a stress on various taboos, a ritual hunt, the ritual brewing of beer, the partaking of sacramental food, and the consecration of seed.

There is little evidence of any kind of gratitude or love for the gods, but I would hesitate to describe Bondo religion as one of fear: it is rather a religion of the battlefield, in which the fortunes of war swing to and fro. Man suffers many casualties, economic and psychological, yet on the whole the Bondos feel, I think, that they are on top of the situation; their apparatus of appeasement is enough for all ordinary occasions, and they have a well-trained force of priests and shamans to deal with the malice of sorcerers and the territorial ambitions of the supernatural world.

Bondo ceremonial is of the ordinary type, expressing a mixture of supplicatory and purely magical ideas. Altars with witch-baffling decorations, temporary booths, a great pother with leaf-cups, plates and little bundles, grass dolls and wooden carts to carry away disease, the casting of rice to the four quarters of the globe, offerings at hearth and threshold, protective gestures of waving and sprinkling, taboos on looking back, going in or out, speaking to strangers — these are the common materials of religion and magic all over tribal and near-Hindu India.

The megalithic elements in Bondo culture compare with those of the Gadabas, Jhorias, Parengas and Didayis, but although there are points of contact with Saora funerary customs, the general atmosphere of Saora religion is strikingly different. Its absorbed interest in the other world, its priestesses with their spiritual husbands, its hosts of disease demons, its scores of demigods, its pictographs, shrines and images, are features alien to the more practical and commonplace Bondo mind. So also from other not too distant neighbours, the Marias and Murias of Bastar, where again ideas and practice about funerary memorials largely coincide, there is a great difference in the general spirit of religion. Bondo festivals, for example, are elaborate and interminable, but they lack the colour, dignity and excitement of the splendid public displays of Maria and Muria ceremonial dancing.

If men make gods in their own image, a study of Bondo theology will throw some light on the Bondo character; we shall learn much from a survey of the strange personality of Mahaprabhu, the equalitarian position of the priests, the heroic battle against ghosts and furies, the relation of ethics and religion. To such a study we must now turn.

2. The President of the Immortals

The Supreme Being, or President of the Immortals as he may not inaptly be described, is usually called Mahaprabhu by the Bondos. This word, which, in varying forms, is common in east and central India, is of purely Sanskrit derivation and means 'great master'. In Sanskrit it may be used of any mighty lord, human or divine. Its use throughout Orissa is probably due to the fact that Chaitanya, the founder of the Bengal school of Vaishnavite Hinduism,[1] was known as *the* Mahaprabhu. After he settled in Puri, where he was later identified with Jagannath himself and called a living, peripatetic Jagannath, the title was also attached to the latter deity. Puri is the key which unlocks many of Orissa's secrets, and I have little doubt that the word Mahaprabhu spread from the great pilgrim centre even to the Bondo hills. As a term of

[1] A recent account is by S. K. De, *Early History of the Vaisnava Faith and Movement in Bengal* (Calcutta, 1942).

address, the Bondo applies it to any demigod, demon or human being whom he wants to please; a Bondo priest will in one breath invoke the sacred sword Pat Khanda and flatter a constable with the same word, Mahaprabhu. But as a descriptive term, its use seems to be confined to the Supreme Being, and in this sense it is frequently used with no further modification or descriptive epithet. The Marias and Murias of Bastar State use the title in the same way; in their legends it is sufficient to speak of Mahapurub as doing this or that; there is no doubt as to whom is meant; it is the Creator, the first and greatest of gods.

FIG. 32. Representation of the sun on the door of a house at Goyiguda

But the Bondos, unlike the Marias and other tribes of middle and western India, appear to identify the Creator with the Sun. Mahaprabhu's proper name is Singi-Arke, or Sih-Arke, and Singi or Sih is the Remo word for Sun. *Arke* in Remo means 'moon' or 'month', but in Gadaba it means 'star',[1] while *arka* in later Puranic Sanskrit (it is not a vedic word) is the 'sun'. So also in Hindi, *arkdin* is a solar day, or Sunday; *arkvarsh*, a solar year; *arkmandal*, the sun's disc; *arkopal*, a sunstone or crystal lens. In Orissa the famous temple at Konarka represents the chariot of the sun. We shall see presently that there are grounds for doubting whether the Bondos direct equal reverence to the sun and moon, and I suggest that it is possible that the *arke* in the compound Singi-Arke is not the Remo word at all, but the Sanskrit *arka*, and is a sort of 'echo-word' to strengthen the sense.

The use of such compounds containing 'Sing' is common among the tribes speaking the languages of the Munda family, for *singi* is the Mundari word for 'sun' or 'day'. Thus the Mundas regard Sing-Bonga as the Creator; [2] the Santals describe him as Sing-Chando or Thakur; [3] the Hos say Sing-Bonga,[4] so do the Birhors,[5] the Barae blacksmiths,[6] the Asurs,[7] and doubtless other tribes and castes. In each case there seems to be some degree of identification of Sing-Bonga

[1] Our records of the Gadaba vocabulary are greatly confused: Grierson gives *arke* as meaning 'moon' in Gadaba.
[2] S. C. Roy, *The Mundas and their Country* (Calcutta, 1912), p. 470.
[3] C. H. Bompas, *Folklore of the Santal Parganas* (London, 1909), p. 402.
[4] D. N. Majumdar, *A Tribe in Transition* (London, 1937), p. 135.
[5] S. C. Roy, *The Birhors* (Ranchi, 1925), p. 297.
[6] J. Hoffmann and A. van Emelen, *Encyclopedia Mundarica*, Vol. II, p. 416.
[7] M. G. Hallett, *Ranchi District Gazetteer* (Patna, 1918).

with the Sun, though this is often obscured in the course of mythological narratives.

The Uraons, however, use the word Dharmes; 'the older name,' says Roy, 'still sometimes used, is Biri-Belas or the "Sun-Lord", and the sun is still sometimes referred to as the visible symbol, if not the actual representation, of Dharmes'.[1] Throughout western Bengal, the cult of Dharma Thakar, who is identified with Vishnu and the Sun, is maintained by the Doms, who may have carried it south to the Bondo country, for the Bondos also refer to Mahaprabhu as Dharam-Deota, particularly in the oft-repeated formula: 'Below is Bismotin (the earth); above is Dharam Deota.' The expression is obviously Hindu and has reference to the 'righteous' (*dharmi*) character of the Supreme Creator.[2] His righteousness is proved by the fact that he may give a man leprosy for not offering sacrifices properly.

Another identification is that of the sun and moon with Ramai-Bhimai, of whom I shall have more to say later on. Ramai-Bhimai, or sometimes Bhimai alone, performs some of the functions of the Creator, especially with regard to rain and harvest.

Mahaprabhu therefore is Singi-Arke or Ramai-Bhimai, the Sun-Moon, or simply the Sun, a 'righteous' Creator (Dharam Deota), President of the Immortals—the demigods, demons, furies and ancestral spirits—over whom he rules. '*Uribalog ursi buribalog bursi*,' say the Bondos. 'When the riser rises, the setter sets; the dying die, those to be born are born,' and they salute the Sun, 'You rise to give us light and set to give us darkness'. Mahaprabhu created the world, mankind and the gods and demons, and also—with curious inconsistency—the sun and the moon. He determines when men should die and in what form they are to be reborn. But the Bondos visualize him far more anthropomorphically than they do the lesser demigods; in the legends he assumes the aspect of a regular cult-hero like Nanga Baiga or Lingo, and often behaves in all too human fashion. Let us now consider some of these legends.

The Bondos have an unusually large variety of creation stories; in common with most Indian tribes they recall an original world which was submerged by a great flood and describe how it was re-created. One such story comes from Katamguda.

A Raja had a son and daughter and the two were always playing together. One day the girl got a gourd seed and threw it away on a rubbish heap. It grew and a great flower came from it and a mighty

[1] S. C. Roy, *Oraon Religion and Customs* (Ranchi, 1928), p. 19.

[2] A connexion of the Sun God with leprosy is widely found. The Saora Yuyungboi (Sun God) affects with leprosy those who offend him. The Dom devotees of Dharma Thakur make offerings to him for its cure. The first Sun Temple at Konarka was traditionally founded by Samba, son of Krishna, in gratitude to the Sun for healing him of the disease.

gourd. The boy made a hole in the gourd and hollowed it out. He said, 'If ever it rains too much, we can hide in the gourd'. One day the rain poured down and the brother and sister went to play in the shelter of the gourd. Several days passed but the rain did not stop and the whole world was flooded with water. The gourd floated on the surface and presently the children grew hungry and began to cry. Mahaprabhu heard them and came to ask what was the matter. He sent for the wild boar[1] and it went down to the Under World and stole earth from Kermo. With the earth it stole seven kinds of trees — mango, tamarind, mahua, sago palm, dumar, pipal and banyan.

The boar smeared the stolen earth over its body and dipped itself in the water. It came out and shook itself, making the earth fly all over the ocean. In this way the new earth was made. Some of the boar's hairs came out and turned into grass. The seeds of the seven trees were also scattered across the world and from them came the jungle.

Then Mahaprabhu took the brother and sister out of the gourd and changed their appearance by smallpox so that they did not know each other. They married and mankind has come of it.

This story of the boar is common among the Bison-horn Marias who live not very far away across the Malkangiri plain, in Bastar State. In Bastar also, and indeed all over Orissa, is known the motif of the brother and sister who are enabled to marry each other by an attack of smallpox which makes them mutually unrecognizable. The next story has affinities with a legend current among the Konds.[2]

Kidramati Rani, the squirrel, said to her son one day, 'On Sunday it will thunder; on Monday there will be rain; on Tuesday the world will be flooded. Eat all you can today, for it will have to last a long while.' Kotramati Rani, the barking-deer, heard what the squirrel said. She was pregnant. A Bondo was sitting by a stream. The deer saw him and was afraid to go to the water to drink. But the creature in her womb said, 'Go for water; if he kills you your life will depart and that will be good. For if you live, in two days you will drown.' The Bondo heard the voice and promised not to shoot the deer if she told him who was in her belly. Then from the belly came a voice: 'I am Mahaprabhu and I have come to warn you. Take your children into a gourd with food and every kind of grain.' The Bondo went back to his village and said, 'In two days the world will sink down below the waters. Let him with two wives give one of them to him who has none. Let us enjoy ourselves while we can.' He put his children in a gourd. Then the rain fell and the world sank below the water.

Mahaprabhu wondered if any men were left. He made a crow from the dirt of his body and it said, 'How am I to fly? Where shall I sit

[1] This is a curious variant on the classical Hindu tradition. 'In the Taittiriya Samhita and Taittiriya Brahmana this animal [the boar] appears in a cosmogonic character as the form assumed by the Creator Prajapati when he raised the earth out of the waters. A later development of it is the boar incarnation of Vishnu.'—A. A. Macdonell, *Vedic Mythology* (Strassburg, 1897), p. 151. The spelling of the Sanskrit words has been simplified.

[2] See my *Myths of Middle India*, p. 41.

Girl building a wall at Andrahal

Plate XXXVII

Plate XXXVIII Girl feeds the pigs at Bodoballe

Plate XXXIX Sukro Kirsani and Semang Mundli at work on a house at Tulaguram

Plate XL Bondo fetching sap from a sago-palm

Plate XLI

Plate XLII Typical scene of forest clearing prepared by axe and fire for cultivation

XLIV Girls carrying their fish-traps to the stream at Tulaguram

to rest ?' Mahaprabhu made a bombax tree and threw it onto the water for the crow to perch on. But the crow could do nothing. Mahaprabhu himself broke open the belly of the crab, but there was no earth there. Then he caught a worm and found some earth. The gourd settled upon it; brother and sister came out. After a time Mahaprabhu gave them smallpox and separated them. When they met again they did not know each other and became man and wife. Bhimai gave them pills to excite them and taught them how to copulate. He gave the girl medicine to make her menstruate and by and by children were born and the number of human beings greatly increased.

The crow and earthworm motif is distributed all over tribal India; it occurs in greater detail in another Bondo legend, which shows Mahaprabhu sowing the earth, brought by the crow, over the ocean as if it was a field. In this story, Mahaprabhu gives the girl a squint and makes her brother a leper — a rather drastic method of instituting human marriage.

A Pinnajangar story emphasizes the part played by the blacksmiths.

The world sank down and water covered it, destroying men, animals, the hills and jungle. Mahaprabhu was living in a golden palace in the sky. He wondered how to remake the world, but he had no means of drying up the water. He made Bhui from the dirt of his body and said to him, 'Go to the Under World and suck the water down'. He lowered a silken thread from the sky and Bhui slid down to the Under World. He sniffed the water up his nose till the earth appeared again. But it would not dry — there was nothing but mud. Mahaprabhu had a little body-dirt left and with this he made a Kommar blacksmith and gave him tools — hammer, tongs and bellows — and sent him down to Samudra Hill to make the earth steady. The Kommar built his shop; he heated the whole hill and beat it with his hammer. The earth was frightened that everything would be heated and beaten, so she dried herself in a hurry and became as before. Then the Kommars made iron pillars and spread the sky upon them. Wherever the earth was unsteady, they threw lumps of ore and made it strong.

It will be noticed that in this tale the method of recreating the world is different. In the other versions Mahaprabhu makes a new world by scattering earth on the face of the ocean; here the old world is salvaged from beneath the water.

Yet another creation motif is found in a legend from Bodapada. Here the transformation of a human body into the world is in the ancient Sanskrit tradition of the Purusha who is changed into the material universe. The Juangs and Marias also have legends of this type. Here we are not concerned with the re-fashioning of the world; we begin from the beginning, with a new world.

There was no world. Mahaprabhu stood up and spat. A tortoise swallowed the spittle and conceived.[1] Its belly swelled and swelled, but the child could not be born — for there was no way by which it could come out. Mahaprabhu came to see what was the matter. The tortoise was so big-bellied that it could not walk. When Mahaprabhu heard its story, he took a knife and cut a hole in its back parts and a girl was born.

When the child grew up she asked the tortoise where her father was. The tortoise said, 'Go to Mahaprabhu; you were born of his spittle'. The girl went to Mahaprabhu and said to him, 'You are my father'. 'How can I be?' asked Mahaprabhu. 'You are of a tortoise's belly.' But he let her stay with him. After a few days the girl said to her father, 'Lie with me'. She caught hold of him to force him to it, but Mahaprabhu killed her with his knife. Her blood fell and the earth was formed by it. From her left eye came the moon, from the right eye the sun; her bones turned into hills, her hair into grass and trees. Mahaprabhu cut open her belly and two children, a boy and a girl, came out. The two lay together and mankind was born.

In this legend we get our first hint of a tradition that Mahaprabhu was older than the sun and moon and that it was by his agency that they came into being. An elaborate version of a tale known all over tribal India emphasizes this point.

After the earth had been created it lay in darkness, though there were sometimes flashes and gleams of light. For the Sun and Moon were man and wife, and the Moon was so beautiful that the Sun would not leave her for a single hour, but was always in the house, fondling her and lying with her. It was only when he went outside to relieve himself that the world got a little light. The Sun was so powerful that every time he copulated a child was born. He did not like girls and threw away the girl babies, but the mother loved them and picked them up again. When the children grew up a little, the boys used to chase the girls and take them by force. The girls wept; the Moon complained to her husband, and there was a quarrel. For the Sun regarded the boys as his and the girls as the Moon's.

One day Mahaprabhu thought in his mind, 'This is all wrong. The Sun never leaves the house to do his work. He spends all his time copulating and soon there'll be so many children that there'll be no room for anyone else in the world. And this darkness is very bad for people; they'll soon be dying of it.' So Mahaprabhu caused a great famine and even the Sun and Moon could not get any food. Presently the Sun got so hungry that he even forgot to copulate and went out to find something to eat. The Moon at last was left alone. Mahaprabhu went to her and said, 'Those boys of your husband's are great rascals; they are planning to kill your sweet daughters'. The Moon said, 'What can I do?' Mahaprabhu gave her a bel fruit and told her what to do. When the Sun came home, he found his wife's mouth reddened with the fruit — she had hidden her daughters in the knot of her hair — and he asked her what she was doing. 'I was so hungry' she said, 'that I've eaten my daughters; you had better eat your sons.' The Sun had not

[1] For some account of the magical power of spittle, see my *Folk-Tales of Mahakoshal*, pp. 365 f.

been able to get any food, so he called his sons and ate them one by one till all were finished. Now his hunger was appeased and he wanted to copulate as usual. But the Moon said, 'First let me take these children out of my hair', and there were her daughters alive and well. But the sons were dead. The Sun was furious at this and broke the Moon's head open. She ran terrified from the house and hid in Mahaprabhu's lap. The Sun came to find her but Mahaprabhu cursed them both: 'You two will never meet again. Go now and do your work and give light to the world.'[1]

Bondo legends about the eclipse similarly suggest that Mahaprabhu is distinct from the sun and moon.

At first men did not eat grain, but only leaves and fruit. Seed was in the sky. One day the Sun and Moon went to get some and as they were carrying it home, it began to rain; they slipped in the mud and the seed fell down with the rain onto the earth.

A Bondo and his wife saw it. 'What is this?', they asked. They took it to Mahaprabhu. He taught them to cut the forest, burn the branches and sow the seed in the ashes. When the grain was ready Mahaprabhu's wife showed the Bondo woman how to husk and cook it, and made a pestle and fan for her. But the Sun and Moon were in difficulty. Their grain had fallen down from the sky and they could not repay the merchant from whom they had taken it. And now whenever he comes to their house to recover his debt, his shadow falls on the Sun or Moon and there is an eclipse.

There are many versions of this legend. Sometimes it is Mahaprabhu himself who takes the loan, and Sun and Moon are his sureties. Sometimes the creditor is not a merchant, but a bear, a caterpillar or a scorpion.

There was a great famine and seeing the world dying Mahaprabhu went to the bear and caterpillar, who had a store of grain and took a loan, giving the Sun and Moon as his sureties. Every now and then the bear or caterpillar come to demand repayment; their shadow is an eclipse.

A total eclipse is a 'Bear Eclipse';[2] a partial one is caused by the scorpion or caterpillar.

But all these stories are obvious borrowings and it is evident that they have been adopted unaltered; there has been no attempt to relate

[1] For an account of similar tales in other tribal cultures see my *Myths of Middle India*, pp. 51ff.

[2] A bear eclipse is lucky; it means good crops and many children; a scorpion eclipse, however, is a warning of smallpox. A pregnant woman should be careful to keep indoors or her child may be born with a hare-lip. After an eclipse, the first woman to go for water in the early morning should take a lighted brand and throw it into the water, to frighten away the bear's shadow which may be in the water. 'If we drink shadowed water, we will have a famine.' Fowls are often offered before grain-bins to prevent the eclipse removing the grain under the impression that it belongs to Mahaprabhu. Where they have Dom neighbours the Bondos imitate them by beating drums and gongs.

them with the main conceptions of Bondo mythology. Other sun and moon stories have nothing to say about a separate or earlier Mahaprabhu. For example, these earlier legends explain the eclipse:

The Moon, the Scorpion and the Bear were cooking, each at his own hearth, under a tree. When the food was ready, they picked leaves for cups, but the Moon had no bamboo pins for hers and had to borrow some from the Bear. Next time, again she had no pins and now she took some from the Scorpion. By and by the Bear demanded its pins back, but the Moon hadn't any and the Bear seized her and she turned black. Then the Scorpion seized her and she turned red.

I will give some other stories about the sun and moon, which seem to me to belong to an older and more original stratum of legend.

The Sun was wandering on earth in the form of a black bull. It came to a threshing-floor at Kichhipoda. Three or four people were threshing millet; they saw the bull and caught it and tied it up. That night the Kichhipoda boys visited the girls' dormitory at Mundlipada. They played with the girls till they wearied but the morning never came. One of the girls gave a boy a mushroom and he tied it in his cloth. When they saw that the dawn would not come, the boys returned home in the dark. They reached the place where the bull was tethered, and the mushroom jumped out of the boy's cloth and fell to the ground as an egg. The egg broke and a cock came out crowing. When the cock crowed the bull jumped into the air, breaking the cord that held it, and the dawn came. All over the world birds broke from mushrooms as from eggs and sang to the dawn. Ever since the sun has risen at the voice of the cock. It raises its arms as it comes up from bathing in the eastern sea.

In another story the identification of Mahaprabhu and the sun is evident.

Men used to have wings, great wings like a vulture's and flew in the air. One day a man flew up to Mahaprabhu and said, 'As you got a wife for yourself, so get one for me'. Mahaprabhu gave him a girl and said, 'Take her away and marry her'. 'No,' said the man. 'You marry her and give me your wife[1] instead.' Mahaprabhu was very angry at this and cut off the man's wings and cursed him: 'As you go home you'll die by the roadside and turn into a cock, and every morning when I bathe a little water will fall in your ear and you'll have to get

[1] Mahaprabhu's wife is not, as we might expect, Bursung or Mother Earth but, where she is not left anonymous, is often named Sita Mahalakshmi. Sita is the sacred grain, the cow that gives prosperity; she gives birth to every kind of seed and the 'red love-charm' tobacco. She gives the milk of her breasts to every virtuous soul who goes to her after death. 'The idea of Sita as a goddess of agriculture is very ancient and possibly reaches far back into the Vedic period. She is invoked to bless the land in a hymn of the Rigveda (iv. 57. 6); the Grihya-Sutras have preserved for us prayer-like formulae, in which she is personified as "lotus-crowned, radiant in every limb....black-eyed" (Kausika-Sutra, 106). The idea that Sita comes out of the earth and that Mother Earth receives her back again recalls one of the most ancient themes of folklore.'—Private communication from Mr Saurindranath Roy.

up and crow.' Ever since, when it is time for Mahaprabhu to rise into the air from his ocean bath, the cock crows.

In a Tulaguram version of the creation legend, it is the boar, not Mahaprabhu, which made the sun and moon.

At first there was nothing but water. A boar lived in it. It brought earth up on its tusks and scattered it over the water and the world was formed. Then the boar went up into the sky, but it got nothing there It came down and made the Sun and Moon by cutting branches of the sago palm into bits and throwing them up into the air. It threw the sago pith up and it turned into the stars.

An interesting variant of the story, of which the protagonists are usually either Pat Khanda Mahaprabhu or Sita and Lakshman, comes from Goyiguda.

The Sun and Moon were brother and sister. At first they lived under the water. The Sun's name was Tunku. Sun and Moon came to the surface of the water and made the earth and lived upon it. One day when the Moon was husking millet, the Sun took his bow and arrow to the forest to hunt. It was hot and the Moon removed her cloth and was husking naked. The Sun saw her and shot an arrow at her to warn her of his coming. The Moon saw him coming and said to herself, 'My brother has seen my whole body; can I ever look him in the face again ?' The Sun too thought, 'I have seen my sister's body; we cannot live together any longer '. So they separated and now never appear at the same time.

Here the identification of Mahaprabhu the Creator with Singi-Arke is complete. So far as I know, this particular legend is peculiar to the Bondos (even though among them it takes several different forms) and it may represent the old original theory of the beginning of things.

But what of Ramai-Bhimai, or rather Bhimai as he is often called? Bhimai (Bhima, Bhimul, Bhimsen) is worshipped all over Middle India as a rain-god,[1] but I do not know of any other tribe which associates him with the Sun or the Supreme Being. But the identification here seems to be evident. Bhimai is a sky-god, so is the sun; he is associated with fertility and seed, as the sun is; he witnesses the affairs of men just as the sun does.

Bhimai sleeps in the sky. When he gets up and washes, it rains; when he puts on his cloth, it is cold; when he goes naked, it is hot.

This can only refer to the sun. Why should the wearing of clothes by a mere Rain-God make it cold ? Obviously it is the shrouded deity who is cold, the naked sun who gives heat to the world.

[1] See my *The Muria and their Ghotul*, p. 184.

Bhimai watches from the sky. When he sees it is time for it, he gives the Sisa a dream saying, 'Now observe the Sume Gelirak, now perform the Giag'. When he fires his gun it thunders.

Here Bhimai is the witness, and to watch mankind is one of Mahaprabhu's most important functions, as we shall see. In another story the creation of the *Bassia latifolia* tree and discovery of ardent spirits is attributed to him — the greatest compliment that can be paid to a tribal hero. One might indeed make a sort of Honours List of immortal beings to whom the credit for this achievement has been ascribed. Nanga Baiga would be there, so would Lingo and the Bondo Mahaprabhu. The Santal Marang Buru, the Kol Singbonga, the Bhuiya Boram Burha and the Muria Tallur Muttai are among those who invented rice-beer.

Bhimai got a lot of sweat from his armpit. He wiped it off and dirt came with it. He threw away the dirt and the *Bassia latifolia* tree was born. We call spirits the 'sweat of Bhimai' and the 'leavings' of the pressed corollae his 'dirt'.

The association of Bhimai with grain is important. Like Mahaprabhu, Bhimai is a cutter-off of wings.

In the old days, rice had wings and could fly about. Once it said to men, 'I'm going to eat you'. They said, 'Eat us if you will. But first let us count how many names we have. How many have you got?' Rice told its names; there were many of them.[1] Men told their names, and found they had one more. Then rice was afraid; it thought, 'I am weaker than men; they will devour me'. But the millets said, 'Don't be afraid; we'll help you'. But all the same rice decided to run away. Bhimai told it not to go, but it took no notice. He drew his sword and cut off its wings. Since then men have eaten rice.

Another legend describes how heavy rains rotted the grain throughout the world, and Mahaprabhu had to consider how to send seed to mankind. He tore off a bit of his loin-cloth and made a peacock, and persuaded it to take his brother Bhimai down to earth. He put the seed on the head of Bhimai, who went down and gave it to mankind. The wind carried him back into the sky.

Like Mahaprabhu, Bhimai is of dubious character. He appears as the seducer of Jalkamni, mother of countless frogs. He stole some of them and put them in his tank which was empty of water. He persuaded his lover to throw water from the sea into his tank; the water came down as rain, and thus by his seductive influence (in the classical tradition Bhimsen was the most successful lover of the five Pandavas) rain and frogs came to the world.

[1] Samples of three hundred different varieties of rice have been collected in the Koraput District.—Bell, op. cit., p. 108. In Bengali folklore, Siva is the god of agriculture and Bhima is his attendant.

In these last stories the general tradition of Bhimai as a rain-god has obviously had its influence. But I think it is fairly clear that to the Bondo mind the real place of Bhimai is with Singi-Arke and Mahaprabhu as a solar deity, creative, fertilizing, supreme.

I have already said that in some ways Mahaprabhu is more like a tribal hero than a Supreme Being. We see him wandering in his fields, making and using a plough, living in a pit, digging for roots, fashioning a bow and arrows, getting drunk. He is married and afraid of his wife. He has an intrigue with a beautiful woman, murders her husband and finally kills her too. Coarse in language, rough with animals — he knocks out a cow's teeth and twists a dog's tail — he is a typical Bondo peasant. But he is a Bondo not only in his faults. He is kindly and affectionate, intensely interested in the world he has made and constantly interfering in its affairs.

For the world that Mahaprabhu created was at first a singularly imperfect one; it lacked the solace of beer, its inhabitants had no idea of the pleasures of sex, there was very little to eat. There was no rice, no tobacco, no fish; such useful trees as the mango and tamarind were unknown; cows ate men and had not yet begun to be eaten by them; there was no money, no law and order. Mahaprabhu set himself to remedy these defects. He made mango and tamarind trees, and lied to birds to divert their attention from the fruit, thereby preserving it for mankind. He changed the cow's anthrophagous habits, made it dumb so that it could no longer quarrel with the pig, and instituted the custom of eating beef. He (like Bhimai) discovered ardent spirits and taught their use to mankind. He planted tobacco and taught men how to smoke. He instructed men and women in the art of copulation.

Mahaprabhu also taught the different tribes and castes their various crafts, how to weave, to make pots, to distil liquor and to cultivate; he got seed for them; he created the earthworm to make the earth porous; he taught men how to hunt and made the spider that from its web the fishermen might learn how to weave a net. He even tried to ration men and sent the bullock to tell them to eat only once a day. Fortunately it forgot the message and told them to eat twice.

Mahaprabhu also put the gods in their proper places, fixed the routine and expense of religious obligation, and established the social order. He divided men into castes, and set Rajas and the police to rule over them. He invented money and had two hundred rupees presented to every household.

At no time is Mahaprabhu represented as able to create anything *ex nihilo*. He has to tear a bit off his loin-cloth to make a peacock; a necklace from his wife's throat is needed to make an earthworm; he uses the thread round his own neck to create a snake. His method of manufacturing a scorpion is instructive. 'Mahaprabhu went to a river and caught a young crab. Down its backside as far as the belly he pushed a bit of irritating bark to make a sort of tail. He caught and killed five snakes and removed the fangs and poison. He put four of the fangs in the crab's belly and one in its tail. Then he put it under a stone and said to it, 'If anyone sits here, bite him and it will really hurt, for the poison of five snakes is in you'.

Mahaprabhu, then, is the President of the Immortals, but he is not omnipotent, nor omniscient. He has to enlist the aid of a crow to bring him information about the survival of mankind after the flood, and of a boar to assist him in the re-creation of the world. When men beg him for grain, he cannot bestow it upon them by a mere exercise of his will; he has to go and find it and gets into difficulties with a moneylender. He cannot introduce death into the world save by a rather mean trick and can only induce the sun to shine by a thoroughly murderous one.[1]

Yet such ambiguity of character and limitation of power does not alter the Bondos' regard for this deity as the supreme lord of the world. None of the demigods or demons can compare with him. In his hands are the issues of life and death; he is the witness of sin and virtue; oaths can be taken on his name; he can be invoked to punish an enemy and called to help in sickness or danger.

Mahaprabhu is not entirely benevolent. I have heard him called 'the trouble-giver'; Singi-Arke may give high fever and has been known to make a child cry itself into convulsions. Children should not be allowed to lie on their backs gazing at the sky, for this tempts the sun to attack them and he must then be propitiated with the sacrifice of a white hen on a path running east out of the village. Offerings are regularly made to Singi-Arke and Bhimai to ensure their benevolence. This is unusual. The Supreme Being in tribal India is commonly regarded as neutral, and it is not considered necessary to offer him sacrifice.

But on the whole, Mahaprabhu is kindly and benevolent, a homely god whom one is glad to have about, every sacred inch a Bondo. He may be well honoured in some words with which Thomas Hardy once described the sun.

> The Sun, on account of the mist, had a curious sentient, personal look, demanding the masculine pronoun for its adequate expression. His present aspect explained the old time heliolatries in a moment. One could feel that a saner religion had never prevailed under the sky. The luminary was a golden-haired, beaming, mild-eyed, God-like creature, gazing down in the vigour and intentness of youth upon an earth that was brimming with interest for him.[2]

[1] I have recorded over seventy of the Bondo legends. Some are given in this book; the rest will be printed in full in my forthcoming *Tribal Myths of Orissa*.

[2] *Tess of the D'Urbervilles.*

Plate XLV Bondo youths fishing in the stream near Tulaguram

Sukro Mundli of Mundlipada bathing before the Susu Festival

Plate XLVI

Young wife assists her husband in a bath at Tulaguram

Plate XLVII Two girls, Sonki and Mangli, throwing away cowdung at Bodoballe

Plate XLVIII Bondos preparing rice-fields near Basupada

Somwari of Andrahal brings *kereng* branches from the forest

Plate XLIX

Budhai Bodnaik of Bodoballe prepares *kereng* fibre

Plate L

A Dom woman sells coloured mill-yarn to a group of Bondos at Bodoballe

Plate LI The Sisa of Pinnajangar extracting *kereng* fibre, work generally done by women

Plate LII Bondo ploughing near Basupada

3. The Sword in the Banyan

High in a great banyan at the centre of the grove above Mundlipada an ancient sword is hidden, and three times in the year—at Dassera, at the full moon of Magh and during the Giag-gige, it is brought down and worshipped. It is evidently a royal sword, for its cultus is subsidized by the Maharaja of Jeypore and its name, Pat Khanda, connects it with the Jeypore armoury where there is a great and honourable weapon with the same title. Swords are worshipped throughout Rajput India and Tod has given a lively description of the homage paid to the 'monstrous blade', the double-edged *khanda,* honoured by the chivalry of Mewar.[1] Next to his sovereign's throne the most powerful oath of the Rajput was by his arms; similar traditions prevailed in western antiquity. For Bondo psychology this sword is of great importance; it has immense snob-value, it fortifies the tribe's self-respect by establishing that fragile link with the Rajput nobility which it is the ambition of every aboriginal to maintain.

Today the sword has become the symbol of an important local deity, Pat Khanda Mahaprabhu. He is the special god of the twelve Jangar villages, but is not worshipped in the other Bondo settlements. There is a vague tradition that he came from Nandpur, which he still sometimes visits; he is indeed rather an active deity, going to Bastar and the Godavari, and causing sickness in his own villages by the withdrawal of his protecting presence. One legend attributes to him certain incidents more commonly recorded of Lakshman and Sita.

In Nandpur lived Pat Khanda Mahaprabhu and his sister. One day Mahaprabhu went hunting and his sister sat at home husking grain. It grew warm and she sweated and removed her cloth. Presently Mahaprabhu returned from his hunt and from a distance saw that his sister was husking grain without her cloth. He shot a club-arrow first and it fell short, then a barbed arrow and it fell in front of the girl. She realized that her brother was coming and in her fright she went down below the earth, taking her broom and pestle but leaving the cloth behind. Mahaprabhu rushed to the spot and was in time to catch her by the hair. But the hair came out in his hand; he threw it away and it turned into thatching-grass.[2] The girl went down under the ground to the Kingu Bodak spring, but her brother followed, and when she saw him she went below the hills to Gumma. She came above ground there

[1] J. Tod, *Annals and Antiquities of Rajast'han* (New edition by W. Crooke, Oxford, 1920), Vol. II, p. 680. There is an interesting account of the Mewar *khanda* at p. 691: it is supposed 'to be the enchanted weapon fabricated by Viswakarma, with which the Hindu Proserpine girded the founder of the race, and led him forth to the conquest of Chitor'.

[2] This is a common motif in Indian folk-tales. See p. 65.

and sat by the road, determined to beat Mahaprabhu should he approach her. But he watched her from the great banyan above Mundlipada. People went by her and for shame she turned into a stone. There can still be seen, on a rock on the banks of the stream which flows from Mundlipada to Gumma, the marks of the broom and pestle. When Mahaprabhu saw his sister turn into stone, he turned himself into a sword.

FIG. 33. Sisa climbing the banyan at Mundlipada to bring down the sword of Pat Khanda Mahaprabhu

It is said in Mundlipada that the presence of the sword became known by a dream, wherein Pat Khanda appeared to the Sisa and gave directions for his worship. There is no record, however, of a formal presentation of a sword by one of the Nandpur or Jeypore kings to the Bondos.

I was present, on 18 February 1946, at Mundlipada when the Magh celebrations of Pat Khanda were conducted. The festival was taken very seriously. There was a great bustle with pestles and grindstones, pots and gourds; everybody bathed and rubbed themselves with oil, cut their hair, made fresh headbands, gathered flowers; the girls wore bright new skirts. For this is an occasion when the headmen of the other eleven Jangar villages are present, each with his followers and his gifts, to be superseded or reappointed for the coming year. It is significant that this official business should take place under the aegis of Pat Khanda Mahaprabhu, whose official status is thus confirmed.

After a good deal of receiving and distributing grain brought by the visitors, offerings were made at the Naiko's *sindibor,* and then a great crowd of men, women and children pressed their way through the thick undergrowth of the grove above the village until they came to the banyan with its rectangular stone altar and its hidden sword. The special Sisa of Pat Khanda brought a goat, a fowl and some water. The altar was cleaned and the tree saluted. Then the Sisa climbed the tree—he went up about forty feet — and brought out the sword with his right hand.[1] He came down and poured water over it and sacrificed the fowl. Then another Sisa killed the goat after the usual preliminaries and poured the blood over the sword. There was a wild scramble to get a few drops of this blood to mark the forehead. As the goat was killed the Sisa recited the following charm :

O Nandpur Mahaprabhu, O Pat Khanda Birkam, O Budha Bhairo of Nandpur,[2] O Dhular Dhoi, O Siri Maoli ! There is night in Nandpur, but light in Jangar. Ground incense, leaves of bel, rice, haldi roots and flour we give to you. A black cock, a black goat we give to you. Let children be well. Let kingdom, earth and country be well. Let the crops be plentiful. Let us have no trouble. Let us be like the washed rice and the blossoming flower. O Pat Khanda Mahaprabhu, let the kingdom, earth and country be well.

After this the Sisa, still holding the sword in his right hand, climbed the tree again and restored it to its hiding-place. The people returned to the village and the other business of the festival was resumed.

Bondo ideas about Pat Khanda Mahaprabhu reveal themselves in the reminiscences of one of the most prominent of his devotees, Ghasi Mundli of Mundlipada now an elderly man approaching seventy. I will

[1] Afterwards the Sisa told me that as he took it in his hand, the sword increased in length; the dirt and rust disappeared and 'it shone in his eyes, *dag-dag* with bright jewels.

[2] The name Birkam or Vikrama is common in the annals of the Rajas of Nandpur and Jeypore; indeed the name of the present Maharaja is Sri Vikrama Deo Varma. A Bhairava Deo was Raja of Nandpur from 1510-27.

quote him in full, for these autobiographical records are valuable for the light they throw on the complex Bondo character with its ambivalent attitude to this world and the next.

Once when I went to cut my clearing someone sent magic against me; it came violent as a gust of wind and knocked me over. I got to my feet and managed to stagger to the bottom of the hill. It felt as though someone was pushing me down. When I reached the bottom I felt so giddy that I had to rest under a tree. My son and brother were with me, but neither of them felt the great wind and could not understand what had happened. A week later I again went to cut my clearing, and again my enemy sent magic against me; there was another gust of wind and I fell down with a bit of wood between my legs and fainted. My son and brother picked me up and took me home. That night, while I was asleep, Pat Khanda Mahaprabhu, wearing a strip of cloth as a turban and an axe over his shoulder, came to see me. Many ghosts of the dead were sitting round me. The magic (*eloto*) was by me and they shouted to it, 'Look, Mahaprabhu is coming; he will kill you if you don't escape'. The magic was frightened and ran away. Mahaprabhu chased it, flourishing his axe, but it ran so fast that it escaped from him.

When I awoke that morning I thought it over; then I sent for some water by the hand of an unmarried boy and washed my hands. I took a little rice and offered it to Pat Khanda, calling on him to aid me. I was soon well again and next day performed the sacrifices I had promised.

The magic came for this reason. Once Guru Kirsani was ill. The Dissari at Salanpada said, 'This man is too sick to recover; he's going to die'. But I said, 'No, he isn't; I can cure him if he'll do what I say'. This led to a quarrel and the Dissari sent the magic to pay me out.

I easily cured Guru Kirsani by promising a brown goat to Pat Khanda Mahaprabhu. Unfortunately I forgot about it afterwards, and this annoyed Mahaprabhu. He came to me in the form of a Paik, wearing a dhoti and a new cloth over his shoulders. He struck me on the back, shouting, 'What are you doing lying asleep?' I started up, but there was nothing there; only my back where he had hit it was so painful I thought it must be broken. I called a Dissari and a Dora Guruma,[1] but they could do nothing. After a time I managed to get up by myself, slowly and painfully, and after washing my hands I offered some rice to Mahaprabhu. That night he came again in a dream and said, 'You promised me a brown goat; why haven't you given it to me? Get it for me at once and you'll also have to give me a brown cock as a fine for your neglect. Then you'll be all right. Why did you send for that Dissari and Guruma? As long as I am with you, no ghost or demon will be able to touch you; no one but I will trouble you.' Next day I felt much better and after sacrificing a goat and cock I was soon quite well again.

Once at the Giag-gige Festival Mahaprabhu gave me a dream. 'Don't go hunting tomorrow,' he said. But I forgot the dream when I awoke and went with the others to hunt as usual. A tiger attacked me and in terror I called on Pat Khanda Mahaprabhu. Directly I took his name,

[1] A female shaman.

the tiger swerved aside and went past me into the jungle. That day we got nothing. When I went to sleep, Mahaprabhu came again and said, 'Ha, sister-copulator.[1] I warned you and you took no notice. But, I saved you; otherwise your life would certainly have left you.'

I have done the Dagoi-gige for both myself and my wife. For two years we had poor harvests and when I called the Dissari he could not tell me the reason. Then Mahaprabhu came in a dream and said I must do the Dagoi-gige for myself. After that the crops improved. Three years later my wife got a wound in the breast and Mahaprabhu told me to do the Dagoi-gige for her. I did so and she recovered.

There have been two great epidemics in my village. In the course of the first, one night I saw a large number of women dressed Paik fashion in coloured cloth going to visit Mahaprabhu. They said to him, 'We get nothing to eat and we are starving. Give us something and save our lives.' He replied 'Go! There is my village. You can eat anything you like there.' I awoke and next morning I found many of our people were ill. I prayed to Mahaprabhu and he came in a dream and said, 'Don't offer sacrifice for anyone, or you'll die. But if you obey me, you'll have nothing to fear and will be quite safe.' For fifteen days the sickness was in the village and many died. Then again I prayed to Mahaprabhu and now at last he allowed me to sacrifice. I offered two she-goats on the path to Thakurani and Pat Khanda Mahaprabhu and the sickness stopped.

The second time, Mahaprabhu was away on a visit to the Godavari. Goats and fowls died first, then men and women. The epidemic started in my own house. My first wife died of it. I too was ill for a time. I sacrificed in the name of Mahaprabhu and the sickness stopped.

My father was also a Sisa of Mahaprabhu and a very famous one. He used to take me with him whenever he went to sacrifice and I sat beside him and learnt what to do. I used to clean the altar and fetch water and gradually I learnt all that my father knew. At last one year at Dassera, when everyone was there and the Naikos of twelve villages were present, my father said, 'I am old now and can sacrifice no more. From today my son will be your Sisa.' They said, 'It is good'. My father sat me down and cried to Mahaprabhu, 'I'm an old man now and can serve you no longer. Now accept ghee, wheat and bel leaves from your grandson instead of from me.' As he spoke he put a mark of rice on my forehead and a knife in my hand. Each of the twelve headmen marked my forehead and I was able to begin my work. That very night Mahaprabhu gave me a dream and said, 'I will accept you as my Sisa, but you must remain in *sato* (truth or virtue)'.

I have performed the Dagoi-gige for many people, and by my sacrifices I have saved many lives.

Once I went to my sister's house and while I was there I had a dream. Pat Khanda Mahaprabhu came by riding on a red horse, a gold umbrella in his hand. He had on the finest clothes, garments of silk and gold. There were many gods attending him. He asked me, 'Where have you been? Come with me.' I said, 'How can I come with you? My children will mourn for me.' Mahaprabhu said, 'I am on my way to

[1] The language of all Bondo deities is deplorable.

the Godavari. There will be no rain till I return. On the day I get back it will rain, but not before. Keep this in your mind.' This was in Chait. Two months went by and there was no rain. In Jeth the people sowed their seed. They began to make sacrifices for rain. Asadh began and they went on sacrificing. But I did nothing; I knew it would be useless.[1] Then on a Saturday there was a noise in Kingu Bodak as of a drum going *gud-gud gud-gud,* and I said, 'Don't go to the bazaar tomorrow. It is going to rain.' That night the clouds gathered and at dawn Mahaprabhu returned from the Godavari and the rain poured down. Everything was flooded. The women who started out to fetch water returned home afraid. I offered a fowl in the grove at Kingu Bodak and the rain grew less.

That night Mahaprabhu said to me, 'Ha, eater of my wife's excreta, sister-copulator, do you remember what I said ? What gods have you been wasting my money on while I've been away ?' Next morning I offered rice and begged forgiveness.

What are we to make of this strange narrative, this mixture of nightmare and epopteia, the relations between the wayward, irresponsible god and his favoured priest? Ghasi quite obviously believed every word of it; these fantastic experiences were far more real to him than the drab events of every day; he trembled as he described that really awe-inspiring experience when he sat surrounded by the ghosts of the dead, and 'the magic was by him'. One thing is certainly obvious and that is the absence of any moralization of the character of Pat Khanda Mahaprabhu. He appears as a rather despicable Paik soldier, arrogant, foul-mouthed, irresponsible. He knows that his absence will bring disaster on his own special village, yet he has no hesitation on going off to the Godavari. When a party of disease-demons, in the habiliments of Hindu women, come to him, he sends them to destroy the very people who are most devoted to his worship. I show later that Pat Khanda may be directed by some angry devotee to avenge a personal wrong, but I have not been able to find any evidence of his interest in human morality or of his automatic punishment of human sin.

4. The Misanthropy of the Demigods

At first there reigned alone, in direct correspondence with his subjects, the bright and dazzling Singi-Arke Mahaprabhu, to whom we may apply (in full consistency with Bondo thought) the title, 'God of gods and Lord of lords'. Those were the days of peace and happiness

[1] This refusal of a Sisa to act is not uncommon. At the time of a smallpox epidemic at Katamguda, Budha, the Sisa of the village, was warned in a dream to do nothing about it. The people were very angry at his inactivity, but when he explained that if he offered sacrifice his entire family would be destroyed, they accepted the situation and waited patiently for the calamity to pass.

for mankind, before religion was invented, before priests and shamans came in, before ghosts and demons and demigods were made to humble and discipline mankind. The origin of the demigods is explained by the Bondos in two very significant legends which I must quote in full.

First men were made, then the demigods. But in those days men were so busy cultivating, copulating, eating, drinking, dancing that they had no time for the demigods and gave them no sacrifices. The demigods lived in the forest on fruit and flowers, wind and water. So, untroubled by religion, men grew rich.

But when Mahaprabhu saw the prosperity of men, he was worried. 'If men get as rich as this, they'll not be afraid of anyone. I must think of some way of getting their money out of them.' He called the demigods[1] and made them stay with him for six months; during that time he made them very comfortable with rich meals of milk and sugar. Then he said, 'Now go and live among men. There is one Seti Sisa; go to him; he is a friend of mine. He'll make arrangements for your camp and will get you all the supplies you need.'

The gods went to the Sisa — it was like the coming of the police in a case of murder — and he made arrangements for them and showed them where to stay. He gave them names — Dumbar he sent to live in the sacred grove outside the village; Orseley, the tiger god, he sent to haunt the approaches to the hill-clearings. Another god he named Runkta and put him to live in the stream where people went to bathe. He sent Saoruli to live in the hill above the village, Bugabor to the forest, Dagoi and Gurangpoi to his own house, Singraj to the spring. For Sindibor he made a stone platform.

To feed all these demigods the Sisa had to levy supplies from the villagers. And the gods were no longer content with roots and fruit; they had grown soft in Mahaprabhu's palace and they demanded meat and grain. Men soon became poor again.

This story comes from Pinnajangar; another version was recorded at Basupada. It concerns the origin of fowls.

Everything was made, but there were no fowls. The demigods were born, but they did not at first live among men; they were in the forest and made their own arrangements for food and wood and water. But this was most bothersome, and after a time they decided to make their camps among human beings and to trouble them until they got the food and service they wanted.

The demigods went in a party to Sukro Sisa. This old man had three daughters: the demigods began by making them desperately ill. Sukro Sisa, torn by anxiety for his children, promised to get supplies for his

1 The relationship between Mahaprabhu and the demigods and furies is similar to that of the Uraon Dharmes and the lower divinities. The Uraons, says Fr. Dehon look on Dharmes 'as their creator, but they have a very poor idea of his providence. He is far above everything, and has given the management of the world into the hands of tutelary divinities and *bhuts*, or devils whom they have to propitiate. As there are bad men and good men in the world, and God does not interfere, so there are good and bad divinities whom God leaves quite free to act as they please'. — P. Dehon, 'Religion and Customs of the Uraons', *Mem. A.S.B.*, Vol. VII (1906), p. 125.

visitors and they let the girls be and they recovered. Sukro went about collecting pigs, goats, grain and wine; there was everything there but fowls. Singraj wanted fowls for his dinner; he said, 'I'll never let your girls alone unless you give me fowls'. The poor Sisa did not understand; he had never heard of fowls, so he went to Mahaprabhu and told him all about it.

Mahaprabhu was suffering from a very bad cold. He began to cough and suddenly out of his mouth there shot an egg. He gave it to the Sisa saying, 'Take this away; make a hatching-nest of bamboo and for fifteen days let your eldest daughter sit on it'. Sukro did as he was told and after fifteen days a cock and a hen broke out of the egg. Soon they had many chickens and were able to satisfy the demigods.

These two legends give, in an unusually lucid manner, the common attitude of all Indian aboriginals to the outsider, whether demigod, official or (I have no doubt) anthropologist. These people are a very great nuisance; the more corrupt demand supplies and service, even the most generous want information. The ruling passion of the Bondo is to avoid being bothered. And of all disturbances of Bondo life the greatest nuisance is the demigod. You never know when he will turn up; you can get no warning of his arrival; it costs something even to discover that he has come. He is a worthless accretion on human society; he does no good, he inspires no lofty thought, no humane desire; he is jealous, touchy, exacting, a nagger about trifles, a formalist in cult, a rigorist in behaviour. He began with simple demands for food and drink; he has ended by interfering in private life; today there is no aspect of Bondo existence into which he had not poked his all-inquisitive, if invisible, nose. The demigod is the blackmailer; unseen he watches, and when he catches you, he demands his price. And there is nothing to do but to pay up.

Long and bitter experience has acquainted the Bondos with the names and habits of many of these demigods; their tariff has more or less been stabilized; their spiritual finger-prints, so to speak, can now be spotted by the most immature Dissari.

Prominent among the demigods is Bursung or Hundi, who is none other than Mother Earth herself. Those who so charitably talk of 'the good earth' and think of this fertile mother feeding and delighting mankind with her bounty, must not forget the sinister aspect she has so often assumed in the minds of primitive people. It is the earth which, among the Kond neighbours of the Bondos, cries out for the blood of human sacrifice; she is generally the most terrible of primitive goddesses. She feeds, but she also starves, mankind. She creates, but in time she receives again the dead.

Bursung is vaguely imagined as female, and the *sindibor* is her seat and dwelling. Hundi is honoured with circular stone shrines, as at

Plate LIII Bondo women transplanting rice

Plate LIV Young boys, Sonia and Sukre of Andrahal, playing on *kinding-sa* drums

Plate LV Donker Kirsani playing the *tolia* at Bodapada

Plate LVI Youth of Andrahal playing split-string instrument of bamboo

Beating a ball of yarn

Woman spinning yarn

Plate LVII

Winding the yarn

Plate LVIII Bondo women weaving at Katamguda

Plate LIX Woman weaving a skirt at Mundlipada

Plate LX Woman weaving outside Mundlipada village

Pinnajangar and Katamguda, and where her cult is prominent the sacred attributes of the *sindibor* are transferred to her shrine. At Pinnajangar, for example, I was told that it would not matter very much if the *sindibor*

FIG. 34. Shrine to Hundi at Katamguda

stones fell out of place, but it would be disastrous if the stones of Hundi did so. At Andrahal, on the top of the hill above the village, is a stone for Bursung with some stone seats near by. The earth, as Bursung or Hundi, is worshipped with elaborate and expensive ceremonies, known as Bursung-gige, at the Gebursung or Giag Festivals to ensure the safety of children, success in the hunt and fertility in the fields.

Unhappily even such respected citizens of the other world seem unable to keep their tempers and allow themselves to be exasperated by the merest trifles. For example, there is a trivial rule that on the special day of the Fowl of Bursung (Bursung-gissing-gige) during the Giag Festival, everyone except certain dedicated persons should stay outside a village. One year Hadi Kirsani of Bandapada forgot the rule and, needing some tobacco from his house, went into the village to get it. This annoyed Bursung and when the man went later in the day to hunt she took the form of a wild boar and knocked him down, inflicting some unpleasant injuries. Hundi is equally sensitive and even more vindictive. It is taboo to touch cowdung on the last day of the Giag Festival.

'Long ago,' I was told at Gokurupada, 'when Lachhim Kirsani was a baby, his mother collected cowdung in the cattle shed on this day and threw it away. His father told her not to, but she made light of it and took no notice. Hundi was very angry and that night when poor little Lachhim was sleeping with his mother by the fire, she threw him into the flames and burnt his left arm so badly that he has never used it since. Indeed if his father had not immediately sacrificed to Hundi, he would have perished.'

The cult of Maoli has spread, possibly from Bastar, into the Bondo country. Maoli and Hundi are said to be man and wife, and are often worshipped together, though Hundi — as the village mother — has her own stone shrines. Maoli and Hundi, if properly tended, save the village cattle from danger and keep disease far away. But Maoli, like his consort, is apt to explode at the least irritation; he then sends wild animals to kill goats and fowls and snakes to bite the children.

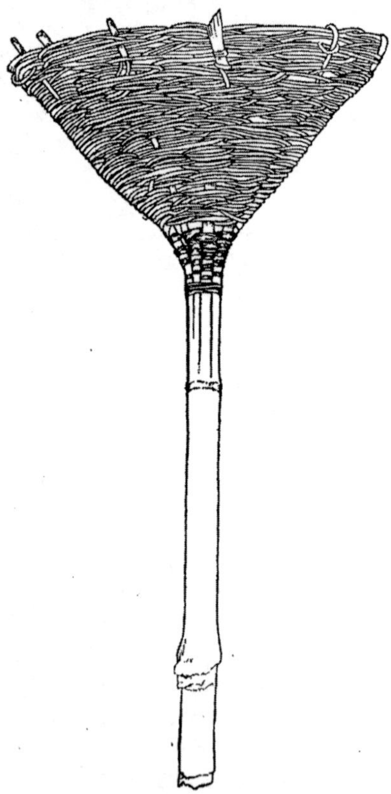

FIG. 35. Bamboo nest for sitting hens

There are a number of stories illustrating Maoli's tiresome misanthropy. One of the *angto* days of the Giag Festival is dedicated to Maoli; and it is regarded as a particularly dangerous time. The Sisa must not speak to anyone; until midday no one should break anything — wood, leaves, toothtwigs. The reason is that 'this is Maoli's day of happiness. He is dancing and playing among the trees.' It is said that the ceremonial hunt on this day is expected to be lucky. But any breach of the rules is risky. Some twenty years ago one Soma Kirsani went to get honey on this day and cut a tree before midday; that evening, during the hunt, a tiger attacked him. But he called on Maoli and was saved. More recently, Budha Sisa of Kadamguda was punished for unpunctuality. He was late for Maoli's sacrifice and, still worse, gave some of the sacrificial meat and rice, which he alone should have eaten, to his children. As a result the hunt was a failure and he himself fell ill. Godra Bodnaik of Dumiripada also failed in his ceremonial duties; he failed to contribute his share of rice to the festival. Maoli was angry and made him ill and he did not recover till he offered the offended deity an egg and a black cock.

The countryside is haunted by these demigods, kindly or vindictive according to their mood, but most often dangerous to mankind. Singraj lives in the mountain streams; if she is pleased she gives good rain, but if neglected sends itch and sores to the people and may cause a drought. Kunda presides over the hills and cultivation-clearings. He must be worshipped on the spot and he then keeps wild animals from damaging the crops. It is taboo to eat anything from a clearing before the offerings have been made to Kunda; any mistake will give a man sores on his head and cause his face to swell.

Mali Bebur is a forest god who has some control over tigers; neglect of his worship may bring these animals down upon a village. Bangaur is the divine grazier of wild animals. He lives in the jungle and has some association with the bombax tree. He can be very helpful if suitably honoured before a hunt.

The Bondos are beginning to recognize a number of the disease-demons which range so freely over the Hindu countryside. There is first and foremost Thakurani Bakorani, the hateful goddess of smallpox, for whom a special *jatra* ceremony, borrowed from the plains is performed. At Tulaguram she is specially associated with a *Pterocarpus marsupium* tree, where she once took up her abode during an epidemic. Offerings are made below this tree whenever smallpox threatens the neighbourhood. With Thakurani is identified Kankali, so called because she brings *kankal*, ruin.

Then there is Ganga-sabota, who gives people pneumonia, fever and vomiting; Gurang, who torments with belly-ache 'like the sharp pricking of a thorn'; Mata Bangta, who brings cholera. These are probably modern accretions to the Bondo gallery and there will no doubt be many more as the tribe comes into touch with the Hindus of the plains.

Special notice must finally be paid to Karandi, who is a sort of fire elemental and makes himself known by arson, but whose influence is strictly localized. So risky is it to offend him that the three villages where his cult is strongest — Basupada, Bandiguda and Salanpada — are beginning to show some small divergences of custom from other places. For example, some of the Basupada women observe menstruation taboos for fear of offending the god; in all three villages women are forbidden to sit on the *sindibor*, though they may do this in other places. No visitors are permitted to camp in Basupada: even the police have to stay outside the boundary.

The story of Karandi's origin is worth quoting. The general motif is a familiar one; the expression of demonic rage is somewhat unusual.

Long ago an old Sisa and his wife lived on a mountain-side alone. They had no children. One day a tiger killed a deer near their house and the Sisa saw it in a dream. He found it and calling his wife began to cut up the carcass. He skinned it, cut off the feet and was about to slit the belly, when a voice said from within, 'Old man, cut carefully so as not to hurt us'. He was alarmed when he heard the voice and dropped his knife, but his wife said, 'Go on, I'm getting hungry; what are you stopping for? The Sisa began to cut the belly and saw inside the god Karandi and his wife. Karandi said, 'Take us out and put us in your basket. We are going to live in your house, and whenever there is any trouble we will help you.' When the Sisa looked again he saw that there were two stones in the belly; he made a new basket for them and took them home. He divided the venison among his friends, but directly they ate it, they fell ill. Everyone was ill except the Sisa and his wife. Karandi gave a dream. 'Offer a goat and a she-goat in my name and your friends will recover.' The Sisa obeyed and all was well for the time being.

Shortly afterwards the old woman conceived and in due time gave birth to a child. The next year she had another child. The boys grew up and found wives; the years passed and the Sisa and his wife died. The elder son became Sisa in his father's place and made it his special care to attend the rites of Karandi. But one day when his wife was in her menstrual period she went near the stones of the demon and he was very angry. 'You are trying to ruin me,' he cried, and in his temper set fire to the house. Now this house had three doors. Karandi broke all three open and, leaving his wife in the burning hut, fled away to somewhere near the Dudma Falls. The house was burnt to the ground, but the basket containing Karandi's stones was untouched by the flames. And now when the people examined it they found one stone was missing, though there had been two when they went to the fields that morning. Presently the Sisa had a dream explaining why his house had been burnt and where Karandi had gone. He offered many sacrifices, but the demon would not return. He stays now at Dudma and only comes occasionally with a party of other demons to visit his wife; when he comes the villagers fall ill.

At the beginning of May 1945 the entire village of Bandiguda was destroyed by fire. Soon afterwards the Sisa of Basupada — a descendant of the same Sisa whose house had been burnt long before — had a dream. One day in April, it was revealed, the wife of one Hadi Kirsani of Bandiguda went with her child to Basupada. She put the child down on the *sindibor* and went into the village for her business. When it was done she returned to the platform and called the child. But he could not get down and the mother, forgetting the taboo that forbade a woman to mount the *sindibor* in this village, climbed up and brought him down. That evening, the Sisa learnt in his dream, Bursing, Hundi, Maoli and a few other demigods collected and gave Karandi a good thrashing. 'We look on you', they said, 'as a very important demon, and yet you allowed a woman to climb onto the *sindibor* and humiliate us.' Karandi was furious at this and next day, a Sunday, when many of the people were away at the Mundaguda bazaar, he went over to Bandiguda and set fire to Hadi Kirsani's house, whence the conflagration spread throughout the village. In the evening Karandi appeared to the Sisa at Basupada, told him what had happened and threatened to destroy that village also. The Sisa hurriedly spread the news and the people of both villages offered goats and grain at their respective *sindibor*.

Karandi's irritability is indeed proverbial. Soma Kirsani of Basupada told me how once he failed to attend the usual sacrifice and the demon sent a bear to knock him down when next he went out hunting.

To the student of Indian village life these instances will seem sufficiently commonplace, but they had to be given if our picture was to be complete. The Bondo theory of the demigods and furies is clear: they are inflicted on man to keep him in his place. They have succeeded in destroying his self-confidence in the face of the unseen, in lowering his economic standards and in damaging his health. At best they are an expensive nuisance; at worst they are a menace to the nervous energy and progress of the people. There is no trace of love or affection for any unseen being.

5. The Watchers in the House

The little Bondo hut, theatre wherein the whole human drama of birth and love and dissolution is played over, is watched and guarded by its own demonic powers. These, like the other members of the family, are all right so long as they get enough to eat and drink. If permitted to feel hungry or neglected, they become obstreperous.

In the inner room of the house, in a corner, on a small platform, is the forked branch of the *Eugenia jambolana* tree, from which depends a small gourd. The gourd represents Angkui, the branch Siniboi; the two spirits are not clearly imagined, but it is believed that they watch over the affairs of the family and house. 'By relying on Siniboi,' I was told at Mundlipada, 'we can leave the house open and unguarded; the grain stored in the bins is in her charge.' Seed is always placed before her.

Siniboi seems to be the same as the Vedic goddess Sinavali who presided over fecundity and an easy birth. She is represented at harvest-time by the drawing of a plough on the piles of winnowed grain.

Angkui and Siniboi are worshipped on all major occasions with offerings of crabs and fish, sometimes with rat's-meat, and always with a few drops of beer or palm-wine.

Dagoi is another watcher, though he has no local symbol; he may be honoured thrice in the life of every Bondo. He can cause fertility or barrenness, according to his whim, in either human beings or in the fields. 'He can control a man's fate' and must be worshipped 'to avert bad luck'.

FIG. 36. Gourd of Angkui suspended from branch in corner of Bondo house

The ghosts of the dead, as we shall see later, naturally have a great interest in their descendants. There is no regular Pot of the Departed, as among the Marias, but the Bondos do sometimes dedicate a gourd (*sairem-kuntung*) for the soul of a person who has not yet been satisfied with a *gunom* menhir. When the family, having decided to pay this tribute to the dead, sets aside a pig to be fattened and preserved for sacrifice, they put samples of every kind of seed and some husked rice into a gourd; they worship it and hang it up in the name of the deceased. When the time comes for the erection of the menhir, they empty the contents of the gourd into a fan, put some pebbles with it, and exclaim, 'Here is the seed stolen by the dead; these stones are the cattle he destroyed!' This seed is then mixed with the other seed in the bins, and the gourd is thrown away. Seed is also usually kept in a gourd hung above the Angkui as a sort of consecration; it is brought out at sowing-time and festivals.

This seems to be the right place for a reference to the mysterious and sacred drum known as the *kinding-sagar*. The sanctity of drums is widely accepted by the aboriginals; the Murias worship their *mandar* before a wedding, and sometimes keep in the dormitory a large *dhol*-drum which is regarded as the local habitation of Lingo Pen or Bhima. The *kinding-*

sagar[1] is a small drum, of the mradang type, double membraned, one end smaller than the other, which is kept in the Sisa's house, supported on three small stones.[2] It is strictly taboo to look at it except on the proper occasions and the nature of the demonic power possessing it is obscure. The drum is used at the Giag Festival; anyone who is fasting may beat it then; its sound brings luck to the ceremonial hunt, improves the crops and keeps away alien demons. At the Sume-Gelirak, it is beaten during the castigation. If any animal is obtained in the hunt, it is first offered to the *kinding-sagar* and then taken to the *sindibor*. On all occasions the conventional offerings are made before it.

Should the drum break of its own accord, when, for example, it is not in use, it is regarded as the worst possible omen: the Sisa trembles for his life and the people expect tigers to appear in the neighbourhood. But if anyone breaks it accidentally during a festival, it does not matter; a bit of cloth is tied round it as a sort of shroud and it is buried.

6. The Intermediaries

The Bondos are the least priest-ridden of men. Their independent and democratic spirit does not take kindly to the idea of certain individuals being privileged above their fellows. Every householder is a potential priest and may be called for the time being a 'Pujari', for he has to perform special duties for his own home and family at every festival and when there is a death in the house. The priest is not a specially gifted person; he has no deposit of doctrine to guard or transmit; he is a religious hack on whom a great burden of responsibility and many an arduous duty is laid. The Sisa, as the village priest is called, may be deposed if he does not do his work properly and every year he has to offer himself, along with the other village officials, for re-appointment.

Every village, or rather every *sindibor*, should have two of these Sisa-priests, a chief and his assistant. The Sisa appears to be attached to the *sindibor* rather than to the village, for where — as at Mundlipada and Andrahal — there are several *sindibor* in the different quarters of the main settlement, each has its special staff. The Sisa, in addition to his assistant, has two or more young unmarried boys to serve as acolytes;

[1] As usual there is diversity of custom and even of name. The *kinding-sagar* is sometimes called *kinding-sangar*. At Bodapada it was not supported on stones but hung on the wall: 'It must be strong as a stone,' they said, 'and not break.' At Andrahal, a stone was hung up with it.

[2] *Sangar* means stone, and there is a stone deity called Pasangar who is worshipped under the form of three small stones outside a village to ensure success in the hunt and the fecundity of the crops.

these, if there is more than one *kuda* in a village, should be representative of each of them. The Sisa is priest only of his own *sindibor*. He has no authority in other villages and it would be considered an improper thing, an *angto*, where he to usurp the authority of a Sisa elsewhere.

A Sisa's importance in his own village derives from the fact that without him the routine duties of religion cannot be performed. He must perform sacrifice at every festival and on all public occasions. His own house is the shrine of the mysterious *kinding-sagar*; if there is no *sindibor*, as at Tulaguram, it is the scene of important ceremonies. His wife has the duty of making special rice-beer and must observe the prescribed behaviour calculated to improve the luck of the ritual hunt.

The Dissari is the Gunia or Bhagat of the Bondos, the shaman or medicine-man. The word may be connected with Dasari (though Dissari stresses the second syllable and Dasari the first), the name of a caste of mendicant Vaishnavas in southern India, some of whose members practice divination,[1] or with Desayi, which means 'of the country' and is applied to headmen in the North Arcot District.[2] Desai, which in Western India means a Deshmukh, or Maratha revenue official, is one of the titles of the Pardhans, a tribe noted for its commerce with the supernormal world.[3] The Mundari *disi* means 'native' or 'country-made'—it is ultimately, of course, a Hindi-Bengali word, and I think that probably the Dissari is so called because he is of the country; like the Baiga or Bhumia, he is the old inhabitant of the soil and thus in touch with its gods and demons.

The Dissari is at once more independent and more important than the Sisa for ordinary, though not for festal, life. He does not derive his authority from the people; he is not subject to election or deposition; he is a Dissari by the favour of the gods and must prove his title by the accuracy of his diagnosis and the efficacy of his advice. Nor is he confined to any one tribe; there are Bondo Dissaris, many of them, but the most popular Dissari in the Mundlipada area was a Gour who succeeded a famous Didayi Dissari who was widely consulted by the Bondos. Similarly Andrahal and Katamguda people often summoned a Gadaba Dissari from Onagelu to their assistance. If one could trust them, I gathered, the Kond Dissaris would be the best of all, 'for they are full of magic'.

The Dissari is free to go anywhere and, when he becomes known, he may develop an extensive practice, which becomes a full-time job. His remuneration is more generous than that of a Sisa, and I think he is

1 Thurston, op. cit., Vol. II, pp. 112ff; H. V. Nanjundayya and L. K. A. Iyer, *The Mysore Tribes and Castes* (Mysore, 1930), Vol. III, pp. 101ff.

2 Thurston, op. cit., Vol. II, pp. 121ff.

3 R. V. Russell and Hira Lal, *The Tribes and Castes of the Central Provinces of India* (London, 1916), Vol. IV, p. 352.

Plate LXI At Andrahal, the Dissari offers a fowl on behalf of Soma Challan (see p. 164)

Plate LXII A Sisa makes an offering on the path leading out of Bodapada to expel disease from the village

Hadi Mundli avoids responsibility — The women join in the discussion

Plate LXIII The election of the Naikos at Mundlipada

Six of the Naikos take their seats — Tying the official turban on a Naiko's head

Plate LXIV Preliminary amenities Concluding embraces
The Castigation The course of the fight

A mother treats her son's wounds with oil

Plate LXV

Boys worship their sticks after the ceremony

Boys engaged in the fight; the *kinding-sagar* is being played in the background

Women preparing grain for the Susu feast

Plate LXVI

The Sisa offers a fowl to the dedicated seed at the Susu festival

Plate LXVII Women of Mundlipada, on their way to a festival, wear their leaf-cups as hats

The Sisa worshipping at the Dagoi-gige described on pp. 108f

The Sisa worships before the *sindibor* at the Susu festival at Andrahal

The Sisa with strips of meat at the same ceremony

Plate LXVIII

generally able to make a normal living. It would be wrong, in my opinion, to accept the opinion of unsympathetic European observers who suggest that the tribal medicine-man exploits his patients. His income is meagre enough compared to, shall we say, that of an Archdeacon or a Harley Street specialist. Yet his value in preserving tribal morale, in freeing sick people from their fears, in inspiring them not only with the will to live but with the faith that to live is going to be possible, is in a way comparable to theirs.

The Sisa is for routine, the Dissari for emergency. When cholera or smallpox strikes a village; if someone's wife runs away; if the cattle sicken and die; if a child goes down with fever; it is the Dissari, not the Sisa or Pujari, who is consulted. He diagnoses the cause of the trouble by means familiar throughout aboriginal India; he falls into trance and prophesies; he commands the winnowing-fan and the gourd; he gets drunk and his ravings are interpreted as the voice of god. He is the bailiff of the gods; he decides the fees that are to be paid, he mortgages the future against a successful cure. When he has had his say, he may himself perform the rites he has prescribed or he may leave them to the householder, who becomes a Pujari for the occasion. His great function is the banishing of fear.

The offices of Sisa and Dissari may be hereditary, but this is more a matter of convenience and training than of any right. Budha Sisa of Katamguda, for example, was the son of the old Sisa. 'My father taught me a lot, but Maoli and Hundi themselves instructed me in dreams. They told me never to touch anyone's leavings of food or liquor and always to sacrifice fasting. When my father got too old to sacrifice, I did it for him.' So too Ghasi Mundli of Mundlipada took over the task of conducting the worship of Pat Khanda Mahapurub from his aged father, who put the sacrificial knife into his hand at a meeting of the elders on the *sindibor*.

7. Ceremonial

Bondo ceremonial is beginning to show many traces of Hindu influence. It is none the worse for that; indeed the combination of ancient and modern practice is often fruitful. External influence has made Bondo ritual more picturesque and complicated; it has introduced many new incidents and gestures; it has undoubtedly improved it, rendering it less messy and disorderly, less a mere orgy of beef and beer.

The materials of worship are of the simplest, yet it is remarkable how effective they can be. The Bondos succeed in conducting their ceremonies with a minimum of expense — all they need are leaves, leafy branches to make a booth, sometimes tiny earthen pots for liquor, grass to make dolls, turmeric and rice-flour, coal-dust, flowers; sometimes they make a little cart, or mud animals, or bamboo fans.

Gifts offered in sacrifice are equally simple: eggs are often used, so are crabs and fish. Grains and fruit are offered or dedicated according to the season. Cattle are sacrificed at marriages and funerals, though not at the *sindibor* worship. There, the usual offerings are of fowls, goats and pigs.

At every ceremony a little altar is made on the ground with witch-baffling patterns. These may be simply a series of lines drawn vertically within a frame, like the lines of a Bondo woman's skirt; or the lines may have a diagonal running across them. Fig. 37 shows a pattern made with rice-flour at a *jatra* for Mahaprabhu.

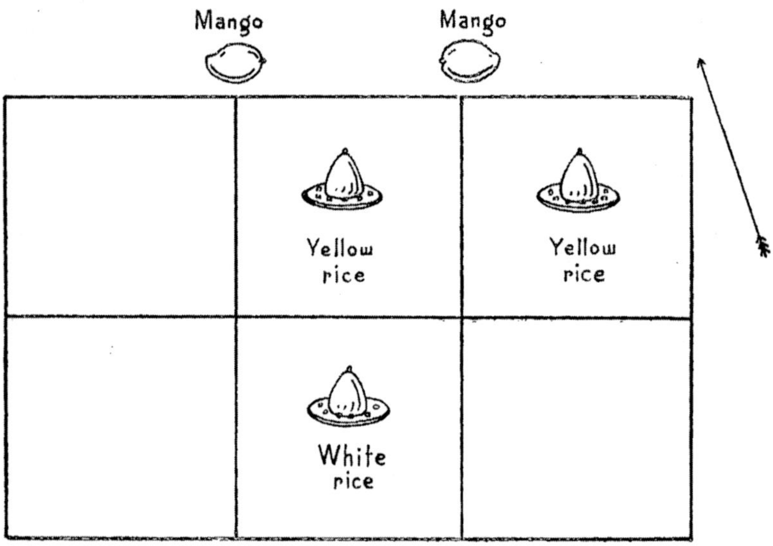

FIG. 37

Yellow and white rice is arranged within the six squares, with mangoes beyond them, and an arrow at the side. Another arrangement is shown in Fig. 38. Here little heaps of white and yellow rice are arranged alternately, and a bow and arrow placed before them. An egg is placed in the centre, with a hole in the broad end which faces downwards. These patterns are drawn in three or four colours — red earth, yellow turmeric-flour, white rice-flour and black coal-dust.

On important occasions a booth is erected near or above the altar, and scraps of cloth (flags) and little offerings are suspended from its roof.

Blood is an essential ingredient of almost every sacrifice. Cattle are killed with a blow on the back of the neck with the blunt edge of an axe; as the creature is dying, the Sisa may slit its mouth and take some of the blood to offer on the altar. A pig has its throat cut, and the head may be removed and placed by the altar. A goat is decapitated with an axe. Fowls are killed in what appears to be a particularly cruel manner. Before any creature is sacrificed, it must be made to eat a little rice or millet: the grain is placed on the altar or, where a rite is intended to protect an individual, on the subject's head. Before a fowl

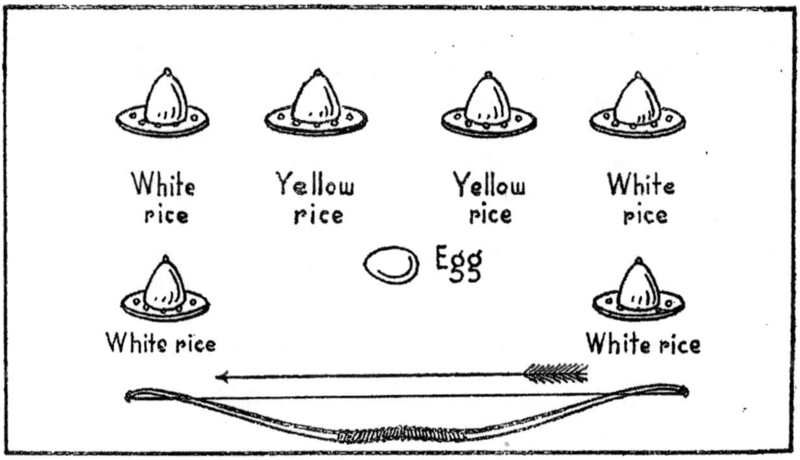

FIG. 38

is given its last meal, the tip of its beak is cut off and the unfortunate bird picks up the grain with its tongue—'the gods stop its pain and help it to eat', I was once told. Then the Sisa cuts off one wing of the still living creature, then a leg, and only then the head. A fowl is not always torn to pieces in this way, but the cutting of the beak is normal. There is a special value in blood from the beak or mouth of any sacrificial creature; a pig too may have its snout struck with a knife, while still alive, until the blood flows from it. The blood is, of course, sprinkled over everything; it dedicates grain and makes it fertile, it makes every offering acceptable to the gods.

A feast on the sacrificial food invariably follows and may only be shared by members of the same community and village; it is usually cooked outside, near the place of sacrifice, and by men.

Where the aim of ceremonial is protective, the Sisa engages in a number of stylized gestures. He waves things round his patient; if he is sacrificing a fowl, he makes it sit on his head; he sprinkles him with water; he may tap him all over with bits of iron. All the materials of ceremonial must be taken out of a village; a grass doll, whatever it may represent, must be taken out and cut to bits with an axe; a little cart bearing disease or danger, is driven forth and broken beyond the boundary. On the way home no one may look round.

Another feature of most Bondo ritual is repetition. Everything is done over and over again, so that there shall be no mistake, no doubt of one's intention. Every ceremony, festival, wedding, funeral is thus drawn out in tedious monotony, yet the Bondos seem to enjoy it — it gives them a lot of leisure and it makes things sure.

I will give briefly a few examples of Bondo rites of protection to illustrate what I have been saying. On 10 March 1945 I assisted at Andrahal in a ceremony calculated to relieve one Soma Challan of a troublesome cough and fever brought on him by the demon Ganga-sabota. The Dissari diagnosed the trouble and prescribed the offering of a fowl. In the early afternoon the Dissari himself began the proceedings. He prepared yellow earth and coal-dust and tied it up in castor leaves. Soma made some rice-flour; someone else spent a long time parching rice. The Dissari who was fasting, went to have what he called a bath. An unmarried, what is officially designated a 'virgin' boy, brought a pot of water. Then the Dissari made a 'litter' of fig leaves; inside he made three little compartments, and filled them with parched rice. He had left the ends of the leaves sticking up and he tied them round with a new cotton thread, and hung from it bright red flowers. Then carrying the litter in his hand, he led the way along a path to the east out of the village. Only men — some fifteen of us — attended. Once we were well outside, the Dissari halted, and sprinkled a little water on the path; on this he made his witch-baffling patterns with red, yellow and white lines. At each corner of this altar he put a heap of yellow rice. He made his patient sit in front, facing east. He put a pinch of rice on his head, made a fowl eat some of the rice on the altar and then some from Soma's head, and threw a little rice to east and west. He picked up the 'litter' and laid it for a moment on Soma's head, then killed the fowl above the altar, and allowed the blood to fall upon it. He threw the body along the path to the east away from the village. Finally he sprinkled water round Soma, placed marks of rice on his own and Soma's foreheads, and then led the way home, carrying the dead fowl with him.

A year later, in the same village, I watched an attempt to cure a baby of a fever caused by a jealous *sairem*. The Dissari discovered that this ghost had made its abode in a hollow mango tree on the bank of the stream that flows below the village. The Sisa therefore took the mother to the bank opposite the tree, made her sit with the sick baby in her lap, recited charms over her and put on her forehead, and the baby's, marks of yellow rice. He then went across the stream to the mango tree, and drew an altar pattern on the ground before it, making seven piles of yellow rice. The mother built a hearth, and cooked a mixture of tamarind, eggs, rice-flour, turmeric and salt; in another pot she prepared rice. When it was ready the Sisa took three cups of rice in his hands and stood above mother and child repeating charms. The mother removed a few grains of rice with her little finger and marked the baby's forehead with them. The Sisa returned to the mango and offered the cooked rice. He made a fowl eat, and killed it slowly in the manner I have described. Finally he returned to the woman, made offerings of rice before the hearth and then gave the mother a dish of rice and curry. He also helped himself and they ate together, giving a few morsels of this *soru*-food to the baby. The Sisa sprinkled mother and child with water, and they all went home.

These examples, and the many given in the course of this book, will suffice to give the reader some idea of the character of Bondo ceremonial. It is rather fussy, it goes on too long, but it is economical and in its way effective. The altar, the blood, the feast, the dedicatory or protective gestures are well calculated to impress the simple-minded, and serve their purpose in maintaining morale and strengthening the will to live.

8. Seats of the Mighty

Like the Hill Saoras, the Bondos often build their villages among rocks, a preference which may go back to the days when cave-shelters were their only form of habitation. They use stone for ordinary domestic purposes, to wall a field or garden, to make a hearth or grindstone, to serve as a seat when weaving. Circular stone enclosures surround young trees or dung-pits. But stone is much more important for ceremonial purposes. The *sindibor* is a stone-circle dedicated to the worship of the earth and the service of the community; *gunom* table-stones are placed by the paths to still the trepidations of innumerable ghosts; sacred stone walls pierce the forest; stone shrines enclose stone symbols of the gods.[1]

The localization of the demigods is always in stone. The goddess of the Kingu Bodak grove at Mundlipada is represented by a stone; so are the dead, lords of the Pinnajangar grove. At Tulaguram, the deities Maoli, Pasang and Singraj are indicated by three stones ringed in a

[1] At Kichchipoda I saw a sacred stone hearth, obviously connected with the fertility of the crops, on the edge of a little cliff overlooking a long stretch of irrigated fields. There were two sets of stones used for cooking and when not in use they were carefully covered with large flat stone slabs. I was told that it was the custom, when the rice was ready for reaping, for the people at first to gather a few handfuls only and these, after the covering slabs had been removed, the women cooked in new pots on the hearths. The Sisa made appropriate offerings and everyone ate a little and then went to complete the reaping.

circle. At Andrahal, on the top of the hill near the village, is a stone for Bursung with some stone seats near by, and at the bottom of the hill close by a stream is an old stone building which was formerly the girls' dormitory. There was a pit and a stone wall some three feet high built up around it. In the old days this was covered with bamboos and earth. Today there are four upright stones in the middle of the house which have come to be regarded as the symbols of Maoli, but were probably (as the boys informed me) originally used by the girls as a hearth.

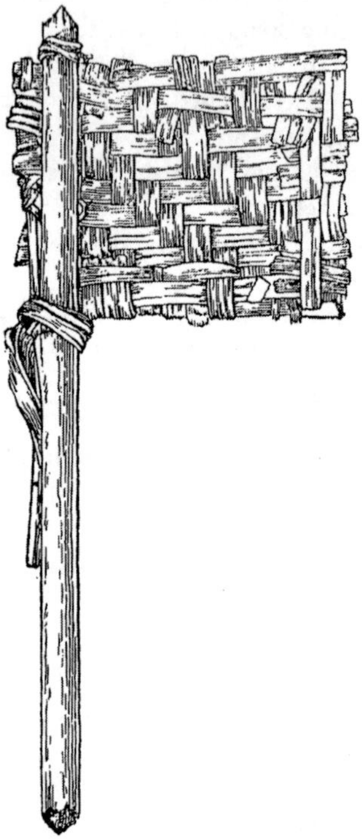

FIG. 39. Ceremonial fan

In several villages there are stone shrines for Hundi, who is often identified with Bursung, Mother Earth or perhaps the Village Mother. At Pinnajangar and Katamguda circles of rubble are built up around a small upright stone which represents the deity. At Semiliguda slabs of stone compose a wall above which rises a thatched roof. At Kadamguda Hundi appears as a stone slab with a small menhir not far from the *sindibor,* which here is not of stone but made of a great bamboo mat stretched over wooden piles. Where the cult of Hundi is strong, some of the sacred attributes of the *sindibor* (which I shall describe immediately) are transferred to her shrine; it was said, for example, at Pinnajangar that if the *sindibor* stones fell out of place it would not matter greatly, but it would be disastrous if the stone of Hundi did so. Festival offerings are made at the shrine instead of at the *sindibor* in these villages.

Traces of megalithic culture are also to be found in the sacred groves which are still maintained in a few villages. There are fine groves, beautiful, holy and enchanted, at Mundlipada, Andrahal and Pinnajangar. At Mundlipada there are two famous groves. One is known as Kingu Bodak in Remo or Kappor Chua in Oriya. In the midst of the trees is a spring of exquisitely clear water built up on either side with stone walls, while among the surrounding rocks are a number of menhirs. This is the traditional site of the origin of the Bondo tribe, the very place where Sita was found bathing by the Bondo women, whence flows a stream down the hill to Gumma and the stone figure of the sister of Pat Khanda Mahaprabhu. In the spring lives Singraj (whose full name is Singraj-Bongraj-Lengodak-Trangodak, which means Singraj of the Spring and of the Falls) and she is worshipped with an egg at each of the great festivals, and enjoys special celebrations every three years at Dassera. Today the Bondos cannot explain the meaning of the menhirs in this grove and deny that they have any association with the dead. I find this hard to believe, especially as similar menhirs, explicity connected with the dead, are found at Andrahal. I suggest that it is possible that there was a very old custom of erecting memorial menhirs in such groves, but that the tradition has died and has been replaced by the custom of placing table-stones by a path.

In the other grove at Mundlipada is the great banyan of Pat Khanda Mahaprabhu, already described, with a stone altar at its foot.

The Andrahal grove has several menhirs and table-stones scattered about in its shade; on the surrounding trees are carvings of the vulva.

Just outside Pinnajangar there is a fine grove, across the middle of which is a low wall of rubble with a gateway flanked by menhirs. Many other menhirs — over twenty of them — stand in and near the wall, which in general plan is just like the sacred *runnukbor* walls to be found elsewhere. The stones and walls are covered with moss, but one stone looks fresh and clean; this is for the dead, lords of the grove, and before it is a flat altar stone for sacrifice. At the Gewursung and Giag Festivals, the people come here with a great display of drums and beer, and the Sisa offers a red cock and sprinkles the wall with its blood. Every three years there is in addition the sacrifice of a pig.

The grove is *angto,* or taboo. Women do not generally enter it. Within its shade it is forbidden to point with the finger, and no one may cut down a tree on pain of death, which the dead will certainly send on the offender. The Sisa declared that if there was any failure in the prescribed sacrifices, the village would be ruined.

In another chapter I describe the use of stone in the appeasement of the dead. Here, we must now proceed to describe the most important and significant of the Bondo megalithic monuments, the stone-circles known as *sindibor.*

The custom of making a convenient sitting-place in the middle of the village, where people can gather and offerings be made, is common in Orissa. In Hindu villages the circular seat is generally of earth or of earth-plastered stones; sometimes it has a roof above it. The Saora *sadru* is only used as a shrine; it is too small to sit about in. In Kond villages the stones and pillars for Dharni Pinnu are occasionally enlarged with stone seats. Regular stone platforms appear more frequently as we move south; then we find the Gadaba *sodor*, the platforms of the Didayis, the Parengas and the Jhorias. In this area certain Hindu castes, such as the Ronas and the Doms, have learnt to make their platforms of stone instead of earth, in imitation of their tribal neighbours.

The *sindibor*[1] is a sort of stone lounge, usually raised one to three feet above the ground and often well placed where there is a good view and in the shade of a mango or jackfruit tree. Large slabs of stone are laid irregularly in a rough circle on a rubble platform and are held in place by small menhirs; these are often set at an angle to serve as back-rests. In the middle is a slightly depressed space where a fire can be kindled. The menhirs are occasionally set to make a sort of wall. There is a definite attempt at comfort, and indeed it is possible to rest with some pleasure among these carefully adjusted stones.

FIG. 40. *Sindibor* at Bandiguda

Not every *sindibor* is of the standard pattern; at Bandiguda it takes the form of a circular stone seat which is built up to a height of three feet round an open space in the middle. There is a 'gate' into this central space which is flanked by two menhirs, one some seven feet high. The slabs are held in place by smaller menhirs and sacrifices are offered to one of those which stands inside the circle. At Kirsanipada, the *sindibor* has seven uprights, one of them seven feet high. At Tula-

[1] The *sindibor* is also known, but mainly I think in poetry, as the *rangtabor* or *junnukbor*.

Plate LXIX Funerary sacrifice at Dumiripada described on pp. 216ff

Men bringing in a *gunom* stone at Andrahal, (pp. 225ff)

Plate LXX

Tying cloth to the bombax branches planted behind the newly-made *gunom* at Andrahal

old cremation sites

Plate LXXI

The procession carrying these offerings, during the *gunom* ceremony at Andrahal

The Orpa ceremony at Dumripada. (p. 218)

Plate LXXII

Women visit the crematic
ground to examine the ash

guram there is no *sindibor* at all, the people here are simply a colony which has emigrated from Bodapada and they have their ancient platform there.

Apart from Tulaguram, however, every Bondo village has a great central *sindibor* dedicated to ceremonial purposes with its own staff of priests; in the larger villages, not only does each hamlet have its *sindibor,* but there are a number of additional platforms, some for the different *kuda* (at Bodapada, for example, there are, in addition to the main *sindibor* for the whole village, special platforms for the Bodnaik and Kirsani clans) and some of prominent individuals or families. 'A Naiko may say to himself, "Here am I, an important person. When my visitors come, where are they to sit?" And he makes a *sindibor* in front of his own house. But sacrifices are not offered to such platforms.' The private *sindibor* of the Naiko of Mundlipada, however, rivals in importance the central platform, for it is here that the preliminaries of the Pat Khanda worship are conducted and the administrative affairs of the Bara-jangar villages discussed.

The *sindibor* is dedicated to Bursung, whom we have already described. She is a female deity of the mother type, probably Mother Earth, an important agent of fecundity. One of the stones is specially sacred to her. At Bandiguda it is a small stone in the middle of the platform; at Bodapada the stone is in a hollow of the over-shadowing tree; at Mundlipada it is at the foot of the tree.

In spite of its sacred character the *sindibor,* even the central *sindibor,* is treated very casually. There is no taboo on women, even on menstruating women, and men and boys are usually to be found lounging, chatting, bathing, cooking or lying fast asleep on one or other of the village platforms. More than once the Bondos have built my camp round a *sindibor,* a convenient arrangement, for everyone has somewhere to sit.

The *sindibor,* in fact, occupies the place in Bondo social life that the *darbar* dormitory club has for the Bhuiyas or Juangs. It has its ceremonial importance, but even more evident is its use as a club, where the elders gather to pass judgement on tribal offenders, plan the programme of a festival, or settle the distribution of portfolios to village officials. The platforms are also used as convenient places for work. Mats and baskets may be made; I have seen women shredding the *kereng* fibre, mothers bathing their children, girls preparing brooms or yarn; at Bandiguda, when I was there, great bundles of thatching-grass had been piled up over the main *sindibor* and had rendered it unusable for days.

The building of a new *sindibor* may be a slow process. At a new hamlet in Kichchipoda, founded in 1944, the villagers were transforming a natural outcrop of rock into a platform by gradually breaking and levelling the stones and piling rubble in the gaps. I was told that whenever anyone saw suitable stones, he told his friends and they brought them in one by one. When it was ready the platform was to be dedicated at one — any one — of the greater festivals and there would be a special feast (to which the whole village would contribute) and a dance

FIG. 41. A *sindibor* at Andrahal

to celebrate the occasion. At Goyiguda, where a *sindibor* was made within living memory, the women played an important part in its dedication. Every woman and girl in the village, and their female relatives from elsewhere, came with a pot of wine or beer on her head and a bundle of leaves under her arm, and offered it on the platform.

From time to time stones fall out of place and a very old *sindibor* may have to be repaired. If a stone falls of its own accord, it is considered unlucky; there is the usual apprehension of sickness and the aggression of wild beasts. The platform may be repaired at any time, but naturally if a festival is approaching, the people wait for it, as it is more economical to telescope one's sacrifices. But the Dissari may declare that it is dangerous to delay and in that case the stones are set up with the ceremony known as Bursung-gige. This, which simply means Mother-Earth-sacrifice, is conducted with variations at each of the main festivals and when a *sindibor* is first dedicated or repaired.

New stones may be added to a *sindibor* to make it more comfortable or commodious or, if it is a private platform, to commemorate a recently deceased member of the family. In 1942, for example, the people of Bandiguda had purchased a pig from someone at Cheliguda for sacrifice at a cost of four measures of grain. As they were on their way to deliver payment, someone noticed a fine flat stone not far from the path. 'We have no stone like this on our *sindibor*', he said. 'Let us take it back and then at the Giag Festival it will do for the carcasses of any big animal we get.' They paid over their grain, borrowed drums and trumpets, and on the way home six of the men tied the stone to bamboo poles and took it to the *sindibor*. The Sisa poured palm-wine and a little beer over it and sacrificed a fowl. But there is no rule about it, they said. 'If we see a stone we like and there is room for it, we remember where it is and then next time we are vigorous with liquor we say to one another, "Let's go and get that stone" and we do so.' During the *gunom* ceremonies which I witnessed at Andrahal in February 1946, a large stone was placed on the private *sindibor* of the family concerned in the name of the dead man 'so that his name will be remembered'. In this case the *gunom* memorial was placed opposite the platform, a thing which was not allowed, I was informed, in the case of the Bursung *sindibor*. There were no ceremonies at all when this stone was added to the platform—but of course there was a general atmosphere of expensive ritual surrounding the incident.

At Cheliguda, Fürer-Haimendorf was told that 'only at the time of a lunar eclipse may new stones be added to the *sindibor*', but he adds that he could find no confirmation of this in other villages. I made further inquiries and I think that what actually happens is this. There is a general belief that the performance of the correct *sindibor* ritual not only assists the crops but is also beneficial to the annual ceremonial hunt. In some villages, therefore, the Sisa tells the people to collect 'two or four small stones and put them on the *sindibor*' at the time of a lunar eclipse. 'If we do that,' I was told, 'then when we go to hunt at the Giag Festival, there will be no mistake and many animals will be killed. If we disobey the Sisa, the hunt will be a failure.' But the stones are little ones, even pebbles; and although a lunar eclipse is a time of good omen, it is not a time for adding large slabs to the platforms. No Bondo is going to do something that will land him in avoidable expense, and if he can put his stone on the *sindibor* during a ceremony or festival when someone else will pay for it, he certainly will.

As a matter of fact, it is a very rare thing to add stones to a platform once it has been made, and few people know the rules. I doubt if there are any. The Sisa or Dissari decides at the time what is to be done.

Every year important ceremonies are conducted at the *sindibor*. At the Gewursung Festival at the end of the rains, the emphasis of the Bursung-gige (as the special ritual performed on each occasion is called) is on the fertility of the crops and success of the harvest; at the Sume-Gelirak an exciting drama aims at the cementing of village fellowship; at the Susu-gige a month later the stress is laid on the regularity and order of village administration; at the great spring festival of Giag the sacrifice is directed to the success of the ritual hunt.

The essential features of the Bursung-gige are — the sacrifice of a pig (and sometimes a fowl) but never of a cow or buffalo, the sprinkling of the stones with blood, the dedication of grain or game, and a feast on the *soru* sacramental food.

I will describe the course of events at each festival in another section.

The ritual importance of the *sindibor* is now sufficiently clear. The seed for the coming year must be vitalized by its magic touch. Each animal taken in the hunt must be laid on its stones as on an altar. No consecration of a priest is valid unless made within the charmed circle; even the secular officials must be appointed beneath its shadow. The *sindibor,* where everyone can meet and chat, is the symbol of village unity, perhaps the chief instrument in promoting village fellowship.

9. Feasts and Holidays

The Bondos spend a great deal of time on their religion, and its feasts and holidays are an important part of Bondo life, which can hardly be understood apart from them.[1] They express and fulfil the Bondo's love of relaxation, his delight in gorging himself with meat and drinking with his cronies, his excited interest in ceremonial, his sense of the need to protect himself against the unseen powers.

In all descriptions of tribal festivals there is a danger — if I may coin a phrase — of missing the wood for the trees. The endless repetitions, all those fowls and goats of different colours, the little bundles of grain and turmeric, the reverences to east and west, the lustrations, the confarratio, the askesis — there is no end to it, and what is worse, there is no fixed standard, no established liturgy: every year and in every village there are little differences due to the convenience of the people or the inspirations of the priest. I have exhaustive notes of the chief Bondo festivals, most of which I have witnessed, but I do not propose to give them here in full. I shall instead attempt to indicate the main features of each festival in turn and to assess its meaning for Bondo life and character.

[1] I was present, with Mr H. V. Blackburn and Mr H. Milham at the Sume Gelirak at Bodapada in January 1946; with Mr Shamrao Hivale at the Susu-gige at Andrahal at the beginning of February of the same year, and at the Feast of Pat Khanda Mahaprabhu at Mundlipada later in the month. My assistant, Sundarlal, an assiduous and trustworthy observer, was present throughout the Giag-gige celebrations at Tulaguram in April 1944; he was only permitted to do this after offering the elders five rupees and sacrificing a chicken to Bursung and a fowl to Hundi. Bondos dislike outsiders being present at their ceremonies and they are apt to postpone them if a visitor is in the neighbourhood.

Certain features are common to every festival; a reference here will save repetition in each case. In the first place, the festivals are real festivals and holidays; on each occasion certain days are set apart as *angto* or taboo days, on which no field-work may be done; every festival is marked by very heavy eating and equally heavy drinking. Perhaps it is wrong to call these occasions a waste of time, for time is not wasted when it is enjoyed, and the Bondos certainly enjoy their feasts enormously. Before they begin there is a great business of collecting grain; the women husk and clean it; rice-beer is brewed, palm-wine accumulated; new skirts are hurriedly completed and boys overhaul their dance attire.

Dancing accompanies each festival and there is some relaxation of the rules which forbid men and women of the same village to dance together with any kind of freedom. These dances begin after supper and continue till dawn.

At every festival there is a routine worship or placation of every demi-god and demon in the calendar. Householders make offerings to Angkui and Siniboi, and bless mortar, hearth, threshold and cattle-shed; the Sisa and his staff tour round the shrines and stones with gifts of beer and grain. Nor are the dead forgotten; they are honoured in each home and worshipped officially by the Sisa.

The little rite known as Bursung-gige is invariably performed in order to flatter the earth into fecundity and in honour of the *sindibor*. The ceremony is conducted by the Sisa at the main *sindibor*, only *soru*-brothers of the village may be present. A male pig is sacrificed and its blood sprinkled on the stones of the deity and the platform. Samples of seed are collected throughout the village and these are placed on the *sindibor* and also consecrated with the blood. A special feast of sacramental *soru*-food is prepared and shared by the village fellowship. At the time of sacrifice the Sisa exclaims,

> Bursung, we worship you. Let the harvest be good. Let our children be well. Let no sickness come to the village. Below is Basmoti, above is Dharam.

At Diwali, when the Bursung-gige is conducted during the course of the Gewursung Festival, the stress is on the fertility of the harvest, and the feast serves as the first-eating of the new dry rice and millets. At the Sume-Gelirak and Susu Festivals, the emphasis is again on fertility. At the Giag-gige more attention is paid to the success of the ritual hunt, and the Sisa adds to the usual formula the words, 'May our hunting be successful'.

The Sume-Gelirak Festival

All the year round young men look forward to the Sume-Gelirak.[1] 'Even middle-aged women', they say, 'look pretty then.' If the Giag is the most serious, the Sume-Gelirak is the most exciting event of the religious year. It is a moral holiday, a week off from inhibitions, a relaxation from the tedious round of agricultural operations, a break in the dietetic monotony of every day. The normal restraints that check the relationships of boys and girls in a village are largely forgotten; members of the same *bonso* or *kuda,* relatives in the forbidden degree, find every freedom to flirt, excite themselves with obscene horseplay and very occasionally even retire together to the woods. In a dance a girl may steal a youth's cloth and wear it; this gives him the right, later on, to drag her away into the darkness, and she must not object.

But of course this great festival is something much more than a mere orgy. Held in the month of Pus (January-February) round about the time of the full moon, after the rice and *Panicum miliare* has been threshed and stored and the *Eleusine corocana* crop has been reaped, it regulates a number of important activities: no new grass may be cut before the celebration;[2] no *kereng* branches may be fetched from the forest; yarn should not be spun, though old yarn may be woven.

According to Bondo legend, the festal programme was laid down in detail by a bean-vine in the days when vegetables could talk.

A Sisa's wife was pregnant and when the moon of Pus came up, she got a craving to eat beans. She sent her husband to get her some, but as he stretched out his hand to pick them, the bean-vine said, 'Don't pluck my fruit'. 'Why not?' asked the Sisa. 'Because the gods should enjoy me first, then men.' 'But how can gods eat you?' The vine replied, 'On a Saturday clean your houses, on the Sunday make offerings along the path and eat me in the name of the gods with rice and goat's-flesh'. And it proceeded to detail the whole programme. 'If you fail in this,' it added, 'your race will be destroyed.' Since then beans have lost the power to talk, for the child in the womb cursed them, saying, 'I had a

[1] Known in Oriya as Pus Parab, the festival is celebrated by many different tribes, as well as by village Hindus. Its orgiastic character appears to be universal.

[2] Sometimes the grass is cut, but then it must be put aside; it must not be thatched on the roof. In Goyiguda in 1943 I saw a household living in a roofless house, wth the grass piled up all round, but the thatch could not be made because the festival had not been celebrated.

longing to eat you, but it was denied me, so from this day you will never speak again '.[1]

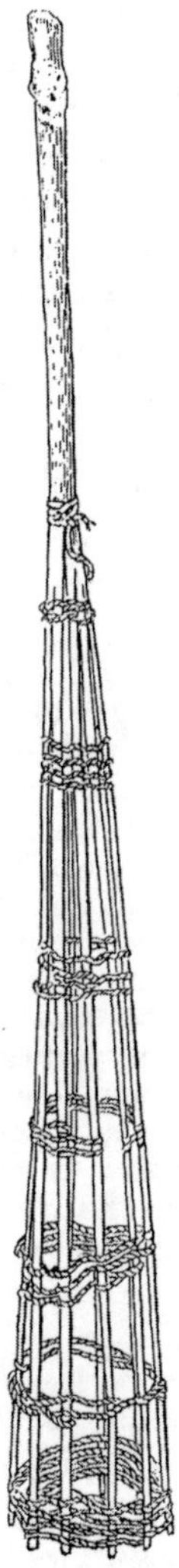

FIG. 42.
Rat-trap

The Sume-Gelirak begins on a Sunday and lasts ten days, though only some of these are *angto*-holidays. Beginning with routine propitiation of demi-gods and demons, it proceeds to a series of heavy meals, one of which is the first-eating of the new beans. The dramatic castigation ceremonies follow; boys and girls make dancing expeditions to neighbouring villages ; Bursung is worshipped; and finally the Sisa goes to the forest and performs a token cutting of grass and *kereng* branches. Dancing begins on the fourth day and continues till the end.

Let us briefly examine the outstanding features of the festival. The first is that it provides a welcome change of diet. Three special kinds of food — beans, rats and what is known as *kirimtor* — are enjoyed. The Bondos are voraciously fond of rats; sometimes they catch and fatten them in cages; at the beginning of this festival the boys go into their hill-clearings and set traps. Some of these are ' fall-traps ', stones propped up by sticks and baited in such a way that the least touch brings the weight down on the intruder; others are long bamboo tubes which are placed in a rat's run — when the unlucky creature enters it cannot back out, and the boys then kill it by cutting its throat with a knife through the bamboo slats or by squeezing the tube till it dies. Sometimes Bondos breed rats and you may see the sleek overfed creatures, but always with their teeth knocked out for a reason that will appear, in their cages, waiting for the festival to put an end to their captivity.

In the evenings the youngsters come home, each with a score of rats. They sit down by a fire and skewer the bodies on a stick or a bit of wire and roast them slowly in the flames. They keep some of these as presents for their girl-friends, hand over a few for ceremonial use, and use the rest to flavour their meals during the rest of the week.

[1] The *Dohada*, or pregnancy-craving, as a motif in Hindu fiction has been studied by Bloomfield (*J. A. O. S.*, Vol. XL, pp. 1-24) and I added a few notes in my *Folk-Tales of Mahakoshal*, pp. 456-7. The reference at the end of the Bondo legend depends on the belief that the mother's craving is caused by the hunger of the child in her womb.

There are a number of legends to account for this. One tells how the rat, which originally had a mighty organ, seduced the wife of a Bondo Raja. When the Raja discovered the intrigue, he cut off the rat's penis and stuck it on his own body. 'Since then women have eaten rats with pleasure, for they feel they are taking revenge for the way they were once deceived.' Another story attributes the enmity between man and the rat to the fact that it was the rat which nibbled a hole between the legs of the first Bondo woman and so created the vagina. The woman was very angry when she saw the blood flowing, and she killed the rat and ate its flesh with beans. This is why the Bondos knock out a rat's teeth if they propose to fatten it as a pet, for 'who knows what would happen if it got to nibbling another hole ?' Men too are said to enjoy rat-flesh for it is supposed to increase potency.

The rat also taught men how to husk grain by breaking open a grain of rice with its teeth. But the most significant of the rat-legends is connected with the discovery of fire, and I will give this in full.

Men had no fire; they sought it in the hills. They found a clump of dry bamboos; in one of them lived a rat. It said, 'If you'll get me out of this, I'll show you how to make fire'. The Bondos cut the bamboo and the rat came out and showed them how to rub one bamboo across another till fire came. Then as the Bondos were carrying their fire home, the rat said, 'I'll come with you' and it went to live with them in their village. After a little while there was a festival and the Bondos said to each other, 'What can we sacrifice?' The rat said, 'You've plenty of children, far too many of them. Sacrifice one of them and the gods and the dead will be pleased.' The men thought its advice good and they killed a fine boy. They cooked and ate the flesh and gave some of it to the rat. But when it sat down to eat, it could hardly swallow the food for laughing. 'What are you laughing at?' asked the Bondos. 'Because you are such simpletons: I told you to kill your own child and you obeyed me, a rat,' and it laughed again. This made the Bondos so angry that they killed it on the spot and swore that henceforth they would kill rats and offer them at their festivals.

In parts of Middle India, the crab is offered as a substitute for human sacrifice,[1] and it is notorious that the Konds use a buffalo for this purpose. It is just possible, though I would not press the point, that the grim little tale just narrated has some basis in fact, and that the Bondos eat rats at the Sume-Gelirak instead of a very ancient and long forgotten sacrifice of a human being.

A third rather pleasant variant on the normal diet enjoyed by the Bondos at this time is the crude delicacy called *kirimtor,* a vegetarian

[1] See *The Muria and their Ghotul*, p. 311.

sausage, which is very popular, though to my palate it was extremely insipid. It is made of rice-flour and boiled pulse, mixed into a paste and shaped as sausage-like cakes four inches long, which are wrapped in leaves and steamed in an earthen pot. The first prepared in each household is offered to Bursung at the *sindibor,* and the rest are distributed among the neighbours and given to boys during the Castigation to spur them on.

In fact every festal meal at this time is marked by an attractive habit of sharing and exchange. Householders, taking rat-meat in one hand and a gourd of beer in another, go on a series of ceremonial visits to their *moitur* friends and the leaders of their *kuda*. There is a traditional formula repeated by the visitors when they do this:

The Raja has Dassera; the Doms have Diwali; the Remos have the Sume-Gelirak. In the plains they set the fish-trap and catch fish; in the hills they set the rat-trap and catch rats. The labour of twelve months is harvested in one; we have come to the Pus Parab. For the dead we give food by the roadside; for the living we put food in their mouths. *Soru*-brothers and *moitur*-friends are demanding food and drink.

It is a nice time to camp in a village, for there is a lot of friendliness about; groups of people wander round, chatting and laughing; there are little drinking parties everywhere.

But the most serious and dramatic incident of the festival is the Castigation. Here we have the same notion already noticed for the marriage by capture. There was a substitute for the thrills of kidnapping and rape under socially approved conditions; here is a surrogate for a violent quarrel and mutual assault in an atmosphere of vinous friendliness.

The Castigation begins with little boys. Someone takes the *kinding-sagar,* the sacred drum, from the Sisa's house and begins to beat it on the *sindibor.* Other drummers join him and the people assemble. Small boys arm themselves with long switches — sago palm branches stripped of their leaves — and two by two stand up before the *sindibor* and hit each other as hard as they can. It is no pretence; soon the backs are covered with weals, and the little fellows bite their lips and go at each other with all the strength they have, while the drums chatter and the crowd applauds. When a couple has had enough, they salute each other and embrace, and another pair takes their place. Mothers hover round with oil which they smear on the wounded limbs and backs. When all the boys have completed this piquant exercise, the Sisa gives them *kirimtor* cakes 'to stop all their quarrels', and delivers a little lecture: 'Never beat one in anger. If during this dance someone's stick is knocked to the ground or breaks, let him catch his opponent by the waist and so stop him beating him. Let everyone treat his fellow as a brother. Never make other people angry.'

The boys then carry their switches out of the village and pile them up beside the path; someone offers them a little rice and meat.

The following evening, the Castigation is repeated, and now it is a little more serious, for it is the youths and men, even old men, who beat each other. The Sisa and his assistant begin; they bow to each other with folded hands, dance round and round, and then with all their strength hit one another with their switches. Blood soon flows from the wounds and when they have had enough the two men touch each others' feet, and warmly embrace, each hugging and lifting the other into the air. Where young men, perhaps jealous rivals for the same girl or old murderers just out of jail or the notoriously violent or morose goondas of the place take part, there is a real tension, and it says much for the spirit of the festival that, so far as I know, the combatants invariably accept their injuries with good humour. There is no doubt that the Castigation does something to counteract the Bondo tendency to feud and quarrel; it teaches people to keep their tempers; it lets off steam; and it serves as a surrogate for the grosser emotions.[1]

The Sume-Gelirak concludes with a series of dancing expeditions, four *angto*-holidays when people sleep off their hang-overs, the consecration of seed by the Bursung rite at the *sindibor*, and a ceremonial cutting of grass by the Sisa which is imitated the following day by the whole village.

The Susu-gige

The ten days of the Sume-Gelirak are grouped around the rising at the full of the great licentious moon of the Hindu month of Pus; the Susu-gige falls at the next full moon, of Magh. The Susu-gige is a fecundity festival, consecrating the seed. But this, one feels, has been done before. So it has, at Diwali and the Sume-Gelirak; the Susu rites reflect

[1] May's account of this, written in 1872, is worth quoting, though it misses, of course, the central purpose of the rite. 'Their religious ceremonies, like those of their neighbours, consist in offerings to some nameless deity, or to the memory of deceased relations. At each of the principal villages the Bhondas congregate once a year, in some spot conveniently situated for their orgies, when a chicken, a few eggs, and a pig or goat are offered, after which they retire to their houses, and next day assemble again, when the salop juice is freely imbibed, till its intoxicating effects have thoroughly roused their pugnacity; the processes of cudgelling one another with the branches of the salop now begins, which they apply indiscriminately without the smallest regard for each other's feelings; this, with the attendant drums and shrieks, would give one the impression of a host of maniacs suddenly set at liberty. This amusement is continued till bruises, contusions and bleeding heads and backs have reduced them to a comparatively sober state, and, I imagine, old scores paid off, when they return to their houses. Thus ends the grand festival of the year. Their other festivals have nothing remarkable.'—May, op. cit., pp. 237f.

the highly-strung and nervous temperament of the Bondos, who can never be quite sure, who are always worrying about their precious harvests, who repeat everything to complete exhaustion. Did the Bursung-gige really work? Was the Sisa truly abstinent? Suppose a sorcerer had intervened or some fool of a woman broken a taboo! It is better to do the whole thing over again, and again.

But we are not to suppose that because this may seem tedious to the observer, it is in any way tiresome to the Bondos. Far from it. They get more holidays, more opportunities for blissful bottled relaxation on the *sindibor*, yet another excuse for an all-night dance.

The essential features of the Susu-gige are a consecration, a sortilege and a scramble. First of all a quantity of seed-grain, contributed by every household in the village, is presented on the *sindibor*; a fowl is sacrificed to Bursung, blood is sprinkled on the seed and stones, and the Sisa salutes the sun, saying,

Johar, Mahaprabhu! Let our children be well. Let our seed be fertile. Let not the bean-poles break. Let the children be well. Since the earth was made we have honoured you. We have brought your offerings. When we sow a handful let us reap a basketful.

FIG. 43. A Sisa of Andrahal consecrates seed before the *sindibor* at the Susu-gige

Then the Sisa performs his sortilege by measuring the grain. He fills a bamboo-measure with rice-seed, first putting in a little, then filling it up, pressing it down with his right hand, covering it and setting it upside down on the ground. He sacrifices another fowl, pouring the blood over the measure and setting the feathers round it. After some hours the Sisa returns and measures the grain a second time. If the quantity has decreased — or rather, settled better in the measure — the omens are unfavourable; but if there is any surplus, there is jubilation, for it means the harvest will be good.

When this has been determined, especially if the omens are good, there is a wild scramble to obtain a few grains of the dedicated rice; these are taken away and mixed with the rest of the seed to make it fertile.

The Susu-gige is a convenient opportunity for the appointment, or re-appointment of village officers. This has to be done every year. The elders gather on the *sindibor* and discuss whether the existing staff should continue or whether there should be any changes. At Bodapada an old man gave a fertility blessing to ensure that the hard-worked Naiko, Sisa and Bariko should have many children and good crops. It is interesting that the Bariko, who nowadays is always a Dom, is included in the ceremony. A reminder, perhaps a rather half-hearted one, is given that these officials must be obeyed.

At Andrahal, I assisted at the appointment of a new Naiko. A venerable old man, of no particular status other than of age, made the candidate sit on the *sindibor*. He put a mark of rice on his forehead and crying, 'From today you are Naiko,' thumped him on the back with his clenched fist. Then he went on, 'Should any officer, great or small, come here, you must attend him and not go elsewhere. Explain things to the villagers and look after them. If anyone here kills another's fowl or goat and eats it, if anyone beats another or murders him, it is your duty to report the matter to the Government.' Then everyone there thumped the new Naiko on the back and he rewarded them by giving a rupee for the purchase of liquor.

There was a more elaborate ceremony at Mundlipada on 18 February 1946. After the consecration of seed and the worship of Pat Khanda Mahaprabhu, mats were spread in front of the private *sindibor* of the Naiko of Mundlipada who is, of course, the hapless Raja of the Bondo tribe. These mats were for the twelve Naikos of the Bara-jangar villages, who have to be re-appointed or superceded every year. The ceremonies were characteristic of tribal mentality. Some of the Naikos did not turn up at all; one was too drunk to sit on his mat; all the others announced their intention of resigning. The Naiko of Mundlipada himself said — with considerable reason — 'What is the use of my being Naiko? No one takes any notice of me. When an official comes,

I and my family have to do all the work, and the people say to me, "You are the Naiko, aren't you; then you can go and fetch water and wood; we don't want these people here, you can look after them".' And the old man, who is a most admirable and dignified old man, refused to take his place on the mat. This, of course, was news, and a big crowd gathered. Some people tried to make one of the Naiko's brothers, Hadi or Mangla, Naiko in his stead. Both refused. Other names were proposed, but no one wanted the thankless task. Round a milling throng of men hovered the women, mothers and wives of the disputants, trying to push their way forward and rescue their menfolk from disaster. Fortunately on this occasion, in spite of a lot of posturing and talk, there was no actual violence, and in the end the old Naiko was persuaded to accept his usual portfolio. The Naikos of the other villages, after endless discussion, were persuaded to join the old man on the mats. The Bandiguda Naiko went off in a temper, so someone else was appointed; a substitute was found for the drunken headman, and yet another for the Naiko of Gokurupada who did not appear at all. When they were all in a row, the Naiko of Mundlipada got up and assisted by the Dom Barik, tore a bit of cloth (provided from his own pocket) into strips and tied one of these round the head of each Naiko; he gave a 'turban' also to the Sisa of Pat Khanda Mahaprabhu, whose secular dignity was thus recognized. He put marks of rice on knees, shoulders and forehead (in that order), tied the cloth round the head, and thumped each recipient on the back in token of his appointment.

The 'refusal' psychology of the Indian aboriginal was very prominent during these proceedings. By 'refusal' I mean the habit, which to the visitor is rather distressing, of looking a gift horse in the mouth. If you give 'baksheesh' to an aboriginal, it is ten to one that he will return it, hoping for more. At a marriage or a funeral, no one will accept the hospitality offered without a protest; a Pardhan measures the liquor provided by his host at a wedding by putting his leg into the pot. A wife who wants something from her husband will not ask for it in the conventional manner, but will practice the *khatpatti,* lying on her bed with her back to her distracted partner who is forced to abase himself before he can understand her needs. This is the psychology of the Neng, whereby it is proper to resist every act in a birth-ceremony or a wedding until one has been bought off by a present. It is connected with the mentality behind the policy of 'sitting dharna' or offering satyagraha. Not one of the Bondo headmen thought it consonant with his dignity to allow himself to be appointed to his not undistinguished post without expressing his complete detestation of it and demanding that he should be forced into an office for which he said he had no attraction.

The Giag-gige[1]

This great festival, which usually falls in April, at the beginning of the hot weather, lasts for over a fortnight, and is distinguished by strict *angto* rules, ritual hunting, First Fruits ceremonies and the worship of every demigod in the pantheon.

As the programme of the Sume Gelirak was detailed by a bean-vine, so that of the Giag-gige is said to have been instituted by a mango — the First Fruits celebration of the new mangoes being an important moment in this festival.

A youth loved a girl of his own village, *bonso* and *kuda*. How could he wed her ? The girl loved the boy the more and begged him to elope with her. But the boy refused. The girl said that she would force her way into his house. He was afraid of jokes in the dormitory and judgement on the *sindibor* and decided to rid himself of his lover. He took her to the forest and killed her there, burying her among the trees. Presently there sprang from her body a mango tree; the flowers in her headband became its flowers and her breasts its fruit. The boy missed the girl who loved him and one day went to weep for her by the place where she was buried. He found the tree and stretched out his hand to pick the fruit. But the mango said, 'No, you must not taste my flesh until the gods have eaten it. Prepare for me a great festival; its name will be Giag; at such a time offer me to the gods.' The mango explained all that was to be done, and the boy returned home and told the elders how to perform the Giag.

The festival opens with several days devoted to the worship of the village and house demigods, the satisfaction of the dead and the appeasement of demons. The ritual hunt begins from the first day and continues daily for a fortnight. On the third day rice-beer is prepared by the Sisa's wife and drunk a week later when it has matured. On the sixth and seventh days there is a ceremonial burning of the forest clearings. The tenth day is the chief and witnesses special offerings to Bursung, the Earth Mother. This is followed by the First Fruits of the new mangoes. Hunting and dancing continue for another week and the festival is concluded by a rite designed to reinforce the fertility of the seed. The fundamental aim of the Giag-gige, which precedes a time of great agricultural activity, is to promote fecundity: the demigods and furies are propitiated to check any action hostile to the fields, the dead are persuaded to leave well alone. The ritual hunt foreshadows by its success or failure the nature of the crop. The worship of Bursung ensures the favour of the Earth herself. The ceremonies of burning the

[1] Under the name of Chait Parab, this festival — with varying rites and greatly reduced duration — is celebrated all over this part of India by Hindus and aboriginals alike.

hill-clearings and of blessing the seed complete the process of fecundation.

The importance of the Giag-gige is shown by the many taboos that hedge it round. Throughout the whole period no one should go in or out of the village area, the area under the control of the local manifestation of Bursung. To come in may bring spiritual infection from another village; to go out may be to carry away the fertility of the soil to alien ground. At the height of the festival, all paths leading to the village are fenced with thorns. The Sisa and his assistant must observe sexual abstinence throughout the festival, but this is demanded of ordinary folk only on special days. On the day dedicated to Maoli no one may break anything — branches, leaves or tooth-twigs — before midday. On the special day of Bursung, no one except the Sisa and his attendants is permitted to remain in the village; the whole population must camp in the forest until a blowing of horns announces the end of the Bursung sacrifices. No woman may eat the head or liver of an animal killed in the ritual hunt; this is equally taboo to the husband of a pregnant woman. No mangoes may be eaten before the First Fruits ceremony. On the last day of the festival it is, for some reason, taboo to touch cowdung. There are no fewer than four days on which no alcoholic refreshment may be consumed. On the other hand, the normal taboo on men and women of the same village dancing together is lifted and there is much more freedom than usual in the relations of the sexes.

Nowadays there is little forest left on the Bondo hills, and the ritual hunt has lost much of its excitement on account of the scarcity of game. The hunters wear their dirtiest and oldest clothes and are not permitted to cover the upper part of the body. 'If we dress like that,' I was told, 'the animals will not recognize us as men but will think we are trees.' It is very unlucky to miss an animal. 'If any creature comes out in front of a hunter and escapes without the fellow even shooting at him, we abuse him, calling him an eater of his wife's excreta. If he shoots and misses altogether, it does not matter so much. But if he shoots and the arrow just grazes the animal we get hold of the bow and arrow and break it, for there is something wrong with it: it must not be used again.'

Various means are adopted to improve the success of the hunt. Every day, before the men start for the forest, the Sisa's wife hides indoors and lets no one see her. She only comes out if the hunters bring something home. If they get nothing, she slips out secretly and bathes in a stream. Before the great hunt, at which every male in the village must be present, on Bursung's day, chastity must be observed in every home. On this day hunting-horns are blown continually and are regarded as very lucky.

There is a ceremony for the worship and consecration of the bows and arrows. The Sisa collects all the weapons and places them beneath a tree. His assistants take hollow bamboo tubes and go round the village begging for water. Each housewife throws water mixed with ash on to the roof of her house, and the assistants catch a few drops in the tubes. From each house they also take a little grass from the roof, and return to the Sisa.

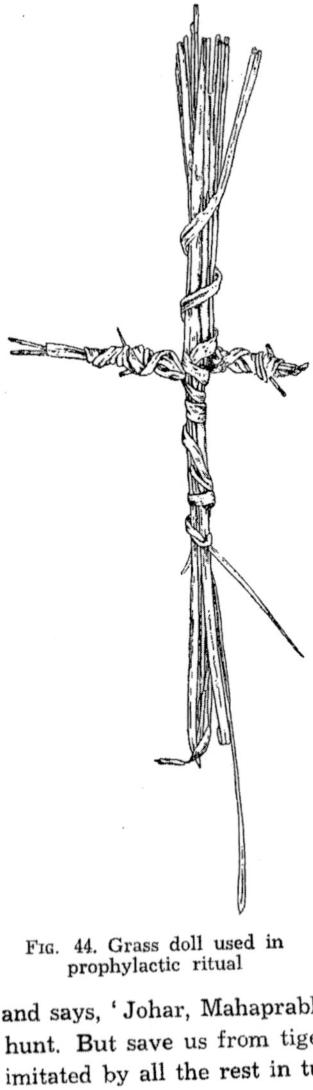

FIG. 44. Grass doll used in prophylactic ritual

The bows and arrows are then taken to an ebony tree, for here lives Bangaur the grazier of all wild animals. The Sisa makes a rough altar of the bows and arrows, cuts a green branch from the tree, bends it in half and sticks an arrow in the join. This he offers to Bangaur and breaks a rotten egg in his honour. He makes the grass brought from the village into a doll and offers it with the water to Bangaur saying, 'You are the grazier of the wild animals. When we go to hunt drive them out in front of us.' Then he sprinkles the weapons with the water and breaks the bamboo tubes. One of the assistants throws a bit of the broken bamboo into the air and the Sisa hits it with an arrow as it falls. They throw a second bit, and examine the two pieces to see which way they are lying. If both pieces are face downwards, it is a bad omen; if they are opposite, it is fair; if both lie face upwards, it is very good. Then the Sisa carries the grass doll along the path, breaks over it another rotten egg, and cuts it up with his axe. He distributes the bows and arrows.

Meanwhile the assistant Sisa has been making offerings to a bombax sapling, which he cuts down. He plants it on the path along which the party will go to hunt. The men gather about twenty yards away and the Sisa bows towards the tree and says, 'Johar, Mahaprabhu! I greet you. Let us get animals in the hunt. But save us from tigers and bears.' He shoots at the tree and is imitated by all the rest in turn.

On the last day of the festival each hunter should wash his bow and arrows and salute them saying, 'After today I am not going to look at you or you at me. So let me kill something today at least.'

If an animal is killed, the man who actually hit it immediately smears the 'head and tail' of his bow and arrows with the blood. They take the carcass to the *sindibor,* singe off the skin and remove the liver. The Sisa cuts it into small pieces. He places the lucky bow and arrow on the *sindibor* and offers a bit of liver to it. He tosses scraps of liver over the heads of the assembled company, then roasts what is left and, after eating a bit himself, distributes it to the others. They also roast the head and feet on the *sindibor* and eat the meat then and there. The successful hunter gets one whole leg as his special share and the rest of the meat is divided among the party equally.

If an animal is killed on one of the great days of the Giag, the hunters decorate the carcass 'as if it was a woman', putting rings in the ears, necklaces round the throat, bands and beads and fibre about the head, and bring it dancing, singing and drumming to the *sindibor.* The women come out singing to greet it.

Nowadays the shortage of game and scarcity of forest growth means that the hunters often return empty-handed. On such occasions, their exasperation is increased by the behaviour of their womenfolk, who meet them with taunt-songs and throw ash and cowdung over them.

> Our rice was wasted,
> Our blood [the sacrifice] was wasted,
> You have not once killed an animal
> And brought it home.
> Why has not Ispur helped you ?
> Why has not Bangaur helped you ?

The men reply,

> You did not sweep,
> You did not cowdung.

This suggests that it was the women's fault that the hunt was a failure; much depends on the conduct of the Sisa's wife during the absence of men. The women retort,

> We gave rice and blood,
> But you did not hunt properly.

The men sing,

> We hunted well, but Ispur gave not,
> Bangaur gave not; what could we do ?

The ritual hunt both assists and foreshadows the fertility of the crops. Two other ceremonies aim even more directly at guarding and blessing the forest-clearings. On the sixth day of the festival, the Sisa goes very early in the morning to his own clearing. This will have been cut already and the timber burnt, but he now collects any unburnt wood and cuts the few shoots that may have sprung up since the firing. He piles these together and lights them with fire made on the spot with a bamboo drill. He comes home, bathes and eats his lunch. Then he takes rice and curry in one leaf-cup and water in another and returns to his clearing, where he offers the food and water to the dead. The following day all the people, after observing a night of abstinence, go to their own clearings and each acts as his own priest in clearing and blessing the soil.

At the very end of the proceedings, the Sisa performs another rite for the consecration of the seed. Early in the morning, while it is still dark, he takes his hoe, a bundle of seed and some fish curry and rice to his field or clearing. On the way he digs up a little earth at a place where two paths cross. When he reaches his clearing, he makes a grass doll, mixes the earth he has brought with a little water and offers this with cooked fish to the dead and Bursung. He breaks the doll, and digs up a little patch of ground and scatters the seed over it. The following day, the villagers, fasting and after a night of abstinence, repeat the rite, each in his own clearing.

The First Fruits of the mango is celebrated during the Giag. The Sisa first worships the mango and then the whole village follow his example. He ties a string of mango leaves and one green mango over the gate of his house-enclosure; then on the threshold he offers two mangoes and some leaves to Hundi and on the veranda a similar offering to the dead. Each householder does the same.

Then the women go down to a stream and bathe. They bring water in new earthen pots. In these each housewife cooks four mangoes, and she herself offers a little rice to Hundi and the dead. If possible, fish also should be offered.

After this everyone is free to pick and eat mangoes.

The Gewursung Festival

The Gewursung [1] Festival is the Bondo substitute for Diwali, the Hindu Feast of Lights, which falls in the month of Kartik (October-November). The Bondos recognize the occasion as Hindu —'It is really for the Doms; it is they who make *dumdām* on this day' — but the rites are their own.

[1] The word is apparently sometimes used as equivalent to Bursung-gige. In any case the central purpose of both rites is the same.

They aim at doing honour to Bursung (or Hundi) and the *sindibor*, and yet again to ensure the fertility of the seed.

The ritual seems to vary considerably from place to place, which is what might be expected if the festival is a comparatively modern one. I have not had the opportunity of witnessing it, but I will reproduce an account given me at Mundlipada.

When the time for the festival arrives, the dormitory boys go round the village on a Friday begging for rice. When they have enough, the Sisa and two boys sacrifice a fowl and a pig on the central *sindibor*: the sex of these two creatures must be opposite — if the fowl is a cock, the other must be a sow.

FIG. 45. Seed tied in bundles and hung above a *sindibor*

The Sisa places two new brooms erect before the *sindibor* and makes little heaps of rice and other seed. He sacrifices the fowl and pig before them on the ground, not on the platform. He rubs turmeric on his body and on his assistants and kills the fowl. He takes the pig in his hands and makes an incision in the snout, allowing the blood to fall on the seed; then he makes the pig eat a little and his assistants kill it. The boys cook the blood-stained rice and eat it with the Sisa on the *sindibor*. They give the pig's head to the Naiko and cut up the rest of the flesh, distributing it carefully throughout the village. Every house must get a little. The housewife cooks it outside and then takes it in and offers it to the dead; after offering, it is eaten by members of the family. As usual at a Bondo festival, gifts of food are sent to and fro between neighbours and relatives. The blood-stained rice cooked on the *sindibor* is divided into many little shares, tied up in bundles with leaves and sent to every house, where each member of the household eats a little, and preserves the rest to mix with the other seed.

This is an *angto* day. No ordinary work should be done. No one should pick anything, not so much as a leaf. No one should drink gruel of *Eleusine corocana* until the festal food is finished. Nothing must be left over; the meat and rice must be finished up, otherwise it should be thrown away. The Gewursung is performed, as I was told at Dumiripada, 'that the seed may be fertile'.

The First Fruits Ceremonies

The First Fruits ceremonies are ritual feasts, designed to celebrate the gathering of a crop and to protect it during the critical period of harvesting and storing. We have already seen how the feasts of new beans and new mangoes fall during the Sume Gelirak and Giag Festivals. The eating of rice at the Gewursung Festival may serve as a Harvest Thanksgiving for that crop, though some Bondos say that neither dry nor wet rice is celebrated in this way.

In the middle of the rains there is a feast for the kernels of the new mangoes, gourds and roselle; a month later for *Sorghum vulgare*, and in October for *Eleusine corocana* and *Panicum miliare* and other small millets of the same family. Each feast is marked by *angto*-holidays, offerings to the local demigods and the dead, and a ceremonial meal, prepared household by household and then shared widely, of the commodity which is to be honoured and preserved.

Pulses seem to be ignored, and in some villages there is no ceremony for rice. The Bondos say that this is because these are 'new, or modern, crops' and they only feast ceremonially on their ancient ones.

10. The Malefice

Bondo ideas about sorcery and the *maleficium* follow the classic models. 'We should never forget', says Kittredge, 'that the essence of witchcraft is *maleficium*. The hatred and terror which a witch evokes is due to her power to inflict bodily injury. Every witch is prosecuted, not because she amuses herself with riding on a broomstick or because she has taken a fiend for a lover; she is hunted down like a wolf because she is an enemy to mankind. Her heart is full of malignity. For a harsh word or the refusal of a bit of bread, she becomes your mortal foe. And her revenge is out of all proportion to the affront, for she is in league with spirits of evil who are almost infinite in strength. She sends blight upon your crops, the rot upon your sheep, the murrain on your cattle; your house takes fire; your ship is cast away. She visits you and your family with strange wasting diseases — with palsy, with consumption, with raging fever, with madness, with death...The witch is a murderer, or may become a murderer on the slightest provocation. She cannot be spared, for there is no safety for life, body or estate until she is sent out of the world.'[1]

If we are to apply this passage to the Bondos, we have first to shift the sexes, for their practitioners of black magic are generally

[1] G. L. Kittredge, *Witchcraft in Old and New England* (Harvard, 1918), p. 4.

considered to be male, and we have then to consider the curious fact that although the dangers of sorcery are fully realized the sorcerer appears to be but seldom penalized. Only one out of twenty-five homicide cases was due to a suspicion of sorcery. I have heard no tales of witch-hunts or ordeals such as are common in Hindu India. One reason may be that the accused are usually men, another that a man rarely works alone. Bondo sorcery is a corporate affair; a family, a clan, a village co-operate in their hateful task, and the strength of numbers lends them security.

Let us examine some examples of sorcery classified according to the ancient European mode.

Emissor Tempestatum.[1] A favourite means of injuring an enemy is to send against him a violent storm of wind to knock him over. It is not quite clear whether the wind goes, as it were, of its own accord, or whether the *eloto* (the Bondo word for magic) clothes itself as a wind, or whether the *tempestarius* is able to summon a horde of demons to raise the storm. I have already described how Budha Mundli was bowled over by a blast of ventose magic. Lachhim Kirsani of Dattipada, now an old man of seventy, had a similar experience. One day, he recalls, while he was still unmarried, he went at the time of the Sume-Gelirak to take part in the mutual Castigation at Dumiripada. Thence he proceeded to Bodoballe for the same performance and there hit one of his competitors rather harder than the conventions of the festival allowed. 'The Bodoballe people were annoyed that I could perform unconquered in two villages and when I went home they sent magic to chase me. Like a gust of wind it struck me and knocked me over. My friends picked me up, but I was so giddy that I could not see, and they had to carry me home.' Many years later Lachhim had another experience of the same kind. He was now a fairly prosperous farmer. 'I had a good crop and sold most of it, keeping just a little for food. From Kumharput came Gour and Kumbhar traders to buy our Bondo grain. They tried to make me sell, but I refused. They went away in a temper and a week later sent magic to trouble me. I was working in my clearing at the time and the magic came like the wind and hit me so violently on the chest that I had to sit down and rest. I walked home slowly and went to bed. Soon my chest began to hurt so much that I thought I would die.'

The Elfshot. The custom of sending small material objects to penetrate an enemy's body and so injure him is of world-wide distribution. It was once common in Britain, and has been reported from Africa,

[1] The author may perhaps be pardoned the vanity of a reference to Margaret Elwin who was executed in 1615 for devising a plot to burn the town of Wimondham in Norfolk and 'to raise the wind by conjuration that the fire should not be stayed nor quenched in haste'.

Australia, Malay and Melanesia; Lhota and Sema Nagas extract from their patients bits of stone, scraps of bones, teeth, chewed leaves, brown juices, pebbles, hair 'or any old thing', which has been deposited there by an adept foe.[1] The Bondos too believe that an enemy can send the bone of a chicken or indeed of any other creature into one's body, where it will cause death unless removed by the Dissari. At Mundlipada, I was told, a sorcerer sent fish-bones into the chest of a man who had offended him and these were only removed with great difficulty. A thread of bark fibre is one of the most dangerous of these missiles, but it is said that the combination of a fish-bone with a chillie is irresistible. The victim of such an onslaught cannot be saved.

One day at Bodapada, a few years ago, Sonia Bodnaik, being drunk on palm-wine, was so indiscreet as to quarrel with Sukra Kirsani (a member of another,, and in this village, opposed, clan), accusing him of having stolen wine from his palm. The two men went to it with their fists and had to be separated by the neighbours. 'So Sukra wanted revenge and sent magic in the form of little thorns against me. My liver, chest and belly were tormented with pricking shoots of pain.'

Sonia Kirsani of Kadamguda was the victim at once of shot and buffet. 'One day long ago I went to dance at a wedding in Puchaguda. It was a big affair and there was a buffalo to be killed; people came down from the hills for it, from Bodapada and other places. When the buffalo was killed, I struggled with the others to cut off a bit of the jaw or tail. We were all pushing and fighting, but the Bodapada folk caught hold of me and stopped me cutting the jaws, which I could have done but for their interference. I was furious and hit one of them. They kicked and slapped me, and one of them drew his knife. I struck again, and got one of them very hard in the face and blood poured out of his mouth. But our host stopped the fight and we all went home. But that wasn't the end of it. The Bodapada people, who are mostly murderers anyway, brooded over the matter; they bought some very powerful magic from the Konds and sent it to me in a hollow bamboo.

'At the next Giag Festival we went to hunt in the hills near Tulaguram. Suddenly a violent gust of wind forced its way through the trees and a bamboo pole fell on me and knocked me senseless. The others thought a bear or a tiger had got me and ran to help. They found blood flowing from my nose and mouth. They carried me home, and there I managed to swallow a little gruel, but I couldn't get up; I felt as if my back was broken.'

[1] J. H. Hutton, *The Sema Nagas* (London, 1921), pp. 213f., 231f.; J. P. Mills, *The Lhota Nagas* (London, 1922), p. 166. Kittredge gives references 'ad libitum' to such practices (op. cit., pp. 134, 455).

Metamorphosis. The witch-creed recognizes two forms of metamorphosis. Demons may take the form of animals and in this guise may serve the sorcerer as familiar spirits to fulfil her sinister designs. Or

FIG. 46. Carving on a door at Bodapada

the witch or sorcerer may personally be transformed into the shape of bird and beast; in this case, if the creature is wounded, the culprit suffers in similar fashion.[1] The Bondo, like everyone else, believes that a sorcerer can turn himself into a tiger; indeed it would be hard to discover, in tribal opinion, a tiger of a purely zoological character. But the Bondos also, for some reason, connect the peacock — that splendid bird which in other cultures has a generally sacred reputation — with malefic magic. At Andrahal, for example, I was told that 'a peacock, which is a witch in bird form, goes into a house while the people are asleep and drinks their blood, making a hole in chest or belly. The victim gets very sick; no one can cure him.'

Venefica. Venific magic may be taken to cover all those cases where an enemy causes destruction by a magic poison in food or drink, or by a curse which brings disease and death. I have recorded a number of such cases, one of which led to murder. Thus, Hadi Kirsani, an old Bondo of Bandapada, is one of those who are always quarrelling with the Didayis of Patroputtu. Once a Didayi youth named Manglu eloped

[1] Cf. Kittredge, op. cit., p. 174.

with a girl and hid her in Bandapada. When her relations came in pursuit, Hadi, always glad to make trouble among the Didayis, told them where she was. They beat Manglu senseless and took the girl home. Manglu's father came for his son, and when he saw the state he was in and heard that it was Hadi who had betrayed him, he cursed the old man. A few days later Hadi fell ill—'my throat swelled up, my chest was painful and I had high fever. I called for a Kond Dissari and he said, "It is *eloto* (magic) sent you by the Didayis". We sacrificed a pig and I recovered.'

In another case, however, the Dissari who diagnosed the case refused to give the name of the sorcerer for fear that it might lead to murder. Soma Kirsani of Basupada, a quarrelsome and aggressive man, but an excellent farmer, had a bumper crop one year. 'My clearings and fields alike were full of grain, and the people at Salanpada got jealous. They called me to drink with them, and slipped *eloto* into the liquor. At once I fell ill with pains in the head and back; there was blood in my motions and for two months I could not work in the fields so that my harvest suffered.' Magic is commonly administered in this way. The wife of Lachhim Kirsani of Gokurupada, to give one more example, went one day on a visit to Dumiripada and an enemy there slipped some magic into her liquor and made her ill for a month.

The most serious case of this kind occurred at Tulaguram. An elderly inhabitant of this village, Soma Kirsani, had four grandnephews—his brother's son's sons—Gopa, Sonia, Sukra and Budha, and he quarrelled with them about the possession of a field. A meeting was held and Soma gave the younger men a cow and took charge of the field. But after a time the brothers decided that they must have it back; they collected a lot of palm-wine, killed the cow they had been given and gave a feast to the village, after which they seem to have felt they had the right to regain possession. Not unnaturally Soma asked for the return of his cow. 'We've eaten it. How can we give it back?' Soma cursed them in his rage. 'You have deceived and tricked me out of my field. Now as my cow has died all four of you will die.' Nothing happened for a time. Then some twelve months later Gopa fell sick and died. Soon afterwards Sonia and Budha also died. Sukra carried on for a little longer and took one harvest from the disputed field, but then he died also. On the day the villagers cremated his body, a distant relative, Mogla Kirsani, came from Bodapada and abused Soma. It is not clear why he should have taken the matter so seriously, for his family and economic interests were not greatly involved. But he declared, 'You have bought *eloto* from the Konds and the Gadabas and even the Doms, and by its power you have killed my brothers; now I am going to kill you'.

That night he went to the veranda where the old man was sleeping and killed him with an axe.

When anyone actually dies as a result of *eloto*, the cremated bones are expected to be black and hard. On 17 May 1945 an old woman died at Kirsanipada. She was Aiti, the widow of a fairly well-to-do man called Sonia Kirsani. When the mourners went to the burning-ground a week later to examine the bones, they found them 'black, strong and shaped like a bow'. From this they knew that the woman had died of magic and popular report credited her young brother-in-law with the crime. Aiti had been the mother of a son and daughter. The boy died young and the girl married a man from Bodoballe. Sonia, the father, had four fields and two pairs of bullocks and did well, but was continually being bothered by Lachhim who had two idle sons to feed and was very poor. The two families lived apart and there were constant quarrels, for Sonia refused to help his brother but was very generous to his daughter and her husband. He would call them to his house and say, 'Stay here with me and look after me; when we die all these things will be yours'. But Lachhim and his two sons said to the girl, 'If you and your husband come here, we'll kill you. You're not going to get this property.' Lachhim, it is said, was so eager to gain his brother's possessions that he killed him by *eloto,* thinking that it would be easy to trick the widow out of her inheritance. But she proved unexpectedly obstinate and sent her husband's things secretly bit by bit to her daughter's house in Bodoballe. When Lachhim discovered what was going on, he is supposed to have performed the necessary rites and killed the old widow also, and so got possession of the property. It is noticeable that no one thought it necessary to take any kind of action against Lachhim.

That is perhaps the first point we may make about the Bondo attitude to sorcery: the comparative unimportance of the sorcerer or witch. There does not seem to be a professional class; anyone can take up the malefic art if it becomes necessary; in many cases the actual *eloto* is purchased from outside and can be used even by an amateur. Along with this it should be noted that sorcery is frequently the work of a number of persons; a village or a family acts in concert against an enemy. Again, revenge by magic has the great advantage over ordinary crime in using invisible weapons and acting at a distance. This kind of murderer always has an alibi.

Eloto is often described as if it was some material substance. Naturally enough, I have never been able to see it or even to obtain a clear description. The victims who do not see it are voluble enough; the sorcerer will always hold his tongue. But Budha Kirsani speaks of the *eloto* as 'being by him' and of its running away when chased by Pat Khanda Mahaprabhu. Others are hit by the *eloto* in the form of a gust of wind or pierced by it in the form of thorns. The normal way of curing an attack of sorcery is to sacrifice a pig or fowl to the *eloto,* as though it was something with an independent existence, after which it goes away. Sometimes the *eloto* is persuaded to go into a grass doll, which is then taken out of the village and thrown away, or cut in half with an axe.

On the whole, however, sorcery and witchcraft is not one of the major disturbances of Bondo life. Only one recent murder was due to it. The word 'witch' is not among the terms of abuse used in women's quarrels. Employed by an individual, *eloto* is described as the worst of sins; as a corporate weapon, to be used for example against the Didayis, I am not so sure that it is condemned.[1]

11. Ethic

The formal Bondo ethic (which is far from being the whole story) centres round two important words, *bissas* and *angto. Bissas* appears to be the Mundari *bisi* (pollution) which among the Hos, for example, describes the period of a woman's impurity after childbirth, or it may be related to the Uraon *bisaha,* a wizard who can distil magic poison, *bis*, against his enemies. The Bondos, however, equate *bissas* with something more than mere ceremonial impurity; it is that, but it is also *pāp* or sin, of which there are three great manifestations—incest with a real or *soru*-sister, murder and *eloto* (black magic). Each of these brings its appropriate punishment—incest leads to blindness, murder to rheumatism and sorcery to leprosy. Theft, adultery and lying are comparatively minor forms of *bissas,* but they too may entail retribution.

But I think that the essence of *bissas* is that it is a pollution; the sins it describes pollute a man, put him out of a state of grace and thus expose him to the attacks of hostile forces. This suggestion gains support from the fact that *bissas* can be transferred to another. Two examples of this are instructive. On one of the days during the Giag-gige when it was taboo to pick anything before noon, the daughter of one Soma Mundli of Tulaguram picked some fruit and ate it. Her mother caught her at it and abused her for doing such a thing on that morning. 'As a result of this abuse the girl's *bissas* passed to her mother. For the rule is that if anyone witnesses such a breach of taboo he must not refer to it or the *bissas* and its punishment will pass to him.' In this case the retribution was swift and terrible. Later

[1] In 1943, in a little hut at Goyiguda, I saw a scene that was reminiscent of the illustrations of classic witchcraft in Europe. A hideous and deformed old hag stood before the door, over which hung a python's head, a turtle-shell, the root of a bamboo and the skulls of two large lizards.

in the day, when the men were out hunting, the women went to a stream for fish and crabs. Soma's wife and daughter were turning over the rocks, when the daughter saw a leopard approaching. She screamed and the mother asked what was the matter, for her eyes were blinded by the *bissas* that had passed to her. 'Cannot you see the spotted thing ?' cried the girl and ran away to safety. But the mother's eyes were blind, and she went on turning over the stones to find her crabs, until the leopard sprang on her and killed her. On another occasion, during the Sume-Gelirak Festival at Mundlipada, the son of Sonia Dangra-Manjhi picked some beans before the taboo on doing so had been lifted, and roasted and ate them. His mother saw him and gave him a beating, with the result that the *bissas* was transferred to her. The following day, when she was out fetching wood, a bear attacked and wounded her.

The Bondo word for taboo, breach of which is not only *bissas* (in the sense of sin) but brings *bissas* (in the sense of pollution) on the transgressor, is *angto*. '*Angto* means No', I was once told and it is a good definition. But it also implies something spiritually dangerous, something 'not done', a mistake, a fault, but not quite a sin; I do not think theft or murder, for example, would ever be called *angto*. But it would be *angto* to steal the sacred *kinding-sāgar* from the Sisa's house or to leave your village during the Giag-gige in order to murder someone outside. *Angto* is not, however, a Remo word. In various forms it appears to be of fairly wide distribution. Thus, in Gujarati and Bengali *aentu*, and in Telugu *antu* means 'touch', and is used for anyone in a state of ceremonial pollution, such as the menstrual period. The Bengali word is often used of 'leavings' of food, which are taboo to all but certain relatives.

The word is in fact specially used in connexion with the taboo on doing ordinary work or going outside a village area on ceremonial occasions. The ten central days of the Giag-gige, for example, are *angto*; no one may go to the bazaar, do his ordinary work, bring wood or leaves from the forest (except on the way home, casually, from the ritual hunt), or drink certain kinds of gruel. The ten days of the Sume-Gelirak are also *angto*, and so are the days before and during the Gewursung and First Fruits ceremonies. The Dagoi Gige involves an *angto* for those observing it, though not for a whole village. After death, the first few days are *angto* for the close relatives, and the tenth day *angto* for the whole village; 'If we did not observe *angto* on this day the crops would die just as the dead man has died.' In fact, any ritual performance, any activity which brings one into touch with unseen powers, may involve an *angto*, which must be carefully observed.

The word is used very much as the Marias use *polo*. I once wanted a great drum in a Maria shrine in the Abujhmar brought out for my inspection. '*Polo, polo,*' they said and there was nothing more to be done. Another day I was about to walk behind a house, forgetting that was the ground trodden by menstruating women; a Maria darted for ward and stopped me, simply saying '*Polo*'. So if you want a Bondo to do some work or go somewhere on a forbidden day, he just says '*Babu, angto*', and there is no more argument. If you pass a group of Bondos engaged on a sacrifice and speak to them, they will not answer, but will simply say '*Angto*'.

But Bondo formalism is not merely negative. An Oriya word *sato* (truth) is used to denote the kind of life expected of someone who, like the Sisa or Dissari, is frequently having to perform religious rites. To live 'in truth' does not mean that a man must bind himself to the often embarrassing duty of avoiding lies. It does not imply that a Dissari will be in closer touch with the divine — will enjoy a more open vision — if he is kind to animals and goes on the wagon. To live in *sato* means that a man must keep the tribal rules. He must observe the *angto* taboos. He must perform exactly the prescribed ceremonies. He must pay attention to his dreams. He must fulfil the obligations of ritual askesis on important occasions, and be particularly careful about his sexual relations before a ritual hunt or during a festival.

I am not sure how tribal opinion would regard a Dissari who became involved, say, in an open scandal with another man's wife. On such a point opinions given to the inquirer are of little value, unless they can be supported by actual instances, and I have not heard of such a case occurring, for after all in Bondo society adultery is rare. A Sisa or Dissari can certainly murder and steal, lie and be drunken without any loss of spiritual authority or efficiency. On the whole, just as a Bondo priest does not enjoy a superior social status, so I do not think he is expected to be morally better than other people.

This is not to say that the Bondos have no moral ideas. They have very definite opinions about what is good or bad in the realm of conduct. 'A bad man', I was told at Andrahal, 'is one who quarrels when he gets drunk; he beats people or kills them, not because he is just in a bad temper, but because he has thought about it and does it deliberately; he steals other people's palm-wine, fowls and pigs; he is too proud to talk nicely to his neighbours; he is rude to everyone and always cross.' On the other hand, a good man is one 'who when he gets drunk just talks but does not mean anything by it. What he says is not from his heart. If he tells you to eat his wife's excreta, he doesn't really mean that: he simply wants to say something. So his words do not lead to feuds and murders. He treats good and bad, rich and poor, alike. He is not jealous if his neighbours are better off than he is. When other people are in trouble he helps them, and if there is a quarrel he tries to make peace. When visitors come to his house he receives them with honour.'

In the instructions given to a young wife at her wedding, great stress is laid on the duty of hospitality and proper reverence for the aged. At a funeral the survivors are urged to 'work in unity with their relations', to avoid quarrels, to be hospitable and to fulfil their civic duties. During the Castigation of the Sume-Gelirak, the combatants are reminded 'never to beat anyone in anger', never to annoy other people and to treat all men as brothers.

This Sermon on the Bondo Mount is not ignoble and I have little doubt that the people make a sincere attempt to live up to its simple yet far-reaching ideals. Bondo society does treat all men as equals; it is very hospitable — at least to its own people; it tries to make and keep the peace; in spite of many internal feuds, it is a closely united body.

How far are these moral and formalist principles derived from divine beings and supported by supernatural sanctions? The character of Singi-Arke is ambiguous, that of Pat Khanda despicable, that of the demigods grasping, arrogant and misanthropic. Mahaprabhu, as Singi-Arke or Bhimai, has been clearly made by the Bondos in their own image. He is a typical Bondo, coarse, rough, generous, affectionate, quick-tempered. He has no hesitation in telling lies; he is cruel to animals; he has scant regard for human life. Indeed his sexual morals fall far below the normal Bondo standard. He conducts a particularly disgraceful intrigue with the beautiful Diyamoti, murders her husband and, when he finds her sexually importunate, kills her too. Bhimai also seduces Jalkamni, though it is not recorded that he committed murder to achieve his end.

But Singi-Arke Mahaprabhu is at least a large, generous, hospitable being compared with the despicable Pat Khanda Mahaprabhu. Pat Khanda reveals himself as an egoistic, arrogant, irresponsible Hindu swashbuckler, a goonda among the gods, treacherous even to his own worshippers. Of the great company of demigods, demons and furies, the less and the better; they seem mainly interested in food; without hesitation a demigod will kill a beautiful little child to get a fowl, or destroy a young mother for a meal of pork. Not one of them ever shows the slightest interest in any kind of moral idealism.

Such being the gods, how far is human morality protected by divine sanctions? The answer to this question is complicated by the extent to which Hindu ideas have infiltrated into Bondo thought. A Bondo who has mixed with Hindu prisoners, who are sometimes rather pious, in jail,[1] or has come under strong Dom influence at Pinnajangar or Mundlipada, will tell you that Mahaprabhu is the witness of human sin and virtue and that he immediately punishes any deviation from the highest moral code. Fürer-Haimendorf was told that Pat Khanda Mahaprabhu punished murderers by sending policemen to put the murderer in jail. There is only one way to decide how far such professions of morality are genuine and that is to find concrete instances of such punishment by the Supreme Being. But in spite of exhaustive inquiries in all the major Bondo settlements, I was unable to find any examples of Mahaprabhu or Pat Khanda punishing men for what we — or even they — call sin. There are many cases of drastic retribution on those who break the *angto* rules, ignore the warnings of dreams or show themselves lax in the performance of their religious or funerary obligations. But it was never Mahaprabhu who inflicted these punishments; it was always a demigod, a fury or the dead. For example, when Hadi Mundli of Andrahal went one night to steal from his recently-deceased *moitur*-friend's sago palm, it was not Mahaprabhu, but the outraged ghost, who threw him down and injured his foot. Indeeed I was frequently told quite explicitly that Pat Khanda Mahaprabhu did not punish men for adultery or murder. It is the *sairem* of the murdered man, not the Supreme Being, who torments a murderer in jail.

But there is one way in which Singi-Arke and Pat Khanda can be employed for the support of moral standards. They can be invoked to punish an offender; a human being can use the Supreme Being just as a witch can use a familiar. Perhaps because of some latent sense of impropriety in this, I was told that such invocations are but rarely made. I know of two examples. Ten or twelve years ago — and there has not been a single instance at Mundlipada in the interval — Kurri Mundli invoked Pat Khanda Mahaprabhu against his neighbour, Mangla Dangra-Manjhi. Kurri's cow got by mistake into Mangla's shed. Mangla tried to drive it out, lost his temper and knocked it on the head. The cow died and Kurri quietly removed the carcass and sold the meat to the villagers. He made no fuss and started no quarrel, but next morning he took a ritual bath, threw rice towards Pat Khanda Mahaprabhu and said, 'This man killed my cow for no reason; now punish him'. That very night, as Mangla was sleeping by the fire, he rolled over into it and was burnt so badly that he lost the use of one leg.

After the murder described at pp. 237-9 Muliya told his friends that when the police came he proposed to confess what he had done. They suggested saying that the dead man had fallen drunk from the palm and

[1] And not only Hindu prisoners. 'Prison populations show an overwhelming majority of those who claim some religious affiliations.' — H. E. Barnes and N. K. Teeters, *New Horizons in Criminology* (New York, 1946), p. 223.

had been killed by accident. 'For he is dead and we have one widow on our hands. If you go to jail, we'll have another. It will be enough if one is widowed.' But Muliya, or so he says, refused. 'I will never tell a lie; let Government do what it will. For if I tell a lie, the crops will fail, my children will die, I myself may be bitten by a snake.' Muliya, after four convictions, has become a little vociferous in his protestations of virtue, and I fancy the truth is that, knowing that a number of people proposed to give evidence against him, he decided that his best chance was confession. Even so, he produced what I believe was not a deliberate lie, but a myth which he persuaded himself to accept as a form of refuge and escape. He was arrested and in due course appeared before the Sessions Judge and was confronted by the prosecution witnesses. Muliya recalled the strange fantastic myth which I print later in this book, but the witnesses denied that Muliya had had provocation: his enemy, they said, had not enchanted him or threatened to murder him; there was no question of his acting in self-defence; it was simply a sordid quarrel about a field. This evidence, at least in Muliya's opinion, got him a longer sentence and he was annoyed.

'As I was going in the train,' he told me, 'I saw the electric light and it reminded me of Singi-Arke. I saluted it and said, "If these witnesses told lies against me, without fail punish them". And presently the first of the witnesses fell from a tree and was killed; the second went lame; the third was bitten by a snake; the fourth lost one of his bullocks eaten by a tiger and his son died.'

Singi-Arke may also be invoked in oaths. When I was camping in Mundlipada in February 1946, there were a number of petty thefts from the camp. One night, there was a festival dance attended by people from Bandapada among others and I lost a shirt and Sundarlal a dhoti. When we investigated the matter the following day, there were many witnesses who had seen these things in the possession of the Bandapada people. We called them and, after a lot of discussion, they proposed to prove their innocence by solemn oaths. We went out onto the hillside, and one by one they stood up and faced the sun and cried, 'O Mahaprabhu, below is Bismotin, above is Dharam Deota. O Mahaprabhu Singi-Arke, be witness! I salute you with ten million salutations. If I stole and anyone saw me, let my eyes be blind, my arms and legs break, my crops be ruined. O Mahaprabhu, I salute you; be my witness.' Since it was quite obvious, not only that the oath-takers were guilty but that they knew we knew they were guilty, it occurred to me that perhaps they took a somewhat modest view of the likelihood of Mahaprabhu reacting in any very definite way against them. And in fact, though we waited a bit for something to happen, I noticed that no one seemed very surprised when they all walked home unblinded and unlamed.

On the whole, then, I conclude that while the Bondos have a far from ignoble standard of conduct to guide their everyday life, it is the ritual offence, or those acts of commission and neglect which directly affect the prestige or comfort of unseen beings, which are supported by supernatural sanctions. The character of the gods is less admirable than that of men, and none are likely to serve as exemplars of exalted conduct.

CHAPTER SEVEN

FESTIVITY IN BLACK

1

To understand the reactions of the emotional and affectionate Bondos towards death, the ethnographer must not only be present and share to some extent in the grief of actual bereavements, record legends and statements and study the supposed fate of the soul, but he must also examine in detail the rites which are performed after a death, for it is ultimately in these rites that beliefs are expressed.

Death really has no business in the world at all. Like many other tribesmen, the Bondos regard death as unnatural, an innovation to prevent the world from being over-populated. A legend about this comes from Andrahal:

> Formerly people did not die, and Mahaprabhu thought, 'If nobody dies, how will there be enough room in the world for everybody?'[1] He went to Goigecko, the lord of death, and said to him, 'These Remo people do not die; you must arrange that they do'. Goigecko sent his messenger, but the Remos shot and killed him with their arrows. Then Goigecko made a tiger and sent it to kill the Remos, but they killed it also. Then Mahaprabhu himself intervened; he took a hair from the head of Sita-Mahalakshmi, turned it into a snake and sent it to kill the Remos.
>
> When the snake reached the Remo village, it saw a little child playing in the street and his mother sitting by. The snake bit the child and he fell down. The mother took a stick and killed the snake. But the child also died. The mother said to the dead snake, 'Because you killed my child, I am going to roast and eat you'. This she did and her body was filled with *eloto* (sorcery). Because the child was killed, death came into the world.

Bondo eschatological ideas are very confused and I doubt if it is possible to say at this date that 'the Bondos think this or that about the after-life'; the truth is that some think one thing and some another. There is, however, more uniformity of practice, and it is just possible in some cases to track down the ideas behind it. Like most Indian tribesmen, the Bondos have a number of contradictory notions, which they

[1] This notion of death being introduced by the Supreme Being to limit the population is common in primitive Indian mythology. See my *Myths of Middle India*, pp. 411ff.

hold all at the same time, about the fate of the soul. It goes to Mahaprabhu and is sent back to be reborn as an animal or human being. At the same time it is believed to remain on or near the earth as a shade and to wander restlessly in the forest until it is mingled in the company of the ancestral dead by the performance of the appropriate ceremonies. The Bondos do not, however, still further confuse the issue, as so many other aboriginals do, with a ceremony of 'bringing back the dead' whereby the soul, which at one moment the people are doing everything to avoid, is at the next ceremonially brought back to the house. The discrepancy in Bondo thought is thus comparatively simple.

The Bondo word for the dead is *sairem*,[1] which appears to mean 'shadow' and this is used in a vague general way like the Oriya *duma*, or the Muria-Maria *hanal*. It is the *sairem* which returns to make itself unpleasant to the living and must be appeased by elaborate obsequies.

I rather doubt, however, if a Bondo would speak of the *sairem* as 'going to Mahaprabhu'. The word usually used in this connexion is the Oriya *jiwo* (I have also heard the word *diyo*) and this is perhaps what we would expect. The idea of an ascent to the Land of Mahaprabhu and rebirth in animal or human form must be comparatively recent and probably dates from the time of the Hindu Dom settlements in Bondo country. Similarly, the Marias and Murias, Juangs and Gonds use *jiwa* or *jiv* for the soul which goes to heaven and is reborn, and their own words, like *hanal*, for the earth-bound ghost which has to be propitiated. Fürer-Haimendorf was given a word *siorem* as used in the sense of *jiwo*, but extensive inquiries failed to discover any confirmation of this. *Siorem* means 'testicles' in Remo, and it is possible that the Bondos once held, as the Baigas now hold, that the seat of the soul was in these organs. But the word, and even the idea, has evidently passed out of general use.

After death the *sairem* is excommunicated, 'for who knows where it may have wandered or whether it has eaten with Dom *sairem* or no'. It is, in fact, in the position of an ex-convict who, on his return from jail, must be purified of all defiling contacts before he can be readmitted into the community. This is why the *sairem* is so restless, for it has no fellowship either with the living or with the other dead, the majority of whom have been readmitted to their tribal privileges by the Kungdak or Gunom ceremonies.

For the fundamental aim of these rituals is to regularize the ghost's social standing in the unseen world; only when it is admitted into

[1] 'Both Bondo and Gutob have a belief in, and a name for, the spirits of the daparted (*sayirẽ or se'arrai*), who seem according to their ideas, to exercise some beneficent influence on the crops.'—Henderson, qu. J. C. Molony, *Census of India, 1911*, Vol. XII, Part I, p. 167.

the tribal fellowship of the Bondo dead will the restless spirit be at peace. For this reason, at a *gunom* ceremony the mummers who represent the deceased are themselves regarded as outcaste for the duration of the rite and have to be purified at its close.[1]

The *sairem* wanders to and fro in the jungle; it cannot get proper food; and if its ceremonies are delayed or indifferently performed, it has to draw attention to itself by attacking some surviving member of its family with sickness or by damaging the family crops or cattle. These ideas are clearly displayed during the funerary rites and prayers; food is frequently offered to the *sairem* at the burning-ground and on the paths near the village — the idea, of course, being that if it is fed outside, the ghost will not enter the village and frighten the inhabitants — and at every festival and sacrifice food is given to the family dead in case any of them should be hungry. It is always, I think, the recently deceased who have to be propitiated in this way. Once a menhir has been erected, the offerings that are made to the stone are more for affection and remembrance than for propitiation.

But at the very same time that the *sairem* is imagined as wandering about cold, hungry and restless, the *jiwo* is pictured as flying up into the comfort of Mahaprabhu's bosom; and side by side with the attempt to mingle the *sairem* with the ancestral dead for ever, there is the rite of marking a corpse with oil and charcoal so that the *jiwo* can be recognized when it is reborn. The new Hindu ideas have in no way been assimilated but co-exist with the ancient beliefs in an undigested form. Nor is there any certainty about the new ideas. Some Bondos say that the *jiwo* is bound to be reborn as a human being and in the same family. Others believe that it may return first as an animal and only after several reincarnations as a human being. I will give a typical example of the modern Hinduized theory from Pinnajangar.

When a man dies his *jiwo* goes to Mahaprabhu. When Mahaprabhu sees that the man is at the point of death, he sends two of his constables with iron rods and a rope to catch him. They say to the *jiwo* as it leaves the body (where its dwelling-place is in the chest), 'Come along quickly now. Whatever you have given away, you will have to eat; if you have given nothing, you will starve.' They beat it, tie it up and carry it away. As they go, if the dead man has been virtuous, the guards give him *dharmo-pāni,* water of virtue, to drink; if he has been wicked, all he gets is *pāp-pāni,* water full of worms.

Mahaprabhu and his wife sit together in their place; the wife takes the *jiwo* on her lap and if the dead has been virtuous, gives it her breast to suck. But if he has been vicious, the *jiwo* gets nothing to drink but

[1] There may be a similar notion behind the Bison-horn Maria custom of excommunicating the drummers at the ceremony of erecting an *uraskal* menhir.

the spittle and urine of the virtuous. Mahaprabhu now sends two other constables to the burning-ground in the form of insects; they grind up some of the dead man's bones and bring them to Mahaprabhu, who fashions the bone-flour into a little cow. His wife puts the *jiwo* of the virtuous man into it and he is reborn as a cow. But if the man has been wicked, Mahaprabhu makes his bone-flour into a dog and sends him back to earth as a dog. Then, when the cow or dog dies, its *jiwo* goes again to Mahaprabhu, who now sends it back as a human being into the same family, and it is given the same name that it had originally.

I have quoted this highly ethicalized statement as illustrating the extent to which Hindu beliefs have already penetrated into the Bondo country; eschatological ideas are always sensitive to external influence, to which in this case the Bondos are unusually exposed. For it is natural for murderers to think and talk of death, and the released convicts are the chief missionaries of Hindu thought. In the above quotation, the punishment or reward for life on earth is in the different kind of reception one gets on arrival at Mahaprabhu's house and in the rebirth immediately following. It does not seem to be considered that a dog or a cow is capable of sin or virtue; the *jiwo* is automatically reborn as a human being, and the earlier sin or virtue is forgotten.

But it is said that executed murderers and suicides do not go to Mahaprabhu at all, nor do the *jiwo* of women dying in pregnancy or childbirth or the *jiwo* of men killed by tigers. These have no further rebirth in material form on this earth. This is not part of the Hindu doctrine, which regards freedom from rebirth as the highest reward of sanctity and devotion.

From the opposite side of the Bondo country, at Andrahal, I recorded a very different myth, an example of those personal experiences which may be one at least of the sources of stylized legend.

Gulong Sisa was very ill. Jam Raja, looking just like an old Bondo woman, with shaven head and a little skirt, came to him. 'Come to my kingdom and have a look at it; if you like it, you may stay there; if not, you may return.' Gulong's *diyo* got ready. Jam Raja had some rope and was going to tie it up and carry it, but the *diyo* said, 'You needn't bother: I'll go quietly'. Down they went to Jampur and there the *diyo* found houses in long straight rows, houses with thatched roofs standing in their own gardens, separate quarters for the Bondos, Doms and Gadabas. Jam Raja took the *diyo* to the Bondo quarter and made it sit down. There was a great trough full of rice-gruel. The people there were only two feet high; they were sitting round the trough, climbing up over the side, and scooping out the gruel with bits of plantain leaf. The *diyo* recognized its old father and mother and many other relations; they were delighted to see it and begged it to stay two or four days.

Presently it saw a goat's head brought in by some youths dancing with drums the size of one's hand. 'Where did that come from?' it asked. They said, 'The Bodoballe people gave it to us'. And in truth there had been a sacrifice of a goat to the *sairem* at Bodoballe that day, and the head went right down to the Under World.

Then Gulong's *diyo* saw a boy, Sonia Bodnaik of Andrahal, who had died not long before. He was sitting apart from the rest, and when the *diyo* asked why, it was told, 'He only came last week and we haven't admitted him yet'. Then the *diyo* got up and climbed a long flight of steps to Jam Raja's house; the Raja led it by the hand; once it nearly fell. The Raja's house too was thatched with grass; it had an enormous door. But just as the *diyo* was about to enter, it heard his friend's daughter crying, and ran back to its body.

And presumably awoke. This cthonic experience of a Lilliputian other-world is much closer to the general tribal tradition, and I have little doubt that something of the sort is the original Bondo view, onto which the whole business of heaven and Mahaprabhu has been grafted in comparatively recent times. Even here, however, the words — Jam Raja and Jampur — are Oriya, not Remo; I have only rarely heard the name Goigecko for the Lord of the Dead.

I have met one attempt — only one — to reconcile these two conceptions. That was at Mundlipada, where I was told that 'When a man dies, his *diyo* goes to Mahaprabhu but his shade becomes a *sairem* and lives here. But if Mahaprabhu does not entertain it properly, the *diyo* goes to its *sairem* and says, "I can't get enough to eat" and sends the *sairem* to pester its relations on earth.'

The Bondos are an affectionate and emotional people, and their sorrow for the dead is genuine. But they do not have the intense preoccupation with death which is the fundamental characteristic of Saora psychology. A rather cynical account of the Bondo attitude was given by Muliya Dangra-Manjhi of Mundlipada, whose indifference to the value of human life was after all notorious.

When a wife dies, the husband makes a lot of fuss and his sorrow for her lasts at least a fortnight. During this time he does no proper work. It is an *angto*-holiday for him. He says to himself, 'Now my wife is dead; where am I to get another? How can I afford a new one? I will have to go to Assam and work for the money. And while I am hunting for a wife, who will look after the children, who will care for the house and fields?' And the thought of the expense and trouble which his wife's death is going to cause makes him very sad.

But when a young husband dies, his wife is content to weep for two to four days. She is careful to let her tears fall whenever she goes for water or to the field and when there are people about. She stands weeping at the foot of the sago palm. For she thinks, 'If I don't weep, they'll laugh at me'. But directly a new man so much as winks at her, away she goes with him and her sorrows are forgotten.

It is true that one great disadvantage of death is its economic implications. The loss of a son or daughter means one less pair of hands to work in the fields; the death of a wife involves the expense of getting a new one; the death of an old man may mean the cost of a *gunom* ceremony. But this, no more than in civilized society, is the whole story. For lovers the separation is intolerable; old couples who have lived long years together cannot face parting; there are children whose death takes the brightness from a home; there are friends whose alliance is as dear as life itself. The lengthy course of funerary ceremonial is not due only to a desire to propitiate the ghost; it is intended to give the mourners an opportunity of separating themselves psychologically from the departed object, a protracted and painful process. 'Mourning', says Freud, 'is entrusted with the task of carrying out this retreat from the object in all those situations in which it was the recipient of a high degree of cathexis'. It is painful because of 'the insatiable nature of the cathexis of longing which is concentrated on the object by the bereaved person during the reproduction of the situation in which he must undo the ties that attach him to it'.[1]

Freud elsewhere makes a comparison of mourning and melancholia. 'The distinguishing mental features of melancholia', he says, 'are a profoundly painful dejection, abrogation of interest in the outside world, loss of the capacity to love, inhibition of all activity, and a lowering of the self-regarding feelings to a degree that finds utterance in self-reproaches and self-revilings, and culminates in a delusional expectation of punishment.'[2] The same traits are met with in grief, except that usually the fall in self-esteem is absent. Bondo mourning however, includes even this. The dejection is obvious to every observer of a Bondo household on the morrow of a funeral; there is no interest in any active effort that is not connected with thoughts of the dead; love-intercourse is, I understand, inhibited for the entire period of mourning; activity is forbidden by the *angto* rules. In Europe where death is regarded as the natural result of biological causes, there is no lowering of self-esteem or 'delusional expectation of punishment'. But where death occurs in an aboriginal family, it means that something has gone wrong; someone has blundered; there is a definite possibility that the death itself is a punishment and that further punishment is in store for the survivors.

I will quote another passage from Freud which, to my mind, gives in modern and psychological terms an exact picture of the Bondo funerary routine.

[1] J. Rickman, *A General Selection from the Works of Sigmund Freud* (London, 1937), p. 291.
[2] ibid., p. 143.

The testing of reality, having shown that the loved object no longer exists, requires forthwith that all the libido should be withdrawn from its attachments to this object. Against this demand a struggle of course arises — it may be universally observed that man never willingly abandons a libido-position, not even when a substitute is already beckoning to him. This struggle can be so intense that a turning away from reality ensues, the object being clung to through the medium of a hallucinatory wish-psychosis. The normal outcome is that deference for reality gains the day. Nevertheless its behest cannot be at once obeyed. The task is now carried through bit by bit, under great expense of time and cathectic energy, while all the time the existence of the lost object is continued in the mind. Each single one of the memories and hopes which bound the libido to the object is brought up and hyper-cathected and the detachment of the libido from it accomplished . . . When the work of mourning is completed, the ego becomes free and uninhibited again.[1]

This explains why Bondo funerals and their sequelae take so long; the task of liberating the mourners can only be carried through 'bit by bit'. No one who has endured the endless prolongations of Bondo grief-ritual can doubt the 'great expense of time and cathectic energy involved'. In the wailing of the women, which is largely reminiscent, 'each single one of the memories and hopes which bound the libido to the object is brought up and super-cathected'. Above all, 'the object is clung to through the medium of a hallucinatory wish-psychosis'. Here is the reason why the Bondo cannot bring himself to let the dead get away. An elaborate wish-psychosis creates the myth of the *sairem* as pathetically dependent on those that loved its warm and breathing personality in life. The belief that we are necessary to other people is one of the most consoling of man's delusions, and the Bondos readily convince themselves that without their gifts of scraps of meat and drops of liquor the dead would be disconsolate and starved. Bondo eschatology creates a hallucination by which the beloved dead are attached for as long as possible to the living. When at last the dreams are no longer seen, and the Gunom ceremony reluctantly performed, the work of mourning is completed and the mourner's ego is free and uninhibited again.

2. The Revenants

The dead come back. This belief, at once the despair and the joy of the mourner, dominates a wide field of tribal practice. On the whole, the sex of the revenant makes a great difference to the manner of the visitation. It is only rarely that women return at all; those who do are generally the victims of some unlucky death; when a female ghost appears she often takes a seductive and entrancing guise. Very different are the

[1] Rickman, op. cit., p. 144.

visits of the masculine dead; irascible and touchy, they are constantly on the watch for any breach of taboo or tribal law, and are sensitive to the least sign of neglect.

I will give a few examples of the supposed reaction of the *sairem* to irregularities in the performance of religious rites or breach of taboo. Sonia Bodnaik forgot to offer an egg to the dead at a First Fruits ceremony in Bodapada. As a result his arms and legs were paralysed. 'I sacrificed to the gods,' he said, 'but it did no good. Then the dead came to me in a dream saying, "You ate the First Fruits and forgot to give us our share". I sacrificed a pig and recovered the use of my limbs.' One year the wife of Lachhim Kirsani of Gokurupada brought home some mangoes during the Giag Festival at a time when it was taboo to do so. 'All our dead collected in the house; they were very angry; it was terrible. They started her vomiting till I thought she would die. When I saw the mangoes I realized what the trouble was and threw them away. I promised two cocks to the *sairem* and my wife got better.'

It is very dangerous to ignore a ghost's instructions. Soma Mundli of Bodapada once had a dream wherein the *sairem* appeared to him saying, 'Remember us whenever you go hunting'. But, as so often happens, Soma forgot his dream. 'I went to hunt and a wild boar charged me. I shot at it and missed. I was so frightened that I fell senseless to the ground. When I got up my whole body was full of pain. The others abused me, threatening to break my bow and arrows. For a week I lay ill; then I remembered my dream and fed the *sairem* on fish, crabs and pork and so recovered.'

Sometimes ghosts act in a wanton and unpredictable way. Soma Kirsani of Basupada, for example, told me how his wife had a very difficult labour at the birth of his first child. The Dissari who was consulted declared that the ghost of a man in Mundlipada, who was no relation and had never had anything to do with the family, had been wandering along the path by which the woman went for water, and 'having nothing else to do' had caught her.

Any failure or delay in offering the prescribed funerary sacrifices is believed to bring disaster, and—as we shall see—this probably does cause real trouble by inducing a form of melancholia in the minds of the bereaved.

There are strange tales of the association of the dead with animals which they meet when wandering out in the forest immediately after death. A story from Basupada runs:

An old man and woman had one son. He was married but presently he died. At night his ghost came to lie with his wife. In time she conceived and when her parents-in-law saw her state they were angry at her wantonness, for she must, they thought, have taken a lover. One night, the mother-in-law hid behind a grain-bin and watched to see who the man was. Her son's ghost came and she caught it. When she saw who it was, she begged it to remain. The ghost said, 'I cannot stay with you, for if I do you'll have to feed my friends'. She replied, 'As long as you'll stay with us, I'll feed whoever you bring with you'. She hurriedly cooked five measures of rice, and presently her son's friends — a tiger, a bear, snakes and birds — came to eat it. After that all these creatures and the ghost lived in and round the house.

This association with animals is one of the reasons why the dead are feared. 'We are more afraid of the dead than of the demons,' I was told at Andrahal. 'The dead are great; the demigods are small. For when the dead are angry, they call tigers, snakes and even witches to help them.' And a significant sentence was added: the dead are very stupid, 'they are slow to understand what men say' and so often cause unnecessary trouble.

At Andrahal, when Gulong Sisa's father died, and Gulong did not satisfy his *sairem* sufficiently, it went to a tiger and arranged that it should kill two of Gulong's bullocks. It called deer and pigs and other *sairem* to wreck Gulong's fields.

I do not know how far the ghost of a husband can visit his wife; I know of no actual, and only one legendary, example. I have not heard of a female *sairem* visiting her bereaved husband for intercourse. Erotic dreams are more commonly of an incestuous character.

The ghost of a woman dying in pregnancy or child-birth is known to the Bondos as Tillarpoi; a Gurangpoi is either the *sairem* of a girl who dies during the menstrual period or a phantom which was created by Mahaprabhu to show mankind how to perform the sexual act. Both spirits visit men in dreams and, after enticing them to sexual intercourse, leave them exhausted.

There are many stories of these encounters current in the villages. I was told at Bodapada how 'the Gurangpoi comes as a beautiful girl and sits beside a man as he lies asleep. She brings millet chaff and some *kereng* bark, and sits there shredding the bark and throwing the chaff at the sleeper. He begins to itch and she scratches him; they struggle and play together, until at last she falls prostrate and he is upon her. When he awakes, he feels as if he had enjoyed a drunken orgy, but he is very weak.' Gulong Sisa of Andrahal confirmed this from his own experience. 'A Gurangpoi, like a lovely unmarried girl, came to me in a dream and played with me. She threw millet chaff over me. I was sleeping on my face, but she turned me over and sat on my body, with her own hands putting my organ into her. This went on for eight days. I got very weak, my stomach ached and I had bloody motions.' Soma Kirsani of Basupada had experiences of an incestuous nature. 'The

Gurangpoi came night after night and forced me to it. Sometimes she came as my sister, sometimes as my younger brother's wife; she came again and again until I fell ill with exhaustion.'

Such fantasies resemble the European traditions of the vampire, except that there does not seem to be any extraction of blood. Their explanation is obvious. 'A nightly visit from a beautiful or frightful being, who first exhausts the sleeper with passionate embraces and then withdraws from him a vital fluid: all this can point only to a natural and common process, namely to nocturnal emissions accompanied with dreams of a more or less erotic nature. In the unconscious mind blood is commonly an equivalent for semen.'[1] The uninhibited Bondo mind does not require this distortion; it frankly accepts the withdrawal of semen, rather than blood, as the main danger of the Gurangpoi encounter.

Both Gurangpoi and Tillarpoi may also attack people directly, just as any demon may do. The Tillarpoi comes as a whirlwind 'throwing leaves into the air'; if in this form she catches a man, she strikes him on the back of the neck and knocks him down. Since this assault is usually fatal people run for their lives when they see a whirlwind coming. The Gurangpoi sometimes attacks children with fever and weakness; she may give a woman pains in the womb. The idea is probably that the frustrated spirits, who have never known the joy of motherhood, are jealous.

To guard against these attacks, various precautions may be taken. They begin at the funeral. Women dying in pregnancy, childbirth and menses must be buried; a foetus is not removed (indeed it is the bones of its knees and elbows that turn into the Tillarpoi and fly with the wind); and no visits should be made to the grave.

A man afflicted with visits from a ghostly lover may stop them by the usual sacrifices. Soma Kirsani was taken by the Dissari into the forest; there he offered two fowls and an egg in order to confine the Gurangpoi in a tree. A Tillarpoi in a whirlwind may be 'killed' if a man strikes it with a certain kind of stick made of the wood of the *kurso* (in Oriya, *kukra-hadiya*) tree.

I have twice assisted at rites intended to remove the danger of hostile assault by a Gurangpoi. At Katamguda, on 4 February 1946, there was a simple rite to protect a little girl, Gora, who had — it was supposed — been given fever by a Gurangpoi. The Dissari put six grains of rice on a leaf and, taking water in a gourd, went into the street before the house. He faced east and said, 'Below is Basmoti; above is Dharam Deota. Listen to my words and leave this child alone. Let her be like the washed rice and blossoming flower. I will give you a feast if she recovers. Should I speak falsely, Mahaprabhu is watching. O Maha-

[1] E. Jones, *On the Nightmare* (London, 1931), p. 119.

prabhu, you are witness.' He went into the house, where the child was sitting with her mother on the veranda, and placed the leaf on her head and repeated the words above her. I was told that if the child recovered and there was no relapse, the family would give a pig to the Gurangpoi later on.

A more elaborate ceremony was performed by the Naiko later in the same month when I was camping at Mundlipada. A Gurangpoi had given his wife fever and pains in the womb. One evening, therefore, he prepared an altar on the floor of his veranda with patterns of flour and coal-dust. There were seven patterns, and on them seven pice, seven iron nails, seven heaps of rice and millet, and in a basket some *Panicum miliare* chaff and seven flowers, some *kereng* thread and a black fowl. He recited the following charm:

> O Gurang of the road, let there be no belly motions, no madness, no fever! O Gour Gurang! O Brahmin Gurang! O Karan Gurang! O Gurang of the road! O Gurang going along the cattle-track! O Gurang of the cave! O Gurang of the hills! Go away! Go dancing, go happy and content, go laughing, go tickling yourself, go leaning on your stick! With medicine I send you away, with medicine. O Bondo Gurang! O Mathia Gurang! O Ghasia Gurang! Go away!

Then the Naiko tied bells to his ankles and danced in and out of the house seven times and called on the Gurangpoi spirits by their names — Kindri, Lachhma, Buddhai, Mangli, Sukri, Sunki and Kinker —bidding them depart. He cried *kurkurkurkur* and whistled as though he was calling pigs. That was all he did that night, but at dawn the next morning he took all his paraphernalia out of the village and sacrificed a fowl.

The use of *Panicum miliare* and the calling to the pigs during this ceremony requires explanation. According to Bondo legend, pigs were created for the special purpose of being sacrificed to the Gurangpoi.

> In the days when the demigods were first born and went to live among men, villages were very dirty, for there were no pigs to clean them. Gurangpoi was displeased with the sacrifices she received and spread disease among the Bondos. One day Mahaprabhu came on tour to a Bondo village and found nothing but excreta everywhere. He said to himself, 'Since these people cannot clean their villages themselves, I must give them some creature which will do it for them'. He told the people, 'You must sacrifice pigs to Gurangpoi if you would be well'. But they did not know what a pig was. Mahaprabhu returned to the sky and there made a model pig, put life in it and took it to Samudra Hill. There it had a large litter. Presently when there were many pigs living on the hill, Mahaprabhu told the Bondos about them. They brought them to their homes, and the pigs kept the villages clean and when they were sacrificed Gurangpoi was pleased and the Bondos' health improved.

In fact, so close is the association of the Gurangpoi with the pig that at Andrahal there is a tradition that the real origin of the spirit was from the chaff left over after the cleaning of *Panicum miliare,* which is usually given to the pigs. A store of this is always kept in a house, and it is said that if a pregnant woman gives birth to her child before the stock that was there at the time of conception is exhausted, a Gurangpoi is born from it. For this reason, when a woman is pregnant she tries to finish the store of chaff as early as possible.

These conflicting theories of origin appear to me to be rationalizations intended to conceal even from the free and simple Bondo mind the true meaning of his erotic dreams.[1] I feel certain, however, that the Tillarpoi and Gurangpoi are the Bondo equivalent of the Churelin of Hindu India, which is associated closely with the cult of the dead.

3. The Funeral

The Bondos bury women dying in pregnancy or child-birth and the victims of cholera or smallpox, but they burn all others. The burning-ground (*raisang-bo*) is always some distance, in any direction, outside a village, and usually under trees, any trees. For adults a pyre is built, but babies are often placed inside a small oven of stones. After cremation, the ashes are regarded as important evidence for the cause of death; an oval ring of stones is made round them, and they are covered with a lightly thatched shed with a lean-to or double roof. I have witnessed a number of funerals and will describe two of them.

[1] But another type of legend admits the sexual character of the Gurangpoi without pretence. 'The first brother and sister did not know how to do it. They slept together night after night and nothing happened. Mahaprabhu was worried by this. "If they don't work together," he thought, "how will children ever be born?" So thinking he rubbed a little dirt off his body and made a boy and a girl. They were both very beautiful and very lustful. Mahaprabhu said to the girl, "Take the form of the sister and go to her brother in a dream. Teach him what to do." He said to the boy, "Take the form of the brother and go to his sister in a dream. Teach her what to do." The phantom girl went to the boy and tickled him; he soon learnt his part. The phantom boy went to the girl and pressed her breasts and forced her legs apart; she too was not slow to learn. When the two woke in the morning, the girl said to her brother, "You did such and such things to me in the night". And the boy said to his sister, "Certainly, I did such and such things, and you also tickled me and taught me what to do". They laughed and in this way the great work came to the world. But once they had started the boy and girl did not stop for a single moment. They did nothing else; they were always at it. And now Mahaprabhu had a new cause for worry; how would there be food in the world if men and women did no other work? One day he went to see them and found them tumbling together. When they saw him they were ashamed and hid themselves. Mahaprabhu said, "There's nothing to be ashamed of. You are man and wife and may do what you will. Only spare a little time for your other labours." After that, marriage also came to the world. The two phantoms made by Mahaprabhu turned into Gurangpoi and now visit men and women in their sleep.'

On 27 December 1943, a very old man, Sonia Mundli, died at Bandapada. He had been ill for several months and expired at three in the morning. The women of the house wept loudly till dawn and then

FIG. 47. Lean-to thatched roof erected over the remains of a pyre

carried the body from the house and laid it on the ground in front; they bathed it and anointed it with a little turmeric oil. Meanwhile a number of men had gone to the burning-ground and were preparing the pyre, which apparently can be made of any kind of wood. Two men, *soru*-brothers of the deceased,[1] tied up the corpse with its sleeping-mat into a sort of bundle, attached it to a single pole and hoisted it onto their shoulders. They went out followed by unmarried youths carrying the dead man's bows and arrows, a pot, his hoe, a quite good leather bag, a bunch of peacock-feathers and a stick to place beside the pyre. A brother carried a handful of thatch pulled from the roof and some smouldering embers in the leaf-cup.

The procession took a direct route to the pyre; there was no divagation to deceive the ghost. I found the pyre propped against two trees.

[1] If this is done by men with whose families the dead man's family could have matrimonial relations, they must pay a pig as a fine.

The bearers put the corpse down beside it, and the brother cut the nails of the little finger and little toe of the right hand and foot, pulled out the tuft of hair with a sharp tug, and put nails and hair on a leaf beside the pyre. He broke the pot and threw away the hoe. The other things he put by the pyre. He untied the mat and with the help of another brother lifted the corpse onto the pile of wood with the head to the north. The spectators who hitherto had been standing at a distance, now came forward and each threw a small twig onto the body. The two brothers stood at either end, each with a bundle of thatching-grass in his hand. They ignited the grass and ran round and round in opposite directions until the wood was alight. When everything was well ablaze, the party went down to a stream and had a wash.

When a woman dies, the great mass of her necklaces and her numerous bracelets are removed, only one slender necklace being left around her throat. Her bark cloth is also removed, but the body is covered with a piece of Dom cloth until immediately before the wood is fired, when even this is pulled away. For, as the Bondos say, 'At the time of birth naked, at the time of departure naked'.

On 7 March 1945 a rather well to-do Bondo named Lachhim Mundli died at Dumiripada. The news went round and relations hurried in from the surrounding villages and prepared a substantial pyre. The corpse was taken out of the house and laid on a mat. A *soru*-brother threw water over it. A brother took some soot off the bottom of the pot in which the dead man's last meal had been cooked and made a mark on the forehead so that he would be recognizable when he was reborn. Two *soru*-brothers tied the corpse up in its mat, slung it on their shoulders with a pole and so carried it out.

On this occasion the dead man's property was taken to the burning-ground before the corpse; his plough and yoke, bows and arrows (with the barbs removed), the shaft of his axe (but not the iron head), a brass bowl, a cooking-pot. On the north of the pyre where the head of the corpse would rest, someone put a little rice and vegetable.

When the bearers reached the burning-ground, they laid the corpse on the pyre after removing the nails and hair. The onlookers threw twigs on the body and two brothers ignited the wood in the usual way. After the fire had blazed for some time, the watchers went to see if the body had been sufficiently consumed; then they went down to a stream and rubbed their bodies with bits of mango bark 'to prevent the *sairem* from going home with them'.

That day the mourners were fed by their neighbours; there was no work done in the house. In the evening they cooked a little ceremonial rice for the *sairem* and carried it to the burnt-out pyre. Then Lachhim's father's brother broke an egg into a leaf-cup, mixed it with water and sprinkled it over his house and the Sisa's. After that there was no further taboo on anyone cooking or eating in the building where death had occurred. But that night no one was willing to sleep there.

The next morning, however, the women cleaned and cowdunged the house, and by nightfall they were feeling better and slept at home as usual.

At Bodapada, where I witnessed, on 7 December 1947, the funeral of the ten-days' old baby son of Sonia Kirsani, the father carried the corpse in his arms. He was accompanied by three young boys. At the pyre, one of the boys dug a shallow hole in the ground and the father laid the body for a moment within it and then placed it on the wood. After a brief invocation to Mahaprabhu, two of the boys ignited the pyre and they all left immediately. The child's death was attributed to a Gurangpoi.

Such is the course of a Bondo funeral; many of its elements are common to the whole of tribal India. The treatment of the corpse is unusually casual and there is no expenditure on it — no clean cloth and very little turmeric. The huddling of the human frame into a bundle in an old and tattered mat seemed to me most pathetic. The sleeping-mat, scene of love's raptures, where the dead had performed the supreme act of passion and creation, was now as worthless and undignified as the body it enclosed. The cremation ceremony was equally casual and marked by the strongly economical habits of the tribe. Everything worth saving must be preserved; the iron arrow heads must come off, even the little strip of cloth over the genitals must be removed.

Yet the general sequence of the mourning was adapted to effect the psychological ends described by Freud.

4. The Bud Ceremony

On the third day after a death, there is a simple ceremony for diagnosis of the cause of death, to feed the *sairem* and to free the mourners of spiritual infection.

The Sisa or any adult male of the deceased's household gets up before dawn. He breaks an egg into a leaf-cup, mixes it in water and with a bit of grass throws a little of the mixture onto the roof of every house in the village saying, 'Today we perform Bud!'

I watched this at Bandapada and Dumiripada. The women went to examine the ashes of the pyre to see if there were any signs. They made tongs of bamboo, lifted up the bones, turned them this way and that, and wept loudly. The tradition is that if the bones are calcined and brittle, breaking at the first touch, it means that Mahaprabhu has taken the dead and that the death was natural and in due time. But if the bones remain black and strong, it means that some witch or sorcerer has caused the death. This may be connected with the idea that where a death is natural, Mahaprabhu sends his constables in the form of insects to grind the bones into flour, whereon they will naturally break directly they are touched.

Any visit to the burning-ground is risky, and so on the way back the Sisa kindled a fire of grass and, as they passed, each woman warmed her hands and feet before it. The Sisa broke an egg into a scrap of earthenware, put some water into a leaf-cup, made a grass doll and stood beside the path. The women passed him in file and each touched the water with her left hand as she went by. Then the Sisa broke the potsherd, tore the grass doll in places and put the leaf-cup down beside the path. This was supposed to prevent any danger of the *sairem* accompanying the women back into the village.

Then the mourners in the house sacrificed a fowl, and cooked *soru*-rice. They put rice and curry in one cup and some water in another and carried them out of the village along the path leading to the burning-ground. There they left the food and water for the hungry desolate *sairem* who in the Land of the Dead would, they knew, receive the most indifferent entertainment.

When a child died at Dumiripada on 21 December 1943, I watched the women returning from their examination of the ashes. The Sisa stood by the path holding in his hand a potsherd containing leaves and fire. He rolled some bamboo leaves into a tube and pushed them through an eggshell. As the women passed him in file, he made passes at each of them with the eggshell; when they had all gone by, he carried the potsherd with its contents and the leaves and shell some way down the path and threw them away.

5. The Kungdak Ceremony

On the tenth day after death falls the Kungdak ceremony, the last of the usual funerary celebrations, which are sufficient for all but the most important persons. I will describe the course of the Kungdak for Lachhim Mundli, witnessed at Dumiripada on 17 March 1945.

From dawn visitors began to stream in to Dumiripada, coming from Andrahal, Dattipada, Mundlipada, Bodapada, even from the lowland Pandraguda and Kadamguda. Every member of the family, however distantly related, brought some rice and gourds of palm-wine, for this was a big occasion and the resources of a single household could hardly meet it.

Early, about seven o'clock, the Sisa offered palm-wine at the hearth of Lachhim's house in the name of the *sairem* 'so that all the dead may be pleased, the food well cooked and no pots broken'. *Soru*-neighbours began at once to cook rice and to heap it, in great piles, on mats when it was ready. The Sisa went round the village with a cup of egg and water, offering it in every house, 'so that the *sairem* may keep far from us and the harvests be good'. Otherwise, he declared, 'as death comes to a man, so death may affect the crops'. He pronounced the day an *angto*-holiday on which no one should leave the village or do any ordinary work.

By about ten o'clock quite a lot of rice was ready in the temporary kitchen, a shed near the house of the deceased. A bullock was tethered near by and a vigorous youth killed it with a single blow from the back of his axe. A number of men began at once to cut up the carcass. Meanwhile the Sisa performed what is sometimes called the Bobring rite. For this he made fourteen leaf-cups with a pinch of *soru*-rice in each. Lachhim's sister and daughter each took seven of the cups and went weeping to the pyre, followed by all the women present. When Lachhim's sister reached the burning-ground, she put her seven cups in a straight line before the burnt-out pyre and about four yards away from it. The daughter put her cups in two lines, first four cups and then three, near the head of the pyre. Then other relatives searched through the ashes, removing anything of value that remained undestroyed, and took out three large bones. They were black and hollow; the women tried to break them but failed. They cried, 'This man died of magic,' and it was whispered that a sorcerer had filled a hollow tube with *eloto*-magic and had sent it to murder the unlucky man.

Lachhim's daughter found a few copper coins in the ashes and threw them away. But the others said, 'No, keep them, for they will bring wealth to the house when he is reborn'. So she picked them up and put them back among the ashes. The women then went to wash their hands and feet and rubbed them with mango bark.

As the women returned to the village the Sisa met them and sprinkled them with water 'to keep the *sairem* out' and later they made a fire with thatching-grass and fanned their hands and feet with the flame, as a final precaution against the deadly infections of the burning-ground.

In Lachhim's house rice and beef was cooked in a new pot. The Sisa offered rice, in the name of the ancestral dead, in the courtyard and to the four quarters of the earth. He carried cups of rice and beef and water along the path towards the burning-ground and left them there so that the *sairem* could join in the feast. He threw a little rice towards the burning-ground.

Now began the feast of the guests.[1] But there was not enough meat, so a second bullock was killed.

All through the afternoon little processions of women, late arrivals, went weeping to the burning-ground to examine the ashes. Each visitor had to throw a twig onto the pyre and bathe before returning.

In the evening the proceedings concluded with an Orpa (in Oriya, Satreng) rite which was calculated finally to free the celebrants and assistants at this 'festivity in black' from any fear of supernatural infection.

At about six o'clock the Sisa, with the help of a couple of dormitory boys, carried branches of *Bauhinia vahlii, Flacourtia ramontchi* and *Albizzia procera* down to the village spring, a beautiful spot where abundant water came bubbling up through the rock and there was open space sufficient for a ceremony. Here the Sisa built an arch across the water and on a flat stone in front of it he placed an axe and some pieces of the cathartic mango bark. He had his usual paraphernalia of leaf-cups and *soru*-rice which he offered to the *sairem* of the four quarters and below the arch itself. Meanwhile a number of youths carried food down to the spring, basket after basket of rice and meat; then they set to work to make leaf-dishes and to divide the rice and meat in exactly equal portions. *Soru*-brothers and visitors gradually assembled and stood by the spring.

Then Lachhim's daughter, a charming child of about fifteen, came to the spring with her broom and fan and sat on the stone before the arch. Her girl friends watched giggling and excited from behind a fence at the top of the cliff above. The Sisa waved a handful of rice round the girl's head. She picked up her broom and fan and ducked under the arch while the Sisa put some rice which he had pounded up with mango bark on her back. She washed her hands and feet in the water on the far side of the arch and went away.

Then all the men present, everyone in fact who had played any part in the day's ceremonial and all the visitors, went down one by one to the spring and passed beneath the arch. As each went through, the Sisa touched his back with the rice and mango bark, after which the man washed himself and climbing up onto the bank sat down for supper.

The *soru*-brothers sat in one row, visitors in another, and they were served by the dormitory boys of Dumiripada. There were no women present. But before the visitors departed, one of the elders went to the house and gave a little lecture to the widow and daughter of the dead man.

[1] During a Kungdak ceremony which I saw a year later at Bodapada, the young men who were assisting in the preparation and distribution of the food, bathed themselves with water mixed with dung from the dead bullock's belly.

He who was to go has gone. Those who are to stay behind must look to their labour. Let them pay their taxes to the Maharaja and do his *begar*. But it is no use mourning longer. Weeping, or even to die oneself, will not ensure a meeting with the dead. Look well to Lachhim's sons and daughters and work in unity with the rest of the family. Let there be no quarrels. Feed the people of twelve *kuda*-clans. There are cows and bullocks; there is a field and garden; sell the produce and live happily. Do not worry about things. But if you do not work, how can you live? We have come to see you and now, satisfied, we are going away. Do not sorrow any longer. All has been done well.

The Orpa rite is the culmination of the funerary ceremonies that immediately succeed a death. For most people, for all ordinary ghosts, these are sufficient. They pacify any ordinary *sairem*; they ensure a good harvest in the coming year; they are an insurance against the contagion of the funeral pyre; psychologically, the elaboration and excitement of the ritual gradually effects a separation of the cathexis of longing from its object and assists the mourners to overcome their sense of loss. Where the psychological adjustment is incomplete, and the mourners continue to be tormented by dreams of the dead and anxiety for the future, further ceremonies are necessary — ostensibly to pacify the dead, in fact to remedy the melancholia of the living.

6. The *Gunom*

The importance of the anthropologists' contention that a fundamental purpose of any megalithic culture is the fecundity of the soil is somewhat discounted, to my mind, by the fact that nearly all tribal religious activity is directed to this end. In particular, the Bondo broods over his seed-grain like a mother with her child, dedicating and rededicating it, and reinforcing its potency at every rite and festival. The *gunom* ceremony, at which stone memorials are set up, is thus only one of many efforts made by the Bondos to protect their fields, increase their fertility and bring success in hunting. Its deeper aim, as I shall suggest shortly, is psychological rather than social or religious; it is the cure of a melancholic condition that affects the mourners under certain conditions and which the earlier funeral ceremonies fail to resolve.

Before I discuss this, however, I will give an account of the *gunom* stones and of the ceremonies which attend their erection.

The *gunom* is usually a flat capstone laid across three or more smaller stones, which is dedicated with expensive ceremonies some time after the death either of a person of importance or where a *sairem* is believed by its survivors to be unusually importunate. When such a dolmen is made it is supposed to benefit and appease not only the *sairem* in whose name it is primarily given, but also all those who may have died since the last dedication of a *gunom* in a village. This is one reason why there are so few of these stones to be seen; one dolmen may be considered sufficient for all the *sairem* of a decade.

FIG. 48. A *gunom* outside Katamguda

Sometimes the the capstone stands by itself; more frequently an erect menhir is placed behind it. As a result the Bondo *gunom* looks very like the Maria *uraskal* or *kotokal*, but in fact the function of the stones is reversed. In Maria custom the erect menhir is the real stone and the table-stone before it is a combined seat and altar for the Departed to rest on and for the offering of sacrifice. But for the Bondos it is the flat stone which is the essential part of the *gunom*; the menhir behind it is an additional superorogatory honour, placed there by a son-in-law of the deceased, and if there is no one in this relationship it is omitted. Occasionally, however, only a menhir without its dolmen is erected and I am inclined to believe that the menhirs to be found in walls and groves are of this kind. Above Kichhipoda, again, I noticed a dolmen surrounded by menhirs; near Togebeda a menhir stood on the top of a cairn and there was a flat stone before it, while near by there was a dolmen in front of a cairn. All aboriginal custom is subject to the inspirations of the priests and shamans with the result that uniformity is rarely achieved.

Why are the *gunom* dedicated for only a few persons, and indeed why are they made at all, at such expense and often long after the subject's death? I suggest that in certain cases the immediate funerary rites fail in their psychological purpose of enabling the bereaved to overcome their sense of grief; they have not succeeded in separating the cathexis of desire or interest from the object, which is not accepted as having been lost for ever. The result is that one or more members of the bereaved family is affected with a form of melancholia. This is certainly suggested by the events which precede the decision to hold a *gunom* celebration.

FIG. 49. Dolmen surrounded by menhirs near Kichhipoda

The melancholiac displays one symptom which is ordinarily lacking in grief — 'an extraordinary fall in his self-esteem, an impoverishment of his ego on a grand scale. In brief the world becomes poor and empty; in melancholia it is the ego itself which becomes poor and empty.' The patient abases himself, regards himself and proclaims himself to be morally despicable; he is unable to summon interest in his affairs. 'This picture of delusional belittling — which is predominantly moral — is completed by sleeplessness and refusal of nourishment.'[1]

These symptoms are clearly evident in many cases of what we may call *gunom*-obsession. Hadi Kirsani of Bandapada did not recover from the shock of his brother's death. He lost confidence in himself, took no trouble over the harvest — which naturally suffered — and developed such significant symptoms as pains in the back and indigestion. His sleep was constantly disturbed by fearful dreams in which his brother's ghost appeared to him, rebuking him for not having done what he should to make him happy. This created that 'dissatisfaction with the self on moral grounds which is far the most outstanding feature in the clinical

[1] Rickman, op. cit., p. 148.

picture of melancholia'.[1] Once Hadi had restored his self-esteem by making arrangements for a *gunom* ceremony, he recovered.

Lachhim Kirsani of Dattipada was a sensitive nervous man; he lost his father and, as he said, 'my father's ghost ruined the crops for two years after his death'. Obviously what really happened was that Lachhim was unable to do his work properly and the harvest suffered. He dedicated a *gunom* pig, and the harvest and Lachhim's own health at once improved. But soon afterwards his wife died, and Lachhim and his son fell ill; they attributed their sickness to the woman's ghost—it was, of course, her memory. Lachhim could not sleep, for he was unable 'to withdraw the cathexes necessary for sleep'. He became subject to acute moral self-condemnation; his wife told him in a dream, 'You are enjoying yourself in the world, playing with my children, stuffing your belly, comfortable and warm in my house. But I have to wander naked in the jungle; I am hungry and thirsty, with no one to look after me. So I'm going to take my child so that I will have someone at least with me.' Lachhim was contemplating suicide—another common symptom of melancholia—when the Dissari advised him to dedicate a pig and perform the *gunom* ceremony. Directly he put himself to a form of activity calculated to cure his grief, Lachhim recovered.

Many such examples could be given. The general picture is always the same. There is a drastic impoverishment of the ego, a complete fall in self-esteem, the bereaved person becomes convinced that he has wronged the dead, he cannot sleep properly, he has appalling dreams, he suffers from headache, backache and indigestion, he has no interest in anything—he neglects his cattle and loses them, he ignores his fields and the harvests fail.

The *gunom* ceremonial is well adapted to remedy this condition. Its lavish display, the expenditure and generosity, restores the mourner's self-esteem; the general social approval, the praise of a man who is doing his duty by the dead, saves him from the danger of further 'delusional self-belittling'. His belief, based on religious tradition, that the offended *sairem* will now be at peace, saves him from bad dreams and lets him sleep again. The fertility motifs of the *gunom* ceremony inspire him with the conviction that his crops will be good and he sets to work with vigour and they really are good. The world, and the mourner's own ego, once more becomes rich and full.

The first act of the *gunom* ceremony is the dedication of an unblemished pig, which is used as a kind of living sortilege: it is kept for three years and if, during that period, the condition of the mourner and his fortunes improve, a *gunom* stone is made.

[1] Rickman, op. cit., p. 148.

The pig is fed on rice and then castrated; an iron digging-stick is driven into the ground with its flat end upwards, the testes are laid across it and they are crushed with the wooden mallet used for pounding *kereng* fibre. The pig is feasted again, rice is offered to the *sairem,* and promises are made of a great celebration should things improve. For three years the pig is carefully guarded, for should anything happen to it, it is supposed that the worst misfortunes will follow.[1] But if all goes well — and it is generally the dedication of the pig which begins to effect a cure — the *gunom* rites are performed at the end of the third year. If things do not improve, the mourners give 'the *sairem* a chance for one more year'. If even then things are no better, they sell the pig: members of the household must on no account eat it, for there is something wrong with it and 'the dead are not pleased'. They may get another pig and repeat the process.

There are resemblances here to the Laru Kaj of the Central Provinces but the Bondo pig is not regarded with anything like the elaborate affection which is lavished on the Laru pig. Nor is the Laru pig associated with the dead, but is dedicated to keep disease from the living.[2]

A *gunom* stone is usually dedicated in the month of Magh (January-February), it was on 19 February 1946 and the following days that I assisted at the ceremonies at Andrahal for the *sairem* of Gulong Sisa, one of the men injured in the great feud of 1930. There were three brothers (the full story is given at pp. 244-5), Gulong Sisa, Ghasi Sisa and Tio Sisa. Ghasi and Tio were killed outright, and Gulong survived them for five years; but his was a miserable life: there was a 'leak' in his throat and his palm-wine used to dribble out of it; it is said that he was not altogether sorry to die. Ghasi's son, Sukro Sisa, performed the Kungdak rites for his father and Tio at the time and then for his uncle Gulong when he died. In his lifetime Ghasi had been fairly well off — he had ten or twelve bullocks and cows, herds of goats and pigs, and even his own private *sindibor.*

Sukro's position, however, in spite of his inheritance of the family property was not altogether enviable. The shock of his father's death, the police inquiries, the mutual hatreds and antagonisms in the village, the natural dread of the ghosts of murdered men, the apprehension of what would happen when the murderers came out of jail, the subsequent tragedy

[1] At Mundlipada Donker Mundli dedicated a *gunom* pig for his two brothers. But a few months later it got into the garden and ate some maize. Donker saw it and killed and ate it in a drunken temper. The ghosts got a tiger and sent it to kill Donker's cattle and goats; they spoilt the young rice-crop, and made Donker himself ill for a month. Donker had to dedicate another pig and sacrifice a bullock before things began to go well again.

[2] For a full account, see Shamrao Hivale, *The Pardhans of the Upper Narbada Valley* (Bombay, 1946), pp. 125-42.

when his brother murdered one of the other party in revenge, induced in due course the usual melancholia. Sukro grew thinner and thinner; he could not sleep; the cattle died, the crops failed; there was no life in the house. At last he sent for a Gadaba Dissari who recommended the dedication of a *gunom* pig.

After this Sukro cheered up, took some trouble over his affairs, and sufficiently improved them to be able to purchase cows and bullocks, and make arrangements for a substantial feast.

For a fortnight before the determined date, Sukro's household was busy with their preparations, brewing rice-beer, husking grain, sending invitations. A week before Sukro sat with the elders on the *sindibor* and they discussed their programme. 'On the Sunday', they decided, 'we'll go to the bazaar and buy what is needed; on Monday we'll build a booth to cook the feast; on Tuesday, visitors will come and we shall call on the *sairem* to attend; on Wednesday we will sacrifice and make a *gunom*; on the Thursday it will end.' I am told that this sequence of days, as so often among the Bondos, is strictly adhered to everywhere.

On the Tuesday, which was 19 February, the visitors, as planned, began to arrive, coming in file over the hills with gourds of wine and pots of beer. Two men were chosen to represent the *sairem* and were dressed up a little with long turbans and bells round their ankles. These men are known in Remo as *sairem-ba*, 'fathers of the dead', and in Oriya as *kamri*, a word widely used for an officiant at a funerary rite. The two men are very definitely set apart; they are dangerously full of other-worldly power. No one may speak to them except 'officially', and no one should touch or even approach them.

That evening, near Sukro's house, the *sairem-ba* drew a number of lines, on a specially-prepared piece of ground, with rice-flour in the name of the dead, and Gulong's daughter offered a little rice and meat. While they were doing this, the dormitory youths beat their drums and someone did a special dance in Gulong's honour. The visitors drank, danced and slumbered the night away.

Early on the Wednesday morning, the Dissari examined the lines made by the *sairem-ba* the previous night. Had the dead man returned to life in the form of pig, ox, cat or dog the footprints of one of these would be found. There was nothing, however, to be seen and the flour was swept up and thrown away.

The rest of the morning was spent in preparing the feast. Long ditches were dug in one of Sukro's fields near his house; fires were lit, water brought, rice prepared and piled on mats. The Sisa offered *mahua*-liquor to the fire so that the food should be well cooked. At a little distance the Sisa cooked some special *soru*-rice and offered sacrifice to the *sairem* before a small booth of leafy branches. The *sairem*-gourd was brought from Sukro's house and hung up here.

Then someone killed a bullock with the blunt edge of an axe. The Sisa offered the dying animal liquor and slit its mouth. He took some of the blood to the *sairem*-gourd and placed marks upon it and on the foreheads of the *sairem-ba*. Presently a number of boys caught the pig that had been dedicated long before and cut its throat. They bled it into a pot, then cut out the jaw and tusks, which boys carried off triumphantly to make into knife-handles, such knives being very lucky. They washed and singed the body and cut it up for cooking. Another group were cutting up the carcass of the bullock and preparing the meat to be cooked. The Sisa took some of the flesh and offered it to the *sairem* at the booth saying,

> *Hānum*! May mother, father, ancestors, sisters, daughters, house and door be well. May the millet seed be well. Let children, cows, bullocks, goats, pigs, fowls be well. O Mahaprabhu, we give food to you. Do not be angry, give us all good things. We have offered rice in little cups at the hearth; we have persuaded the gods with ground turmeric and flour of rice. O Mahaprabhu, salutation! Below is Basmoti, above is Dharam Deota. For seven days and seven ages I have persuaded, I have explained, I have won them to my side. O Mahaprabhu, salutation! Give us complete happiness.

Then the dormitory boys twisted strong slings of stripped creeper bark and went out to find stones. When they had found them, they brought them one by one drumming and dancing to the village. It had been decided to build the *gunom* opposite Ghasi Sisa's private *sindibor* which was under a great tree near his old house. The boys first placed the supporting stones in position and then laid the capstone over them. Ghasi's son-in-law and a *moitur*-friend cut three bombax branches and planted them behind (that is, on the side farthest from the path which ran between the *gunom* and the *sindibor*) the stones, and the son-in-law erected an upright menhir in front. They placed little earthen pots full of liquor on the stone and tied scraps of cloth to the branches. They poured beer over the stones and relatives threw coins on them. Several rupees' worth were collected and Sukro returned them to the donors.

At the same time a stone was placed on the *sindibor*, without any separate ceremonial, 'so that the name of Ghasi Sisa might be long remembered'.

The next incident was the procession to the burning-ground. One of the *sairem-ba* stuck bits of beef on either end of a small carrying-pole; in a winnowing-fan he put four cups of liquor, two cups of meat and two of rice. He slung the pole over his shoulder and with the fan in his hand, led a long procession of boys each carrying cups of rice, pork, beef, turmeric and flour, with earthen pots of liquor, to the burning-ground. They went first to the spot where Gulong had been cremated

FIG. 50. *Gunom* stones with bombax branches raised above them

and then, near by, to where Ghasi and Tio (who had been cremated at Mattili) had had their bows and axe-shafts ceremonially burnt. The *sairem-ba,* followed by the boys, made their offerings here, and the man cried, 'Look, you have been troubling your children. You have killed their cattle. You have ruined their crops. Now we have brought you back into the tribe. You are no more an outcaste. Now live at peace with us. Now let our harvests be good; the cattle, goats and fowls you took, return.' The *sairem-ba* then picked up two small stones and some earth and put them into his now empty fan. He carried it thus loaded and placed it on the newly-built *gunom*; the stones and earth are a symbol of the goods and cattle that the dead are now pledged to restore.

Now the feast began. First members of the Sisa *kuda* who also belonged to the Ontal *bonso* ate the special *soru*-rice cooked by the *Sairem-ba*. After that the hosts fed their visitors, neighbours and Doms.

As the sun went down, the *sairem-ba* danced before the door of Sukro's house, where Ghasi had once lived, the scene of the shocking events of fifteen years ago. The mummers held branches in their hands and reproduced incidents of the murder; one pretended to have his throat cut, another got his head broken, they fell to the ground in agony and 'died'. They went on to the *gunom*, danced round and round it, and one of them put an anna bit on the stone saying, 'We have tried to please you. Here is some money. Buy some plantains, parched rice or sugar and enjoy yourselves.'

They returned to the house, and Gulong's *sairem* came upon one of them and he cried, 'Why have you sent for me?' The other answered, 'You took my cattle and my harvest and sent sickness on my children. Give me back all that you have taken. I have brought you back into our tribe. Before this you were wandering about, lost in the jungle, eating anywhere you could, often altogether starving. Now we have brought you home.' The *sairem* replied, 'That is true. I got no food, I wandered from hill to hill, and now you have brought me back. I have already returned all that I took away.' Then the *sairem* left the man and the party sat down and had something to drink.

While the feasting and drinking was going on, the two *sairem-ba*, in the dark and with no one watching them, cooked some *soru*-rice and took it secretly to the *gunom*. They brought back the fan with the stones and earth and placing it on the ground, heaped onto it a variety of objects — a cow's tethering-rope, every kind of grain, scraps of meat, a goat's rope — and poured liquor over it. They called Sukro and the *sairem* came again onto one of the celebrants and said, 'Take this. Here is the harvest I took away. Here are the cattle I took away. Here is everything I took from you.' Sukro accepted the fan in both hands and took it home. The *sairem-ba* ate the *soru*-rice they had prepared and drank some beer, and one of the elders accepted food at their hands in token of the fact that they, like the *sairem* they were representing, were now admitted into the tribal fellowship. For throughout the ceremony they had been excommunicated, 'belonging to the caste of the dead'.

Finally the *sairem-ba*, by now completely drunk, staggered into Sukro's house and tried to perform a final divination ceremony. They were supposed to make patterns on the floor and tie a thread from the roof above them. But they collapsed into a drunken slumber; in the morning, however, they thought it advisable to tell Sukro that the omens had been good and that he would recover everything he had lost and would have no more trouble in future. Sukro was pleased at this and himself carried a pot of beer and a basket of rice and raw meat to their houses. He said to each wife in turn, 'For a long time your husband was occupied in dancing and singing, and you had to live as a widow. It was in my work that your husband was entangled. From today live happily.'

FIG. 51. Menhirs — perhaps the relics of a *runnukbor* — at the top of a hill between Pinnajangar and Kichchipoda

With these kindly words Sukro, now a new man, entirely cured of his melancholic obsessions, concluded the proceedings.

After a *gunom* has been erected, it is customary for anyone who was acquainted with the deceased or his family to pause for a moment as he passes by and offer on the stone a tiny pinch of tobacco, touching it with his hand in salute. It is quite in order to sit down and rest on the stone, which may be pleasantly shaded by the trees that were planted to give shade and comfort to the *sairem*. At Mundlipada I was told that at the Giag Festival, a 'son' or 'brother' of the dead should make offerings at the latest *gunom* to be built and should continue these every year until a new stone was erected.

As the people go to hunt during the Giag Festival, somebody offers the latest *gunom* two sticks of tobacco, two leaf-pipes, two mangoes, a cup of water and a cup of rice, finally laying his bow and arrows on it saying, 'I am going to hunt. Let no tiger or bear attack us. But let the sambhar and barking-deer come.'

He throws a pinch of rice over the bow and arrows, picks them up and goes off to hunt.

7. The *Runnukbor*

A *runnukbor* is a stone wall some four feet high which runs along the top of a pass separating one village area from another and cutting the path which, however, it lets through by a gateway flanked with menhirs on either side. There are not many of these walls; the most striking is the one above Andrahal and there are others near Goyiguda, Basupada and in the grove at Pinnajangar. There is a Gadaba *runnukbor* on the ridge between Guttalupada and Thal Duralu; here there is a cairn and a row of menhirs at right angles to the wall which are said to be in honour of Kot Deota.

The origin and purpose of these walls is obscure. Many Bondos are unable to say anything about them except that they are very old. In some villages, it is said that Runnukbor is himself a god; the more Oriya-minded declare that Runnukbor is the same as the Hindu god Kot Deota. At Mundlipada official opinion decided that the wall was dedicated to Bunumpa, but at Andrahal the people said that 'Bunumpa' was simply a term of salutation like 'Johar' or 'Salaam' and was used when a passer-by saluted the wall with the offering of a twig.

At Basupada the *runnukbor* was associated with the unpleasant fire-elemental Karandi (see pp. 156-7).

One day a Bondo, cutting wood in the jungle, saw a sambhar. He turned himself into a tiger and leapt upon it. The sambhar broke free and escaped to the spring near Basupada where it fell down. The Bondo chased it there and drank its blood, but a lot of people chased him away and he ran to Thagavada and died there.

But Sukro Sisa and the villagers took the sambhar into Basupada and cut it up. Karandi came out of its belly as a human child. The Sisa adopted him but presently he disappeared. But he returned in a dream and said, 'Make a *runnukbor* wall for me on the Banapasari Hill (above Basupada) and I'll live there'. The Sisa and other villagers built a wall on the hill and offered a goat and fowls there. Then said Karandi: 'From today I am to be called Runnukbor. Whenever a stranger comes to the village, turn him out before night falls. If any stranger sleeps in the village I will burn it down.'

The general form of the *runnukbor* suggests some connexion with the *gunom* cult. The walls are built up with and supported by menhirs, and menhirs (sometimes with altar stones before them) flank the gate through which the path takes its way. At Goyiguda I was told that the *runnukbor* there had grown up gradually from the accumulation of a number of menhirs; when there were enough of them, a rubble wall was built up between them. At Mundlipada I was informed that a *gunom runnukbor* was made when a very rich man died; his bones were taken to the top of a hill and buried with treasure and the wall built above. The menhirs in the groves at Mundlipada and Pinnajangar, on the hill above Kichchipoda and by the *runnukbor* everywhere suggest that the original form of the Bondo memorial-appeasement stone was upright and that the flat capstone is an imitation of the Gadaba stone or even of the Maria *danyakal*.[1]

But the Bondos agree that, whatever their ultimate significance may be, the *runnukbor* walls are of the first importance and that the ancient demigods or ghosts who dwell therein must be carefully humoured. Whenever a Bondo passes through a *runnukbor* gate he should break a small twig from a tree near by and place it on the altar stone saying,

> Let there be no trouble on the way!
> Let not my hands and feet be injured!
> Let there be no quarrels where I go!

And I have more than once been told that the special stress of the prayer is always on the prevention of quarrels, a matter in which the ancestral dead (so many of whom have been murdered) are naturally interested.

[1] For detailed accounts of this dolmenic memorial in Bastar State, see W. V. Grigson, *The Maria Gonds of Bastar* (Oxford, 1938), p. 281 and my article 'Funerary Customs in Bastar State', *Man in India,* Vol. XXV (1945), pp. 108ff.

CHAPTER EIGHT

THE PROBLEM OF MALADJUSTMENT

1

THE formation of society, says Kinberg, is a 'phenomenon of adaptation involving a limitation of the desires, efforts, and actions of each individual primarily for the benefit of the whole, and secondarily for the benefit of the individual through the protection afforded him by society. Criminality must therefore be regarded as a sign of social maladjustment, expressed in such acts as are by the penal code considered criminal.'[1] Let us now turn to a consideration of Bondo crime.

In doing so we must bear in mind certain important considerations. For the Bondos, as for the Marias and most other tribesmen, an offence against the penal code does not necessarily imply a maladjustment to tribal society; it is a breach of regulations imposed by another, and different, culture; these regulations are often loftier, more 'civilized' than those of tribal society, but they are alien to it. The result is, that while the Bondo who breaks the rule of village exogamy may suffer from an acute sense of guilt, the Bondo who kills a Didayi during a quarrel over a gourd of wine or the man who avenges his family or clan on some ancient foe, does not feel guilty at all; he thinks he is a very fine fellow and has done exactly what he should.

A further result of this is that tribal society is very slow to condemn an offender against the police code. Many Bondos, of course, speak in terms of detestation of theft and murder to the visitor and even to the anthropologist, but the excellent position which society gives the murderer who has served his term in jail suggests that this is mere lip-service to the supposed standards of the investigator. In the old days Bondo justice was mainly revenge; to some extent it still is; but the interest of the elders in most major crimes is confined to reporting them to the police, which they have to do, even though they may not take them very seriously.

On the whole, the Bondos keep their own rules fairly well. They observe the taboos on incest or adultery and their religious obligations

[1] O. Kinberg, *Basic Problems of Criminology* (Copenhagen and London, 1935), p. 15.

with such fidelity that the few exceptions are long remembered, and the swift vengeance of the immortals makes almost superfluous the functioning of tribal justice. The Bondos are also, in the main, singularly innocent of the more conventional and sordid offences against the penal code; they rarely steal or cheat — at least among themselves; offences against children are unknown; the mean and cowering crimes of blackmail and defamation belong to another world. Their one great trouble is their bad temper.

The majority of Bondo crimes are due to this defect. A Bondo village is an arena of continual quarrels and disputes; the majority burn themselves out in a flare of verbal exaggeration and dramatic posturing, but there are other arguments that go too far, blows that reach an oversensitive target, abuse that advances from the more or less humorously insulting to the unforgiveably obscene. There is a spark, a flash, a hand to knife or arrow — and two lives are ruined.

It is not always, of course, as simple as this. There are family and village feuds, strange fears of persecution, the passion for revenge; sometimes it is just plain downright hatred that torments the simple minds of these men. And many tragedies are due to some form of alcoholic paranoia or at least to such intoxication as, by removing fears and inhibitions, prepares the way to murder.

Not all Bondo murders are intended. The Bondos live hard; from childhood they learn to be unusually rough; the knock-about life of the dormitory, the harsh struggle with field and forest, a general tradition that one should hit hard and swiftly, has taught them to be far too ready with their blows, which sometimes fall on bodies ill adapted to receive them.

It would perhaps be better to describe Bondo crime as an excess rather than as a maladjustment.[1] There is no Bondo criminal class; the whole tribe is in it; anyone, you feel, may exceed and become without warning or preparation a murderer.

A discussion of Bondo crime thus becomes inevitably a discussion of Bondo homicide. The Koraput police were good enough to furnish me with a list of murders committed by members of the tribe during the nine years, 1936-44. The list, especially in the early years, is probably incomplete, for the Courts did not formerly distinguish very carefully between the different classes of Poroja, and the administrative changes of the past decade have made it difficult to obtain access to old records.

[1] Cf. Hooton: 'The criminal is a person distinguished by the commission of an overt act against society and he exemplifies for us an extreme of human conduct.' E. A. Hooton, *The American Criminal* (Harvard, 1939), p. 8.

Table V

NUMBER OF BONDO HOMICIDES CONVICTED UNDER SECTIONS 302 AND 304 OF THE INDIAN PENAL CODE

Year	Number of Murders Committed	Number of Persons Convicted	Number of Persons sentenced to Death	Transportation	
1936	1	-	-	-	
1937	1	5	2	3	
1938	1	1	-	1	
1939	1	1	-	1	
1940	4	6	1	5	
1941	4	4	1	3	
1942	4	3	-	2	(1 shorter sentence)
1943	6	6	2	3	(1 shorter sentence)
1944	5	8	-	1	(7 shorter sentences)
Total	27	34	6	19	

This table gives, for the five years 1940-4, a total of 27 convicted murderers, which out of a population of roughly 2500, shows an astonishingly high incidence-rate. Comparative figures are not easy to obtain in India, but I worked out the average annual homicide-rate for the Bison-horn Marias at a little over 69 for the years 1931-40. The rate for the whole of Bastar State during this period was just over 40; in Mayurbhanj State in 1935-6 it was about 28; in the Central Provinces and Berar in 1939 it was only 11.[1]

Bonger gives tables, collected in rather haphazard fashion, for other parts of the world. Thus, a survey of men in prisons in the U.S.A. for the years 1926-34 gives for manslaughter (both homicidal and by negligence) a figure of 39 to the million for Whites and 328 for Negroes.[2] Another table, quoted from Hacker, gives comparative figures for certain European countries in 1925-32; these indicate convictions for murder and manslaughter per million of the adult population.[3]

Bulgaria ..	223	Italy ..	38
Lithuania ..	139	France ..	16
Latvia ..	110	Germany ..	9
Portugal ..	56	Sweden ..	3
Finland ..	51	England and Wales ..	2

It is generally considered that aggressive criminality is high among the Mediterranean peoples: in Italy in 1880-84, the rate for the whole

[1] See my *Maria Murder and Suicide*, pp. 37-9. In view of the very rough and ready statistics available for the Indian population, there is no point in working out figures exact to several decimals; only a general indication can be given and a profession of greater exactitude would be misleading. This precaution is particularly necessary for the Bondos where the Census figures are certainly unreliable.

[2] W. A. Bonger, *Race and Crime* (English translation, New York, 1943), p. 45.

[3] E. Hacker, 'Statistique Comparéé de la Criminalité'. *Revue Internationale de Droit Pénal*, Vol. XIII (1936).

country was 70, though in the Sicilian and southern regions it rose as high as 300 to the million. In Spain at the same period the rate was 64·9, but in Italy at least the incidence of violent crime has sharply diminished in recent years.[1] Aggressive criminality is also high in Russia, particularly in Asiatic Russia, where in 1908-12 the Armenians showed for 'crimes against human life' a figure of 160, the Caucasian mountain people 148 and the Georgians 104.[2]

Against even the highest of these figures, the Bondo rate stands out catastrophically, as high as, if not higher than, any in the world. For if we take the population figures of the 1941 Census, the annual rate is over 2000 to the million.

Besides the figures given me by the police, I was also able to examine the old criminal files in the Record Room at Koraput. Some of these appear to have been eliminated; others are scattered in various offices in Orissa and Madras. I was only able to obtain particulars of 25 cases. I was able to verify details of several of these by inquiries on the spot and even by discussion with such of the convicted men who had finished their sentences and had been released.

It is hardly possible to base conclusions on so small a number of cases yet the figures give some hint of the Bondo homicide situation, which is strikingly different from that, for example, of the Bison-horn Marias of Bastar. Thus, among the 25 murders there was only one arising out of a domestic quarrel (the Maria figure was 16 per cent), not a single sex-murder (as against the Marias' 17 per cent), only one caused by fear of sorcery, and not a single case of human sacrifice. On the other hand, murder for revenge and from fear of persecution was much more common. No woman figured as accused in any of the Bondo case-histories that I examined.[3] The motives for homicide may be very roughly tabulated as follows:

Table VI

MOTIVES FOR HOMICIDE IN 25 BONDO CASES

Domestic quarrels	1
Fear of sorcery	1
Fear of persecution	3
Revenge	4
Disputes about property	10
Drunken unmotivated quarrels	4
Post-bazaar quarrels	2

1 Bonger, op. cit., p. 68.
2 ibid., p. 99.
3 'Female criminality is generally slight in lands where aggressive crime is frequent.'—ibid., p. 107.

I have already discussed elsewhere in this book the cases of murder for domestic causes and fear of sorcery; I will now proceed to a detailed examination of the others.

2. The Fear of Persecution

In the changing conditions of modern life the aboriginal finds himself in a setting where it is inevitable that he should suffer many kinds of anxiety and fear. To the supposed attacks of demigods, ghosts and furies, there is now added the menace of administrative provisions — new taxation, new laws about the forest and the hunt, new prohibitions of ancient custom. Indian aboriginals today are nervous people, and the Bondos are no exception to the rule.

Where the general background is in disorder, where there is frustration and repression afflicting society as a whole, it is not surprising if individuals develop the prevailing tendency to anxiety right up to breaking-point. Freud distinguishes objective anxiety which is concerned with a known danger and neurotic anxiety which is anxiety about an 'unknown, instinctual danger'. But both are real. 'There are two reactions to objective danger. One, an affective reaction, is an outbreak of anxiety. The other is a protective action. The same will probably be true of instinctual danger.' The two reactions can co-operate, the one giving the signal to the other to appear.[1] The element of tragedy is introduced when a surplus of anxiety drives the victim to a reaction that the objective danger does not really justify. Moreover, neurotic anxiety 'has a quality of indefiniteness and lack of object'.

Hadi Kirsani of Kichchipoda had for several years suffered from just such a type of neurotic anxiety about his affairs. The person about whom his phobias mainly revolved was an unpleasant, pushing fellow named Mangla Mandhara of the same village. One day Mangla removed some wood which Hadi had just chopped up. Hadi retaliated by stealing one of Mangla's pigs. But Mangla was a Dissari and Hadi grew more and more anxious about the dangers of a physical or magical revenge falling upon him. In Court, he described how, as the Sessions Judge put it in his judgement, 'Mangla for some reason not explained attacked his father and mother and then himself....He told another very incoherent story about the deceased chasing him for many days and beating his wife and sister.' To the Court these statements were unsupported by evidence and did not appear 'to have any basis in reality'. But to my mind they are all too real. 'The quality of indefinite-

[1] Rickman, op. cit., pp. 281f.

ness and lack of object' which Freud describes does not make the anxiety neurosis any less acute; the instinctual reaction will be just as inevitable. And so it was. The persecution delusion — if it was a delusion — grew stronger and stronger until at last, on 9 January 1941, Hadi came up behind his enemy as he was warming himself at a fire against the morning cold and shot him in the back with an arrow. He was sentenced to death, but I do not know whether he was executed or reprieved.

Sukra Bodnaik was more fortunate; he only got two years for killing one Lachhim of the same *kuda,* who — he believed — was seeking his life in order to get exclusive possession of a field which they were jointly cultivating. For three years Sukra's life was dominated by this anxiety; he used to wander from village to village dodging what I am told was a quite imaginary foe. At last, one night when he was told that Lachhim was coming for him, he got his blow in first. In yet another murder, at Goyiguda in 1937, one of the motives for the killing was a son's fear that his father's murderer would kill him also.

But the most important example of an anxiety fantasy occurs in the tragic life of a very nice person, a friend in whose company Fürer-Haimendorf, Hivale and myself have all found pleasure, Muliya Dangra-Manjhi of Mundlipada. Muliya is now a man of about forty years, of which he has spent several in jail, for he has served four sentences, one of them for murder. Jail life has made him a little conceited; he feels rather superior to the unsophisticated savages around him; he believes that what Mundlipada wants is a school and a railway-station with trains running to and from Jeypore. At times he seems wayward and casual — but perhaps the truth is that he is not really interested in anthropology and has something better to do than to sit all day with an inquisitive foreigner discussing endogamy and acculturation. He has good manners, he is a good fellow, with a pleasant kindly face, and his career of crime began with what was little more than a tragic accident.

I will give his story in full, though much of it is irrelevant to the point under discussion. But it is very interesting, not only as giving a true picture of certain aspects of Bondo life, but even more important because parts of it are obviously false. Muliya, in describing his great crime, not only suffers from the normal 'errors in recall' to which all writers of autobiography are subject; he has also created a myth. He has deposited the fears and anxieties that even now haunt him in a fantasy, in which his enemy assumes the dimensions of a legendary monster, a Rakshasa, against whom puny heroic Muliya pitted his strength. Muliya never tells his story twice in the same way, but I will give it as I first heard it.

In Basupada I bought a palm for ten rupees; the yield was so abundant that I had to keep two pots always tied to the tree and was able to sell the wine for a rupee a day. My *mahaprasad* Ghasi Mundli, lived in Mundlipada. He performed the Dagoi-gige for his wife and his guests went to my tree to steal the wine; they also helped themselves to the pots, the rope and the knife. When I next went to the tree for my morning drink, I found nothing. I went home and sat on the veranda. I said to myself, 'If I attend this Dagoi-gige without a gift of wine, I shall be shamed'. So I did not join the party till the afternoon when all the people went out along the path for the final offerings. Ghasi said, 'Why didn't you come this morning?' 'Because I had no wine to bring,' I replied. 'Never mind,' said Ghasi. 'There's plenty in the house,' and he took me in and gave me wine from my own tree in my own pot to drink. When I recognized my pot, I said, 'There is no pot tied to my tree and the sap is trickling down wastefully. Pour this wine into something and let me have this pot for my tree.' He did as I suggested and I tied a cord round the neck of the pot and hung it over my arm. I ate and drank and got ready to go home.

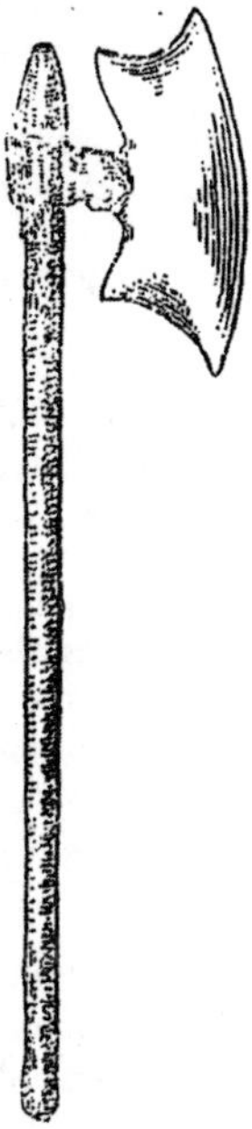

FIG. 52. Axe, of a kind commonly used in murders

But Budha Mundli caught me by the arm and said, 'Come and have a drink'. He took me to his house and there was my other pot, doubtless also full of my own wine. By a similar trick I persuaded him to empty it and give it to me and I slung it over my other shoulder. But Budha said, 'What do you want with two pots?' and began to shout at me. I said, 'Because both my pots are broken,' and got out of the house and away to Basupada as quickly as I could. I climbed the tree, tied the pots in place and, meeting three men going towards Mundlipada, went with them back to my house.

When I got back I went to my two friends, Ghasi and Budha, and said to them, 'You robbed me of my wine. Never mind. It was meant to be drunk and you have drunk it. But now give me back the three other pots you took and the rope and knife.' They were annoyed and picked up their axes to beat me. I ran home and got out two knives and my axe. As I was going back I saw under a tamarind tree a pregnant she-goat belonging to one of the Doms. I had a knife in each hand, and I stabbed the goat and it fell dead. I was very drunk, I cut the creature in half with my axe. Out of the belly came two kids. Everyone was pleased and we all, friends and enemies, roasted the flesh on the spot and ate it. But I kept the kids for myself. Presently along came the Dom demanding compensation. The others said, 'We didn't kill it; you'll have to get the money out of Muliya'. I had gone home by then but the Dom followed me and sat down in my house and wouldn't go. I gave him wine and some of his own roast meat. It was dark and while he was eating the fellow secretly got hold of one of the kids and hid it in his cloth. Next morning he went to the police and made a report against me.

The police came and arrested me. They took me to Mattili first and then to Malkangiri. The Magistrate said, 'You are fined eight score rupees'. I said, 'I haven't got so much in the world. The most I can pay is forty.' He said, 'No, you must bring it all or go to jail for a fortnight'. I said to myself, 'Why should I waste such a lot of money? In jail I'll get good food; there'll be nothing to worry about and I'll save my cash.' So I went to jail. All the same, I got my own back on the people who stole my things. I too made a report and they were fined twenty-five rupees each. When I returned from jail I had to pay five rupees to the village for a purification feast. But on the whole I saved a lot of money.

I wasn't married then. A year afterwards I took a girl and two years after that I took another. I lived very happily with my two wives.

Now my father's name was Mangla Dangra-Manjhi. There were four brothers — the eldest Muliya, the next Ujje, then my father, and the youngest Gulong. We had some very good harvests and this Gulong, my uncle, grew jealous of me. He thought in his mind, 'Mangla has only this one son; if the boy were to die, then I would be adopted and in the end I would get these fields and cattle'. With this in mind he sent *eloto* against me, and I was desparately ill for a fortnight. My parents called the Dissari and had me cured but for a time I was very weak. When I got better the first thing I thought of was palm-wine. I longed for it with all my heart. So one day — it was a Wednesday — very early in the morning, while it was still dark, I took two annas and went to buy some at Dattipada. At the same time my father went for his drink to our own tree.

That very morning Gulong had decided to murder both of us. He took his bow and arrows and came to my house. One of my wives was warming herself at the fire and the other was husking grain. Gulong asked where I was. They said, 'He has gone somewhere or other for wine'. Gulong shouted, 'If he and his father had been here I would have eaten their flesh with stale rice; but as they have gone to the palm I will eat their flesh with new wine'. He hurried home, called out his wife, and armed with an axe and a knife went to our tree. On the way he met the Naiko of Mundlipada and abused him. A little further on he met my father coming home and quarrelled with him. He and his wife beat my father and knocked him senseless. They thought he was dead and left him lying there. When I got back from Dattipada I was already drunk, but I had some more wine in a gourd. I went to my tree at Basupada and lay down at its foot. In the evening my father recovered and came in search of me. When I saw him covered with blood, I asked him what had happened, and he said he had fallen from a tree. He did not tell me about the quarrel for fear I should get excited and try to kill Gulong.

In the evening I went home and my wives gave me water for a bath. After I had finished my supper, I was preparing to sleep on the veranda, but they told me what Gulong had been saying and insisted on my sleeping indoors with the door shut. Next morning, the Thursday, my father was up very early and took his bullocks to the field to plough. I went for a drink to a palm near the field and took with me Sonia, Ujje's son. Soon after I had left Gulong again came to the house and told my wives what he was going to do to me. He followed us down to the field. There he abused my father and smashed the plough with his axe. When I heard what was going on I shouted at him and this diverted him from my father and he came to attack me instead. He came up waving his axe about, but I too had an axe and I struck his, cutting it in half. Then I hit him hard with the blunt edge on the side of his head and knocked him out. Sonia picked up the axes and hid them. I sat down at the foot of the tree and had a drink.

But as we sat watching him Gulong sat up slowly and twirled his moustache at us. He said, 'Now I'm going to get my bow and arrows and I shall kill father and son and throw their bodies away together'. I said to myself, 'This man is certainly going to kill us'. So I seized my stick and before he could do anything I struck him on the head and back and belly. But he took no notice; he just stood there abusing me. I broke his arm; we could see the bone sticking out; but he rubbed it and it healed. His head swelled under my blows to double the size, but he rubbed it and it healed. Then I struck the front of his head and the stick sank in as if it had been an axe, and the blood spurted out, but he rubbed it and the place was healed. At last I hit him very hard on the back of the head and he fell forward, and I added five heavy blows on his back. But he just turned over and said, 'Now hit me on the chest,' and I beat him there until he lost consciousness. Now, I thought, he will certainly die, so I sat down and had another drink and then went home.

In the evening Sonia and I went down to the palm tree again for our evening drink and found Gulong still alive. I gave him two cups of wine, for I thought, 'He is bound to die, but let him have a drink before he does'. Then I went home. The next morning, while it was still dark, we went again to the tree, and there was Gulong, sitting up and warming himself at a little fire. When I saw him I was really frightened. I did not dare approach, for I thought, 'Nothing can save us now. It is impossible to kill this man.' However, I sent Sonia to get our wine. He gave some of it to Gulong and brought the rest to me. Gulong drank and then looked up, twirling his moustache at me. I drank also, then quietly picked up a heavy stone and went near and hurled it down on his head with all my strength again and again till the head was smashed and he was quite dead. We sat down and finished the wine and at last went home, leaving the body there.

Even when the police took the corpse to the hospital, the doctor broke two or four of his knives trying to cut open the head, it was so hard.

Muliya was arrested and sentenced to two years' imprisonment. Even then he was not free from the threat of Gulong's enmity. He told me how he was often tormented in dreams by Gulong's ghost (*sairem*). 'He used to come and abuse me and in my dreams it was always I who was killed. As long as I was in the jail his ghost troubled me. He used to offer me palm-wine, which I greatly missed there, but I knew it was full of his magic and I dared not drink it.' It was only when Muliya was released that he felt himself free from these visitations. This appears, indeed, to be the usual tradition. Until the penalty has been worked out, a murderer is liable to a supernatural punishment, to visitations from the victim's ghost. But once the sentence is finished he seems to be safe; the ghost's honour is satisfied. A Bison-horn Maria once said to me — he was referring to a released convict; 'If Government has forgiven him, why shouldn't the gods forgive ? '

Muliya's improbable story is interesting, not because it is true, but because it is partly false. It is his own private myth, which he repeats with endless variations, like Ghasi Mundli's private myth about Pat Khanda Mahaprabhu. Such fantasies restore the narrator's self-respect and help him to overcome the frustrations and anxieties of jail life. In jail Muliya, for example, suffered several forms of anxiety. He was constantly worrying whether his two wives were remaining faithful to him, whether his father was alive or dead, what sort of crops his fields were bearing, and whether Gulong's family were trying to take revenge. His greatest deprivation in jail — and this is true of most aboriginal convicts — was that he was unable to anaesthetize himself against his anxieties with alcohol.

3. The Blood-feud

So strong is the impulse to revenge in the Bondo mind that regular blood-feuds develop between families and even villages. At a wedding in Semiliguda, Mogla Kirsani just released from jail came over from Bodapada with a party of friends, quarrelled with some of the other guests from Kurriguda and killed one of them. Shortly afterwards the Kurriguda people raided Bodapada and killed a man and his son. For ten years Bira Naiko of Goyiguda cherished plans of revenge against Lepa Bodnaik who had murdered his father with a pestle. When Salai Mundli's two sons heard that their father had been assaulted on his way home from the Mundaguda bazaar, they grabbed their bows and arrows and hurried off to rescue and revenge.

The two most notorious examples of the blood-feud are both connected with Andrahal, at once prince and villain of Bondo settlements. They are of sufficient importance for our understanding of Bondo character to be described in detail.

About six miles from Andrahal to the south-west, somewhat down the hill and not far from the Machkund River, is the attractive Didayi village of Patroputtu with its fertile palms, broad cultivated fields and comparatively civilized appearance. Between the people of this village and those of Andrahal there has developed a bitter enmity.

It began in 1944. That year, the Agar Sumsum, or Feast of the First Mangoes, which is part of the great Giag Festival, fell on 21 April. This is the occasion for an important ceremonial hunt preceded by special rites. These were performed and a large party of Bondos went out into the woods. There was Gulong Mundli, Lakshmi Sisa, Budha Mundli, Soma Sisa, Gulong Jigri and a number of others. They had no luck in the forests round Andrahal and wandered down the hills into the area near Patroputtu. Its gets very hot in this valley on an April afternoon and the disappointed hunters grew tired and thirsty. But every Bondo knows where refreshment is to be had, and the Andrahal men knew all too well (for they had often robbed it) that there was a fine sago palm belonging to Somra Sisa, a Didayi of Patroputtu. They found the tree and Gulong Mundli climbed it and brought down the pot of sap. Somehow the news reached Patroputtu and Somra Sisa himself, with his brother Lachha Sisa (who had long suspected the Andrahal people of stealing his fowls) hurried, full of indignation, to the spot. They found the Andrahal party pleasantly intoxicated at the foot of the trees and a violent quarrel began. The usual phrases flickered to and fro — 'Eater of my dirt!' — 'Eater of my wife's excreta!' — 'Fruit of a dog's copulation!' — and soon Gulong Mundli staggered to his feet and struck Somra Didayi on the head with the back of his axe. Somra turned to flee, but Gulong had his bow and he shot at him, driving an arrow into his left leg. Somra fell down crying that he was dead.

When the Didayi Lachha heard this he lost all control of himself and shouting that the Andrahal men had murdered his brother, he drew his bow and shot an arrow right into Gulong's mouth. Gulong pulled it out and with blood pouring from him fell at Lachha's feet, begging to be forgiven. But Lachha was mad with rage and he beat the unfortunate man with his axe until he was certain he was dead. The Bondos now rallied their forces and one of them, Lachhmi Sisa, shot at the Didayi Lachha and hit him in the right fore-arm. Lachha, who had run out of arrows, pulled it out of his arm and shot it back. He dropped his bow and struck Lachhmi to the ground with his axe; then he picked up a great stone and smashed his head with it. Meanwhile the other members of the Andrahal party had run away; they were not afraid, they insist to this day, but they were so drunk that they knew they had not a chance against a sober and determined foe. Lachha then went to his brother and finding him alive laid him comfortably in the shade of some bushes and hurried back to the village for assistance.

The next day, the headman and the Bariko went the thirty-two miles through the forest to Mattili to report the matter to the police. Lachha

Sisa was, of course, arrested, but the Court, taking into consideration the grave and sudden provocation and the fact that he undoubtedly believed that his brother had been killed and he himself was in danger, sentenced him to only two years' imprisonment.

This started the feud. Soon after the village officers had departed to fetch the police, young Lachhmi Mundli of Andrahal arrived in Patroputtu. He seems to have been driven into a sort of frenzy by the news of the death of Gulong, who was his cousin, for he broke the strictest of *angto* taboos by visiting another village during the Giag-gige and he came down the uneven street of Patroputtu waving his bow and arrows in the air and shouting that he would kill every Didayi in the place. There were few people about, but a feeble ancient called Mongla was sitting in front of his house and Lachhmi made for him. The old man took to his heels and the Bondo sent an arrow whistling after him; it struck a key hanging at his girdle and glanced aside. The youth fired again and this time the arrow grazed Mongla's waist; he fired again, and this time the arrow pierced his left forearm. Before he could shoot a fourth time, a number of Didayis caught hold of the boy and disarmed him. He was sentenced to seven years for attempted murder.

But this did not deter the Bondos of Andrahal from seeking their revenge. They began to make armed raids on the Didayi villages of the valley; they robbed their palm trees, killed their cattle, carried off their fowls. By 1946 the once populous village of Patroputtu had been reduced to a wretched hamlet of half a dozen huts. The people of Mundlipada joined in the feud. In January 1946 they, with some support from Bandapada and Tussayipada, raided the Didayi village of Gumma across the Madras border, beating up the people and carrying off two bullocks and many fowls. Other Didayi villages in Madras also suffered; Gobarpada was raided and cattle stolen. In Chindiguda the Bondos killed a goat in the middle of the village and roasted and ate it on the spot. The Didayis did not dare make reports to the police, for fear that Bondo revenge would take an even more ferocious character.[1] For, as a Didayi once told me, 'Every part of a Bondo's body is armed with weapons'.

[1] On 7 February 1946 a party of Doms returning to their village, Badguda, from the Phanasput bazaar, were set on by a number of Bondos, who robbed them of their purchases of cloth. The Doms made no report to the police for fear of retaliation. There have indeed been very few cases where members of other communities have dared to attack Bondos, but one such occurred on 2 June 1946, when two drunken Ronas brutally murdered Salai Kirsani of Banspada on the bank of the Damdei River as they were returning from the Mundaguda bazaar. Salai had offered to buy some palm-wine from the Ronas; they refused to let him have it, and he abused them. The Ronas attacked him with such ferocity that when the police inspected the body, they found the head hanging loosely almost severed, a great wound in the forehead, and a gaping cut across the wrist.

The other notorious blood-feud was a domestic one. It involves the charming, if ambiguous, character of Sonia Sisa, from whose lips I heard the story which was indeed confirmed by common report. Sonia is a dear fellow; he is good-looking, courteous, obliging, thoughtful. He stands out in any company. He is obviously liked and respected by his own party, while naturally feared by the opposite faction. He has matured in a hard school. He has seen the world. He has contacted civilization—for he has done a life sentence in the Orissa jails—and has, on the whole, survived it. He is still simple and unsophisticated, his tribal loyalties unimpaired. He made no apology for what had happened, no attempt to protest his innocence, no claim that he had been badly treated. But he did not for a moment, of course, believe that he was guilty in any moral sense. He had done his duty and looked on himself, not as a convict, but as a prisoner of war.

Here is his story. It happened in 1930. I give it as Sonia tells it, checking its main details by village gossip. Unfortunately I have been unable to find the official records of the trial.

Kaliya Mundli of Andrahal had a field. But one day Ghasi Sisa said, 'This field is mine. Long ago your parents gave it to me in payment for a sacrifice I performed on their behalf.' Kaliya said, 'I have never heard of this before; I have been ploughing this field all these years; why have you come to me now?' The discussion went on and on, until at last Ghasi brought a bullock and tethered it at Kaliya's door saying, 'We gave a bullock to your parents when they gave us the field; now I return you your bullock; give us the field and we will have no more quarrels'.

But Kaliya said, 'I don't want your bullock, anl I'm going to keep my field'. He untethered the animal and drove it away. That evening—it was a Tuesday—Kaliya called the elders to the *sindibor* and they discussed the matter. Kaliya's father's elder brother, Sukro Mundli, said, 'This field is ours; when did our parents give it away? We have been cultivating it all our lives and now Ghasi suddenly claims it. Who has taught him this trick?' Ghasi was very angry at this and he got up and with a heavy stick hit Sukro over the head and broke it open. The next day—Wednesday—I myself went with Kaliya, Sukro and one Lachhi Mundli to make a report to the Nandpur police.

Now Gulong, Ghasi and Tio Sisa were three sons of the same parents and of the Killo *bonso*. I, who am also one of the Tiger people, am distantly related to them through my grandparents. Soma, Kaliya and Somra Mundli, of the Ontal *bonso*, were three sons of three brothers, who in turn were the sons of the same parents. In this way the Sisa men who belonged to the Killo race were opposed to the Mundli men of the Ontal race. But I threw in my lot with the Mundli party.

While I was away getting the police, the three Sisa brothers went to the Mundli houses and beat up the womenfolk, dragging them out and damaging the walls and verandas of the buildings. The police kept us hanging about till the Saturday, and in our absence the three brothers spent their time abusing and bullying our families. On the Saturday evening we got back to Andrahal and saw the damage that had been done. But we thought, 'We have called the police and they will soon be here. It is better to keep quiet and not cause any more trouble.'

But the police were a long time in coming; had they been a little more expeditious, they might have averted the tragedy that was so swiftly approaching. On the Sunday, Monday and Tuesday mornings, the three Sisa brothers appear to have spent a lot of time showing off. Naturally, every morning the Mundli party, along with Sonia Sisa, had to go for their daily drink of palm-wine. Nothing could interfere with that; the need for the morning drink is as inexorable as defecation, as certain as the sunrise. Every morning, in their absence, the Sisa brothers went into their houses, frightened and alarmed the womenfolk and did what we may call symbolic damage to the buildings; they pulled straw from the roofs, for example, and relieved themselves against the walls. But it is noticeable that although Sonia and his friends were perfectly well aware of what would happen in their absence, it does not seem even to have occurred to them to give up going to the forest for their morning drink or even to have sent one member of their party to fetch it while the others remained on guard. One reason was probably the not unjustified conviction that no one can be trusted with a gourd of palm-wine; the other was the acute anxiety-tension from which these men were suffering and which they could not endure without the support of alcohol. Sonia may now be allowed to continue his story.

On the Tuesday I went with Soma Mundli to Katamguda (about half a mile away) to drink palm-wine. In our absence the three brothers threw stones at my young brother Lachhim Sisa who was building a house. They did not hit him but they nearly did. Lachhim was frightened and ran to hide in the jungle. When his mother-in-law missed him she decided he had been killed and came screaming after us to Katamguda. We hastened home and, not finding the boy there, searched for him in the forest. At last we found a group of boys — they were all young and Lachhim was among them — sitting under the trees and weeping for fright. We encouraged them, saying, 'We must not be afraid. If they hit us, we will hit back.' We brought them to the village and they took refuge in the house of Soma Mundli's father.

Then along came Gulong with his axe and attacked the door of Lachhim's house. But after he had given the door a few blows he went away, I don't know why. After that we all went back to the forest for a drink of palm-wine and the three Sisa brothers went to their palms. When we returned in the evening we found that Gulong had killed two she-goats belonging to Domu Mundli, who was Sukro Mundli's brother's son. Domu met us with a great outcry about this, but we said, 'Let him kill a few goats; that is better than his killing men'. For we were all afraid of what he might do.

The police still had not appeared on the Wednesday morning and both parties went to get their wine as usual. The Sisa group got home first and offered their routine insults to the Mundli houses. Sonia and his friends now decided that if the police did not come that day they would go on the following morning (Thursday), after their usual drink of wine, to report the matter again.

But on the Thursday morning, Sonia's party was a little late in getting back to Andrahal, and when they arrived they found the Sisa brothers, all drunk, beating at their houses with their axes. They decided to attack at once. Soma Mundli led the way, striking Tio Sisa on the back with his axe.

The blade sank into his back and he could not pull it out. He ran about fifty paces with Soma after him holding onto the handle of the axe, and then fell down. Soma at last got his axe out and chopped at him with it all over his body. Somra Mundli was standing some twenty paces away and when Ghasi Sisa discovered what was going on he came up trembling with rage and shot at him. His first arrow flew wide to the left, the second to the right, but as he was about to shoot a third, Somra caught hold of him and threw him to the ground. He called Soma, who left Tio, who was now almost dead. They struck Ghasi several times on the chest and the man died at once.

Then Gulong came running to me—I was watching the scene at a short distance. He shouted, 'You've had my brothers killed,' and slapped me twice in the face. I had a razor in my hand and I slashed at Gulong's throat saying, 'Yes, and I'll kill you with them'. But Gulong suddenly folded his hands and bowed to me saying, 'No, between you and me there is truth (*sato*); we are of the same *kuda* and *bonso*; we will be friends; at least spare my life'. I let him go and he ran to hide in his house.

The next day the Bariko took a report to the Nandpur police and on the third day a head constable came and on the fourth the Sub-Inspector. They tied me up with Soma Mundli, Kaliya Mundli and Somra Mundli and took us, with the two corpses and Gulong, whom I had wounded, to Mattili. There after the doctor had examined the bodies, we were allowed to burn them. Gulong was soon cured in the hospital. We confessed that we had killed our enemies. If we had not confessed the police would certainly have killed us.

The three men were given sentences of life-imprisonment. But they were not free from their anxieties, any more than Muliya was. Sonia used to have nightmares—that he was climbing his palm to collect the sap and the three Sisa brothers came to shoot him with their arrows, that they were coming to murder him and he hid in a pit or thick jungle to escape them. But he learnt, he told me, to work a paper-machine and this interested him so much that he forgot his enemies.

The chief protagonists were dead or in jail. But the feud went on. In January 1941 Ghasi Sisa's son, who was now old enough to avenge his father and uncle, murdered Domu Mundli whose two she-goats had been killed and eaten by Gulong long before.

Gulong himself survived the death of his brothers by five years. But he never fully recovered. There was a 'leak' in his throat, the villagers told me, where Sonia Sisa had slashed him, 'and his palm-wine ran out of it and he died'. Sukro, the son of Ghasi who was killed, a poor, thin, amiable creature, performed the obsequies for all three brothers. This was expensive and he tried to avoid erecting a *gunom* stone for Gulong. But Ghasi had been a prosperous man — he even had his private *sindibor* — and Gulong's ghost, though not for over ten years, insisted on the proper rites being performed. I assisted at this ceremony on 19-20 February 1946 and it was a strange experience to watch the final memorials to the three turbulent brothers being concluded. Yet even now the feud was not over. Sonia Sisa, the real agent of Gulong's early death, now out of jail, insisted — in spite of my persuasions — on being present at his victims' final obsequies. During the dance on the night of the 20th, Sonia took charge of the proceedings, ordered everyone about, rebuked them for not dancing with sufficient zest and, at last provoking a quarrel with yet another member of the Sisa family, fought with him and inflicted a frightful wound on his right arm. I dreaded Sonia's return to jail, and managed to persuade the two parties to compromise the offence; no report was made to the police and, even more important, further fuel was not heaped upon the fires of hatred.[1]

4. Disputes about Property

While murders due to some reaction against anxiety or to the desire for revenge may be taken as examples of psychological maladjustment, those arising from disputes about property illustrate the problems of social maladjustment. In its extreme form, that of theft, this type of maladjustment is uncommon in Bondo society. In 1942 a small gang of

[1] A pathetic incident, on Sonia's release from life-imprisonment, is worth recording here. Sonia was given a railway pass as far as Bobbili, fifty rupees in cash and his freedom. His journey, by bus from Bobbili to Koraput and thence home on foot, cost him eighteen rupees. On the way he bought twelve rupees worth of cloth for his wife and children. He had never had so much cash in his hands before. He was a free man. For a few days he felt like a king. On the train, somehow scenting his simplicity, the beggers thronged round him; to one he gave four annas, to another eight and to a blind man a whole rupee. His face glowed as he described these gifts; he had got a tremendous kick out of bestowing them. He, Sonia, a poor murderous 'savage', was able to give alms to 'civilization'.

men from Kichchipoda and Thagavada — two of them were ex-convicts: Buti Kirsani who had done time for murder and Hadi Mundli who was involved in the Thagavada killing of 1937 — made themselves, according to the police report 'a terror to the neighbourhood'. On 14 June 1942 they attacked two men returning from the Mundaguda bazaar, robbed them of a knife and blanket and beat them up. The police came quickly and found the gangsters drinking with a crowd of other men; most of them escaped up the hill but the gangsters themselves were too drunk to get away.

Kinberg has drawn attention to the fact that 'the general lowering of the moral level by alcohol may give rise to economic crimes. There is thus a class of thieves who only steal when they are under the influence of drink...Sometimes it would seem as though alcohol released an actual passion for thefts.'[1] Two drunken men from Gokurupada, who normally would have never even considered such a thing, robbed an old man of his fowl and when he resisted, killed him. In several other cases drunken Bondos on the way home from Mundaguda have tried to rob their fellows. It was when Muliya of Mundlipada was drunk that he stole the goat which marked the beginning of his criminal career.

The more serious crimes connected with property are not sequelae of theft or cheating; they are the result of hot-tempered disputes or the desire to prevent economic loss. Someone takes a jackfruit and the argument about it ends in his head being broken. Cows wander into a field and when the ploughman injures them as he drives them out, he gets beaten up for his pains. Embankments between fields are broken down; tempers are roused over the problem of their repair and soon there are broken arms and aching heads.

Murders over the possession of land are of more interest to the economist than the student of crime. The mortgaging of land is a constant source of dispute, for the Bondo's attachment to his fields is such that even when he knows he has forfeited his right to it, he cannot bear to see someone else in possession and often tries to take it back. Guru Sisa of Pakkanaguda, for example, gave one of his fields to a neighbour, Budha, as security for a loan. When the time fell due for repayment, Guru was unable to meet his obligations and accordingly Budha took possession of the field and began to plough. When Guru saw him doing so, he came and unyoked the bullocks and drove them from the field. The two men began to throw stones at each other and the matter would

[1] Kinberg, op. cit., p. 211. Scott points out that it is in the early mild stage of intoxication that 'there is committed a considerable proportion of the thefts which may be attributed to the action of alcohol. The weakening of moral feeling and the blunting of the fear of consequences combine to produce a state of mind in which such offences become more likely.'—G. M. Scott, 'Alcoholism and Criminal Behaviour', *Mental Abnormality and Crime* (London, 1944), p. 167.

have taken a serious turn had not the elders intervened, taken the disputants to the *sindibor* and arranged a compromise.

A similar dispute at Bandapada at the end of 1944 did not end so happily. The Dora family in this village had split into two branches which had lived separately for many years. A simple diagram will make clear their relationship.

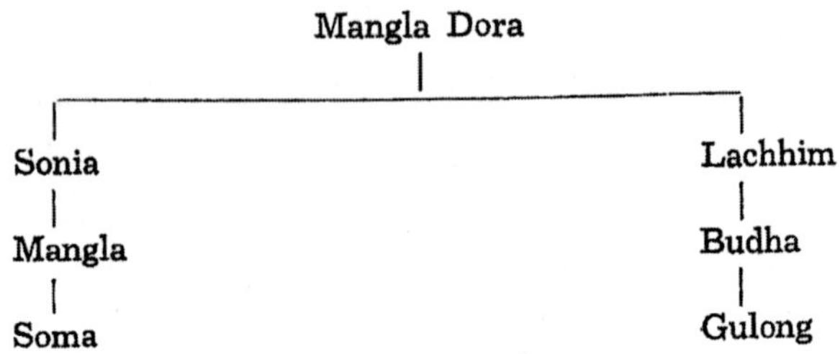

Soma had inherited a field from his father Mangla and used to make his living by it. His wife fell ill and the Dissari prescribed the sacrifice of a goat and a fowl. Soma seems to have been very poor, for he had not even a fowl in the house, still less the money to buy a goat. He was able however to borrow a goat and two rupees in cash from his cousin Gulong; in return he said that Gulong could cultivate his field and enjoy the crop for the next three years. The field must have been uncommonly barren — or the loan exceptionally profitable. The first year, accordingly, Gulong sowed rice and got a good harvest. When Soma saw the grain he could not bear to think of the rich fruit of his own field going into another's hands and he went to Gulong and said, 'Take back your rupees and goat. They are yours, but this crop is mine and I must have it.' Gulong placed the matter before the elders at the *sindibor* and they very properly gave judgement in his favour. Soma said nothing at the time, but privately refused to accept their verdict. After a few days he invited Gulong to go with him to his hill-clearing for a drink and to talk things over. Gulong sat down in the shelter of the field-hut and prepared to take his ease, but Soma, pretending to be fetching the palm-wine crept up behind him with his axe and killed him with a single blow. He hid the body in the jungle, but could not face his friends and stayed out in the clearing, pretending to be busy. But Gulong's relatives suspected there was something wrong; they came to the clearing, searched the hut and found a trace of blood, and in the end discovered the body. When the police came, Soma confessed.

The paucity of our information in all these cases is tantalizing. We have hints, suggestions, but little detailed knowledge. I see Soma, the youngest and poorest of a large family, with his sick wife, his dread of the supernal fury which had attacked her, the despairing bid for the wherewithal to buy it off. There follows a barren year, his field in alien hands, and the sight of a rich crop which might have been his going elsewhere. Society supported his opponent and he could not adjust himself to its decisions.

The Dumiripada murder of 1939 illustrates the same feeling of despair at the sight of another man using one's field. Mangla Sisa sold a bit of land to one Sania Mundli for three rupees. He took the money and allowed Sania to cultivate the land. But when the crop was ready he took it away. Village opinion supported Sania, but Mangla would not submit; there were frequent quarrels and this time it was the new owner who got his blow in first. Sania stabbed Mangla at dawn after an all-night dance which was part of the Sume-Gelirak celebrations.

A dispute about inheritance led to a murder at Bodoballe. Hadi Bodnaik of that village lost his father while he was still a boy. After some years his mother married again and left the village, leaving the boy in her brother's house. Before she left she gave the family cow and calf and entrusted the management of the fields and sago palms to her brother's son, Soma. When Hadi grew up he asked his cousin to return his possessions but Soma refused to give up anything beyond the cow and calf (now a fine bullock); these he gave to Hadi at his wedding. He continued to cultivate the fields, considering that the work he had done on them entitled him to use them. Hadi brooded over this and one November morning he went with his bow and arrows to the field where Soma was busy reaping. He called to his cousin and when the latter turned round Hadi shot him in the chest above the left nipple; the wounded man swung round and Hadi sent another arrow deep into his back and killed him. He was only twenty-two years old and went to jail for life.

Quarrels about the repayment of debts not infrequently end in disaster. At Kichchipoda two men were killed when they demanded the return of a heifer which they had lent for a wedding some years before. On 24 February 1942 Hadi Kirsani, the headman of Kurriguda, was arranging for the collection of the land revenue for remittance to the Jeypore Estate. He was sitting in his house discussing this when one Ghasi Kirsani came in and demanded the return of a loan of paddy seed which Hadi had borrowed the previous year. Hadi, who had naturally been drinking to fortify himself against the exacting business of collecting the rent, said that neither he nor the paddy were going to fly away and there was nothing to make a fuss about. This annoyed Ghasi and he became abusive. Hadi too lost his temper, went over to the fence near his house and, picking up a bamboo stick, struck Ghasi with it twice, killing him immediately.

I will give one last example of a quarrel between two friends over a trivial cause; unmotivated, unintentional, unnecessary, this tragedy well illustrates my belief that many aboriginal murders are little more than tragic accidents. One hot Sunday in May 1942, two Bondo youths, life-long friends, Mangla Sisa and Lachhmi Kirsani went down together from Kirsanipada to the Mundaguda bazaar. As they went along they took pot-shots at birds and grubbed about in the bushes on the chance of finding eggs. Suddenly Mangla shouted in triumph, for he had discovered four peahen's eggs, a real prize. He hid them carefully and the two youths went on down the hill to the bazaar. Lachhmi, however, slipped away early, went to the place where the eggs were hidden, removed them and took them home. There he cooked and ate two of them, and put the other two under a hen for hatching. Mangla came up the hill afterwards, drunk as usual after the bazaar, and searched for his eggs. When he found them gone, he went to Lachhmi's house shouting abuse. 'You are not an eater of eggs but of my wife's excreta. Come and lick the dirt from her body, come and eat the filth of mine.' Lachhmi was not to be seen, but his old father Soma was washing his hands after his supper. Mangla, blind with rage and liquor, struck him a heavy blow on the neck with his axe, severing the jugular vein and carotid artery and killed him at once.

It may be that Lachhmi considered that half the egg-find belonged to him; it is certain that Mangla had no intention of killing either his friend or his old father. All he wanted was some demonstration. But alcohol and possibly fatigue combined to turn it into tragedy.

5. Crime and Alcohol

The problem of alcoholic addiction among the Bondos is by no means easy. Alcohol, says Dent, 'is taken to anaesthetize oneself against too formidable surroundings, to overcome fear, to lessen self-consciousness, to produce sleep, to relieve pain, to act as a quickly absorbed food, to be an appetizer for other food, to stimulate the heart and to raise blood-pressure.'[1] The Bondos, consciously or unconsciously, probably drink for all these reasons, particularly (as I have already shown) as a defence against anxiety and the pressure of 'too formidable surroundings'. It may well be that one reason why so many Bondos get drunk at the Mundaguda bazaar is that they realize there something of the great forces of the outside world that are conspiring to destroy their independence.

[1] J. Y. Dent, 'The Study and Cure of Inebriety', *The British Journal of Inebriety*, Vol. XXXIX (1941), p. 5.

The Bondos are addicts, in a sense that other tribesmen are not. They are not content, as the Saoras are, with their morning drink — as if it was an early cup of tea. They go on drinking all day. There is no end to the drinking parties and convivial gatherings, especially as the sun goes down. Palm-wine is the routine tipple of every day. But at festivals, weddings and funerals large quantities of rice-beer are brewed; at the Mundaguda bazaar *mahua* spirit is preferred.[1]

A study of the occasions of liquor-inspired homicides is revealing. Two occurred at weddings, when the main drink was rice-beer supplemented by gourds of palm-wine. On neither occasion was there any motive or previous enmity; the people were simply blind drunk. In one case a man asked his brother for a drink and stabbed him when he did not get it. In the other, a man accused his fellow guests of finishing up the supply of beer and leaving none for him; there was a general fight and someone was killed.

Two murders occurred during the Sume-Gelirak dances. I have already noticed one; in the other a young buck of Dumiripada stabbed a rival when both were drunk. It was during the Giag Festival, another time of heavy drinking, that the blood-feud between Andrahal and Patroputtu started. One murder occurred during a *gunom* ceremony; there was no special connexion with the rite — it only happened then because the occasion brought together a number of mutually inimical people and filled them up with liquor.

But the majority of these narcomanic tragedies take place on Sundays, in connexion with the Mundaguda bazaar.

It is not altogether easy to understand the fascination that this event has for the Bondo mind. Mundaguda is a very ordinary little Hindu village lying in the flat country, commonplace and humble at the feet of the splendid Bondo hills. But every Sunday there is a bazaar and the Bondos must go swarming down from the highlands to attend it. The way is long and exhausting, the descent — of at least two thousand feet — is precipitous and rough. There is nothing to do at the bazaar, little to buy and the Bondos only meet the people that they see every day at home, the other people there being naturally shy of talking to such savages. The Bondos sometimes take a few mats to sell, perhaps they buy some luxuries for a wedding or festival. But it is not business that takes the Bondo down the hill. I suppose it is some fascination for the excitement and bustle of the greater world, a brief change from the monotony of agricultural labour and domestic care, a chance to overhear the news. But, whatever the cause, the whole of Bondo life, every

[1] The Bondos, like the eastern Finns, must be reckoned among those peoples who are provoked by alcohol to aggressive criminality: alcohol by no means has this effect in every case. See Bonger, op. cit., pp. 93 ff.

festal or funerary programme, circles round the day of rest; these ardent sabbattarians even base their name-system on the days of the week which gain their importance from their relation to the Sunday.

Of course, you can always get a drink at Mundaguda. But here again I have never been able to understand the attraction of walking eight or ten miles to obtain under very risky conditions (for the Excise staff is abroad at Mundaguda) what you can get without any difficulty at home. Perhaps it is the lure of stolen fruit; there is said to be a great deal of illicit distillation of *mahua* spirit all round the bazaar — for this favoured spot is surrounded by thick forest and there are many lonely gullies and thickets which might have been created for the express purpose of foiling the prohibitionist — and the Bondos go to it with enthusiasm. Then as they stagger up the hill in tipsy exaltation, they lose touch with reality and quarrel, beat and kill.

The police supplied me with a list of crimes arising in recent years out of the Bondos' attachment to bazaars. Some incidents occurred at the Mattili and Bodiguda bazaars which, like Guneiyapada, are also visited by Bondos, but the majority come from Mundaguda.

Table VII

LIST OF CASES IN WHICH BONDOS WERE PROSECUTED FOR CRIMES COMMITTED DURING VISITS TO A BAZAAR

Year	Section of I. P. C.[1]	Sentence
1936	326	Discharged
	324	Two years
1937	324	Compounded
1939	325	Fine
	304	Two accused got five years each
1940	325	Two weeks
	326	One year
	302	Life-imprisonment
	302	Two sentenced to death, of whom one was reprieved
	325	Not recorded
1941	325	Not recorded
	325	Two months
	325	Two months
1942	324	Three months
	324	Not recorded

It cannot be denied that this list, which is certainly incomplete, is formidable; indeed so strongly did the police appreciate the evil influence

[1] Section 302 I.P.C. covers murder; 304, culpable homicide not amounting to murder; 324, hurt; 325, grievous hurt; 326, grievous hurt by dangerous weapons or means.

of the Mundaguda bazaar that it was seriously proposed to move it further away from the Bondo hills.[1] But this was not practicable, nor indeed would it have done much good. The Bondos want their weekly holiday and if they do not get it at Mundaguda they will get it somewhere else.

The Mundaguda bazaar stands as a warning to those who desire to assimilate the aboriginals into the culture of the plains as soon as possible. I have no doubt that the Hindu and Mussalman merchants at this market are the mildest and most respectable of men. But the whole contact is too exciting; there is too much corruption behind the scenes; the temptations are too great. To the Bondo 'uplift' means all too often an uplifted axe.

To retail the details of the many drunken brawls which have led to murder in recent years would be an inexpressibly tedious task. I will content myself therefore with giving accounts of two only of the many recorded in my notebooks, the first because it illustrates the development of a quarrel, the second because of the devotion to a father that was displayed.

My assistant Sundarlal was present on two successive days, 24 and 25 May 1945, at disputes in Gokurupada and the neighbouring Mundlipada about thefts of palm-wine from the trees.[2] A young man of about twenty-five, Sukra Kirsani of Gokurupada, had some fine sago palms in his possession. Soma Sisa, a man some ten years senior to Sukra, who lived near by in Salanpada, used frequently to go secretly to the trees and steal the sap. On the evening of 24 May, Sukra was drinking *mahua* spirit in his house with a group of friends. Soma, drunk on the wine stolen from Sukra's trees, came rolling in, loudly demanding something to drink. Sukra himself was a little high and said, 'You steal my wine daily and now you come asking me to *give* you some. I suppose you have to steal my wine because you think I'm so mean I wouldn't give you any.'

SOMA: 'Who has ever seen me stealing your wine? Call him and let him say so to my face. How dare you call me a thief, sister-copulator!'

SUKRA: 'Certainly I say you are a thief.'

SOMA: 'Well, who saw me? Bring him here, or I'll have your wife.'

SUKRA: 'What did you eat on Friday and Monday last? Was it the dirt from my wife's body or the filth from mine? Thu, son of a dog, sister-copulator, brother-in-law!'

[1] In 1947, the bazaar was actually removed.

[2] Sundarlal, who is a careful observer, made full notes of the incidents and conversational exchanges on the very days they occurred. His account may be accepted as authentic.

SOMA: 'If I stole your wine, how is it you didn't catch me at it? You were too busy, I suppose, eating your own excreta. If you dare to call me a thief again, I'll cut you to pieces with my knife.'

At that Soma twirled his moustache, struck an attitude and pulled out his knife, but before he could do anything the others caught and disarmed him.

SUKRA: 'So you'd cut me up with your knife, would you? I'll go to jail for ten years, I don't mind, but I'll take care to kill you first.'

He drew his own knife and attacked Soma. But the women screamed and two of them caught hold of Sukra and held him back while others protected Soma. Eventually Soma was persuaded out of the house and taken home to bed.

The following day, there was another row. Sonia Mundli of Mundlipada went to a palm belonging to his cousin Ghasi, filled a gourd with wine and took it home. In the evening Ghasi went for his usual drink — and found the pot empty. There is hardly anything more exasperating to a tired and thirsty man than to climb one's tree at the end of a long day and find nothing there. Ghasi went home, had several drams of *mahua* spirit which he fortunately had in stock, and went to the Naiko to lodge a complaint. The Naiko took Ghasi to Sundarlal and Ghasi said to him, 'O Mahaprabhu, you are a tiger, I am only an old goat. This Sonia is young and strong; I am worn out and I have no sons to aid me. Sonia will certainly kill me and throw my body away. That tree belonged to my father, yet Sonia is always robbing it.'

There was obviously nothing Sundarlal could do, but he went with Ghasi to Sonia's house; Ghasi stood outside and began to show off a little.

GHASI: 'Come out, thief! Is it your father's tree that you are always robbing?'

SONIA: 'Thu, son of a dog! It's not your father's tree; it's mine.'

GHASI: 'You are a thief. Every day you steal my palm-wine. If you continue I'll have your mother, I'll even report you to the police.'

SONIA: 'Certainly, go, go, dog; go and tell your father about it. And take my pubic hairs with you; you can have them as a present.'

Ghasi pulled out his knife when he heard that, but Sonia ran into his house and shut the door. For a long time Ghasi swaggered up and down in front of the building, brandishing his knife and shouting abusively. At last, very late at night, the neighbours got him to bed.

There was no tragic sequel to this incident, but in 1940 a drunken quarrel on the steep ghat between Mundaguda and Mundlipada ended in real disaster.

Salai Mundli had four sons, of whom the two younger were Sonia and Soma. In the hills near Mundlipada there was an old clearing belonging originally to a man named Sonia Dangra-Manjhi. Finding it abandoned, Sonia and Soma began to cultivate it. The owner, as so often happens, seeing someone else take an interest in his property, revived his desire for it and tried to get it back, but without success. There is, of course, no legal ownership. The boys were actually sowing the clearing, in July 1940, when their father went one Sunday down to the Mundaguda bazaar.

On the same day, the dispossessed and resentful Sonia Dangra-Manjhi also went with an elder brother and both got drunk. On the way home, the two parties met and there was a violent dispute. Salai got the worst of it, and the others went on their way, leaving him unconscious, with some of his teeth knocked out. The news flashed on to the village and Salai's sons, waiting only to fill a gourd with gruel and collect their weapons, went to the rescue. What happened then is not, to my mind, certain. The prosecution story (entirely based on the hardly unbiased evidence of Sonia Dangra-Manjhi's friends) was that the two youths lay in wait for their enemy and ambushed him. They appeared suddenly from behind some bushes, shot Sonia, scattered his party and then beat the injured man to death. The body was found with two arrows sticking in the stomach, the head cut about and many bones broken. Such was the story accepted by the Court.

But the opinion five years later in Mundlipada — and I have rarely found village opinion to be wrong — was that it was Sonia and Soma who were ambushed. This is far more likely; there was no time for the boys to prepare an ambush; on the other hand, their enemies, well aware that retribution would be on the way, had every reason and ample opportunity to get ready. When the boys arrived, Sonia shot twice at them but missed and then attacked them with his axe. The boys shot back — and they were sober and accurate in aim — and both arrows went home. Thinking their father had been killed, they finished off his supposed murderer with their axes and then went on to find his victim. They discovered then that their father was alive, revived him with the gruel they had brought and carried him home.'

This was the story that was not revealed in Court, for the defence was conducted with deplorable indifference to the interests of the accused, and the two boys were sentenced to death. The sentence was commuted in appeal to the appalling mercy of life imprisonment.[1]

[1] Wherever I have had occasion to study them, I have been astonished — and the people themselves are not only astonished but outraged — at the inconsistency in the sentences awarded to aboriginal prisoners. Why, for example, did Lachha Sisa get only two years for the crime described at p. 241, while these two youths, who acted with a precisely similar motive, were sentenced to death? There surely should be some means of controlling the temperamental vagaries of Sessions Judges.

To conclude that the aggressive criminality of the Bondos is mainly, or even largely, due to alcohol would be an over-simplification of the facts. In general, all statistics regarding alcohol as a cause of crime have suffered from our ignorance of the alcoholism rates in the non-criminal population. The Bondos drink a great deal and their homicide rate is high; the Murias and Baigas probably drink quite as much and their homicide rate is low. Moreover, there are many Bondos who drink heavily, yet never commit a crime.

'In general'— so runs an authoritative recent report —'it appears that the studies of the relationship of alcoholism and crime have neglected to take into account the correlative influence of such possibly concomitant factors as intelligence, abnormality, and socio-economic status.'[1] Alcohol certainly appears as a contributory factor in many Bondo crimes; among the Bondos, as among other people, it reduces the inhibitions of self-criticism and self-restraint, which have been described as the brakes which make for safety in social intercourse. But quite apart from alcohol, the Bondos are exceptionally uninhibited by self-criticism and a sense of responsibility, and it is possible that many of them would give way to their love of property or passion for revenge even if they were strict teetotallers.

Kolb has in fact contended that in the majority of cases criminal conduct precedes narcotic addiction and is not caused by it, that criminality is, in fact, somewhat inhibited by addiction to drugs and alcohol. Anxiety and fear, which is anaesthetized by alcohol, is perhaps the main cause of Bondo homicide, and might work even more strongly under a prohibitionist regime.[2]

On the other hand, we must not underestimate the influence of alcohol on aggressive crime, which is most clearly marked in the moderate stages of intoxication, when 'there is frequently seen an almost complete loss of self-control', and when 'outbursts of passionate rage are common, often without any adequate provocation. These outbursts may lead to serious assaults, with or without weapons. There is a complete disregard of consequences, and the most severe injuries may be inflicted or sustained. It has to be remembered that along with the paralysis of self-restraint, there is a blunting of ordinary sensation, and fights tend in consequence to be more violent and more prolonged.'[3] There are some remarkable examples of this in the preceding pages.

[1] J. Michael and M. J. Adler, *Crime, Law and Social Science* (London, 1933), p. 138.

[2] L. Kolb, 'Drug Addiction in Relation to Crime,' *Mental Hygiene*, Vol. IX (1925), pp. 74-89.

[3] Scott, op. cit., pp. 9, 167f.

Even so, to prohibit alcohol to the Bondos would almost certainly cause more evil than good. There would be an enormous increase in the number of short-term convicts, jailed for illicit distillation, and these through contact with hardened criminals would return to introduce new forms of delinquency to their comparatively innocent homes. The sense of grievance, already fostered by restrictions on hunting and axe-cultivation, would be deepened, and the Bondo would become more than ever an outlaw from 'civilization', hostile to its nobler values, assimilating only its defects.

6. The Attitude of the Criminal

The Bondos, like the Marias and other tribesmen, are often exceptionally simple in the face of prosecution. They rarely attempt to conceal their crimes, they seldom abscond, and most of them confess. Sometimes they repeat at the Sessions trial a form of defence which has obviously been provided by the pleader engaged, at Government expense, to defend them. The few exceptions to the prevailing habit, therefore, are of special interest.

It might have seemed that if ever there was a murder difficult to conceal it was the Thagavada killing of 1937, for five persons were concerned in it and there were three bodies to hide. Yet the attempt was made. For some time Chakro Mundli had suspected that people were stealing sap from his three palms on Leveru Hill two miles north of the village, and it was generally assumed that the thieves came from one of the hamlets of Kichchipoda, some distance to the east, for a few Kichchipoda people, like the Mundli families of Thagavada, had their axe-cultivation on the same hill. On 18 November 1937, Hadi Sisa, Budha Kirsani and Sonia Kirsani went with Soma Dora from Kichchipoda to cut Soma's crop of small millet which was growing in a clearing only a quarter of a mile from Chakro Mundli's clearing on the Leveru Hill. They cut the crop and stacked their sheaves on the threshing-floor. Then they felt thirsty. Chakro's palm trees were near at hand. Soma had a drink and went home. The other three stayed on. Soma had a friend with him and the two men were evidently a little merry; they had to pass Chakro's field and Chakro stopped them and accused them of getting drunk on his own wine. They replied, 'Why are you accusing us when the real thieves are still at your trees ?' When he heard this, Chakro took his axe and went hastily to his trees. On the way he was joined by four others — Budha Mundli, Gora Mundli (a boy of eighteen) and two other men, Hadi Mundli and Lakmi Bodnaik. They at once attacked the Kichchipoda men whom they found drinking at the foot of one of the palms; they had the advantage of numbers, though only two were armed, and of being sober. Chakro knocked Hadi down with his axe, then led a general assault, strongly supported by Budha who also had an axe. The Kichchipoda people were far too drunk to resist, and it is not easy to decide what actually happened. But in the end Chakro Mundli had to face one inescapable fact; he had three corpses on his hands.

He slept on it, and next morning sent for three other men, close relatives, whom he let into the secret, and took to the scene of the tragedy. They first, of course, had their morning drink, finishing an entire pot of wine, after which Chakro persuaded his friends to help him carry the bodies to a deep pool below a waterfall two miles north-west of Thagavada. In the meantime, Chakro's wife, previously instructed by her husband, gave out that there was a tiger on Leveru Hill and that it was unsafe to go there.

It took Chakro and his friends all day to dispose of the bodies of the murdered men. They had to carry them, without being observed, to the falls and there tie stones round the necks and waists, lashing them firmly in place with bark-rope. It was not until late in the afternoon that they saw the last of the corpses sink into the dark waters of the pool.

By next morning, of course, the entire countryside knew what had happened; a cowherd, who had watched the previous day's proceedings with much interest, gave a detailed account of them to the headman and he went down to the Mattili Police Station with the report. The police came and arrested Chakro and his friends. Within an hour Chakro was at the falls, showing the Sub-Inspector just where he had concealed the bodies. He refused, however, to go into the water to bring them up and finally the Sub-Inspector had to go in and get them out himself.

Chakro and his four friends admitted the fight and the killing of their opponents, but they claimed that they had acted in self-defence since the Kichchipoda men had attacked them first. But, as the Court pointed out, it is surprising that in a quarrel where the deceased were the aggressors, not a scratch was sustained by any of the accused, while the total number of injuries on the bodies of the deceased amounted to more than twenty-five. Indeed it was evident that the murdered men had been so drunk that they were unable to do anything to defend themselves, and Chakro and his supporters were sentenced to long terms of imprisonment.

In this case, what is so odd — and yet so characteristic of the aboriginal — is that Chakro, after taking all that trouble to conceal his crime, should have at once taken the police to the waterfall and told them all about it. I do not suspect Third-Degree methods, though the police are often successful in bluffing a suspect into confession; I think it more likely that Chakro simply collapsed when he realized that the details of the crime were known.

In other cases, where the accused does not immediately make full confession, he may put up a story of extenuating circumstances. Lachhmi Sisa, who stabbed his brother in a fit of intoxication during a wedding, claimed first that he had forgotten all about it and then that his brother had attacked him and he was only defending himself — which was quite untrue. Sania Sisa who killed Domu Mundli at Andrahal as an act of revenge, declared that Domu threatened him first, but was unable to bring a single witness to prove it. Sania Mundli, who stabbed a rival during a dance, stated that the latter had first attacked him with a crowbar, but all the evidence goes to show that he was absorbed in dancing. Hadi Mundli maintained from the beginning that the crime in which he was involved was no more than an accident; there was a struggle, and his opponent fell on his own knife.

These rather pathetic and certainly futile attempts at a defence are interesting in that they suggest that, after a Bondo has committed a serious crime, he usually falls into a kind of apathy. A civilized man will at once set about devising his defence; few Bondos would be convicted if they had the wit to exploit immediately the strong communal sense of their neighbours and relatives, if they bribed witnesses, concocted statements, persuaded the village officials to their support. But the Bondos seem unable to do this; they collapse, they cannot even run away. Occasionally they spend their few remaining hours of freedom in drinking and debauch.

It is possible that the ease with which the aboriginal criminal usually gives himself away is an example, in conditions of great simplicity, of a tendency which has been made the subject of an interesting study by Reik.[1] The self-betrayal and improvidence of the criminal, his *Verbrecherpech* (bad luck) is proverbial and is often regarded as due to stupidity, an intellectual inferiority due to physiological causes. Reik, however, considers that the criminal's mistakes and self-betrayals are 'indications of hidden mental processes, unknown to the ego, which find expression....It is a question of mental compulsion, none the less compelling because its motive is anonymous'.

'It is clear', Reik continues, 'that in the criminal two mental forces are fighting for supremacy. One tries to wipe out all traces of the crime, the other proclaims the deed and the doer to the whole world.' This second force 'is impelled by the unconscious desire for punishment which expresses itself in faulty acts....Of course, there are criminals who do not react to their deed in this way, but in some cases this un-

[1] T. Reik, *The Unknown Murderer* (Eng. trans., London, 1936), pp. 71ff.

conscious need for punishment becomes so strong that it overwhelms the culprit and from the very outset seals his fate.' This 'internalization of the law of talion' may well explain the conduct of some Bondo murderers; I have found many traces, among Bondo and other aboriginal criminals, of a belief that only mundane punishment can save one from eternal justice.

The extreme brutality of some of these murders must be noticed. When Soma and Hadi Dora beat Saru to death with their axes, they inflicted no fewer than eleven incised wounds; all the bones of the face and scalp, except the mandible, were broken and smashed to pieces, and each of nine different wounds was alone sufficient to cause death. Lachhmi Sisa stabbed his brother with such violence that his knife went right through the abdomen, penetrating the liver, kidney and large intestine, and emerged at the right side of the back. The body of Sania Dangra-Manjhi was found covered with the most brutal wounds; the right lung, stomach, intestine, liver and spleen had been penetrated by arrows and almost all the bones of the head broken by axe-blows. I have already described the shocking death of Gulong at Mundlipada. When Hadi Bodnaik of Bodoballe killed his cousin Soma, he fired his first arrow with such force that it penetrated four and a half inches into the chest above the left nipple, and his second five and a half inches into the diaphragm and stomach. In February 1946 I visited in the Koraput Jail an unusually brutal-looking Bondo youth, Muliya Dhangra Manjhi (not the one of this name already described) who killed a man who had given evidence against him in a previous case. He shot one arrow right through his chest, another into his stomach, then with his knife slashed face and chest in half a dozen places. He pulled the arrow out of the stomach, broke it into three pieces, placed two of them by his victim's head, threw the third into his garden, kicked the corpse and went away, shouting boastfully of what he had done. He was only twenty-five years old.

It is possible that these attempts to mutilate the corpse are evidence, not so much of natural ferocity as of a belief (now almost sub-conscious) that it is necessary so to disable the ghost through the mutilation of the body that it will be unable to take revenge on the murderer. Tylor pointed out long ago that 'the Australian who has slain his enemy will cut off the right thumb of the corpse, so that, although the spirit will become a hostile ghost, it cannot throw with its mutilated hand the shadowy spear, and may be safely left to wander, malignant but harmless'.[1] The Bondos are certainly very much afraid of the ghosts

[1] E. B. Tylor, *Primitive Culture* (London, 1871; 5th edition, reprinted, 1929), Vol. I, p. 451.

of their murdered victims; Muliya and Sonia were both haunted by them in jail.

7. The Attitude to the Criminal

Bondo society is fully aware of the dangers to which it is exposed by the quarrelsome temperament of its members, and it makes genuine efforts to overcome them. The Castigation ceremony at the Sume Gelirak Festival trains the people to accept sharp and sudden pain without losing their tempers. The need of avoiding dissension is impressed on a young couple at a wedding and when they are ceremonially bedded. Whenever a Bondo passes through one of the *runnukbor* walls, he should place a twig upon it and pray that he may not get involved in any trouble at the place he is visiting.

The women of the tribe constitute a sort of perpetual Home Guard to protect their menfolk alike from murdering or being murdered. For them a dance or festival is not all pleasure. During a dance, mothers, wives, sisters, daughters stand round the gyrating throng of turbulent excited performers, watching with strained attention for the first sign of violence. I remember at Andrahal, during a dance one night, how Soma, the Naiko's brother, very drunk, pushed his way into the midst of the throng, broke up the fire by whose light they were dancing, tossed embers and ash over them and scattered handfuls of dust in all directions. This annoyed Sukro, the supremely handsome son of the Bodoballe Naiko; the two men grappled with each other and drew their knives. At once detachments of women darted forward from every side; one group seized Soma, another Sukro. The Naiko went to his brother's rescue, but his mother and two wives were on him in a moment and had him hustled out of the dance and into bed. His brother fell down and some girls took him too to bed. Sukro shook himself free from the women's protecting hands and pranced back again into the centre of the dance.

At Mundlipada too one night I saw an angry husband rush suddenly into the crowd and begin beating his young wife, though she had a baby in her arms. He brandished his knife, but immediately half a dozen women surrounded him, held his arms, clung to his waist, wrested his knife from his hand, keeping him immobilized until he calmed down and began to laugh. Sometimes you may see an old woman dash into the throng of dancers and remove a stick or axe from the hand of a youth who is flourishing his weapon too vigorously. At the appointment of the Naikos of the twelve Jangar villages at Mundlipada, when there was a great deal of heated half-tipsy argument, old women threw themselves into the struggle as valiantly as the men and prevented the pushing and pulling from taking a serious turn. It must be an anxious business to be a Bondo woman.

After a convict returns from jail serious efforts are made to reabsorb him again into Bondo society and to prevent the perpetuation of a feud. This is not always successful, but the attempt is made.

The Bondos have borrowed, perhaps from their Dom neighbours, the custom of subjecting a released criminal to a ceremony of purification before allowing him to resume his normal community life. This is the general Hindu and near-Hindu practice, but it does not seem to me to be an old or genuine element in Bondo culture, for the details of the rite are Hindu in character and the Bondos do not hold that belief in caste which is the ultimate reason behind the demand for purification. The ex-convict is not to be washed clean of his sins; he is to be purged of the defilement of social contact with untouchables in jail. But the belief in caste is growing — no Bondos hold it more strongly than the ex-convicts themselves — and doubtless the demands for purification feasts will grow in rigour. When Sonia Sisa returned to his village after fifteen years' absence, he was not allowed to eat with his children or approach his wife until the necessary rites had been concluded.

The ceremony has four main features — the payment of a fine, a rite of burning or sprinkling, a symbolic enactment of rebirth into a new life, and a community feast in which someone ceremonially accepts food from the culprit's hands. The fine, which is used for the feast, may consist of one or more cows or bullocks, some pots of rice-beer or a money payment. One of the elders heats a bit of gold or a silver coin and burns the ex-convict's tongue and chest seven times and each ear and the back of the neck thrice, saying, 'Never do this again. This time we have taken you back, but a second time we will not forgive you.' Sometimes however the convict is sprinkled with water in which tulsi, gold or silver has been dipped or with a mixture of water and cowdung. Finally a great feast is prepared, and the celebrant at the rite and the convict sit down together and feed one another. The willingness of the celebrant to eat food from the other's hands is regarded as proof that the latter has been forgiven and purified. Often an Orpa rite is performed; a sort of booth is built over a stream and the culprit is made to pass under it seven times while the celebrant sprinkles him with tulsi-water.

But this is not enough. The Bondos further insist that the ex-convict should make his peace with whomsoever he has wronged. It is specially important that a released murderer should make friends with his victim's family. Both households prepare rice-beer. The murderer invites the elders and his victim's family to a party. He touches their feet and says, 'It was my fault. We belonged to the same village (or tribe) but I had hatred in me. Now I have fed on excreta and urine. Forgive me; after this I will never quarrel again.' Again and again he is made to promise both his own relations and those of his victim that he will not attempt to take revenge for the punishment he has suffered. When the company is satisfied, someone exclaims, 'Good; be one with us again'. Then the ex-convict takes a leaf-cup and offers rice-beer to everyone present in turn, emptying the dregs of the cup each time; in this way he 'swallows their leavings' and they return the compliment. After this they all feast together.

This rite has features of great significance. The little booth in the bed of a stream through which the offender has to crawl is surely a symbol of the vagina, through which he is born again to a new life.[1] The insistence on confession may be simply a means to prevent the culprit from repeating his crime; it may be intended as a public warning to others, and particularly, the younger members of the tribe; but there may also be a deep-rooted purpose (possibly unconscious) of self-purification by open admission. The Bondo ex-convict is in a state of taboo; there is something about him which is dangerously contagious: this danger is averted by burning with fire or sprinkling with water (obvious tokens of purification), the confession, and the ceremony of re-birth, and safety is finally guaranteed by the sharing of a common feast which restores the offender to the tribal communion.

So far as I know, for all the expense and trouble it involves, in spite of the further quarrels that may be caused, every ex-convict accepts and even insists on this rite, which alone can satisfy the deep psychic needs of a man who knows he is guilty and realizes he is taboo. 'The breaking of a convention is a very serious thing to the primitive's mind. ....When he obeys the code, he is pure and lucky; when he infringes the code, he is out of luck and unclean — subject to mystic dangers. To know he has broken a commandment puts him at once in a state of terror; it splits him psychically; and he naturally flies to the priest to unburden himself of his guilt.' 'The sinful state is a definite, infectious psychic condition...and a menace to the whole group.' The convict must be cleansed for 'the safety of the group is the supreme subconscious aim of all savage customs and the social instinct overrules all others'.[2]

[1] This symbolism was formerly not unknown in India. Frazer quotes *Asiatick Researches,* Vol. VI, pp. 535f. on the purification of two Hindu ambassadors after they had been polluted by contact with strangers as a result of crossing the sea. 'For the purpose of regeneration it is directed to make an image of pure gold of the female power of nature, in the shape either of a woman or of a cow. In this status the person to be regenerated is enclosed, and dragged through the usual channel. As a statue of pure gold and of proper dimensions would be too expensive, it is sufficient to make an image of the sacred *Yoni,* through which the person to be regenerated is to pass.'—J. G. Frazer, *The Golden Bough; Taboo and the Perils of the Soul* (London, 1914), p. 113.

[2] C. R. Aldrich, *The Primitive Mind and Modern Civilization* (London, 1931), p. 220.

The purification removes the taboo; it does not necessarily eliminate the desire for revenge.

After Salai Mundli's two sons had gone to jail for the murder of Sonia Dangra-Manjhi, Sonia's elder brother wanted to start a vendetta with the Mundli family, threatening to kill the younger children. But the elders forced Sonia's brother and Salai to engage themselves in a special bond of friendship; the two men drank the dregs of each other's beer and henceforward could not injure each other. Salai in fact gave the other a field and both men swore, 'May our eyes break, our hands and feet break, our children die, our wealth be destroyed, if we cause further trouble!' They sat down together and the Sisa threw tulsi-water over them and the neighbours placed marks of yellow rice on their foreheads.

When Sukra Kirsani returned to Gokurupada after six months in jail to which he had been sentenced on evidence supplied against him by Hadi Kirsani, the latter came to greet him with gifts of wine and a fowl. Sukra responded with similar gifts and the two men drank and feasted together and later, I am told, became firm friends.

It does not always, of course, work out quite so easily as this. Some men return from jail with a passion for revenge. While Miliya Bodnaik was serving his sentence for murder, he heard that his younger brother had been killed in revenge and that the boy's murderer was actually in the same prison. In fact he had the somewhat embarrassing task of telling Miliya why he was there. Miliya told me that he constantly planned to kill this man inside the jail, but did not get a chance, and spent many an hour dreaming of how he would finish off his entire family when he was released.

Bitterness is increased by the expense of the purification ceremonies. When the ferocious Mogla Kirsani got out of prison he abused the sons of the man he had murdered. 'For your worthless father's sake I have had to waste my time in jail; give me two cows or I'll kill you as well.' They were sufficiently alarmed to give him one cow, which he used for his fine. When Sukra, a Gour cowherd, who murdered Godra Mundli some thirty years ago in Kadamguda, was released after only a nominal imprisonment, the elders declared that he must pay five rupees towards the performance of his victim's obsequies. Godra's brother tried to make friends and said, 'If you'll pay this we'll be friends with you and you can go on living in the village'. But Sukro exclaimed, 'I will give you five rupees for my pubic hairs!' There was a great quarrel and in the end the family of the murdered man, not the murderer, had to leave the village. It is evidently sometimes quite as bad to let yourself be murdered as to be a murderer, for what a lot of inconvenience you cause the unfortunate man who killed you!

8

The facts related in this chapter should not tempt us to regard the Bondo as a 'criminal tribe'. It is obvious that there is here a far greater tendency to aggressive criminality than in the neighbouring populations, but it must be remembered that our statistics are imperfect and cover only a small range of years. There is a general tradition among the Bondos themselves that violent crime has become emphasized in recent times, and it is possible therefore that this is due, not to any inherent defect, but to the malaise, the loss of nerve, the lack of adjustment which is disturbing all tribal peoples in India today. How far the Bondo character itself, rather than the economic milieu, indulgence in alcohol or the conflict with external forces, is the dominant factor in the situation we will consider in the next chapter.

CHAPTER NINE

CONCLUSION: THE BONDO CHARACTER

The attentive reader should by now have discovered enough about the Bondo to be able to assess his character, both in its virtue and its defect. He will have noticed, I hope, courage, freedom, equality, independence, industry, friendliness. The defects of these qualities are equally evident; courage becomes an indifference to human life, freedom and independence degenerate into ill-mannered aggressiveness, too strong a sense of equality can become bad citizenship. The Bondo drinks too much; he is often lazy and drives his womenfolk too hard; he is not very clean; he wastes a lot of time in the exact, and rather fussy, performance and repetition of ceremonial. But otherwise there is a great deal to be said for him. If he is a savage, he is at least a noble savage. If he is poor, he is at least patient and courageous in his poverty. If he is outside, and perhaps behind, the main stream of civilization, he is at least free of its debasing vices.

It is its freedom and independence that first strikes a visitor to a Bondo settlement. The Bondo receives him, with friendliness and courtesy, but without that nauseating obsequiousness that is so common in the plainsman, all the more distressing because it may mask a heart filled with suspicion and even hatred. The Bondo is free because he does ultimately regard himself as the equal of any man on earth. He is the first-born of mankind and all the rest are parvenus. He is neither priest-ridden nor subservient to the village elders. He is not a bad citizen; in a case of murder he co-operates with the police and state officials very much better than does, for example, the Maria of Bastar. But he does not regard himself as inferior to another citizen simply because the latter may be wearing a dirty uniform. At Bandapada once I heard some Bondos abusing a Forest Guard who had told them to pick up his baggage. 'Why don't you pick it up yourself?' they said. 'You're only a Forest Guard.' At Bodoballe once, when I was reading in the evening, a Bondo came into the camp and, in the most natural way possible, picked up my lantern, carried it to his house, where he wanted to examine something, and brought it back with a friendly grin, not a bit abashed at having left me in the dark.

This freedom and independence can be an embarrassment to the visitor and it sometimes degenerates into a rather excessive contempt for tribal authority. The visitor, of course, must put up with it, and not allow it to influence his judgement. He really must not expect the Bondos to be interested in his tiresome demands for water, firewood and labour. In this respect they are extraordinarily unwilling to oblige. They are prepared to sit round in the friendliest fashion, laughing, joking and chatting, so long as you do not ask them to do anything. They are always ready to give information. But they object very much to giving anything else. They have no apparent desire to earn money, though the plains Bondos have picked up an annoying habit of begging for it. At Tulaguram I offered some boys, who had nothing whatever to do, the equivalent of three days' earnings to catch some fish for me, but they refused. The Bondos are most unwilling to sell any of their possessions. All this, however, may only be part of the barrier which many Indian aboriginals throw up to protect themselves against the stranger, however much they may like him. There is no greater mistake than to judge primitive people by their reactions to yourself.

This strongly democratic spirit makes the task of the village elders very difficult. The headman has less authority than in any tribe I know; the watchman has to argue and persuade, not give his orders as elsewhere; the priest may be obeyed by the gods — he certainly is not obeyed by men. An odd result of this is that the post of headman is often held by a young and insignificant person, who acts as the village drudge on the occasion of an official visit.

This spirit of freedom extends back to childhood. Bondo mothers are not very fond of carrying babies about: they are apt to get entangled in the general decorative apparatus. From an early age, the child is left alone; it quickly learns to crawl and then to walk. Parents rarely interfere; the children play, fight, laugh and cry but nobody seems to mind. You do not get mothers embroiled in their children's quarrels; no agitated father comes to support his son against a neighbour's. The children have few organized games; from the very beginning they learn to act as individuals. One makes a propeller by fixing a leaf to a stick; another plays at rice-husking in a mortar in the ground; a third makes mud-pies or leaf-caterpillars or devises strange animals out of little jackfruits and bits of wood. As they grow older, the boys and girls enter the free unsupervized existence of the dormitory. To be free to love and choose in the most important of life's personal adventures is to be free in everything.

Naturally this freedom is tempered in many ways, notably by the rules and taboos of religious observance. The community always comes first, though among the Bondos the individual has an unusually independent life within it. Sexual freedom is particularly restrained, but the Bondos do not seem to mind. On the whole, the general pattern of life is one of great independence, liberty and equality.

This is doubtless why the Bondos are a people of such marked individuality, positive, explosive, electric, dangerous. They have few of the negative virtues; theirs are the qualities of the blitzkrieg. They would make splendid commandos. But they are the most quickly inflammable people I have ever met.

Yet they live in the midst of meek, peace-loving folk; the poor, thin, oppressed Doms are aggressive only in business; the Konds are quiet enough; the submissive and commonplace Gadabas have all the virtues of the 'good fellow'—humility, amiability, gentleness, good manners. It would be hard to imagine a greater contrast than between the Bondos and their neighbour Gadabas. At Andrahal I was once present at a violent quarrel when a Bondo attacked a Gadaba, who was supposed to have insulted him by exposing his private parts. The contrast between the ferocious Bondo, screaming abuse in three languages (including English)[1] and the meek Gadaba bowing before the storm with folded hands, was striking. Another day I saw a group of Bondo boys from Katamguda invade the Gadaba village of Thal Duralu, and rob its favourite sago palm of its juice. The Gadabas chattered with rage and anguish as they watched their precious wine slipping down the ample Bondo throats, but not one of them dared to interfere. When they had drunk their fill, the Bondo boys paraded the village with an electric insolence and charm. In spite of her rage, every Gadaba girl ran from her house and stood gazing fascinated. After executing a particularly obscene little dance just to put everyone in his place, the Bondos finally departed leaving the village exhausted as a person through whose body has passed a powerful, but not quite fatal, shock.

It is indeed an extraordinary experience to witness a Bondo quarrel. There is first an exchange of words. References to the wife's excreta and a sister's virtue flicker to and fro. Then the Bondo suddenly comes to the boil; the waters rise and topple over. He twirls his moustache. He spits at his adversary. He pulls out some pubic hairs to throw at him. He chatters and bubbles with temper. And then he pulls his knife or jumps for his bow and arrows.

This passionate temperament also derives from childhood. Little boys and girls are very rough; they cover each other with dust and ash, knock each other about, spit, bite and scratch. In the dormitories, at a kidnapping, when a wedded pair is shut up together for the consummation,

[1] The Bondo's knowledge of the language of Milton and Shakespeare is confined to such basic expressions as 'damn' and 'bloody', picked up in jail or Tea Garden.

the boys are hard, tough and pitiless. Bondo youth is a hard school, and the youths are hard on everyone. One day at Mundlipada, four or five elderly women were roasting *Bauhinia vahlii* seeds in the pod, sitting round the fire and pulling out the pods when they cracked, and eating the kernels. Into this homely and domestic scene, there suddenly irrupted a gang of boys; while some distracted the old women by thumping them, and thumping them hard, with their fists, others collected the roasted pods and made off with them. Smaller children grabbed what they could and hid, but the boys got most of them; when they had eaten the kernels they returned and threw the empty pods at the women who, far from being indignant, were chuckling at the manliness of their splendid boys.

A contrast suggests itself here with the Lepchas, about whom Geoffrey Gorer has written one of the classics of Greater Indian anthropology. The Lepchas are distinguished by a complete absence of aggressiveness and an overwhelming obsession with sex. The Bondos have the highest homicide rate in India and their sexual libido is unusually deficient. Gorer suggests that 'the Lepchas' failure to develop any pattern of external aggression may be considered to have been conditioned by their low material development, and the difficulties of wresting a livelihood from their environment.'[1] Within the group, 'there are the social rules' for the control of aggression, 'and there is the treatment of the new recruits to the society, the babies. From the social point of view, the most obvious is their strong social sanction against quarrelling; the Lepchas have not admitted a single situation in which quarrelling or vengeance-seeking is permissible.' Then there is a social arrangement of all sexual relationships so as to exclude jealousy. 'Parents have no role in the sexual life of their children; exclusive sexual possession is legally impossible; the younger are favoured against the elder (since they have access to their elders' spouses).' Yet still more important perhaps, is the treatment of babies for the avoidance of overt aggression. The first is 'the immediate and willing satisfaction of all the infant's expressed physical desires'. The Lepcha baby is rarely frustrated, and so in the first few months of life there are 'few experiences to provoke aggression'. 'But parallel with this gratification of physiological appetites there is the considerable physical restraint which the babies endure through passing the majority of their waking hours firmly tied to the back of their guardian, and also the complete lack of encouragement which their elders give to the babies' earlier self-maximating activities and attempts to acquire body techniques and physical independence. Young babies get no social approval from their attempts to crawl and

[1] Geoffrey Gorer, *Himalayan Village* (London, 1938), p. 448.

walk; on the contrary a mobile baby is more likely to be picked up and placed on its guardian's back, since it is there easier to control.' And finally, Gorer suggests that there is a connexion 'between this partial extinction of self-assertion in early childhood and the adult Lepchas' tendency to judge their fellows in their role of members of society and not as personalities. This impersonal attitude to their fellows seems to me the chief operative factor for the suppression of competition and aggression in adult life.' [1]

How far does this analysis help us, *per contra,* towards a solution of the problem of Bondo aggressiveness. The Bondos' policy of external aggression towards the Didayis, whose villages they raid and despoil, or towards the Doms whom they rob without compunction, might well be considered to have been conditioned by 'their isolation, their low material development, and the difficulties of wresting a livelihood from their environment'. The argument can be turned both ways. The same conditions produce a lack of external aggressiveness among the Lepchas and its excess among the Bondos. The Lepchas have social rules for the control of aggression within the group, but so do the Bondos — prayers on the *runnukbor,* exhortations at festivals, the discipline of the Sume-Gelirak Castigation, the tiresome ceremonies when one gets back from jail. Jealousy again is not a motif in Bondo crime, unless it be jealousy of someone's material possessions.

Do the Bondos judge their fellows as members of society and not as personalities? It is very hard to say. All tribal societies tend to stress the corporate nature of their life, and Hutton has pointed out that the Nagas and Kukis 'where self-assertion and aggression are a *sine qua non'* are dependent for their very existence on 'the spontaneous mutual co-operation of their members'.[2] To the outsider, to Sassoon or Hivale or me, the Bondo stands out as a personality; I remember him vividly, and I am impressed, because I am ashamed to say that I do not remember very many people. But does Miliya Bodnaik and Sonia Sisa, and Muliya Dangra-Manjhi stand out in equally sharp focuss in the eyes of his own people? I doubt it. There is certainly among the Bondos a stress on personal freedom and individuality which is somewhat in advance of that recorded for the Lepchas, but I would not have thought it was sufficient to make what is after all a very considerable difference — the difference between a mild non-aggressive tradition and one that has as high a homicide rate as any in the world.

But what about the babies? Here, I think, Gorer really has something. Bondos and Lepchas deal with their babies very differently.

[1] Gorer, op. cit., pp. 449ff. [2] ibid., p. 26.

The Bondo baby is continually frustrated. Since the women do most of the work and in any case are already over-burdened with a vast mass of ornaments, they give their babies to the older children or their husbands to look after. I have never seen anywhere so many fathers looking after babies, who tug at the small male nipples with an obvious sense of disappointment. Babies are thus not fed for long periods and when they are fed they have to burrow uncomfortably in the thicket of brass chains and beads that adorn the mother's bosom. Moreover, in contrast to the Lepcha child, the Bondo baby is not subjected to much physical restraint; it is allowed its freedom, and learns to crawl and walk very early. After all, there is often no one to carry it about. And then when it gets old enough to be bullied, and all through its childhood, it is knocked about and suppressed by the older boys. In the dormitory especially a boy gets all the frustration he can stand. The self-assertive desires of youth are not really satisfied by being able to bang a pretty girl on the head or smear her face with ashes; they demand something more. The Murias satisfy that demand, and are famous for their pacific, non-aggressive character. The Bondos deny it, with the result we know.

The Bondos are not very clean. They have bad teeth. A man will spit and not bother to wipe his chin of saliva. A woman will urinate and come into your camp with her legs splashed with the stale. A girl will, without embarrassment, appear even before a visitor in her menstrual period with drops of blood running down her legs. Bondo men certainly bathe often, cleansing hair and body with a clay that serves as soap. But the women rarely wash their skirts, and the villages are indescribably filthy. My chief personal mortification in Bondo research was the continual bad throat from which I suffered as a result of inhaling the appalling mixture of human and porcine excreta, decayed food, shavings of old hair, and urine-impregnated dust that is stirred up in noxious clouds whenever the Bondos dance or assemble in any number. The Bondos are quite unabashed about excreta. They seem to like to have it about. After all, it is something for the pigs. Shamrao Hivale saw a girl of twelve relieve herself in front of her house; she had no leaves, so she walked dirty as she was into the kitchen, brought out some leaves, wiped herself, dropped the leaves on the veranda, and went about her duties. I have often seen boys urinate in front of my camp, facing me, without a trace of self-consciousness.

The Bondos are not very interested in material goods. They have as yet hardly learnt the value of money. There is thus no stimulus to do more work than is required to provide the minimum necessities of life. Yet to provide even these is a full-time job, if you would be self-sufficient and have no commercial sense. The women work very hard indeed, for they not only have to labour in the fields and forest, but they have the never-ending business of the loom to fill their time. The men are much more lazy and may often be seen lying in blissful drunken relaxion on the *sindibor.* But when they do work, the men work hard and well.

The Bondos never waste anything, least of all do they waste energy. It is always interesting to watch them returning from the forest. A woman will have a load of *kereng* bark balanced on her head, her sickle stuck through the headband. Under one arm will be a great bundle of leaves, in the hand a gourd freshly filled with water. In the other hand are as many sticks as it can hold. Then comes a youth with a load of grass, two great bundles of it at either end of a pole balanced across his shoulder. In his waistband he has tucked a bundle of leaves for pipes or plates, and in his scanty loincloth are a dozen date-palm grubs and a bit of honey-comb. In his hand is a chick of a jungle fowl. Then comes a girl with a pot of water on her head, a bundle of brooms in her hand, a long gourd slung over one shoulder, a baby over the other. Only the old men are privileged to return home unburdened, save with the double load of palm-wine in the belly.

The Bondos, ungentle savages, yet savage gentlemen, are passionately devoted to their 'race'. They are loyal to one another and to their tribal traditions. Most of them are good citizens of the village community. They love their children and desire them to be free.

And in conclusion, to adapt slightly words from Tod's original dedication to the *Annals and Antiquities of Rajast'han,* the Bondos' 'admirer and annalist may, perhaps, be permitted to hope that the sighs of this ancient and interesting race for the preservation of their present independence' may not go unanswered.

APPENDIXES

Appendix I

SOME BONDO RELATIONSHIP TERMS[1]

Father	*Ba*
Mother	*Young*
Father's elder brother	*Busān*
His wife	*Busān Boi*
Father's younger brother	*Kakka*
His wife	*Umbuk Boi*
Mother's elder brother	*Māmung*
His wife	*Wāng*
Mother's younger brother	*Māmung*
His wife	*Wāng*
Father's elder sister	*Muna Wāng*
Her husband	*Māmung*
Father's younger sister	*Dau Wāng*
Her husband	*Māmung*
Mother's elder sister	*Busān Boi*
Her husband	*Busān*
Mother's younger sister	*Umbuk Boi*
Her husband	*Kākka*
Husband	*Umpor*
Wife	*Kunoi*
Father-in-law	*Unkui*
Mother-in-law	*Kiyar*
Son-in-law	*Ārju*
Daughter-in-law	*Kimi-On*
Son	*On*
Daughter	*On*
Stepson	*On*
Stepdaughter	*On*
Elder brother	*Māng*
His wife	*Imbing*
His son	*On*
His daughter	*On*
Younger brother	*Me*
His wife	*Kimi-On*
His son	*Busaon*
His daughter	*Busaon*
Elder sister	*Ming*
Her husband	*Umbāng*
Younger sister	*Kui*
Her husband	*Ārju*
Father's brother's son	
(if older)	*Māng*
(if younger)	*Me*
Father's brother's daughter	*Ming*
Father's sister's son	*Marenger*
Father's sister's daughter	
(if older)	*Ming*
(if younger)	*Kui*
Mother's brother's son	*Marenger*
(if older)	*Ming*
(if younger)	*Kui*
Mother's sister's son	
(if older)	*Māng*
(if younger)	*Me*
Mother's sister's daughter	
(if older)	*Ming*
(if younger)	*Kui*

[1] These are from the central villages of the Bondo hills: there are dialectical differences in Andrahal on one side and Pinnajangar on the other.

Appendix II

GENEALOGIES

Names of men are given in capitals, those of women in ordinary type.

Abbreviations within brackets give first the *kuda*, then the *bonso* and third the village of each individual.

Kuda : BN = Bodnaik

C = Challan

DM = Dangra-Manjhi

D = Dora

J = Jigri

K (standing first in the line) = Kirsani

M = Mundli

S = Sisa

Bonso : K (standing second in the line) = Killo (Tiger moiety)
O = Ontal (Cobra moiety)

BOOK-LIST

ALDRICH, C. R., *The Primitive Mind and Modern Civilization* (London, 1931).

BELL, R. C. S., *Koraput District Gazetteer* (Cuttack, 1945).

BOMPAS, C. H., *Folklore of the Santal Parganas* (London, 1909).

BONGER, W. A., *Race and Crime* (English translation, New York, 1943).

ELWIN, Verrier, *Maria Murder and Suicide* (Bombay, 1943).

Folk-Tales of Mahakoshal (Bombay, 1944).

The Muria and their Ghotul (Bombay, 1947).

Myths of Middle India (Bombay, 1949).

FURER-HAIMENDORF, C. VON., *The Reddis of the Bison Hills* (London, 1945).

'Avenues to Marriage among the Bondos of Orissa', *Man in India*, Vol. XXIII (1943).

'Religion and Ethics among the Konyak Nagas and other Indian Tribes', in *Essays in Anthropology presented to S. C. Roy* (1942)

'Megalithic Ritual among the Gadabas and Bondos of Orissa', *Journal of the Royal Asiatic Society of Bengal*, Vol. IV (1945).

GHURYE, G. S., 'Dual Organization in India', *Journal of the Anthropological Institute*, Vol. LIII (1923).

GORER, G., *Himalayan Village* (London, 1938).

HENDERSON, C. A., see MOLONY.

HIVALE, S., *The Pardhans of the Upper Narbada Valley* (Bombay, 1946).

KINBERG, O., *Basic Problems of Criminology* (Copenhagen and London, 1935).

KITTREDGE, G. L., *Witchcraft in Old and New England* (Harvard, 1918).

KOPPERS, W., 'India and Dual Organization', *Acta Tropica*, S. Vol. I, Nr. 1/2 (1944).

LAUBSCHER, B. J. F., *Sex, Custom and Pathology* (London, 1937).

MAY, J. A., 'Notes on the Bhondas of Jaypur', *The Indian Antiquary*, Vol. II (1873).

MOLONY, J. C., *Census of India*, 1911, Vol. XII, Part I.

RICKMAN, J., *A General Selection from the Works of Sigmund Freud* (London, 1937).

ROY, S. C., *The Mundas and their Country* (Calcutta, 1912).

The Birhors (Ranchi, 1925).

Oraon Religion and Customs (Ranchi, 1928).

SCOTT, G. M., 'Alcoholism and Criminal Behaviour', *Mental Abnormality and Crime* (London, 1944).

THURSTON, E., *Castes and Tribes of Southern India* (Madras, 1909).

TOD, J., *Annals and Antiquities of Rajast'han* (New edition by W. Crooke, Oxford, 1920).

WORD-LIST

angto	Taboo
Bāriko	Village watchman
bissās	Sin, pollution
bonso	Moiety
Dissāri	Shaman
Diyo	Soul
eloto	Magic
Ghotul	The Muria dormitory-club for unmarried boys and girls
gige	Sacrifice
gunom	A megalith in appeasement and for the honour of the dead
jiwo	Soul
Johār	A form of salutation
kereng	A shrub, *Calotropis gigantea,* R. Br.; yarn from its bark is used for Bondo cloth
kinding-sāgar	A sacred drum placed on small stones
kommar	Blacksmith
kuda	Clan
Mahaprabhu	Great Master. See pp. 133ff.
mahaprasad	A form of ceremonial friendship
mahua	In Remo, *bosisum.* The tree *Bassia latifolia,* Roxb.
moitur	A covenanted friend
Naiko	Headman
podu	Axe cultivation
runnukbor	A sacred stone wall
sairem	Ghost
samdhi	The relationship between two fathers-in-law
sebung	The regular Bondo marriage
Selani-dingo	Girls' dormitory
sindibor	Sacred megalithic platform
Sisa	Village priest
soru	A sacramental food, eating of which is confined to members of the same village

MOTIF INDEX

This Index is based on Stith Thompson's *Motif-Index of Folk-Literature* (Helsinki, 1932). New motifs, which do not occur in the original tabulation, are marked with an asterisk; their numbers, it must be remembered, are provisional and will have to be revised when Dr Stith Thompson issues the supplementary or revised *Motif-Index* which he has promised.

A. MYTHOLOGICAL MOTIFS

A0—A99. CREATOR

A0. Creator, Chap. VI, passim
A1. Sun-god as Creator, 135ff.
A10. Nature of the Creator. The nature and character of the Creator, called Mahaprabhu by the Bondos, is discussed throughout Chap. VI
A32.* Creator's wife, 63, 140, 203
A34. Birds as Creator's servants, 136f.
A37.* Animals as Creator's servants: the boar, 136
A37.1.* Animals as Creator's servants: the crab, 137

A100—A499. GODS

A101. Supreme god, discussed and illustrated in Chap. VI
A112. Birth of gods, 26, 151
A112.5.* Gods born from the belly of a deer, 156, 229
A151. Home of the gods, 137.
A210. Sky-god, 49, 56
A220. Sun-god, 134ff., 141ff.
A240. Moon-god, 134f.
A287. Rain-god, 23, 137, 141f.
A401. Mother Earth, 102, 120, 152f., 166
A411. Household gods, 13, 18, 100, 106ff., 151, 157f.
A411.3.* Sword-god, 145ff.
A425. River-god, 155
A427. God of springs, 151, 166
A431. God of fertility, 140, 157
A435. God of forests, 151, 155
A440. God of animals, 151, 155
A478. God of disease, 155
A487. God of death, 201, 204
A493. God of fire, 155

A600—A899. COSMOGONY AND COSMOLOGY

A700.1. Heavenly bodies from objects thrown into sky, 141
A701. Creation of the sky, 137
A710. Creation of the sun, 138, 141
A711.2. Sun as a cannibal, 138
A714. Sun from object thrown into sky, 141
A715.2.* Sun and moon from eyes of girl killed by Creator, 138
A722.6.* Sun raises arms in morning, 140
A722.7.* Sun bathes in ocean, 140
A722.8.* Sun rises at voice of cock, 140f.
A728.3.* Sun in form of black bull snared by men, 140
A736.2. Sun-brother and moon-sister, 141

A1000 — A1099. WORLD CALAMITIES

A1100 — A1199. ESTABLISHMENT OF NATURAL ORDER

A1200 — A1699. CREATION AND ORDERING OF HUMAN LIFE

A1700 — A2199. CREATION OF ANIMAL LIFE

A2600 — A2699. ORIGIN OF TREES AND PLANTS

B. ANIMALS

C. TABOO

For a discussion of the Bondo theory of taboo, see pp. 194 ff.

C0 — C99. TABOO CONNECTED WITH SUPERNATURAL BEINGS

C100—C199. SEX TABOO

C114. Taboo: incest, 73f., 123
C114.1.* Taboo: clan and village incest, Chap. II, passim, 74.
C115. Taboo: adultery, 74, 95
C117. Nuptial taboo, 49, 58, 183
C117.1. Taboo: intercourse at hunting season, 183
C117.2.* Taboo: intercourse before making rice-beer, 58
C117.3. Taboo: intercourse during threshing, 49
C117.4.* Taboo: intercourse during festival, 183
C140. Taboo connected with menses, 122f., 155
C152. Taboo during pregnancy, 101, 139
C172.* Father-in-law taboo, 102
C181. *Taboo confined to women*
C181.1. Taboo: women not to touch drum, 43
C181.2. Taboo: women not to participate in hunting activities, 43
C181.4.* Taboo: women not to plough, 42
C181.5.* Taboo: women not to climb trees or roofs, 42
C.181.6.* Taboo: women not to put carrying-poles on shoulders, 42
C181.7.* Taboo: women not to offer sacrifice, 42
C181.8.* Taboo: women not to make mats, 43
C181.9.* Taboo: women not to carry a corpse, 43
C181.10.* Taboo: women not to use musical instruments other than a Jew's Harp, [illegible]
C181.11.* Taboo: women not to wear more than a certain quantity of cloth, 64, 66
C181.12.* Taboo: women not to wear anklets, 18
C181.13.* Taboo: women not to be tattooed, 21
C181.14.* Taboo: women not to let their hair grow, 64
C182.* *Taboo confined to men*
C182.1.* Taboo: men not to weave, 42
C182.2.* Taboo: men not to husk or grind grain, 42
C.182.3.* Taboo: men not to cowdung floors, 42
C.182.4.* Taboo: men not to shave hair of adult women, 42

C200—C299. EATING AND DRINKING TABOO

C210. *Taboo: eating in certain place*
C219.4.* Taboo: eating food cooked elsewhere on threshing-floor, 49
C219.5.* Taboo: eating in house on day of death, 215
C220. *Taboo: eating certain things*
C221.3. Taboo: eating certain parts of animals, 52, 183
C230. *Taboo: eating at certain time*
C231.3.* Taboo: eating anything in clearing before sacrifice, 155
C231.4.* Taboo: eating beans before appropriate festival, 174
C231.5.* Taboo: eating mangoes before appropriate festival, 182, 183, 208
C250. *Taboo: drinking*
C251.* Taboo: drinking beer and spirits on threshing-floor, 49
C252.* Taboo: drinking alcohol on certain days of a festival, 183
C253.* Taboo: drinking a certain gruel before festal food is finished, 187, 195
C254.* Taboo: holding ladle by bowl when drinking palm wine, 57

C300—C399. LOOKING TABOO

C312.1. Taboo: man looking at nude woman, 65
C314.* Taboo: sun and moon seeing one another naked, 141
C328.* Taboo: looking at sacred drum when not in use, 159

C400—C499. SPEAKING TABOO

C401.4.* Taboo: priest not to speak on certain day of festival, 154
C401.5.* Taboo: threshers not to speak to stranger, 49
C427.* Taboo: not to speak of broken taboo, 194f.

C500—C549. TABOO: TOUCHING

C526.* Taboo: touching cowdung during festival, 183

C700—C899. MISCELLANEOUS TABOOS

C756. *Taboo: doing thing before certain time*
C756.3.* Taboo: cooking in new house before proper ceremony, 100

C900 — C999. PUNISHMENT FOR BREAKING TABOO

D. MAGIC

D0 — D699. TRANSFORMATION

D800 — D1699. MAGIC OBJECTS

D1700 — D2199. MAGIC POWERS AND MANIFESTATIONS

E. THE DEAD

E200 — E599. GHOSTS AND OTHER REVENANTS

E600 — E699. REINCARNATION

E700 — E799. THE SOUL

F. MARVELS

F0 — F199. OTHER-WORLD JOURNEYS

F200 — F699. MARVELLOUS CREATURES

F700 — F899. EXTRAORDINARY PLACES AND THINGS

F900 — F1099. EXTRAORDINARY OCCURENCES

G. OGRES

J. THE WISE AND THE FOOLISH

K. DECEPTIONS

M. ORDAINING THE FUTURE

N. CHANCE AND FATE

S. UNNATURAL CRUELTY

T. SEX

T400 — T499. ILLICIT SEXUAL RELATIONS

T500 — T599. CONCEPTION AND BIRTH

T600 — T699. CARE OF CHILDREN

Z. MISCELLANEOUS GROUPS OF MOTIFS

Z71. *Formulistic numbers*
Z71.1. Formulistic number: three, 27, 29, 151
Z71.3. Formulistic number: five, 2, 209
Z71.5. Formulistic number: seven, 26, 54, 136, 225
Z71.8. Formulistic number: twelve, 3, 6, 26, 63, 97, 219
Z71.9. Formulistic number: thirteen, 97

GENERAL INDEX